Cultures
of
Growth

How the New Science of Mindset
Can Transform Individuals,
Teams, and Organizations

Mary C. Murphy

Simon & Schuster

NEW YORK   LONDON   TORONTO
SYDNEY   NEW DELHI

100 YEARS
SIMON &
SCHUSTER

1230 Avenue of the Americas
New York, NY 10020

First Simon & Schuster hardcover edition March 2024

SIMON & SCHUSTER and colophon are registered trademarks
of Simon & Schuster, LLC

Simon & Schuster: Celebrating 100 Years of Publishing in 2024

For information about special discounts for bulk purchases, please contact
Simon & Schuster Special Sales at 1-866-506-1949
or business@simonandschuster.com.

The Simon & Schuster Speakers Bureau can bring authors to your
live event. For more information or to book an event, contact the
Simon & Schuster Speakers Bureau at 1-866-248-3049
or visit our website at www.simonspeakers.com.

Interior design by Paul Dippolito

Manufactured in the United States of America

1   3   5   7   9   10   8   6   4   2

Library of Congress Cataloging-in-Publication Data has been applied for.

ISBN 978-1-9821-7274-9
ISBN 978-1-9821-7276-3 (ebook)

For Arya, Conner, Ella, Everett, Friday, Jackson,
Miles, River, and Tyberius.

For my love, Victor.

For you, the culture creators.

Let's build Cultures of Growth together.

Contents

Foreword   ix

Introduction   xiii

PART ONE: MINDSET RESET

Chapter 1   The Mindset Continuum   3

Chapter 2   Organizational Mindsets   15

PART TWO: MINDSET CULTURE

Chapter 3   Collaboration   31

Chapter 4   Innovation and Creativity   52

Chapter 5   Risk-Taking and Resilience   81

Chapter 6   Integrity and Ethical Behavior   99

Chapter 7   Diversity, Equity, and Inclusion   122

PART THREE: IDENTIFYING YOUR MINDSET TRIGGERS

Chapter 8   Mindset Microcultures   151

Chapter 9   Evaluative Situations   161

Chapter 10   High-Effort Situations   176

Chapter 11   Critical Feedback   202

Chapter 12   Success of Others   229

Conclusion   257

Acknowledgments   261

Notes   267

Index   315

Foreword

One momentous day in 2006, Mary Murphy walked into my office. At the time, she was a much-admired graduate student in our department at Stanford. So, I was delighted when she made an appointment to talk with me, and I couldn't wait to hear what she had to say. Little did I know that after that conversation there would be no looking back.

Let me give you some pre-Mary background. Decades of research on mindsets had shown that a person can believe that their important abilities, such as their intelligence, are simply fixed and can't be developed. Case closed. We called this a "fixed mindset," and we showed that it often leads people to shy away from challenges that could reveal low ability; to interpret mistakes or setbacks as reflecting a lack of ability; and therefore, to give up more easily in the face of difficulty. Other people, we found, held more of a "growth mindset"—the belief that abilities can be developed over time through, say, hard work, good strategies, and lots of help and support from others. And we showed that this belief often leads people to take on challenges that can increase their abilities, to learn from mistakes and setbacks, and therefore to persevere more effectively and accomplish more in the long run.

When Mary came to my office that day, she said something like this: I love your work and I think it's important, but you've been treating a mindset as something that simply exists in a person's head. Yes, people do tend toward different mindsets and that can make a big difference—but the environment, the social context, the culture, the organization a person is in can also have a mindset. This mindset can be embodied in the dominant philosophies and practices of the group or organization, and it can powerfully affect the people there, no matter what their individual mindset might be.

Now, we already knew that although people can favor one mindset or the other, they don't just sit there in that mindset no matter what. A big setback or failure, for example, can send people into a fixed mindset even if they are usually in more of a growth mindset. But Mary's idea was more profound than that. She maintained that no matter what personal mindset someone holds, the work or school environment they're in will have a large impact. That is, people can have all the growth mindset in the world, but there are places where they won't be able to use it. Those places are fixed mindset environments, or what she calls "Cultures of Genius."

How, exactly, can a work or school environment have a fixed mindset? Its philosophies and practices may be infused with the idea that abilities are simply fixed and cannot be developed—the idea that some people are smart and some just aren't. Such an environment may value immediate perfect performance with no periods of confusion or struggle. It may value the appearance of genius over the fact of learning and growth. It may value those who seem to have that touch of genius over those that the culture deems do not. And, regardless of a person's own mindset, the environment's mindset will often win. It's hard to take on big challenges or to value and learn from setbacks when you're being judged as smart or not, worthy or not.

In short, Mary's message was: The environment you're in can have its own mindset culture. It can be a culture that believes in and values the development of all people's ability. Or it can be a culture that believes in and values fixed ability, a culture that expects some people to have more of it and some people to (permanently) have less of it.

How did I react to Mary's announcement in my office? I was super excited. I saw at once that this was a really new and really important idea—an important idea for research and, even more so, an important idea for society. So I said, "Let's do it!" And before we knew it, Mary had launched her now-renowned program of research.

In this research, Mary has demonstrated over and over that organizations and teams that hold a growth mindset and infuse their policies and practices with it have employees who are more motivated and committed, more mutually supportive, and more creative and innovative. They are also less likely to cheat, cut corners, or steal each other's ideas. In college courses, instructors who create a growth mindset culture have students who are more motivated, learn more, and achieve higher grades. These Cultures of Growth honor every person, support them to grow their abilities, and create the conditions for every person to make a valuable contribution. In these cultures, great ideas and great contributions come from many people at all levels and in all segments of the organization—not just people who have been identified as brilliant, talented, or having "high potential."

I can't stress enough how new and valuable this perspective was. It meant that it was no longer enough to simply teach members of an organization or classroom to hold a growth mindset. It was no longer just their personal responsibility to act in growth-mindset ways. It was now the responsibility of the leaders of the organization or classroom to create a growth mindset culture, one in which their actual practices motivated, supported, and rewarded learning and growth for everyone. But Mary's impact didn't end with this understanding. She inspired all of us doing mindset research to study how we could help create these cultures—by setting out to develop and rigorously test practices for teachers or managers that they can learn to use effectively. My original excitement about Mary's idea has only grown with time.

Mary has now studied and worked with countless organizations around the world—both "Cultures of Genius" and "Cultures of Growth." She has learned exactly what they look like, how they operate, and how each mindset plays out. In this book, she shares this fascinating and incredibly valuable information so that all organizations and groups can get on the path of growth—creating cultures that support everyone to fulfill their potential and contribute to the productivity, innovation, and success of the whole. Imagine if this happened on a national or even global level. This is the book that can make it happen.

—Carol S. Dweck, PhD

Lewis and Virginia Eaton Professor of
Psychology at Stanford University

Author of *Mindset: The New Psychology of Success*

Stanford, California

Introduction

Picture it: You're starting a new job, and you've got that big, fresh, first-day energy. For years you've wondered what it would be like to work here, and now you've landed it—a coveted position at one of the highest-profile organizations in your field. You know it will be a challenge, but you're up for it. Plus, it's such an incredible opportunity to learn—you can't wait to dive in!

You look up at the clock and see it's time for your first Monday morning team meeting. As the conference room fills, there's a buzz in the air. The man seated next to you introduces himself. "So, you're new; where'd you graduate from?" he asks. You tell him and he nods. "Not bad," he replies. "I graduated from MIT with a double degree." The meeting begins, and when the boss asks project leaders for status updates, each brags about their wins. When it's revealed that a key deadline has been missed, the atmosphere becomes tense; lots of finger pointing about who's responsible, but no clear answer. Finally, the boss asks for ideas about how to solve a thorny problem the team has been stymied by. You're tempted to raise your hand, thinking you have a good suggestion, but you hold back. Considering what you've just witnessed, you worry about missing the mark. What if your idea *isn't* very good? What will your boss and the others think of you? You decide that maybe it's better just to keep quiet.

By the end of the meeting, you have a sinking feeling in the pit of your stomach. You can't help but wonder if perhaps you've made a mistake. Maybe you don't have what it takes, after all.

Now, let's rewind and consider another possibility.

You're feeling that big, fresh, first-day energy, and you look up at the clock. It's time for the Monday morning team meeting. After introductions all around, the boss says, "I know you're going to bring valuable skills and experiences to the team. We're happy you've joined us." The status updates proceed, and the project leads share their successes, as well as a struggle they are dealing with, and the team offers suggestions to help them work it out. A big deadline was missed and instead of finger pointing, the team discusses what can be learned, how they will change their processes to make sure it doesn't happen again, and what they're going to do to meet the next milestone. Finally, the boss asks for ideas about how to solve a thorny problem the team has been stymied by. You wait for a few others to talk, but realizing you have a suggestion that hasn't been offered yet, you speak up and your idea is greeted with enthusiasm.

By the end of the meeting, you're feeling a part of something. You can see how the team collaborates to work through problems, innovates solutions, and takes risks together. You're excited to take on whatever challenges and opportunities tomorrow holds!

It's a tale of two cultures: a fixed mindset culture—what I call a Culture of Genius—versus a growth mindset culture—a Culture of Growth. As you can begin to see from just these two brief examples, when it comes to individual, team, and organizational performance, the culture you're in matters. From the very beginning.

Throughout this book, I'll explain the difference between these mindset cultures, but at the outset it's worth noting that when Satya Nadella became CEO of Microsoft, one of the first things he did was to make a public commitment to transform the company's culture. He knew that Microsoft's success relied on its ability to produce the most innovative and creative products, and then he asked: "How can a growth mindset help us achieve that?" In other words, how do companies not only put growth mindset into practice, but also use it to solve some of their hardest problems?

In 2014, when Nadella took over, Microsoft's stock price was roughly $36. In November 2021, it hit a high of over $340, and when tech stocks crashed in 2022 it remained a strong performer. Microsoft shifted from its heavy dependence on Windows to rivaling behemoth Amazon Web Services in its share of the cloud computing market, becoming, in 2021, only the second company in US history (after Apple) to receive a $2 trillion market valuation. Microsoft is often held up as a case example of employing this or that strategy, and so seeing them highlighted in yet another book could prompt a sigh. And yet most of the successes for which the company has been heralded stem from a single ideal: Nadella's determination to shift Microsoft into a growth mindset culture. Today, as the computing world focuses on the promise of artificial intelligence, Microsoft is trying to improve workplace culture by tasking the technology with helping all of us inhabit our growth mindset more often. In the wake of some cringeworthy stumbles from their chatbot Tay (and more recently, Bing) Nadella directed his engineering team to find ways to tune their products to be more inclusive and growth-oriented. My collaborators and I have joined these efforts and are working together to create AI-powered tools that will help teachers and managers create growth mindset cultures in their classrooms and teams.

But what, exactly, is a growth mindset culture? What is its true promise, what does it look like in practice, and what does a transition to this type of culture entail? In this book, I'll show you. Additionally, I'll show that growth mindset cultures don't just work for large corporations, they also boost outcomes in schools, nonprofits, sports teams . . . essentially anywhere there's two or more people working together. (It's worth noting that three of the four teams to make it to the 2023 NBA final four playoffs were growth oriented, meaning they had coaches or team leaders who've publicly advocated for a growth-minded approach.) We'll also look at the latest science on individual mindset, and how it intersects with what we've learned about mindset culture.

Microsoft's transformation owes much to Nadella's reading of Stanford psychology professor Carol Dweck's *Mindset*, first published in 2006 and now read by more than seven million people in more than 40 languages. Mindset refers to our beliefs about the malleability of intelligence: whether it's largely fixed, or whether it can be developed. Fixed mindset beliefs assert that people either "have it" or they don't, while growth mindset beliefs suggest that intelligence is something you can develop and expand. The concept of mindset has been nothing short of revolutionary in its impact on our understanding of individuals. People's mindsets can tell us how they respond to challenges and setbacks, the goals they are likely to pursue, and their behavior. Operating in a fixed mindset can lead people to give up when they are frustrated, take fewer risks when it comes to their learning and development, and conceal mistakes.

I first became acquainted with Carol when I began working with her as a graduate student in 2006. I was struck by how mindset matters not just individually, but in the context of other people—and especially in groups. The biggest influence on whether you're operating from your fixed or growth mindset at any given moment *isn't* necessarily between your ears—it's outside of you. That's right: Mindset isn't just in your mind. Now as her colleague, I have spent more than a decade working with Carol to examine how mindset operates at the group and organizational levels. The results are transformative and fundamentally shift our understanding of how systems and teams work. And they speak to the power of how we impact one another.

Imagine a fish swimming in a lake. Saying that mindset is a purely individual characteristic is like saying that how that fish behaves comes down to the fish, alone. It completely overlooks what's going on in the water (or the other fish swimming around). Similarly, the mindset culture in which *we* swim significantly impacts our thoughts, motivation, and behavior.

I know that these days, especially in Westernized countries, we're all about personal agency. No matter what's going on around us, we can learn to master our minds so that, ultimately, all is under our control—or so popular thinking goes. This meme is often used to blame individuals and blind us to organizations' failings. I'm not here to undercut anyone's agency or abilities, but I am here to bring to the fore the powerful influences that surround us. We survey the landscape around us to see what the norms are, what is expected of us, and how we can succeed and gain admiration. We derive this information from the culture.

An organization may have a culture that worships and rewards fixed ability. As a result, it may admire and praise those who are deemed brilliant and judge and blame people who don't measure up. How would you act in this culture? What would you strive for? Going against the culture would be like swimming upstream. Sure, it's possible, but the truth is, it's unlikely.

A growth mindset culture is one that values, fosters, and rewards growth and development among all members. Of course, there's the bottom line to think about, but such organizations believe that prosperity and success stem from people learning, growing, and developing in ways that move them and the company forward.

The mindset culture we're swimming in also starts to affect us on a deeper level, shifting how we see ourselves. Often without even knowing it, we may begin to adopt our organization's mindset as our own, and that ripples outward to how we see and value others. We start reinforcing the mindset culture, making it stronger and creating a continuous and intensifying cycle.

Every gathering of people has a mindset culture. Yet the reality is that most organizations have *no idea* what their mindset culture is, or how it influences the group and their outcomes. Throughout this book, I'll be highlighting how mindset culture shows up in many groups whether in workplace contexts, schools, families, sports, or others, and I'll use the term "organization" to refer to these different groups. I'll also use "leader" and "employee" as shorthand, to make for easier reading. But know that fostering a growth mindset culture is possible in almost any setting, well beyond the workplace.

Rather than something that lives inside us, mindset can best be understood as a system of interaction among three concentric circles: Your personal mindset can be affected by the local mindset culture of your group or team, which, in turn, is influenced by the organization's larger mindset culture. Just as with individuals, organizational mindset culture is not fully fixed or growth, but instead functions on a continuum. Over the past decade of research, my team and I have identified the two ends of the mindset culture continuum: Cultures of Genius and Cultures of Growth.

Culture of Genius sounds appealing, right? But consider several leaders emblematic of a Culture of Genius: First, Theranos CEO Elizabeth Holmes, who dropped out of Stanford to found a now-infamous blood-testing company with the backing of Stanford faculty members who thought they had discovered the next Silicon Valley disruptor. After Theranos's leadership not only failed to deliver on its promise but also lied about their problems, Holmes was found guilty of fraud and conspiracy. Then there is Arif Naqvi, who similarly masqueraded as an impact investor whose Abraaj private equity fund was aimed at supporting conscious capitalism. Like Holmes, Naqvi dazzled investors who were impressed with his apparent genius, but it was all smoke and mirrors. In reality, Naqvi stole $780 million from the fund. We also have Charlie Javice, CEO of Frank, a financial aid assistance company Javice billed as the "Amazon of higher education." Javice wowed early investors and quickly became a darling of tech media but was later charged by the Justice Department with "falsely and dramatically inflating the number of customers of her company" to entice JPMorgan Chase to acquire it for a hefty sum.

A Culture of Genius aligns with the fixed mindset. It is one where the overarching belief is that talent and ability are innate, and you either have "it" or you don't. Cultures of Genius value brilliance and smarts above all else—especially if they seem to come naturally. Cultures of Genius focus almost exclusively on high fixed intelligence, so people who apply for jobs in these organizations often feature their IQs, test scores, and academic and intellectual awards and achievements, hoping to be deemed worthy and among the chosen few.

Cultures of Growth, on the other hand, also want smart people, but they want them to be highly motivated and excited about further developing their abilities by learning, trying new strategies, and seeking help when they're stuck. As a result, people's job applications are likely to highlight not only their successes, but also the challenges they overcame to get there, their commitment to their work, and their desire to develop further. A Culture of Growth centers the belief that talent and ability can be honed and enhanced through good strategies, mentoring, and organizational supports.

Just as individual mindset is a strong predictor of behaviors and outcomes, so, too, is mindset culture. Research clearly shows that organizational mindset can forecast the success of individuals, teams, and organizations. It affects whether people collaborate; whether they come up with innovative ideas and solutions; whether they are willing to take risks; whether they engage in ethically problematic behavior like hoarding information, hiding mistakes, and stealing ideas; and finally, whether the company can benefit from the insights and talents of people from diverse groups, or whether their perspective remains limited. You'll see in this book how Satya Nadella created a Culture of Growth that has shaped Microsoft's investment strategy, its capacity to collaborate with Apple and other competitors, and its ability to rebound from technical failures. And you'll see other Cultures of Growth success stories, like how two sisters are using a solution-oriented approach to disrupt the wine market and make top-quality products accessible to a broader and more diverse group of consumers, and how a belief in all students' ability to learn revolutionized instruction and drastically improved outcomes at a community college.

Fortunately, organizational mindset can be consciously shaped. Working with leaders, managers, and individual contributors, my team and I have seen firsthand the power of Cultures of Growth to spur people's motivation and boost individual and organizational performance. We've discovered how to help organizations change to embody and promote a growth mindset. We've uncovered what shapes a company's mindset culture, and how to change policies, practices, and norms to help people into their growth mindset.

Furthermore, we have discovered the link between mindset culture and diversity and inclusion. Namely, organizational mindset shapes whether companies identify, recruit, and retain people from diverse groups. This has led us to create the Equity Accelerator, the nation's first focused research organization to apply social and behavioral science to the challenge of creating—and sustaining—more equitable learning and working environments. Fostering inclusive growth mindset cultures is a big part of what we do there and what I'll show you how to do on your own teams.

Throughout this book, we'll cover the groundbreaking research that reveals how you and your team can inspire growth mindset together. We'll see how well-known companies and organizations in a variety of industries have changed the way their people work together to create Cultures of Growth. We'll explore the worlds of education, nonprofits, sports, and more to see how Cultures of Growth flourish everywhere—as, for example, when a school superintendent in New York State reversed massive inequities for children of color in his district by reshaping the district's mindset culture. And how a combination bakery–foundation has applied growth mindset principles to its hiring and development, creating career opportunities for formerly incarcerated people while running a hugely successful business.

Importantly, I'll also show you how to prompt yourself toward growth mindset, *and* inspire those around you, fostering a Culture of Growth team. This book is full of many exercises, tools, and practices you can start today to change how your organization works together. You'll identify what cues trigger you personally toward your fixed and growth mindsets (spoiler: we all have both within us) and learn how to take the cues that move you into your fixed mindset and flip them around—turning them into situations where you can be inspired and develop. From this vantage point, you'll be able to help others do the same—building the mindset culture you want.

This book will change what you know about mindset, while also providing clarity as you learn new evidence-based insights and actions you, your team, and your organization can benefit from. In Part One, we'll do a mindset reset, recasting our understanding of how mindset works. In Part Two, we'll examine organizational mindset in depth, looking at how it plays out in five key areas:

+ Collaboration, and whether we're more likely to compete with our colleagues or work together;
+ Innovation, and whether we can access new ideas or are stuck repeating the past;
+ Risk-taking and resilience, and whether we're willing to take chances or feel compelled to play it safe;
+ Integrity and ethical behavior, and whether we take shortcuts or break rules to meet performance expectations, hide mistakes, or enhance their reputation; and
+ Diversity, equity, and inclusion, and whether we seek to recruit and retain a workforce with multiple talents and perspectives, or hire based on a narrow prototype for success.

I'll show you how to identify your organization's mindset and mindset influences, explaining how to shift toward growth and stay there. In Part Three, we'll look at how mindset cues affect us as individuals. I'll introduce the four common situational cues that shift us into our fixed or growth mindset:

+ When we face situations where our efforts will be evaluated;
+ When we encounter difficult challenges;
+ When we receive critical feedback; and
+ When we're faced with the success of others.

You'll learn how to recognize which situations tend to trigger you along the continuum, and how you can invoke your growth mindset more often.

Yet even though, as individuals, we are powerful, we can only do so much alone. The best and biggest work of our lives comes from collaborating with others to realize our fullest potential collectively. Mindset is a team effort, and I encourage you to share what you learn. The very nature of a Culture of Growth is to strive for growth for everyone. This can only happen if we shift toward our growth mindset, roll up our sleeves, and work together.

PART ONE

Mindset Reset

CHAPTER 1

The Mindset Continuum

We've gotten mindset all wrong. Well, not *all* wrong, but we've over-simplified it drastically, and to our detriment.

Mindset seems like an easy concept to grasp: Either you believe that intelligence and ability are largely set and can't change much, or you think that we can grow and develop them over time. Yet when you reflect on your own personal experiences, you might sense something more complex than an either/or dichotomy.

Think of a time in the past when you were met with a challenge. How did you respond? Let's say your boss asked you to come up with some fund-raising ideas to help address a projected shortfall. Perhaps you played it safe, suggesting only initiatives that were in line with what the organization had done in the past. Or, maybe you saw in that request an opportunity to try something new, and you stretched yourself to offer unique solutions that went beyond traditional outreach and events. Or, maybe you started by listing the usual ideas, but then decided to push yourself a little.

The reality is that no one has *either* a fixed or a growth mindset. Although we may favor a fixed or a growth mindset, we all have both—and shifting between them is something each one of us does. Moreover, when we shift from fixed to growth, it isn't always like flipping a switch; sometimes it's more like adjusting a dimmer.

Mindset exists on a continuum. And where we fall on that continuum at any given moment often has to do with the situation we're in and the people around us.

However, the way we've come to think about mindset doesn't reflect this complexity. Since Carol Dweck first introduced the concept, we've seen the following illustration displayed frequently in classrooms and on social media:

What Kind of Mindset Do You Have?

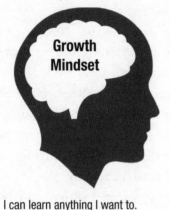 

Growth Mindset

Fixed Mindset

I can learn anything I want to.	I'm either good at it, or I'm not.
When I'm frustrated, I persevere.	When I'm frustrated, I give up.
I want to challenge myself.	I don't like to be challenged.
When I fail, I learn.	When I fail, I'm no good.
Tell me I try hard.	Tell me I'm smart.
If you succeed, I'm inspired.	If you succeed, I feel threatened.
My effort and attitude determine everything.	My abilities determine everything.

What's wrong with this image? Yes, people can differ in the mindset they typically endorse, but by focusing on our brains, this image implies that mindset is located entirely in the head. And it puts it in either/or terms. It asks us to identify *what kind* of mindset we have, implying that it's one or the other. Can you see the irony here? Thinking we always embody either the fixed or the growth mindset is a very fixed way of viewing mindset!

This image also shows a clear preference for one mindset over the other: Growth is good and fixed is bad. Although, as we will see, people and cultures with more of a growth mindset may have many admirable qualities, these misunderstandings have led to the moralization of mindset, especially in the American educational system and in corporations that have taken up the idea. When we view mindset as a fixed trait that resides inside an individual's head, and when we believe that a person with one mindset is a better person than someone with the other mindset, it's easy to use mindset to sort and label people. It also means that we put the onus of change on the individual, instead of considering the context and culture that creates and maintains mindset.

Mindset culture as it exists outside of us is an active, collaborative creation. Still, organizational leaders often focus on individual mindset, as if identifying and retaining "growth mindset" employees will create a growth-minded organization. Many school systems have asked my colleagues and me if there are assessments to rate teachers on their fixed or growth mindsets; and investment firms have requested that I help them create assessments so they can identify which entrepreneurs to invest in. Often, organizations want to use such assessments for selection and hiring. The underlying assumptions behind these inquiries are that: (a) mindset is static; (b) it's entirely individual; and (c) such assessments will reveal the "truth" about someone's mindset—whether they have a growth (or fixed) mindset, and therefore whether they'll be a good employee (or not). And when we affix these beliefs on individuals, they turn around and affix them on others.

In the teacher training institute that my colleagues and I created, we see teachers who endorse this false dichotomy view of mindset labeling students who struggle with motivation or performance by saying things like, "I'm sorry, this kid just has a fixed mindset and there's nothing much I can do about it" or "This generation of students has really fixed mindsets." When we ask teachers what they're doing to help students move toward their growth mindset, they sometimes say, "That's not my job. Students just need to have a growth mindset, or their parents need to be working with them to develop one." But labeling kids as unable to change is the definition of a fixed mindset—on the part of the teacher. And because some teachers may want learning to come easily and quickly (another fixed-minded attitude), they may short-circuit students' struggles—and thereby their learning—by immediately offering the correct answers or reassuring them that, "It's okay, not everyone can be a math person."

All of this misconstrues what mindset is, as well as the factors that determine our mindset in any given moment. And it turns mindset into a blame game, which doesn't help anyone.

Ask someone what their mindset is, and the accurate answer is: It depends. Even among those of us who study mindset, no one leans toward growth all of the time. **Depending on the situation, our fixed or growth mindset can become activated.**

Meet the Mindset Continuum.

THE MINDSET CONTINUUM

Instead of simply having a fixed *or* growth mindset, we are nudged along a continuum either more toward our fixed or more toward our growth mindset, depending on the circumstance. But on this continuum, we also have a default set point. Perhaps you tend to hang out on the growth end of the continuum, or your initial response to challenge is more fixed. (Don't hold too tightly to that idea either, because our set point can change over time and in different situations.)

Understanding our mindset set point can be a helpful starting point, as Carol Dweck's classic work shows, yet none of us lives in a vacuum. In fact, one of the most surprising findings of our research is how people move along the continuum based on predictable, discernable cues around them, which is why mindset assessments aimed at targeting our "one true mindset" often miss the mark.

MINDSET CULTURE

The culture surrounding us is one of the *biggest* influences on our beliefs, motivations, and behavior. This *mindset culture* exists at the group and organizational level.

Mindset culture is so powerful that it can actually block an individual's growth mindset. But when leaders focus on developing individuals, they almost always overlook the impact of the mindset culture they've created. In many cases, they're not even aware of it! For example, Barre3 CEO Sadie Lincoln had built a fitness business that she thought had growth mindset at its core until an anonymous company-wide survey shattered the image she'd worked hard to develop—that of the perfect leader who made it all look easy. "I really tried to play that part, even though it wasn't always true," says Lincoln. "I didn't realize I had created a culture of perfection, and as a result we lost authenticity, trust, and our ability to innovate together." Perfection is one aspect of a fixed mindset culture. In an environment that demanded seemingly effortless, flawless performance (as modeled from the top), employees felt demotivated and demoralized instead of invigorated and inspired to take on challenges. This is mindset culture at work. Even an attentive leader such as Sadie Lincoln was shocked to learn that instead of a Culture of Growth, she'd unwittingly created what I call a Culture of Genius, an organization whose policies, practices, and norms embody fixed mindset beliefs.

Lincoln knew she and her team had to overhaul their corporate culture, starting with taking ownership of her role in creating a toxic atmosphere. (We'll look at how she did that in Chapter 11.) It wasn't easy—and it wasn't without consequences. "I lost team members during this trying time," Lincoln told *Marie Claire*.

Some people who bought into the fixed mindset culture of effort-less perfection found it unsettling to see Lincoln openly acknowledging and owning her failures. But the people who stayed helped her build their new growth mindset culture. And as Lincoln told Guy Raz in a 2020 interview on *How I Built This*, the lessons her team learned during that time later helped them successfully navigate the COVID-19 pandemic—when countless other fitness companies had to close their doors permanently. Within days of closing all of their locations nationwide, they re-opened as an online exercise platform.

But lockdowns were only the beginning of what they would have to grapple with. In response to the Black Lives Matter movement, Lincoln and her team called on experts and began to formulate a plan to address issues of structural racism, diversity, equity, and inclusion that they identified within the business. As Lincoln told Raz, "This is one of the most hard, profound, important moments of our history at Barre3. . . . I am a White woman in leadership with immense privilege, and [I've unconsciously built] a company of leaders who look a lot like me," including franchise owners and instructors. The company has been working with their DEI partner to educate leadership and franchise owners, and to reshape their outreach and hiring practices. They've been sharing their plans publicly through the company's blog, have created a set of internal metrics to measure their progress, and are working to reshape their systems to make DEI-centered policies standard practice throughout the organization.

CULTURES OF GENIUS AND CULTURES OF GROWTH

Organizational mindset refers to the shared beliefs about intelligence, talent, and ability that are held by a group of people in an organization. This mindset is revealed through the group's cultural artifacts: its policies, practices, procedures, behavioral norms, messages from leaders and other powerful people, important organizational materials (such as its website, mission statement, and other foundational documents), and so on.

Organizational mindsets also exist on a continuum spanning fixed to growth. Teams don't just have a static mindset; they move between them in response to opportunities and challenges that arise and the affordances provided by the larger organization. Organizational mindset beliefs—that is, the degree to which a given group believes that intelligence, talent, and ability are fixed or are malleable—not only influence our behavior and how we present ourselves, they also guide our interactions and our expectations of others. These core beliefs shape the way people in a group think, feel, and behave. In workplace settings, mindset culture has a ripple effect that impacts everything: collaboration and innovation; who is hired, fired, and promoted; ethical (or unethical) behavior; diversity and inclusion; and bottom-line economic success. At school, the mindset culture affects students' experiences, engagement, and performance in class, and it influences which students teachers and administrators deem worthy of challenging material and additional investment.

Fixed mindset organizations—or Cultures of Genius—believe and communicate the idea that people's abilities are unchangeable, or fixed. People either "have it" or they don't, and there's little anyone can do to change this. "Star search" and "stack ranking" evaluation practices are a common outgrowth of fixed-minded Cultures of Genius. If leadership believes that some have it and some don't, the focus naturally shifts to finding, recruiting, and promoting stars and either ignoring or firing everyone else. In Cultures of Genius, systems encourage people to compete against one another to prove themselves and to see who rises to the top (often by whatever means necessary).

Ironically, when people hear the term "Culture of Genius" without context, their eyes widen. "Ooh, I like the sound of that!" they exclaim. Our society has a cultural fascination with the idea of genius and the perception that some special people are born with innate abilities and skills that lie beyond the grasp of the rest of us. We even falsify history to retell stories that emphasize the genius or lone hero who, by virtue of innate talent, has a brilliant "aha" moment that changes the world. Paradoxically, the more our daily lives require interdependence, collaboration, and teamwork, the more we seem to cling to these genius narratives. As Harvard professor Marjorie Garber writes in *The Atlantic*, "The further our society gets from individual agency—the less the individual seems to have real power to change things—the more we idealize the genius, who is by this definition the opposite of the committee or the collaborative enterprise. Indeed, some of the resistance to the idea that Shakespeare wrote his plays in collaboration with other playwrights and even actors in his company comes from our residual, occasionally desperate need to retain this ideal notion of the individual genius."

As Garber goes on to note, Joseph Addison, an eighteenth-century chronicler of the history of the genius, described two types of genius popular in the early 1700s: natural and learned. One could display brilliance from an early age, but one could also develop it through industriousness (or what I call *effective effort*). These days, we focus almost exclusively on the former manifestation, to the point of idolizing it. That's why the Culture of Genius, at first blush, sounds so appealing.

When I asked Carol Dweck where she thinks our love of genius comes from, she speculated, "I think a large part of it comes from the legacy of hierarchy," explaining that those in power, born into privilege and educated at prestigious schools, tend to look for ways to justify why they're better. Stanford psychology professor Claude Steele echoed a similar idea: "It's probably a root of a power-privilege sustaining ideology. Once you have it, you have it, and if you don't have it, you're out of luck. That guarantees a certain status to me if I'm a genius and I have high ability—it gives you a sense of exclusiveness that other people might not be able to get there and it's just the natural order of things." Claude added that this type of thinking "legitimizes and launders privilege. The reality is I've gotten good because I've had some pretty good scaffolding, but with the genius idea, I don't have to think about my position that way—I can think about it in terms of 'this is a gift that I have.'" Consistent with these analyses, the research I've conducted shows that the genius mentality helps maintain the status quo. Those who most benefit from the status quo—the few who are considered stars—have an interest, consciously or unconsciously, in keeping it in place. At the same time, it takes the pressure off those who haven't been anointed; after all, if I'm not someone who *has it*, people are likely to expect less of me.

Perhaps then it's logical we'd gravitate toward building Cultures of Genius. With a genius at the helm—and as many as we can find, spread throughout the organization—we should be extremely successful, right? But that's not what my research shows. As you'll see in coming chapters, ironically, Cultures of Genius often produce *less* genius—that is, they tend to show significantly less innovation, creativity, sustained growth, consistent results, and so on. People's drive, their willingness to take the kinds of risks that will lead to the next big idea or breakthrough, their desire to collaborate with their colleagues or folks in other sectors, may all be dampened inside the prove-and-perform culture of effortless perfection that Cultures of Genius establish.

Conversely, with its emphasis on embracing complexity, possibility, and dedicated effort, growth mindset cultures—or Cultures of Growth—can sometimes seem more demanding. In an organization where learning is continuous, there are always more ways to improve and new horizons to seek.

Yet people often misperceive the growth mindset as softer and less rigorous, and Cultures of Growth as ones where leaders provide unreserved warmth, positivity, and endless affirmations while rewarding effort more than results. But this flies in the face of my research, which shows that college students in classrooms taught by faculty who create a growth mindset culture, for example, do not experience those professors' classes as easier or less rigorous. Instead, they describe the classes as quite demanding, and sometimes, downright annoying. When a professor is functioning in their growth mindset while leading a class, they will keep challenging students to stretch themselves to learn and grow. These teachers will not be content if even one student hits a learning plateau; they push for continuous improvement, even among students who are already doing well. From the perspective of students, this is not always pleasant. But they tend to appreciate it in the longer run because they do better and learn more.

People in Cultures of Growth believe that talent and ability can be developed with effort, persistence, good strategies, help-seeking, and support. They are often asked to reflect on their progress and development instead of just reporting whether or not they've accomplished their goal. They are also asked to identify what was done to create that progress (including things that failed, not just things that succeeded). Finally, they are asked to use that knowledge to improve the organization. Cultures of Growth offer tangible strategies and structures that encourage innovation and expand the abilities of their workforce. That is, the Culture of Growth's commitment to development is demanding—requiring effort, attention, and dedication to proactively identify ways to improve—but critically, individuals are not left to do this alone; the organization provides support and resources to help folks along the way.

My research shows that an organization's mindset culture consistently influences five common ways people work well together (or not): collaboration; innovation; risk-taking and resilience; integrity and ethical behavior; and diversity, equity, and inclusion (DEI). These *behavioral norms* (defined as unwritten rules for behavior that are considered acceptable or desirable within a group) are often interlocking, such that when a team has issues with collaboration and innovation, they usually struggle with risk-taking, ethics, and DEI too. In Part Two, I'll show how mindset culture shapes each of these norms and how you can harness them to build organizational trust, employee satisfaction and commitment, and yes, profit.

That's a whole lot, and it's reasonable to ask how we know so much is shaped by mindset culture.

Organizational Mindset as a Meaning-Making System

An organization's mindset may rest on a shared belief, but it has a cascade of implications for people's other beliefs, goals, and behavior. When we encounter setbacks, when we're called upon to channel substantial effort into our work, or when we need to master a new domain, the core mindset beliefs endorsed by an organization tell people how best to respond. In Cultures of Growth, the cues around us prompt us to frame these challenges as opportunities to expand our abilities and develop professionally, and as people. In Cultures of Genius, we're more apt to view these situations as cause to defend and prove ourselves, even at the expense of others, if necessary. Instead of learning, we seek to elevate our status or shore up our standing.

Organizations don't fully embody either a Culture of Genius or a Culture of Growth at all times and in all contexts; they are not monolithic. As with personal mindset, organizational mindset exists on a continuum. And while there is often a recognizable overarching mindset culture at the level of the organization (the cultural set point), within organizations there are often a variety of *mindset microcultures*. For instance, while the organization as a whole may largely embody more of a fixed mindset, certain divisions, departments, or teams may be more oriented toward growth.

Then we have mindset at the individual level. Through research we've isolated four common, predictable situations, termed *mindset triggers*, that lead us to embody our personal fixed or growth mindset. (You and others may have triggers not listed here, but these are the ones that, according to analyses of the literature and anecdotal experiences working with a variety of organizations, show up most reliably.) These situations are useful to understand because they provide insights about when we tend to embody our fixed mindset and how to shift ourselves toward growth. We'll cover all of that in Part Three. (And if you're still a little confused about how it all fits together, don't worry—I'll break it all down as we move forward.)

For now, let's reconsider the illustration of the personal mindset from the start of this chapter. Instead of those two competing heads, here's a more accurate picture of how mindset operates. This version considers the influence of both the mindset culture and mindset cues that move us along the continuum between our personal fixed and growth mindset beliefs.

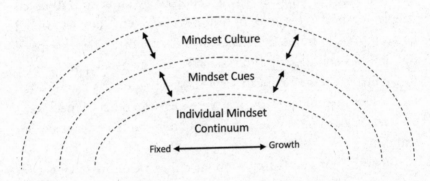

Though individuals have some control over their personal mindset beliefs, external factors such as an organization's mindset culture play a large and underappreciated role in shaping our thoughts, motivations, and behavior.

Your organization has a mindset culture—the question is: Do you know what it is and the ways it is affecting you and others within it?

CHAPTER 2

Organizational Mindsets

William James, often credited as one of the founders of American psychology, wrote that an individual has "as many different social selves as there are distinct groups of persons about whose opinion he cares." You can see this concept in action when you consider who you are in different professional and social situations. For example, if I'm at my friend's wedding in a church, I'll act in a manner appropriate to that context, which will differ from when I'm in a classroom or out with friends on a Friday night. Various parts of our identity emerge and our behavior changes depending on the setting. The mindset culture of groups is a feature of the setting that draws out different parts of ourselves.

One of the first times I noticed how different mindset cultures change people was during my time in graduate school. Like most psychology departments, Stanford's consists of different areas: social psychology, cognitive psychology, developmental psychology, neuroscience. At the end of every year, PhD students in each area are asked to give research presentations to review the projects they've worked on and share the progress they've made. For most students, these talks can be nerve-wracking, and it's especially true for first- and second-year graduate students presenting in front of faculty.

One afternoon in Carol Dweck's office, I mentioned that I noticed how the students from two of the seminars performed very differently. The first seminar had a clear prove-and-perform, fixed mindset culture. It was populated with some of the most eminent and decorated faculty members—many of whom had been voted into the National Academy of Sciences, the most prestigious body of scientists in the country. Charged with competition, faculty members vied to be first to find the fatal flaw in each research talk, to take down the idea most effectively, and to one-up each other with the most devastating comment. With faculty fighting among themselves to be the star of the show, students suffered. Having worked all year, students were the experts on their projects, yet they were suddenly overcome with *ums*, *uhs*, and *hmms*, blanking out on important details of their work. They choked, despite knowing their work backward and forward. Afterward, they were frustrated and dejected: "Why didn't I say this or that? There were so many ways I could have responded to that question. The data don't even support the interpretation that faculty member made!"

Although equally eminent faculty populated the second seminar, the atmosphere reflected more of a Culture of Growth. It was still a critical environment where faculty pointed out flaws and problems, but instead of jockeying to show who was smarter, they took a "break it down to build it up" approach. Faculty believed the seminar to be a place to reveal the challenges of research and learn how to address them head-on. They played off each other to offer suggestions to improve the study designs and analytic approach in order to strengthen the project. Students were still nervous to present to such an esteemed group, but they didn't stumble or freeze in the same way as the students in the fixed-minded seminar. They were able to answer questions and brainstorm together with faculty about ways to improve their work. They left motivated and determined to make the changes that would strengthen their studies.

After describing the way these seminars shaped students' behavior, I asked Carol, "Has anyone ever studied mindset as a cultural factor? As a quality of an entire group or environment?" Her face lit up and with a big smile, she shook her head, saying, "No! No one has ever looked at that. But, Mare . . . we should do it together!" That's when the concept of *mindset culture* was born.

For the previous three decades, mindset was thought to be almost exclusively something that lived within an individual. A large body of research had shown what happens when individuals operate from their fixed or growth mindset, but no one had examined how we think, feel, and behave when we encounter an organization's mindset—or even that there was such a thing as organizational mindset.

HOW ORGANIZATIONS SIGNAL THEIR MINDSET CULTURE

One of the ways my team evaluates how people respond to mindset culture is to present them with company mission statements that align with either a Culture of Genius or a Culture of Growth. In addition to mission statements, other cultural artifacts such as websites, founding documents, onboarding processes, and evaluation and promotion policies all shed light on an organization's mindset culture. Together, a portrait emerges. When companies narrowly focus on outcomes—offering employees "opportunities to prove themselves" and "perform at their very best"; when they boast about being "results oriented"; or when they explicitly value the "best people" and their "natural talents and success," without also mentioning the growth and development that it takes to get there—it communicates more of a fixed mindset culture. These artifacts paint a picture of a culture that is pretty black and white: either you succeed or you fail; employees are either stars or they're not; only the final result, rather than any aspect of the process, is what matters.

Most growth- and fixed-mindset organizations share some characteristics. They all want excellent performance—who doesn't?—to ensure bottom-line outcomes. However, *how* they expect employees to achieve success is different. Organizations with Cultures of Growth focus on progress and provide support to make it happen. They offer growth opportunities to employees instead of "opportunities to demonstrate their abilities." They are passionate about advancement and development—yes, of the bottom line, but just as importantly, of their employees. Organizations with Cultures of Growth are likely to deem more characteristics essential to success besides sheer ability, talent, or intellectual brainpower, like motivation, creativity, problem-solving, and the willingness to develop oneself.

My research shows that organizations with Cultures of Growth enjoy more effective company cultures and have more satisfied, high-performing employees.

The box below summarizes some differences between the two cultures that we can pick up when we analyze company artifacts like their mission statements and job ads.

ORGANIZATIONAL MINDSETS

The following are characteristics that we see in companies at the poles of the mindset culture continuum.

Culture of Genius	Culture of Growth
Offers highest performance opportunities	Offers highest growth opportunities
Emphasizes employees' talents and successes	Emphasizes employees' motivation and hard work
Focuses on results	Focuses on results and process
Atmosphere of bests—best instincts, best ideas, best people	Atmosphere that fosters a love for learning, passion, creativity, and resourcefulness

---

If you've started to suspect that your organization is mostly a Culture of Genius, and you're wondering how to shift it toward growth, know that mindset culture *can* be changed. Like turning a large ship, though, this transition is not easy. Many companies fall right back into that tricky, false mindset dichotomy. But rest assured, it is possible, and in Part Two, I'll show you some ways you can get started, including some concrete approaches you can start using right away, on your own or with the people you manage.

THE MINDSET CULTURE CYCLE

Perhaps you're unsure where your organization falls on the mindset continuum. A natural next question is: "How do I find out?" Maybe you're hoping there's a quiz available to help identify fixed-minded leaders or employees. This desire is understandable, especially in a world obsessed with rankings and static assessments. Yet when it comes to mindset, these appraisals are likely to miss the mark. They may show what someone believes about their ability and intelligence in the moment, but they don't reveal where—and under what circumstances—that person's fixed or growth mindset shows up, or what you, as a supervisor or mentor, might do to support them in realizing their potential.

The question is not: "Are you a person with more of a fixed or growth mindset?" The question is: "*When* are you in your fixed mindset and *when* are you in your growth mindset?" At the organizational level, the question is not: "How can we avoid hiring fixed mindset people?" The question is: "What triggers our employees to adopt more fixed- or growth-mindset views and behaviors? How can we shape the environment to encourage more of a growth mindset more of the time?"

In aiming to evaluate individuals' mindset set points, organizations often end up putting an inordinate amount of focus on what employees bring to the table and not enough on how that table is constructed.

Let's take a look at what happens when we try to label people by mindset. Say a hiring manager is looking for someone brilliant with innate talent. This brilliance heuristic—a cognitive shortcut that looks for the people and patterns that we associate with brilliance—quickly runs into bias. When we bring to mind what qualities indicate brilliance and inborn talent, inevitably the results are colored by society's cultural norms, looking a whole lot like stereotypes. After all, who in our culture are typically held up as geniuses? Just for kicks, you can pull up a Google image search for "What does a genius look like?," and it returns mostly pictures of Albert Einstein. While Cultures of Genius look for individuals who leaders perceive as innately talented, they implicitly exclude people who belong to groups whose skills and abilities have been historically excluded and stereotyped as inferior—not because these groups lack brilliance and innate talent but because they don't automatically come to mind when fitting the genius prototype that Cultures of Genius prize.

Which groups are excluded in a Culture of Genius often depends on industry. In tech and other STEM fields, White (and sometimes Asian) men tend to embody the genius prototype. Think of the most famous tech founders, for example, almost all of whom are White or Asian men. Who doesn't fit the prototype of a natural genius in these fields? Women; Black, Latino/a, and Indigenous people; LGBTQ+ folks; and people from the disability community, among others. In Cultures of Genius, these prototype matching processes often happen automatically and unconsciously, with decision makers forming a picture of whom to hire before considering how someone outside the stereotype might contribute. A Culture of Growth also emphasizes strong skills and abilities, but in addition it prioritizes people's motivation, trajectory of growth, dedication, and willingness to continuously develop over time. No matter what race, sex, age, ability status, or other demographic, willingness to grow is a quality available to all.

This is an example of how a core belief gives rise to behavioral norms. For a more detailed illustration of this process, let's consider a totally different example: beliefs about time. If an organization or team holds as a central tenet the belief that time is scarce and we have to make the most of every minute, then norms about when meetings start (Right on time, every time.) and being late (Don't do it—or else!) are clear. This shapes people's behavior (Get to meetings on time.). In settings where time is believed to be abundant and expansive, it can—and often is—used for thinking. Instead of rushing off to implement ideas and potentially breaking things in the process, this organization may favor a more thoughtful, measured approach. The late Edgar Schein, professor emeritus at MIT, studied organizational culture for decades and demonstrated how such norms arise out of core beliefs. These norms are deeply embedded within organizations and shape the unconscious, taken-for-granted behaviors that constitute the essence of organizational culture.

Like time, mindset is one of those core beliefs about human behavior. Mindset is a cornerstone of an organization's culture. Our core beliefs about the fixedness or malleability of intelligence, talent, and ability drive every important organizational process in self-reinforcing cycles. I call this the Organizational Mindset Culture Cycle.

HOW ORGANIZATIONAL MINDSETS CREATE AND RE-CREATE CULTURAL VALUES

We hire others who demonstrate these valued traits

We self-present fixed or growth mindset traits to get in the door

We demonstrate valued traits at work (evaluation/promotion)

We take on and internalize these valued traits

Depending on what we perceive a company's values to be, we will present either fixed- or growth-minded traits in order to get hired initially or, later, to get assigned to prestigious teams or assignments. Once employed, we will then demonstrate those traits in order to acquire the goodies of the organization—positive evaluations, more promotions, bonuses, and so on. Yet, as we embody the fixed- or growth-minded traits valued by our team (so we can win respect and accolades), we start to believe the act. To make our behavior align with our beliefs, we start to believe that these traits are emblematic of who we are. To further resolve our cognitive dissonance, we internalize the organization's mindset, making it our own.

In my lab's research, we found that when people presented the organization's preferred mindset traits over time, they not only started to celebrate these traits in others, but when in the position to hire, they were significantly more likely to select those who demonstrated these same mindset traits, all of which further reinforced the organization's mindset. These feedback loops shape an individual's experiences within the organization, and that, in turn, can influence their performance, persistence, and engagement and, as a result, have a significant influence on individual and organizational outcomes.

Employees have less trust in and show less commitment to Cultures of Genius compared with Cultures of Growth. Because Cultures of Genius believe that some people have it and others don't, people constantly have to prove and perform, knowing that they are only as good as their last performance. In this environment, colleagues are constantly competing against each other and wondering who might take their place. This culture undermines trust in the people you work with, and it undermines trust in the organization to notice, value, and appreciate your abilities. It's not too hard to see, then, why employees are less committed to companies with strong Cultures of Genius. Employees in these organizations are more willing to entertain outside offers and are more likely to look for early exit strategies, relative to employees in Cultures of Growth.

Organizational Mindset Shapes Behavioral Norms

If a company proclaims its core value is collaboration, then is it more likely to have a collaborative culture? Or is culture more accurately reflected in how people behave and interact with each other? My colleagues and I found that while the values expressed in mission statements can indicate an organization's mindset, the connection is not definitive. To understand how mindset actually influences behavior, we need to look deeper. For example, collaboration, risk-taking, innovation, and integrity are norms often associated with greater organizational trust and commitment, and they impact productivity and economic success. Yet we know relatively little about the beliefs that shape these norms. In other words, what's the interplay? So my colleagues and I decided to look at how organizational mindset influences employees in their actual workplace environments, in this case in Fortune 500 companies.

Naturally, we predicted we'd uncover distinctions between Cultures of Genius and Cultures of Growth, but the significance of these differences was surprising. **In our analysis, we found that employees of organizations with strong Cultures of Genius were 40 percent less satisfied with the company's culture compared with those who worked for organizations with strong Cultures of Growth.**

We reviewed the mission statements of the Fortune 500—which represent two-thirds of the U.S. gross domestic product—and compared these with employee satisfaction data from Glassdoor. The results were clear: Mindset as professed in these companies' mission statements had a distinct impact on employees' experience of their company's culture. Yet simply proclaiming the desired norms and values doesn't guarantee they'll become an actuality.

Interestingly, employees were not less happy in Cultures of Genius in every category. When we focused on compensation and benefits, for instance, we found similar satisfaction results among the two cultures. This showed us that employees weren't simply wearing rose-colored glasses in Cultures of Growth and gray-colored glasses in Cultures of Genius, rating everything in line with key perceptions (what psychologists call a *halo effect*). Instead, mindset culture had clear and unique consequences for the organization's norms and values. It doesn't affect everything. **What organizational mindset does affect is the way people think of themselves, the way they interact with others, and the way the organization performs.**

The question, then, was whether organizational mindset shapes how people actually behave. In another study we undertook with a San Diego–based culture consulting firm, we examined the behavioral norms present in Cultures of Growth and Cultures of Genius. We found that collaboration, innovation, and integrity—which are associated with positive cultural and economic outcomes for companies—were not present in the same way across the two cultures. Employees who worked in Cultures of Genius reported that the organization was less supportive of collaboration, was less innovative, and encouraged less intellectual risk-taking. More than that, employees in these companies reported that folks were more likely to engage in unethical behavior like cheating, cutting corners, hoarding information, keeping secrets from each other, as well as backroom negotiating for prized promotions or assignments. Not surprisingly, employees were less likely to trust their company and were less committed when it embodied more of a Culture of Genius.

Remarkably, we found that organizational mindsets are indeed powerful enough to shape people's behavior. Recall my earlier statement that a Culture of Genius can actually override an individual's tendencies toward their growth mindset. Most of us have witnessed that situation—or experienced it ourselves—where someone who tends to be geared toward growth tries to persist in the face of a fixed and limiting organizational culture, only to eventually either conform to the culture, or give up and leave. As our analysis showed, in stronger Cultures of Genius, employees experienced a less adaptive company culture. Psychologically, employees were less committed too. They reported less trust that their company would treat them fairly and expressed a greater desire to leave the company for other opportunities, compared with employees in stronger Cultures of Growth.

Next, we were curious how managers' perceptions of the company's behavioral norms compared with those of employees, and how they evaluated those they supervised. Again, what we found surprised us. Managers who worked in a stronger Culture of Genius reported that their direct reports were less collaborative, less innovative, and less ethically behaved compared to managers in a stronger Culture of Growth. Managers were also able to detect differences in employees' organizational trust and commitment, reporting lower levels of both in a Culture of Genius. The differences managers noticed among their employees were similar to those that employees had reported themselves; in other words, their perceptions matched. What we hadn't anticipated were the effects of mindset culture on performance and leadership potential. After all, if a Culture of Genius is careful to attract and select the very best talent and value and promote it over time, shouldn't managers think their employees are the most talented and have the most leadership potential compared to managers in a Culture of Growth? Instead, it was the managers in Cultures of Growth who reported higher levels of performance among their employees and felt their employees showed more leadership potential. Those in a Culture of Genius may view themselves as stars with leadership potential, and their managers may initially believe the same, but then evaluations come in, and those beliefs seem to dissipate. And perhaps they're not wrong since in a Culture of Genius, it's difficult for anyone to perform to their true potential.

Now that we understand the importance of organizational mindset, let's figure out how to tell which you're in.

Identifying Mindset Culture Cues

When my team and I are asked to assist companies in assessing and shifting their mindset culture, we've found that one of our most effective tools is a *cues audit*. We educate employees about the dynamic nature of fixed and growth mindset, along with the four common situations that cue people to shift between these mindsets. Then, we ask them to consider the everyday policies and practices they routinely encounter in their organization that might (perhaps even unintentionally) be communicating more of a fixed or growth mindset. Organizations often inadvertently send mixed mindset messages to employees. Cues audits can be particularly effective at not only identifying such inconsistencies, which can be quite subtle, but also engaging employees in remedying them.

These cues are found in what managers say and do. In 2016, a large multinational bank approached our research team to identify how mindset culture might be shaping their employees' experiences. In the course of our work, we discovered that managers' mindsets about their employees shaped managers' behavior. Managers who endorsed more growth mindset beliefs about their employees used more growth-minded strategies to coach and interact with them. These managers normalized struggle and confusion for their direct reports—especially when the employee was working to develop a new skill. They were also more likely to invest their time and energy in all employees, not just the ones they immediately connected with or the stand-out stars, consistent with their belief that all employees can develop and grow. Finally, they recruited the whole team to help when people struggled, viewing challenges as "ours" to overcome rather than an individual's mountain to summit alone.

Managers with more fixed mindset beliefs about their employees preferred star performers who didn't need much development. They believed that a good manager keeps their top performers motivated and happy, so they gave the boring, uninteresting work to those they saw as having less potential. These managers said it was better to reassure a struggling employee by saying that the task in question just didn't seem to be that employee's area of strength. Finally, they offered greater developmental opportunities to those they perceived as most talented, rather than focusing on developing their whole team.

These types of fixed mindset behaviors within the different mindset microcultures that managers create are what happens at most companies.

Intrigued by the findings at this institution and other large corporations, I worked with entrepreneur Ben Tauber and psychologist Christopher Samsa to survey 165 Silicon Valley startup founders. In a separate study with Kathleen Boyle Dalen and Wendy Torrance at the Ewing Marion Kauffman Foundation, we investigated the mindset of 300 more entrepreneurs. Between the two, we wanted to examine how founders' mindsets influenced the cultures they created at their companies. Consistent with the Fortune 500 results, we discovered that founders who self-reported more fixed mindset beliefs created companies with more interpersonally competitive cultures, where people were more likely to engage in unethical behavior, and where employees perceived the organization as being less tolerant of mistakes. Companies led by more growth-minded founders provided more support for employees' risk-taking and were more flexible and adaptable to change. These organizations had more innovative, more ethical, and less interpersonally competitive company cultures. Additionally, employee turnover was lower, with employees having more trust in and commitment to the organization. The culture also impacted entrepreneurs' success in realizing their fund-raising goals. **Not only does mindset impact perceptions and behavior, it shapes bottom lines.**

DOWNSTREAM EFFECTS OF MINDSET CULTURE

Now, let's take a closer look at how mindset influences actual behavior and outcomes within organizations. In Part Two, we'll cover the five sets of behavioral norms and outcomes over which mindset culture holds sway. These are *collaboration*, whether people are willing and motivated to work together or whether they become mired in interpersonal competition; *innovation*, whether employees feel supported and encouraged to think big, or whether their creativity is hampered by narrow reasoning; *risk-taking and resilience*, whether employees feel empowered and are given the resources to take moonshots, and to bounce back if they miss their target, or whether employees and organizations play it safe for fear of failure and become fragile in the face of setbacks; *integrity and ethical behavior*, whether employees are encouraged to do the right thing, or to take dubious shortcuts; and *diversity, equity, and inclusion*, whether organizations can attract and retain broad representation while supporting the success of all employees, or whether they create exclusive cultures that include and support only a select few.

First up: collaboration.

PART TWO

Mindset Culture

CHAPTER 3

Collaboration

As a new professor at Indiana University, one of the first faculty meetings I attended was a discussion about how to distribute the department's merit raises. Like many organizations, these annual raises tend to be minuscule—maybe 1 to 2 percent a year, if there's a raise pool at all.

In the past, a merit review committee would inspect all 60-plus faculty members' annual productivity reports (including how many papers we wrote, how many PhD students we advised, how many grants we got, etc.) and rate and rank each professor in turn. To my horror, I learned that each faculty member would then get a letter in their mailbox showing everyone's ranking from highest to lowest, with your personal position brightly highlighted in yellow. Now our department is incredible—full of some of the most productive faculty in the country whether you measure by publications, grants, awards, national academy memberships, teaching evaluations, or the number of students mentored and placed into jobs. Yet the day the letters arrived in everyone's mailboxes was the day of the year that many faculty dreaded most.

With this system, the junior faculty were almost always stuck at the bottom. How could they compete when their senior colleagues had so many more resources and opportunities, like the ability to build bigger labs with more students and staff, with larger grants that could support greater output? To the senior academics, the inevitable salary compression that occurs over time rendered the system unfair. At 25 years in, because annual raises did not keep pace with rising inflation, their salaries were close to the starting pay of the junior faculty. And nearly everyone agreed that, overall, the ranking system created too much interdepartmental competition, all for a potential 1- to 2-percent increase.

Faculty weren't the only ones who faced problems created by such ranking systems. A few weeks later, when walking by our large teaching auditorium, I noticed a few sheets of paper taped on the wall outside the entrance. Looking more closely, I saw the papers contained the exam grades of all the students enrolled in Introductory Psychology, listed in order of highest to lowest grade. As the students streamed by, some purposely ignored the papers; others gathered around, running their fingers down the lists, looking for their ID number and hoping to find it on the first or second sheet and not the fourth or fifth.

From performance-based classroom seating to corporate ranking systems, we often have to jockey for position. In a society that claims strong (if dated and misguided) meritocratic values, it seems reasonable to distribute resources—whether admission to more rigorous classes, scholarships, promotions, or raises—by ranking people against a set of criteria. However, inside organizations, the internal competition that such practices encourage often has unintended consequences, including crushing collaboration.

If you're ready to leap to your feet and defend the merits of competition, hear me out. *Marketplace* competitiveness does seem to be a necessary component of long-term success, especially for capitalist corporations: You want to be the company, the brand, or the school of choice. What I'm describing is competitiveness not among, but *within* organizations. When people are set up to battle one another internally for status and resources, when the pressure is on to prove oneself over others, and when opportunities for success are limited, problems rather than solutions prevail. Some leaders believe that creating a kind of *Hunger Games* atmosphere is the best way to push people to do their best, yet we know how that story played out, and research backs it up. **When chances to succeed are scarce, people**

tend to be triggered toward their fixed mindset. In the long run (and sometimes even the short one), their resulting behavior can end up hurting their own performance and limiting their potential, and by extension their organization's.

In this chapter, we'll look at how organizational mindset influences the environment to make it more competitive or collaborative. We'll also examine some of the policies and behaviors that shape and reinforce mindset culture, and how mindset affects organizational outcomes. Finally, I'll provide some specific suggestions for how you can encourage a growth-oriented approach to collaboration in your organization.

You might think that competition among employees is necessary for innovation and growth. Yet while competition may produce some positive results among some individuals—by limited measures and over a limited amount of time—as we'll see, the cost of those results can be high. Fostering collaboration isn't just about making folks feel good, but about creating the kind of environment that produces durable and sustainable achievement among more people in the organization.

Because of their emphasis on collaboration, Cultures of Growth seem to some as if they might lack the edge and drive necessary for success. Our work shows the opposite. These organizations have plenty of drive, but they don't view achievement as something that needs to be weaponized and pointed inward, dividing people into winners and losers as often happens in Cultures of Genius. **Cultures of Growth harness the tension between where individuals and the organization are versus where they want to be, and they use it to fuel collaborative efforts that propel everyone forward toward their goal.** Our studies show that Cultures of Growth can be exceptionally competitive in their marketplace performance, and without the collateral damage to people that Cultures of Genius often accrue.

Before diving into how to foster a growth-minded culture of collaboration, let's first take a closer look at why it's more effective than setting people against one another.

HOW INTERNAL COMPETITION CREATES LOSERS—AND HOW WE CAN DO BETTER

Adam Neumann claimed that WeWork thrived on competition. The former CEO was known to personally pit employees against one another. In Jed Rothstein's documentary *WeWork: Or the Making and Breaking of a $47 Billion Unicorn*, a former assistant of Neumann's described an internal performance review which took place in one of WeWork's ubiquitous glass-paneled conference rooms, in which Neumann told her that she was doing a good job. But when another employee walked by, he pointed to the passerby and said, "But you're not her. You could be, but you don't have the confidence that she has." The assistant says she went home and asked herself what she needed to do to become like the other employee. "You're constantly in this fear [that] 'Somebody else is gonna take my job. I have to fight to stay here,'" she said. "I felt constantly like I couldn't just breathe." She added that Neumann would frequently admonish staff, telling them, "I could fire all of you and do this by myself."

WeWork bought into the idea that low-ranking employees should be fired on an ongoing basis, letting go 20 percent of its workforce annually. This process, called stack ranking, was made popular by former GE CEO Jack Welch; but it was unsympathetically referred to at WeWork as "Jen-ocides," a reference to attorney and executive Jennifer Berrent, who was often in charge of the layoffs. For those remaining, staying in the top 80 percent presented its own challenge. Employees were rarely given the resources or support to meet outsized goals, and it became commonplace for employees—many of them millennials who had been lured by Neumann's invitation to "do what you love"—to cycle in and out of the company within just 18 months. They also might have left because they were simply fed up. Employees in their growth mindset become frustrated in Cultures of Genius because of limited opportunities for development. Because they perceive they won't be valued, and must constantly attend to their status, they can't take the risks that real growth requires. All of this impacts organizational outcomes. High turnover is expensive, not only financially, but to an organization's reputation. In a competitive marketplace, when trying to recruit the most sought-after employees, companies with high rates of churn can, ironically, lose their competitive edge.

According to data from the Center for American Progress, companies spend roughly 20 percent of an employee's annual salary to replace workers earning under $50,000 per year, and higher-level employees are even more costly to replace—as much as several times their annual salary. Gallup estimates that churn among millennials costs the U.S. economy alone as much as $30.5 billion per year. Among their top priorities, millennials report that they value feeling a sense of purpose in their work and a company whose values align with their own. As our study of Glassdoor data revealed, employees in Cultures of Genius were less satisfied with their employer than those in Cultures of Growth. If an organization wants to develop a deep bench of talent, especially among younger workers, knowing it's dedicated to investing in them could be key to attracting and retaining people who are—and who can become—excellent and committed employees. When 2021's unprecedented "great resignation" hit, and more than 30 million Americans left their jobs, organizational behavior experts noted that people don't just quit a job, they quit bad workplace cultures. With the potential for a massive employee exodus, Cultures of Growth were better situated to both retain talent and become the landing place for people valuing the higher levels of individual development and support that they offer.

One of the most powerful influences on an employee's experiences, motivation, and performance is their perception of their supervisor's mindset. In fact, these perceptions can be better predictors of these outcomes than a leader's own self-reported mindset. Part of the reason for this discrepancy is that leaders who function more in their fixed mindset are likely to have bigger blind spots in their self-awareness. Only when Neumann's former assistant eventually left the company did she fully realize the gap between the company as Neumann and executives described it and her own experience of the culture.

Putting success or failure at the feet of a single charismatic leader is especially easy to do with Cultures of Genius because they perpetuate this genius mythology. Yet as our research has revealed, the effects of an organization's mindset are most pronounced when its employees buy into that mindset. If we rush to attribute the rise and fall of WeWork exclusively to Neumann and his larger-than-life personality, as many do, we miss the fact that in the culture he created, legions of executives, supervisors, and investors participated in and encouraged this behavior, creating a self-sustaining culture cycle.

Ironically, WeWork sold itself on the strength of its culture, yet people's experiences of that culture were in stark contrast to how the corporate website depicted it or how Neumann presented it. The company did indeed have a strong culture, just not the one it was selling. These gaps between what a company says it values and the real culture people experience (termed *value–implementation gaps*) are costly. Neumann was eventually ousted after a failed IPO in which the company's $47 billion valuation dropped to roughly $9 billion in just a few weeks when it was discovered that WeWork's financials were largely smoke and mirrors propped up by a combination of Neumann's salesmanship and outsized investments from venture partners.

As we see in modern examples such as WeWork and Theranos, as well as older examples including Wells Fargo and Enron, approaches that pit people against one another are common in Cultures of Genius. And disconcertingly, stack ranking seems to be making a comeback in the tech sector. But competition doesn't have to be formalized through such practices to encourage interpersonally competitive behavior. Instead, it can follow directly from people's *perceptions* about their organization's mindset. If people perceive that their company endorses fixed mindset ideas, it's enough to set staff jockeying for position. Employees are likely to behave in ways that selectively demonstrate their superior talents and abilities, while hiding their mistakes and weaknesses. Pressure to showcase their smarts causes employees to compete with one another rather than collaborate; after all, in a Culture of Genius, collaboration makes it more difficult to identify personal contribution. When work products are a team effort, it's harder to be recognized as the stand-out star. In Cultures of Genius, people tend to avoid taking on innovative or risky assignments since risk-taking can lead to failure, and failure can signal low ability. Finally, when people feel pressured to prove themselves, they are more likely to engage in unethical behaviors such as hoarding information or hiding mistakes in service of being perceived as smart and capable. In turn, these behaviors reinforce fixed-minded ideas that some have it and others don't, and the culture cycle continues.

How Mindset Culture Shapes Individuals' Behavior

In my research with Fortune 500 companies, I found that when companies had more of a Culture of Growth—for example, when their websites and mission statements described commitment to employees' development—study participants expected these companies to be more collaborative. Conversely, when companies touted a Culture of Genius—such as when they sought to recruit only the most brilliant people with a single-minded focus on results and performance—participants expected them to be more internally and interpersonally competitive. But to us, outside perceptions of these organizations weren't enough (though they might shape potential workers' decisions to join these organizations). We needed to know how employees and supervisors inside these companies perceived their organization's mindset and how those perceptions shaped the way people behaved toward each other on the ground.

Partnering with a management consulting firm, we recruited several Fortune 1000 companies spanning industries including energy, health care, retail, and technology. We asked employees a variety of questions to ascertain their organization's mindset (such as whether most leaders in the company seem to believe talent is fixed or malleable), along with the behavioral norms of collaboration and competition at their company. They were asked the extent to which they agreed or disagreed with statements such as these:

+ At this company, people get points for working together.
+ It's extremely important in this company to always show everyone how smart you are.
+ It's very important to show that I am more talented than others at work.
+ It's important that my manager doesn't think that I know less than others at work.

The results were clear. Employees in Cultures of Genius reported that most people at the company were more likely to engage in internal, interpersonal competition than collaboration. In Cultures of Growth, people were more likely to work together to solve problems and reach goals. Supervisors noticed and confirmed these differences too. These results are significant because whether employees view an organization as being geared more toward collaboration or competition impacts their trust and commitment. **For employees in Cultures of Growth, the perception that the culture desires and supports collaboration fosters organizational trust and commitment. In Cultures of Genius, the sense that interpersonal competition is the norm makes employees feel less committed.**

Cultures of Genius demonstrate their fixed mindset values by setting up competitive behavioral norms and dedicating fewer resources to employees' growth and development. Since the stars are already stars, those who underperform can simply be let go. As CEO, entrepreneur, and business professor Margaret Heffernan writes, "When we worship outstanding performers, we infantilize everyone else, conveying the message that everyone can—even should—be passive in the face of towering ability." And whether organizations have a star-player- or team-based culture also impacts perceptions outside company walls. Just ask fans of virtually any other baseball team how they feel about the New York Yankees.

As it happens, a team of researchers from the University of Kansas and Murray State University focused on sports franchises to investigate people's affinity for and beliefs about "bought" versus "built" teams. "Bought" teams acquire stars from other organizations while "built" teams develop their talent over time. When surveyed, people consistently preferred the built teams more than the bought ones. And this didn't just apply to sports, but to other professions, as well. When asked why they cheered for the built teams, the most common response was their perception that these teams had to work harder and put in more effort to succeed, which is something they admired and respected. They also admired the organizations for investing in cultivating their people. The teams with acquired stars were viewed as having taken a shortcut to success. The second most frequent response was a perception that the built teams would have a greater "sense of team cohesion and cooperation" as a result of having developed *together*. These studies are consistent with our Fortune 500 findings: Supervisors in Cultures of Growth recognized better performance and more leadership potential in their employees than did supervisors in Cultures of Genius, where "bought" stars were simply expected to demonstrate the abilities for which they had been acquired.

One company that takes the "build" approach is Atlassian, a software developer that creates products, such as project management systems, to support teams. In stark contrast to the sink-or-swim approach taken by many Cultures of Genius in the hiring process, Atlassian tells candidates how they can be successful—an approach aimed not at identifying perfect performers, but rather at nurturing people's potential when the playing field is even. For example, design candidates are reassured they won't be forced to perform under pressure because "when a candidate is stressed, it's hard to understand what they can actually do and whether they'd add value to the team." Additionally, candidates are encouraged to bring their "most authentic selves" to the interview and are given specific information on what to expect and how to perform well, such as "be sure to give us the context we'll need to understand your work before diving in. . . . We understand most projects are collaborations, so be upfront about your specific contributions." There's separate information on the site from three female employees from diverse racial and ethnic backgrounds on how women can succeed in tech. Another page offers a Q&A for interns and recent graduates, including reassurance that "productivity is cyclical," so they shouldn't be overly concerned if they're not always performing at maximum capacity. Conversely, the hard-charging language on the websites of fixed-minded organizations often focuses on superlatives, like stating that the organization is the "recognized leader" and offers a "competitive advantage" to deliver "world-class performance" and "superior results."

Atlassian's philosophy is that "Career development begins within the first 90 days of a new job," so they incorporate a 90-day plan to help employees start out on the right foot—learning the organization's values and processes, along with forming initial relationships that will help them do their job and develop during their tenure. From there, managers and employees work together to create a career development plan, a map for ways to grow in their career and advance within the company. Atlassian also shares the journeys of employees who've moved up through the ranks, normalizing struggles and challenges—"For the first six months [as a new manager], I honestly had no idea what I was doing"—as well as triumphs. They also seek to learn more about employees' career goals continuously, not just on exit. Sarah Larson, Atlassian's head of talent management and development, has encouraged managers not to wait for exit interviews, and to instead conduct "stay interviews" with their team members to gauge an employee's commitment and satisfaction and where necessary identify ways to improve their experience. Larson says managers should ask each team member what motivates them and what they look forward to about their work, what keeps them there and what can keep them there in the future, and when's the last time they've thought about leaving. "Your goal is to connect, build trust, and pave the way for an ongoing dialogue about their current reality and future plans." These are all signals to employees that they work in a culture where they can—and will be expected and supported to—grow and develop. According to Glassdoor data from 2023, 93 percent of Atlassian employees would recommend the company to a friend and the company scored a 4.8 out of 5 on culture and values. And for those concerned that Cultures of Growth must be less competitive in the marketplace, consider this: as of May 2023, Atlassian had a valuation of more than $38 billion and its products, including Jira and Trello, were consistently ranked among the top performers in their category.

Research is clear that too much chronic, ongoing stress—the kind that's baked into an interpersonally competitive culture—can exact a steep price. The Yerkes-Dodson law, which illustrates the relationship between pressure and performance, shows that at a certain point, stress actually impairs learning during challenging tasks. **When employees are motivated to perform out of fear of losing their job to colleague-competitors or stars who will be brought in to replace them, it not only undermines their sense of psychological safety and potentially their long-term health, it's also likely to impair their ability to develop and improve.**

Pressure itself is not the determining factor in performance—after all, having some high-pressure situations and deadlines is part of almost every work setting. The question is whether we can channel that pressure to kindle collaboration, camaraderie, and innovation, reframing the stress as something that we can overcome together by pooling our energy, resources, and contributions; or, whether the stress is exacerbated by the need to constantly watch our back among our coworkers and achieve alone, an approach that crushes creativity and cohesiveness. Over time, employees may just become frustrated (or physically sick) and leave. And again, our research has shown that when employees are in a Culture of Genius, these employees are more likely to be looking to move on.

Now that we've explored some of the negative impacts of internal competition and how it hinders collaboration, let's look more closely at how collaboration *boosts* performance and outcomes in Cultures of Growth.

HOW CULTURES OF GROWTH STOKE COLLABORATION AND BEAT THE COMPETITION

As a young girl, Jennifer Doudna became interested in the story of James Watson and Francis Crick's discovery of the double helix structure of DNA. But what perhaps captivated her most was the contribution fellow scientist Rosalind Franklin made to the discovery. Reading about Franklin was a revelation for Doudna: Women, too, could be scientists. That realization would not only shape the course of Doudna's life, it would change the course of genetics research forever. Doudna, working in conjunction with collaborators within and outside her lab, would go on to make a series of scientific discoveries that directly led to the development of CRISPR—a gene editing technology that may one day eradicate a variety of devastating congenital diseases and is being used to develop new methods for detecting and fighting viral threats.

The fact that Watson and Crick failed to acknowledge Franklin's contribution to their discovery may also have influenced Doudna. Her own career has been distinguished not only by the leading-edge discoveries her lab has made, but also by *how* they've gotten there. Bucking the genius mentality so prevalent in science, Doudna's team displays an unusual degree of camaraderie. This is based on Doudna's own belief that collaboration can produce more effective progress and better solutions than any one or two researchers working in isolation. In 2020 Doudna was awarded the Nobel Prize in Chemistry along with Emmanuelle Charpentier, a scientist outside Doudna's lab with whom she partnered on key research that contributed to the development of CRISPR. When the COVID-19 outbreak struck, Doudna convened a multi-organizational task force to determine ways CRISPR technology could be used in the fight against SARS-CoV-2. She also put aside a long-standing rivalry with fellow gene-editing researcher Feng Zhang. The two agreed to pool their resources and share any findings publicly without concern for patent licensing. The result was a CRISPR-based diagnostic test that received emergency use authorization from the FDA in early 2022.

For Doudna, maintaining the culture in her lab is paramount. As Walter Isaacson chronicles in *The Code Breaker*, when hiring her team, Doudna "placed as much emphasis on making sure someone was a good fit as she did assessing their research accomplishments." At one point, Isaacson challenged the scientist on this approach, wondering if she might be missing out on some "brilliant misfits." Doudna replied, "I know some people like creative conflict. But I like having in the lab people who work well together." As part of her interview process for doctoral students, Doudna has her team weigh in to make sure everyone agrees on who would be a good fit. "The goal was to find people who were self-directed yet collegial," she says. When intrinsic motivation is paired with a growth mindset culture, competition with teammates isn't needed to drive people. They are fueled more by an internal fire to grow, learn, and achieve together. Doudna, herself, is known to be highly competitive, yet within her team she encourages and expects collaboration, whereby the strengths and specialties of each scientist can fertilize a shared territory of research from which novel discoveries can emerge. She sets the lab culture from the top.

In Doudna's lab, instead of cutthroat competition, she and her team achieve advances by collaborating. In one instance, when Doudna noticed that a student wasn't stretching himself, she pulled him aside, telling him, "You're not taking the kinds of projects that a student like you is capable of. Why else do we do science? We do it to go after big questions and take risks. If you don't try things, you're never going to have a breakthrough." With Doudna's encouragement, close guidance, and continued support, the researcher went on to make several discoveries that advanced the field. Doudna applied this same approach outside her lab, cofounding a CRISPR conference to bring together scientists working on gene editing to gather in person, creating a place where they could feel safe to share unpublished data and new ideas.

Doudna's emphasis on collaboration and team coherence has helped to create and sustain a Culture of Growth that makes it one of the most successful, innovative, and financially competitive labs of its kind. But unless it's intentional about fostering collaboration, an organization can unintentionally send its employees a very different message. That's what we discovered in our research with the multinational bank. While messages about mindset come from multiple places, employees glean a lot from supervisors about what behaviors the organization values. In analyzing data from multiple surveys with thousands of employees and managers, we found a set of managerial strategies that influenced whether employees would be more competitive or collaborative with colleagues. One strategy included keeping star employees happy by giving them the more difficult assignments, and, as a result, giving duller work to the less talented to avoid demotivating top performers. Inadvertently, these managers fostered a Culture of Genius, and as soon as employees perceived their managers' fixed-minded behaviors, they started to jockey with one another for position. By contrast, more growth-minded managers divvied out difficult projects across their team and worked with employees to identify how to be successful.

At Patagonia, managers employ this kind of high-engagement, growth-minded approach to hiring and developing staff. From the outset Yvon Chouinard, founder of Patagonia, has been intentional about fostering collaboration. "[W]e don't look for 'stars' seeking special treatment and perks," he says. "Our best efforts are collaborative, and the Patagonia culture rewards the ensemble player while it barely tolerates those who need the limelight." This also provides an excellent example of a case in which the fixed mindset (about collaboration—you either do it or you don't) can provide something positive. (Along with their zero-tolerance attitude toward those seeking to elevate their own status relative to others, Chouinard and the rest of Patagonia's leadership are also inflexible about their sustainability and ethical standards.)

Patagonia still wants high achievers, just ones who are more focused on group and organizational outcomes than individual rankings or results. "We won't hire the kind of people you can order around . . . We don't want drones who will simply follow directions. We want the kind of employees who will question the wisdom of something they regard as a bad decision." That last part is essential for adhering to Patagonia's high ethical and quality standards for its products: Design and production teams work in close collaboration, otherwise one simple design change can require production to shift factories, which might mean a whole new certification process to ensure materials and worker treatment are up to standard.

Patagonia is a culture of builders. They tend to promote from within, which works because, like Doudna, they pay lots of attention to hiring for cultural fit, collaboration, and potential, even if it means it takes some employees longer to hit their stride because there are more role-specific skills they need to learn. Patagonia's model has been so successful that they have had to pull back the reins on their growth from time to time to make sure they stay aligned with their environmental impact standards. Nonetheless, the company has been one of the only major retailers that not only has continued to be profitable, but has grown during major economic recessions.

Leaders like Doudna and Chouinard have an outsized impact on organizational mindset, and my team's research shows that other entrepreneurs do too. In the study I referenced above with the Kauffman Foundation, we found that companies with more of a growth mindset tended to have founders who believed in a positive correlation between effort and ability: The more effort you put in, the stronger your abilities become. Whereas those with more of a fixed mindset asserted a negative correlation between ability and effort: If you have to try hard, it's likely a sign of low ability. Companies led by more growth-minded founders also showcased fewer competitive behaviors and more collaborative ones than companies led by founders with more fixed-minded beliefs. But did the companies with Cultures of Growth pay a price for those collaborative (vs. competitive) norms? Not at all. As I noted above, not only was there less turnover in these organizations, companies led by growth-minded founders were more likely to meet the annual fund-raising goals they set for themselves. And in case you're wondering, it wasn't that growth-minded founders set easier targets for themselves—they were just as ambitious as their more fixed-minded peers.

Still, some of you may still be holding out, believing internal competition can sometimes drive the best results. Perhaps a field in which individual performers really do have to be superstars because the stakes are life or death, such as surgery, would prove the exception where competition confers an advantage. Renowned neurosurgeon David Langer says otherwise, and he should know. Langer is chair of neurosurgery at New York City's Lenox Hill Hospital, which has been rated by *U.S. News & World Report* as one of the best hospitals nationally for neurology and neurosurgery. "If you don't have collaboration," he says, "and you don't have great teams and you don't have people driven to help each other, everything breaks down . . . Our focus and our heart and our collaborative culture is what won the day. That kind of special chemistry is what allowed us to be able to compete against the biggest neurosurgery departments."

CREATING A COLLABORATIVE CULTURE OF GROWTH

Here are some ways to create your own collaborative Culture of Growth, while minimizing negative internal competition in your organization.

Conduct a Cues Audit

When getting to know an organization, my team almost always conducts a cues audit where we identify the policies, practices, and norms in place and whether they're pushing people more toward their fixed or growth mindsets. You can do something similar in your organization. You'll want to focus on the regular, routine ways of operating that might be putting people at odds with one another, undermining group cohesion.

When we do a cues audit, we typically start with the organization's affinity groups, which represent people from negatively stereotyped, structurally disadvantaged, or numerically underrepresented backgrounds. As we know from my research, those individuals tend to be more vigilant to cues in the local environment that signal whether a company practices norms of respect, inclusion, and collaboration. For example, asking racial affinity group members about their experiences of collaboration and inclusion on teams tells me a lot about a company's behavioral norms. Sometimes I hear that groups feel that the company trots them out "like window dressing" and "tokens" to "make the company look good" but, when it comes down to the work, these individuals are not provided with challenging work assignments and access to networks that will allow them to grow and develop. That tells me we have a culture problem. It's not uncommon to hear employees say that some people are afforded opportunities to make mistakes and learn from them, but this flexibility is not widely offered to others at the company (indeed, people tell me these affordances too often fall along race and gender lines).

When we start the cues audit, I often describe the mindset continuum, and then talk about how different policies and practices can communicate these mindsets. I then ask folks, "What are some of the interactions, policies, or practices in your day-to-day work where you feel like fixed- or growth-mindset messages are communicated?" And we go from there. For detailed instructions about how to perform a cues audit, visit this book's website at www.marycmurphy.com.

See What the Data Show

A common misperception is that Cultures of Growth are less data-oriented than Cultures of Genius. In fact, the reverse is often true. Because of the belief in geniuses, people rely more on their (or the genius's) gut; plus, looking at data can challenge one's genius. Running coach Steve Magness, one of the people who blew the whistle on Nike coach Alberto Salazar's unethical and abusive practices, recalls an incident when Salazar was complaining that a particular runner—one who had just made her first world championship team—was "too fat." Magness showed Salazar data charts reflecting that the runner had an exceptionally low body fat percentage. Salazar reportedly fired back, "I don't give a damn what the science says. I know what I see with my eyes—she needs to lose weight." (Incidentally, Magness says Salazar also routinely threatened to have the length of his contract cut if Magness didn't keep "proving" himself.) I can often tell that we are dealing with a Culture of Genius when there is a reluctance to examine data or share it across teams, divisions, and with groups brought in to help the company improve.

In Cultures of Genius, people may insist that interpersonal competitiveness is a key element of their success, and yet if they look at it, the data often tell a different story—one that doesn't match the corporate mythology. In our research, we've seen that teams with stronger Cultures of Growth adopt more cooperative behavioral norms in their work, and this predicts higher performance on their quarterly evaluations (and greater employee satisfaction).

This often surprises leaders who would not have otherwise known without looking at the data. Still, don't take my word for it—see what your own data say.

Recast Competition

On the sitcom *Friends*, Monica is known to be exceptionally competitive—with anyone, about anything. In one episode, Monica is crushed to learn that she doesn't give the best massages, as she purported to. In fact, she gives the worst massages. To soften the blow, her beau, Chandler, reframes the news, telling Monica that she gives the "best bad massages." Recasting competition isn't about catering to fragile egos, but it is about injecting a little fun and creativity into the idea of what competition can look like.

The question is: Instead of having employees go head-to-head to defeat one another in a fixed way, how can you encourage them to compete on the dimensions of collaboration, growth, and development? Tech company DigitalOcean offers nonfinancial incentives and awards for collaborative behavior, including Kindles preloaded with business books handpicked by the CEO. At PepsiCo, employees' annual bonuses are tied to what they've done to help other employees succeed. Consider how you might reimagine incentives and evaluative structures to value the individuals and teams who develop the most or demonstrate their ability to innovate together. What if recognition were given for a project that invoked the most cross-team or cross-departmental collaboration? Maybe even challenge teams to come up with ideas for growth-minded competition as their first task.

Redo Your Rating System

In 2013, Microsoft threw out their stacked ranking system. If your organization uses stack raking (or a similar gladiatorial approach to making people compete for precious resources), consider another method for evaluation and resource distribution that doesn't encourage people to compete against, instead of collaborate with, their coworkers.

When Patagonia started asking questions of their own human resource system, one of the changes they made was to do away with their individual rating system altogether. Dean Carter, head of human resources for Patagonia, says when it comes to managing people, he's learned to follow models from the sustainable agriculture movement. With today's standard agricultural approaches, once a plant matures we pluck its fruit or cut it, then till the ground. As Carter explains, every time you do this you deplete the soil, then you have to invest resources to re-fertilize as you start the process again. It's an approach focused entirely on extraction, which is also how we tend to treat the people who work within an organization. In regenerative agriculture, farmers pay attention to inputs as well as outputs so the soil stays healthier. Carter realized that Patagonia was unintentionally eroding its own soil by focusing almost entirely on what the company could get from its employees without attending to what it gives back. He asked, "What processes in HR do we have that feel more extractive in nature and what are more regenerative?" Those questions led Carter's team to Patagonia's annual performance review process, which he realized created a massive pain point during the year (much as my colleagues and I experienced during the annual merit raise process). As Carter describes, it was a "moment in time that the employee hates and the manager hates and basically everyone has to recover from during the next cycle." People were depleted by reviews, and the company offered raises and bonuses to re-fertilize the soil and try to restore morale. When Carter announced that Patagonia was overhauling its performance management process, employees "literally stood up and applauded." Though the company is known for already giving its employees a broad berth to make determinations about how best to do their work, when it rolled out new sessions to share ideas about how to redo performance management, they had record attendance. "It was standing room only" to brainstorm how they wanted to rethink performance. Now, instead of an annual evaluation, HR provides a tool that employees can opt into to help their performance "and they can lean into it as heavy as they need based on their personal situation and their needs, and the needs of their manager, versus this policed HR effect," says Carter. The new approach has resulted in improved employee performance and has freed up HR to look for interesting insights and data to help people further develop. Through these new dimensions of performance analysis, HR is now getting much more useful information, Carter reports. He adds that the system also "frees up time for the employee and the manager to do better work, or in Patagonia's case to maybe go catch a surf."

As part of its Talent Assessment Program, software developer GitLab encourages managers to evaluate not just past performance, but also employees' growth potential. As the company describes it, "Growth potential refers to the ability and desire of a team member to successfully assume increasingly more broad or complex responsibilities and learn new skills, as compared to peers and the roles' responsibilities outlined in their respective job family. This could include the growth potential to move up to the next level in their job family, and/or a lateral move." By determining an employee's growth potential—which is evaluated against the four primary pillars of adaptability, expandability, consistency, and self-awareness—managers can calculate the best trajectory for them to realize that potential. In true Culture of Growth fashion, the company notes that growth potential can change over time relative to shifts in an employee's skillset and abilities, along with their interests. You can incorporate something similar for your employees, helping them identify and realize opportunities for growth.

At the start of this chapter, I described the cringeworthy way my faculty colleagues used to circulate people's ratings each year. Now we model the extent to which faculty collaborate with each other on papers, projects, and grants; our department's collaboration network diagram is posted in the front office, right by the faculty mailboxes. Consider what metrics you can use in your organization to stoke a collaborative Culture of Growth and challenge the competitive Culture of Genius. Remember Atlassian's highly individualized development plans, where everyone is expected and supported to keep growing. And after your new system has been in place for a time, don't forget to check the data to see exactly how they're impacting metrics like performance, retention, and more compared with the old system so you can adjust as needed.

CHAPTER 4

Innovation and Creativity

When it comes to the future of energy, we have no choice but to change how we've been doing things. Companies built on fossil fuels will have to shift from a model that's relatively tried and true to one with far more unknowns and complexities to work out. Or as Shell frames the question: "How do we move from a world of relatively predictable variability to one of fundamental uncertainty?" A global energy transition is under way. "We don't know how fast, we don't know how big [it is] . . . but we know it's coming," says Jorrit van der Togt, executive vice president of HR at Shell (and, incidentally, holder of a PhD in social psychology). To navigate an unclear future, Shell would need to transform its entire business. But how?

Van der Togt looked across industries to see if other long-standing organizations had successfully managed such a massive shift. He landed on Microsoft and its transformation from laggard to leader in cloud technology. CEO Satya Nadella orchestrated the move by shifting the organizational culture from a Culture of Genius to a Culture of Growth. Van der Togt knew it would take a similar cultural transformation at Shell to meet the changing demands for global energy.

Coincidentally, while Shell was searching for a way forward, van der Togt was also in the process of refreshing Shell's employee development program, and among the candidates for a partner to help them was Stanford. Van der Togt flew to Palo Alto and spent a day listening to faculty presentations about how organizations can meet transformational moments such as the one facing Shell. That's where we met. After my presentation on organizational mindset, things started to click for him. He knew that Shell had an urgent need to innovate and would have to implement every ounce of creativity it had in order to solve the challenges facing it. Perhaps focusing on organizational mindset could help Shell with these priorities as it had Microsoft.

I went to The Hague for a series of meetings with then-CEO Ben van Beurden and members of the executive team, who agreed with van der Togt. They understood that organizational culture is driven from the top, and so the shift would have to start with them: They would need to lead and model it. Each executive worked on their own mindset story—reflecting on situations where they had embodied their fixed mindset, how and why they shifted to their growth mindset, and how that shift had helped them in their career.

Understandably, the executive team wanted to test our mindset culture change model. They could have made the test a low-stakes one so that if it didn't work at Shell, any potential negative impact would be rather minimal. Instead, they made a strategic choice to focus on one of the organization's most important and most challenging priorities: safety. "In our case," says van der Togt, "we work in an inherently dangerous industry, where operations can sadly result in fatalities, so safety was the biggest use case for us."

Historically, Shell had been operating largely as a Culture of Genius, especially when it came to safety. That makes sense, right? Safety is an area where rigid protocols seem appropriate. Everyone at Shell, including the executives, wore lanyards around their necks that described the safety principles the organization prized. The problem was, even though Shell's rigorous commitment to safety was successful at decreasing accidents, no matter how many checklists they adhered to or post-incident analyses they conducted, Goal Zero eluded them.

Set in 2007, Goal Zero was Shell's holy grail of safety: Their target was to ensure zero harm and zero leaks across the organization's en-

tire system, including personnel, process, and transport operations—
from extracting oil from the ground to transporting it by truck, rail,
and ship; storing it in huge tanks; and using it to make products that
would ship across the globe. Despite recognizing that fatalities and
leaks were unacceptable parts of business, Shell had failed to achieve
Goal Zero. They had made steady progress for years, bringing these
numbers down little by little, but they wondered whether a growth
mindset culture could finally help them close the gap. Could people
turn away from fixed thinking and routine ways of operating and
instead lean into learning, especially when, inevitably, mistakes were
made? As Shell shifts its business model and sets new goals for the energy transition while balancing the safety imperative, the challenges
and stakes for innovation are even higher than in other industries.
Together, we worked on ways to help people be actively on the lookout
for ways to improve safety protocols and encourage employees to embody their "learner mindset," as Shell calls it, when it came to safety
issues. Later in this chapter, we'll see how Shell fared as it shifted its
organizational mindset in pursuit of Goal Zero.

Like collaboration, creativity and innovation are influenced by
an organization's culture. Collaboration fuels innovation, so Cultures of Growth receive a dual benefit from investing in collaboration, as it encourages people to come up with new ideas or combine
current concepts in new ways. While Cultures of Genius can and
do innovate, like Shell was doing with safety issues, they are often
working against structural and interpersonal constraints created by
more fixed-minded norms. Operating in Cultures of Genius is like
flying a plane into strong headwinds: You may get to your destination, but your expenditures will be greater, you may be delayed, and
the trip is a lot more stressful. And while Cultures of Genius may
at times produce significant innovations, the question remains as
to what greater accomplishments they might have achieved, and at
how much lower costs, if they'd invoked their growth mindset more
often, instead.

Cultures of Growth are what we think of when we talk about

learning organizations; every day is a treasure hunt, with employees eagerly searching for novel ideas to improve products and processes. Cultures of Genius are primarily *leaning organizations*, which lean on the status quo or how things were done in the past to direct their current efforts. They may at times offer resources and encouragement to innovate, but they usually grant these only to a few special stars or to support leadership's pet projects.

In this chapter, we'll look at how Cultures of Growth and Cultures of Genius innovate differently, along with the specific aids or roadblocks that mindset engenders.

HOW MINDSET FUELS OR FOILS INNOVATION

When thinking about innovation, perhaps the last field you'd expect is accounting. Yet Candace "Candy" Duncan achieved just that, by inspiring people to expand their thinking, and by navigating the delicate balance between creativity and upholding hard legal and ethical rules. Duncan served as the managing partner for KPMG's Washington Metro Area practice, becoming the company's first female managing partner and leading its quality growth priorities across audit, tax, and advisory functions. While her résumé is extensive, those who worked for Duncan at KPMG frequently remember her by a single question she often asked: "How can we raise the bar?"

Duncan said in a personal interview that she's issued the same challenge to everyone who's worked for her: "Do your best every single day. That sounds easy, but try it for the next week. Try it for the next month. Don't cut a corner. I find that setting that goal is helpful, whether you're right out of school or taking on a new leadership position at fifty-one. You will be amazed at how it adds up over a year. Look at how it's added up for me over a thirty-seven-year career." Leading by example has been integral to Duncan's success—"I never ask anyone to do something that I wouldn't do"—a practice supported by an academic study of financial advisors: Those func-

tioning in their growth mindset were more willing to go above and
beyond for clients when they saw those behaviors modeled by others.

Duncan says one of the keys to innovation in a landscape filled
with regulatory constraints is encouraging collaborative, engaged
teams. "I think nine times out of ten a team comes up with a better answer," she said. "A diverse team will bring to the table more
experiences. It's smart business. Why not use the best of everything
you've got?" She adds that this diversity of ideas from employees at
all levels of the organization showed Duncan her own blind spots,
for example. "Sometimes you don't know what you don't know," she
said. "When you're working with someone and you don't understand
why they're doing what they're doing, if you're willing to be educated, all of a sudden you look at things differently." Duncan's core
values of being curious and willing to learn from everyone are hall-
marks of the growth mindset.

When it comes to corporate culture, many companies lean on a
set of organization-wide values. In the case of the ride-sharing app
Uber, several of their original, now-infamous core values indicated
their Culture of Genius mentality: (1) always be hustling; (2) be an
owner, not a renter; (3) big bold bets; (4) celebrate cities; (5) customer obsession; (6) inside out; (7) let builders build; (8) make
magic; (9) meritocracy and toe-stepping; (10) optimistic leadership;
(11) principled confrontation; (12) super pumped; (13) champions
mindset/winning; (14) be yourself. How is an employee simultane-
ously expected to focus on winning and prioritizing meritocracy *and*
be themselves? As *New York Times* journalist Mike Isaac wrote in
Super Pumped, during the early years at Uber, performance reviews
entailed employees being evaluated on qualities such as fierceness,
scale, super pumpedness, and innovation. "Scoring low could mean
termination," Isaac reported, "while scoring high influenced pay
raises, promotions, and annual bonuses." Not surprisingly, the scores,
he revealed, "often depended on how close a given employee was with
the manager or department head who was doing the grading."

Uber's former fixed mindset culture lacked clear and appropriate standards. Yet often people stereotype Cultures of Growth as cultures that are too unconstrained and without precise boundaries. However, in growth mindset organizations, individuals learn where the real boundaries are and exercise creativity and innovation within them. At KPMG, in an atmosphere with significant legal and regulatory boundaries, Duncan faced a challenge where no amount of creativity would get her team to the goal—at least not ethically. When there's a government shutdown but also a government agency has just opened a project for bids, you can't ask federal employees questions about that project because they're not supposed to be working. Duncan recalls a time working under one boss from KPMG's New York office who refused to accept that the DC practice couldn't reach out for more information to help make their bid more competitive. Her team did what they could to get creative, to "interpret the information the agency had given us and address it in our bid." When her boss insisted that they contact the federal employees involved in the bid, she knew they couldn't. "It's not legal," she explained. Duncan solved the problem by recruiting two of her boss's supervisors to explain the potential legal implications. Eventually he backed down. Duncan had modeled what it looks like to hold the line even when pushed to break the rules.

At Uber, by contrast, creativity often had a dark side, such as spending tens of millions of dollars each year to influence lawmakers to work in their favor and using high-tech tools to spam those who didn't. They also surreptitiously tracked the app users' movements after they left Uber; recruited ex-CIA, -NSA, and -FBI employees to spy on government officials; and enlarged the potential driver pool by hiring drivers with sketchy records who would not have qualified for a regular commercial driver's license. One Uber "innovation," which employees nicknamed "Hell," was a high-tech program that monitored the activities of Lyft drivers, many of whom also worked for Uber. One of their tactics was to strategically manipulate Uber's pay rates to try and get drivers to take more Uber fares. These examples are a powerful, if unfortunate, illustration of how an organization's behavioral norms feed off one another, pushing employees to innovate at all costs, which may encourage ethical lapses as part of the price of success.

In a zero-sum world, Uber was playing a game it could lose. It nearly did when a massive #DeleteUber campaign revealed some of the company's tactics and an earlier viral blog post by then-Uber engineer Susan Fowler exposed Uber's culture of sexual harassment. Cofounder and then-CEO Travis Kalanick, who has been portrayed as the primary source of Uber's extensive culture problems, was eventually ousted. However, culture runs deep, as Harvard Business School professor Frances Frei learned when she was hired to repair Uber's culture as senior vice president of leadership and strategy. Frei implemented a massive increase in executive education focused specifically on logic, strategy, and leadership to help correct gaps between managers' duties and their abilities. Yet in her assessment, "it became super apparent that the training needed to go way beyond that." Incidentally, Uber's new CEO, Dara Khosrowshahi, quickly axed Kalanick's 14 values, replacing them with ones focused more on inclusivity and ethics, such as "We celebrate differences" and "We do the right thing." Still, there's much work to be done for Uber to learn from its mistakes, repair its image, and realize its true potential—and a mindset culture shift is a big part of that change.

Now that we've seen some examples of what innovation can look like in a Culture of Growth versus a Culture of Genius, let's dissect a few elements of organizational culture to discern how organizational mindset fuels or foils that innovation.

How Mindset Impacts Creativity

In Cultures of Growth, creativity is the purview of everyone, not relegated to a few gifted "creatives" as in Cultures of Genius. When we're in prove-and-perform mode, research shows that these pressures impair our ability to be innovative. Specifically, when we're preoccupied with how our efforts will be received and how we'll be judged for them, we have fewer cognitive resources to apply to the task at hand. In a series of experiments, researchers gave undergraduate and graduate students a series of math or verbal performance tasks. Then, they gave them a set of not-too-subtle instructions designed to trigger them into their fixed mindset, such as "During this task, the experimenters will assess your performance. It is important for you to perform well and obtain a high score to demonstrate your competence. You should know that a lot of students will do this task so you should try to distinguish yourself positively, that is, to perform better than the majority of students." When provoked into a fixed mindset, these students performed worse, worried about how they'd be evaluated.

These findings support the hypothesis that preoccupation with social comparison and trying to showcase one's ability consumes working memory. When employees are worried about repercussions for underperformance, they have less brainpower to give, and that means less innovation and worse problem-solving. (Incidentally, we term this mental chatter *task-irrelevant thoughts* because they are not what one needs to be thinking about when solving difficult problems.) Conversely, a different set of studies showed that when subjects had a growth mindset about creative ability, they were more likely to have greater interest in creative thinking, along with better actual performance.

Cognitively, creativity is thought to involve at least two different types of thinking: divergent thinking, or searching through multiple directions and solutions, and convergent thinking, or figuring out the single best or most correct solution. Researchers ran a study to measure divergent thinking and, in particular, to look at the relationship between mindset and creative solution generation. Results showed that those who endorsed growth mindset beliefs about their creative capacity produced more diverse and unique ideas than those who believed their creativity is limited.

In another study, researchers measured convergent thinking by giving participants ten minutes to solve a series of insight problems.

For example, "A woman's earring fell into a cup that was filled with coffee, but her earring did not get wet. How could this be?" (Okay, I won't leave you hanging. The answer is: The woman's cup was not filled with prepared coffee, but with coffee grounds.) The results showed that those in their fixed mindset enjoyed the creativity task less, were more likely to experience negative emotions during the task—and performed worse. Those in their growth mindset showed more enjoyment, were more likely to experience positive emotions during the task, and were more likely to put greater effort into solving the problems. **Environments that move people toward their growth mindset around creativity are more likely to stoke employees' self-efficacy and motivation about their own creative abilities, which helps them become more effective problem solvers.**

Fostering Flexibility

As a quote frequently attributed to Charles Darwin goes, "It's not the strongest species that survives, nor the most intelligent, but the one most responsive to change." In psychology, cognitive flexibility describes your ability to shift your thinking or attention in relation to changes in your environment. Given this definition, it's easy to see why flexibility is an essential component of innovation. Yet companies are often faced with a predicament about whether to play it safe and maximize their resources (known as *exploitation*) or look to new products, areas, or partnerships for growth (known as *exploration*). Research shows that individuals and organizations that more chronically inhabit their growth mindset tend to be more flexible.

Jacqueline Novogratz was excelling at her career in high finance, yet she was preoccupied with a desire to make a real difference in the world. So she accepted an opportunity to travel to Africa, where she began working to assist local entrepreneurs through efforts such as microloan programs in Rwanda and other countries. Yet she was dismayed by the broken systems she encountered that made it difficult to offer meaningful support. For instance, organizations trying to assist African entrepreneurs frequently would come in with funding hampered by stringent restrictions for its use that paid no attention to how local economies actually worked, or to what would truly benefit the entrepreneurs and those they were serving. Too often when it comes to impact investing, the people providing the money are also providing the solutions, telling others what will work from their perspective. On the ground, Novogratz saw over and over how this approach falls short; it may make funders feel good about their contributions, but it does little to actually help people in poverty. After cofounding a successful microloan program, Novogratz decided to expand her vision. Her organization, Acumen, is a nonprofit global venture that provides financial and advisory support to help local entrepreneurs—in Africa and elsewhere around the world—develop and scale their own proven concepts to help those in poverty. Rather than a financial return for themselves, Acumen funders expect to see returns in the form of growth, innovation, and financial gain for local communities. The organization's innovative model marries the business sense of venture capital with the compassion of philanthropy and a genuine respect for the people they are serving.

Among the entrepreneurs Acumen has supported is Ankit Agarwal, who was determined to do something to alleviate pollution in India's sacred Ganges River. Every day, Hindus all across India visit the country's temples, toting flowers and food offerings for the gods. As the flowers accumulate, priests typically toss them into local rivers. While the floating florals make for a pretty sight, the flowers are in many cases treated with pesticides that pollute the waterways. Such was the case for the Ganges. Agarwal and his best friend and business partner, Karan Rastogi, came up with a venture that addressed several challenges at once. Their company, Phool (which means "flower" in Hindi), collects flowers from temples along the Ganges, sprays them with an organic cleaner to rid them of toxins, then transforms the flowers into incense sticks. Not only does this keep the pesticides out of the waterways, the sticks are a healthier replacement for traditional charcoal incense, which can negatively impact respiratory health. Agarwal and Rastogi took their vision a step farther by employing workers from India's lowest "scavenger" caste, who typically are relegated to the most undesirable jobs—such as dealing with human waste—and suffer some of the most extreme poverty. Phool provides a living wage and health insurance along with transport, an inviting and comfortable workplace, and rations of clean water for workers to take home to their families. Acumen supports much larger initiatives, as well, including a company called d.light, which provides affordable solar lighting and power solutions for low-income people around the world. By 2023, d.light had helped approximately 140,000,000 people across 70 countries gain access to inexpensive and environmentally friendly products to improve the quality of their lives. According to Novogratz, Acumen now supports 40 companies working in off-grid energy. "We can say with a straight face that we want to bring clean electricity to two hundred fifteen million of the hardest-to-reach people on the planet with off-grid solar and electricity." That is real impact.

So-called stakeholder capitalism often falls short. And many of the problems come down to a Culture of Genius mentality. When I spoke with Jacqueline Novogratz, she shared a story of talking with hedge fund investors about some of the challenges one Acumen-supported company in rural Bihar, India, was facing with rice husk gasification. They replied, "Well, why don't you just let us run your company?" They'd never even been to India and had no experience with the processes of gasification. "It was just the Culture of Genius writing you off," Novogratz said, and it's a common mentality she sees in the sector. "It was a deep assumption that even if they were to do what we were to do, they would be much better at it than we could ever possibly be. Their intellectual frameworks may work in their heads, but they don't necessarily work on the ground."

Conversely, Acumen's approach emphasizes listening, learning, and humility—developing a deep understanding of the problems so they can partner with entrepreneurs in developing the best solutions. When identifying entrepreneurs who they might support,

Acumen isn't swayed by big promises. Instead of charisma, they look for character. "Character is everything," Novogratz told me. Acumen searches for people who can "talk in an unvarnished way about failures and what they've learned from them in a way that's believable and shows resilience. They show an ability to take feedback and demonstrate real listening, and they show that they're genuinely curious about the people they're here to serve. There's also at least some awareness of their own deficits and an attempt to build a team around them that's populated with people who help to compensate for those deficits." Novogratz says that describes the team she's built around herself, as well. That deep, diverse bench enables an organization that's agile and flexible enough to function successfully in challenging markets while solving complex problems.

Marketing to Mindset

Up until now, we've focused almost entirely on how mindset culture is evident *within* an organization. Yet as our research shows, some signals about a company's mindset are obvious—whether consciously or not—to those *outside* the organization's walls.

Do you choose your favorite brand of jeans, burritos, or rental car based on your mindset? Yes, according to multiple studies, including work I undertook with Carol Dweck. If you're in the market for a French cookbook because you're excited to challenge yourself in the kitchen, or because you're excited to show off your culinary skills at your next dinner party, that can indicate whether you're functioning more from your growth or fixed mindset (respectively). Understanding the mindset of its core customers can help a company determine the most effective messaging to connect with consumers' goals.

University of Cincinnati researcher Josh Clarkson and I also demonstrated that mindset steers us toward certain products because it helps us meet either our performance goals or our learning goals. We found that people in their growth mindset orient toward products that enhance their learning by expanding their knowledge of the broader category. For instance, a more growth-minded Merlot lover would lean toward trying an entirely new type of wine (for example Chardonnay) rather than a sub-type of their preferred wine (such as a Merlot–Cabernet Sauvignon blend) because of the greater learning potential. Growth-minded participants preferred new, exotic flavors of chocolate, software that was still in its development stages, songs from a music genre they hadn't heard before, and a new type of electronic sports car because these choices expanded their learning across the product categories.

People operating from their fixed mindset are more likely to set self-enhancing performance goals than learning ones. For example, were they to step up to the tasting counter, they would be more apt to want to show others what they already know—commenting on tannins or terroir, for example—than to ask questions and seek out new information. In our research, participants in their fixed mindset were more likely to pursue products that would reflect well on them and that provide information about the best choice in a particular product category. These participants chose the Merlot–Cabernet blend, chocolates that provided "an enhanced chocolate flavor" (rather than new exotic flavors), a new version of the leading industry standard software (an iteration of a proven entity), a song from their favorite music genre, and a new "high acceleration" sports car that proved its performance right there in the description.

How products are marketed can determine whether they appeal more to those in their fixed or growth mindsets. For instance, a Baby Einstein video, which offers a toddler the experience of passively absorbing the genius that's presented, appeals more to our fixed mindset. On the other hand, Lumosity's "brain training" platform or the language app Duolingo, which promise skill development as a result of consistent hard work, appeal more to our growth mindset. Additionally, organizational behavior studies demonstrate that those in their fixed mindset want to associate with brands that help them prove and perform for others: They want brands that show off the positive qualities associated with the brands. (Think of how many people opt for a luxury purse with the brand's high-end name stamped all over it to signal style, or the proliferation of merch from Ivy League universities to signal smarts.)

People often perceive fixed-minded organizations as more prestigious, but growth-minded ones as more trustworthy. Additionally, when a company shows itself to be in learning mode, consumers are more apt to trust them. This is also one of the reasons for the rental car company Avis's successful "We try harder" campaign, in which it underscored its second-place status (to Hertz) as a means of explaining why it was motivated to go the extra mile for customers. As the company stated in its ads, "We are in the rent-a-car business, playing second fiddle to a giant. Above all, we've had to learn how to stay alive. . . . The No. 2 attitude is: Do the right thing. Look for new ways. Try harder." According to *Slate*, the ads were an instant hit, catapulting the company from $3.2 million loss per year to earning $1.2 million—the first time in a decade the company had turned a profit.

If prestige is what a Culture of Genius is going for, it could work for them, but it could also be at the expense of consumer trust. The rise of Bitcoin and other cryptocurrencies has been fueled in large part by drops in confidence in traditional financial services, especially among younger consumers. A Meta survey of Millennials showed that as many as 92 percent of respondents did not trust long-standing institutions to handle their money. They expressed mistrust of the organizations due to their heavy reliance on practices designed to keep consumers in debt, along with widespread incidents of mismanagement, and said traditional companies don't understand their needs. These types of sentiments open the market to new forms of currency, as well as innovative services or products from companies not typically associated with finance, such as Virgin Group and their brand extension Virgin Money. As it turns out, trust could be a key differentiating factor in your industry, and when trust in one organization or sector declines, creativity and innovation can help you seize those opportunities.

Speaking of Virgin, they've been successful at getting consumers to voyage with their brand through various products, including records, air and space travel, mobile phone service, and beyond, though the company has had some notable flops—Virgin Cola among them. As history has shown us, it's risky to mess with people's soda. That was the message consumers handed to Coca-Cola when it introduced New Coke. Even though the drink had performed well in taste tests, when the company rolled it out, it faced a wave of push-back from Coke drinkers. Coca-Cola was perceived by consumers as a "heritage brand" (like Ralph Lauren's classic polo shirts and those addictive little Werther's Original candies). Such brands often have a harder time launching successful brand extensions because of the fixed mindset they have engendered in their consumer base about the predictable qualities of their products: In some ways, their consumers have learned to count on them never changing. That's why Coca-Cola was forced to launch Coca-Cola Classic and let New Coke fall by the wayside. Another example is a ketchup company's bid to appeal to kids. Heinz's EZ Squirt Ketchup transformed the traditionally red condiment into options such as "Blastin Green," "Funky Purple," and "Passion Pink." Though the product caught on at first, it eventually failed in part because health-conscious parents fretted over a product that contained artificial colors and flavors, making it more like Frankenfood than the more natural options they favored. On the other hand, some brands like Virgin charac-terize themselves as cutting edge and trendsetting. These brands prompt a growth mindset among consumers such that they expect brand extensions from them—even and perhaps especially ones that seem far afield of their original market, such as Virgin expanding from airline to phone service provider.

Organizational mindset also plays a role in innovation when a company undertakes the process to identify its target market. It shapes our beliefs about specific groups of people and what we think would or wouldn't appeal to them. *Intergroup mindsets* refer to what characteristics people believe *other* groups possess and whether they believe those characteristics are fixed or changeable. A fixed approach may make organizations avoid certain markets—such as racially and ethnically diverse consumers when the traditional market has been largely White—because they see those consumers as "unwinnable." Or if they move into new markets and bring their fixed mindset with them, they may introduce products or services that stereotype new consumers and consequently fall flat with them. An example is when Taco Bell launched in Mexico. The company's Mexico managing director stated proudly that the menu they introduced was nearly an exact replica of the one used in the United States. Yet, as any Tex-Mex–loving Texan like myself could have told them, certain items popular in the United States aren't actually authentic Mexican food. Mexicans were baffled and, in some cases, downright disturbed by the chain's offering of hard-shell tacos, something that doesn't exist in that country's native cuisine. "[T]hey're not tacos . . . they're folded tostadas. They're very ugly," one customer complained. McDonald's has done a far better job flexibly attending to local consumers' authentic tastes when expanding into foreign markets, offering beer in their restaurants in France, Belgium, Germany, and Austria; poutine (French fries covered with gravy and cheese) in Canada; and Vegemite (a spread with a rather distinctive taste) in Australia. When organizations approach new consumer segments or markets from a growth mindset, they're more likely to learn about and adapt to different preferences, creating innovations that fit the market even if it means changing the product a bit in the process.

To venture into new territory and to feel comfortable trying uncomfortable approaches requires psychological safety. It is a critical factor when it comes to becoming and staying in a Culture of Growth.

Psychological Safety

"Fear inhibits learning."

So writes Harvard organizational behavior expert Amy Edmonson. Feeling afraid or anxious drains our physiological resources. As we saw earlier, when we're preoccupied with how our performance will be judged, we have less working memory available for complex tasks. Fear (and being in our fixed mindset) disrupts our creativity and problem solving, which are essential to innovation. We want people to feel challenged, but we also want them to have access to resources and feel supported to meet those challenges. Unfortunately, because Cultures of Genius focus on fixed abilities and competition, they often place people in a threat state. As Edmonson summarizes in her book *The Fearless Organization*, "it's hard for people to do their best work when they are afraid." Cultures of Growth encourage people toward their growth mindset by creating psychological safety.

While a first-year doctoral student, Edmonson joined a team studying medical errors in hospitals. Her focus was on looking at the effects of teamwork on error rates. Over a six-month period, while nurse investigators collected data, Edmonson surveyed and observed the medical teams. Going into the study, she hypothesized that the most effective teams would make the fewest errors, yet what the data showed was confusing: Better teams seemed to actually make *more* errors. Upon further investigation, Edmonson found that it wasn't that the highest-functioning teams were making more mistakes, it was that they spoke more openly about them with one another and were more willing to report the mistakes than the other teams, who were more likely to leave mistakes off their reports. Learning, combined with the psychological safety needed to speak up, kept the highest-functioning teams focused on continuous improvement.

Psychological safety is not about avoiding criticism so people feel more comfortable, it's about cultivating respectful candor. When employees see something isn't working, a psychologically safe environment makes it more likely they'll speak up because they don't fear being ignored, ridiculed, or fired for it. However, a growth mindset culture goes a step farther, encouraging employees to actively seek out opportunities to innovate and to improve—both the work product and themselves. Psychological safety tunes the atmosphere to one in which employees feel more comfortable sharing their insights and ideas. To that point, when looking at how shy people's mindset set points influenced how they handled social situations, researchers found out that shy people who tend to hang out in their growth mindset actually seek out more challenging social situations because they believe that such interactions could increase their social skills. Conversely, those who tended toward their fixed mindset preferred less demanding interactions where their perceived social shortcomings won't be highlighted. They tended to engage in more avoidant behaviors during social exchanges.

As Jacqueline Novogratz observed during her initial work before founding Acumen, lack of psychological safety was a huge barrier to effective engagement with entrepreneurs throughout Africa. In several programs she worked with, women entrepreneurs with innovative ideas had learned how to tell funders what they wanted to hear, rather than to express their own insights or what they truly needed to be successful. "People who've always been dependent on others for some kind of charity or goodwill often have a hard time saying what they really want because usually no one asks them. And if they are asked, the poor often think no one really wants to hear the truth," she wrote in *The Blue Sweater*. The same is often true within organizations: Employees are so seldom listened to from a learning mindset that they doubt whether their opinions will make a difference. Novogratz took these insights with her when she founded Acumen. As she tells philanthropists and other partners who want to become involved with Acumen, leadership "starts with listening."

HOW SHELL SHIFTED THEIR MINDSET CULTURE

When Shell attempted to cultivate a growth mindset culture to innovate on safety, not everyone was convinced that a shift in mindset would get them closer to Goal Zero. What if it somehow moved them farther away?

When I arrived at Shell's headquarters, I was offered the requisite safety card lanyard that everyone in the building wears. In the main foyer, a large screen prominently displayed the company's Goal Zero updates. They had the right artifacts that signaled the company valued its safety culture, yet the goal of no safety issues remained elusive. Should the company commit to a significant mindset shift? Would that help them get where they wanted to go?

Shell decided to commit to their cultural revolution, and they understood that a series of brainstorming sessions and a standard safety campaign weren't sufficient. They needed to shift *everyone* toward their growth mindset in each area of the business from finance, technology, legal, and HR to staff and contractors involved in ground-level implementation. This included not just Shell employees and contractors but also other organizational partners, in the offices and in the fields and on ocean rigs. Without total buy-in, how would they get people to commit to the hard work of learning new technologies and a new industry, innovating creatively but safely, forging new partnerships, and learning from the inevitable mistakes that would occur along the way? And while it was essential to have everyone on board, Shell executives also understood that change had to start from the top.

As part of its old Culture of Genius mentality, leaders at Shell had been expected to be know-it-alls instead of learn-it-alls. "If you have middle management trying to do something different, but the top says, 'Leaders know the answer,' you'll have a disconnect," Jorrit van der Togt explains. "So our conclusion was that it had to not be about leaders as teachers who *have* all the answers, but about leaders as learners, helping others, enticing others and enticing teams to *find* the answers. It's not about operating on the basis of our knowledge, but on finding out a better answer, and doing it faster than the competitor." It's not about focusing on *what* you know, but *how* you know. And this know-it-all mindset among leaders was one of the first things I helped Shell shift.

We started with then-CEO Ben van Beurden and his executive

committee, who oversaw each area of the business. The committee asked pointed questions about mindset and how it shows up in the workplace, particularly between managers and employees. Each executive then found examples in their own careers where they recognized that their fixed mindset had held them or their team back. And they recalled times when switching to their growth mindset had helped them persist, innovate, and achieve what they'd accomplished in their careers. They committed to sharing their stories with the senior leadership teams that they each managed, and they created a system by which those leaders would do the same down the organization's hierarchy.

Shell also examined the prevailing behavioral norms that might trigger employees toward their fixed mindset. For example, how were meetings generally run? Were they places to "know it all" or to "learn it all"? What kind of processes could be developed to shift people more toward their growth mindset more of the time?

They examined their evaluation processes to make sure that growth and development were key areas for discussion when employees came up for their performance reviews. Employees were encouraged to set growth-minded learning goals and to review them regularly with their managers and team, especially when they were stuck or encountering obstacles that could benefit from new strategies. More than anything, though, everyone was encouraged and rewarded for seeking ways to improve their work. They also created channels to offer ideas for improvement to managers so that those good ideas (especially with regard to safety protocols) could be tested and implemented at scale. Suddenly, it wasn't just about following the safety routine on the cards around their necks and speaking up when something was not to code; now employees and contractors were encouraged to proactively notice and suggest new ideas for improvement because they were committed to learning how to do things even better (and more safely).

From there, the internal HR and strategy leaders incorporated growth mindset—or as Shell called it, "learner mindset"—into all aspects of the business. On their annual Safety Day, when every year all 86,000 employees gather, Shell discussed their learning initiative, starting with the question: *What do leaders need to do differently?* Van der Togt explained how people need to "listen—to ask four or five more questions before they finally comment. We really shifted our way of thinking on safety, moving away from 'You must prevent mistakes at all costs,' because it's impossible to avoid all mistakes. Now our model is 'Learn to respond quickly when mistakes are made.'" In other words, after the immediate situation is handled, double down on the learning before you move on.

Shell put into practice the research regarding mindset's role in shaping employees' behavior. In a Culture of Genius where only stars can be successful, with people vying to show off their talent and downplaying their mistakes, errors are likely to repeat themselves. These behaviors are particularly dangerous for an organization with safety at its core. Shell's move toward building a Culture of Growth meant that its leadership became obsessed with learning and viewed mistakes as opportunities to develop new proactive strategies that could improve outcomes and learn from those mistakes in the future. A learner mindset among leadership created the psychological safety necessary for people to speak up, air mistakes and vulnerabilities in the system, and be proactively vigilant for ways to improve the organization. Shell learned how to mine mistakes for valuable learning.

"I think we now have a much better response around how we deal with safety protocol situations," van der Togt says, "but over time there has been less focus on just extracting the learnings and more on disseminating them and making sure that all of Shell learns from them, too."

In 2020, Shell took a huge step forward on Goal Zero, achieving zero fatal accidents in Shell-operated facilities worldwide while their competitors sadly still experienced fatalities that year. The shift to a growth mindset culture helped Shell protect and save lives.

HOW TO ENCOURAGE AND ENABLE INNOVATION

There's no end to the ideas you can invoke to help employees view innovation and organizational improvement as everyone's domain. Here are a few suggestions.

Surface Ideas from Everywhere

In Cultures of Growth, great ideas come from anywhere in the organization. Patagonia's philosophy is that their biggest competition is environmental devastation—that's what they're out to beat, and that kind of effort requires all hands on deck to bring their best solutions forward. Throughout their internal operations, Patagonia maintains an "open book" policy so that employees can easily understand management decisions and regularly seek input and feedback from all levels within the company. Such transparent, accessible actions help demonstrate that valuing everyone's insights is not just lip service.

Pixar employs many strategies to ensure that everyone contributes their best, including removing barriers to participation. During their early days, a beautifully designed table sat in the center of one of the main conference rooms, and it was around this table that the creative team would gather to discuss movies in progress. The director, producer, and a few other senior team members would sit front-and-center at the table so everyone could hear them. As the team grew in size, the table overflowed and the remaining team members would squeeze their chairs in along the walls or take standing positions. Eventually, someone started making name cards to save seats for the senior staff, but this had an unintended effect. One day, Pixar cofounder Ed Catmull realized that the only people weighing in at the meeting were the named royalty or those close in proximity to them. Not only had they accidentally created a hierarchy, they'd made it difficult for other folks to contribute. So they did away with the placards entirely and got a larger space with furniture that enabled everyone to come to the table, literally and figuratively.

Emma McIlroy, cofounder of Wildfang—an innovative women's apparel company that incorporates design approaches traditionally used in menswear—shares two simple words that keep her focused on the fact that good ideas can come from anywhere: *Yeah, maybe.* When Emma was seven, she fancied herself a budding paleontologist. One day, while on the beach with her mother in their native Northern Ireland, she came across something she was absolutely certain was a fossilized mammoth's foot. Now, Emma's mom knew that the small, craggy chunk her daughter held in her hand was not a mammoth's foot, but instead of saying, "Yeah, right!" she nodded and said, "Yeah, maybe it is. Let's take it to the museum to find out." When we respond to others' notions with some version of *Yeah, right!* it shuts down conversation and possibility, and often makes the person on the receiving end feel lousy and disengage next time, McIlroy says. *Yeah, maybe*, on the other hand, allows continued thinking and opportunity. A few years ago, when a junior customer service employee came to McIlroy with a new idea for how to do something, she immediately started to mentally poke holes in the idea. It was weird and wacky, she said, and on the surface McIlroy could think of all kinds of reasons it wouldn't work. And yet, she had to admit it was an idea she'd never considered before. Some part of her thought back to that day on the beach with her mom and instead she told the employee to develop the idea—to do some research and preliminary work and see what came of it. McIlroy says lots of young people go to work for Wildfang because they're interested in being part of the culture, which in part is one where "ideas can come from anywhere." Yet, "they don't necessarily have any corporate training" and so some of those ideas are uninformed by real-world experience. "Sometimes when the ideas come to you, you can see the weaknesses and you can see the flaws," and the challenge is to not squash them before they have a chance to evolve. Now, says McIlroy, she's faced every day with a choice: "Whether I'm going to shut down ideas or allow them to grow."

McIlroy says that keeping a *Yeah, maybe* mindset is harder in practice than it is in theory. One of the most helpful things, she's found, is to internalize that question at an individual level. As she sees it, many of us shut down our own possibility, so saying *Yeah, maybe* to ourselves can make a huge difference in our capacity to innovate. It helps that McIlroy has a high tolerance for failure, seeing it as "part of the innovation journey." She learned this mindset while competing on the international stage as a runner for Ireland's national team, understanding that if she wasn't losing enough, she wasn't competing at a high enough level. She sees innovation at Wildfang the same way, crediting every major advance they've had as one that's come from failure. "The culture that we've built is so focused on adopting and accepting failure, and then learning from it and sharing learnings. . . . When from leadership down you accept and own failure, it gives such permission to the rest of the organization and the organization becomes an organism—it starts to grow and move in ways that you didn't realize possible because people feel truly empowered . . . to try and fail." (Oh, and by the way, that rock young Emma found? She and her mom did take it to the museum, and it turned out it wasn't a mammoth's foot. It was a 200-million-year-old ichthyosaur skull, and museum staff told her it was the best example of such a skull anyone in Ireland had ever found. It's still on display at the Ulster Museum in Belfast if you're ever in the neighborhood.)

Whether through philosophical approaches or physical design, Cultures of Growth seek out and remedy roadblocks to everyone understanding that their ideas are welcome.

Dedicate Time to Innovate

Visa cofounder Dee Hock once said, "The problem is never how to get new, innovative thoughts into your mind, but how to get old ones out. Clean out a corner of your mind and creativity will instantly fill it." For some companies, the strategy is to clean out some space on employees' calendars. In Chapter 3, I described the software company Atlassian's penchant for collaboration. Because mindset culture operates as a cohesive meaning system, the same organizations that display growth-minded norms such as collaboration are also likely to embody other growth-minded norms like innovation. Atlassian combines these norms with their ShipIt days, where employees get 24 hours to team up and tackle any problem that appeals to them, from solving problems with the help desk system to resolving the lack of arcade games in the employee lounge. One of the benefits of the quarterly ShipIt days is that they foster collaboration among employees across departments, and that can lead to even more innovation in the future.

Many other organizations have similar structures to encourage innovation, but the originator of the idea was 3M, a multinational conglomerate known for its products like Post-it Notes but that also produces roughly 60,000 products and operates 46 technology platforms. Each year, roughly one-third of the company's sales revenue comes from products developed within the past five years, and that target is purposeful. According to 3M, this ability to churn out successful new products is due to its emphasis on collaboration. In fact, the company is credited with originating "15 percent time"—a program in which all employees are encouraged to use 15 percent of their time to tackle questions and challenges that have caught their personal interest—all the way back in 1948. (And yes, *all* employees, not just engineers, get 15 percent time, because, as the company says, they believe great ideas can come from anywhere—another indicator of a Culture of Growth.) But 15 percent time isn't just meant for lone geniuses to go off and invent. Once employees flesh out their concepts, they present them to coworkers, seeking collaborators who are inspired enough by their work and see enough potential that they sign on to help develop the projects. Perhaps the best-known result of 3M's 15 percent time is their famous Post-it Notes, which scientist Arthur Fry developed using an adhesive created by another 3M employee. As journalist Katherine Schwab described in *Fast Com-*

pany, "Once a year, about 200 employees from dozens of divisions make cardboard posters describing their 15 percent time project as if they were presenting volcano models at a middle school science fair. They stand up their poster, then hang out next to it, awaiting feedback, suggestions, and potential co-collaborators." A manager in 3M's abrasives division says, "For technical people, it's the most passionate and engaged event we have at 3M."

Google allows employees to dedicate up to 20 percent of their work time to self-generated side projects. In fact, the ideas for Gmail and Google Maps originated from side projects. At manufacturer W. L. Gore, these aren't considered side projects, but rather just projects: The culture allows employees to develop their own ideas, then, similar to 3M, sell coworkers on collaborating to bring them into being. This degree of freedom can be challenging for some folks to get used to, so senior managers encourage newbies not to take on more than they can realistically handle and to bring in others to help. While great ideas are prized at Gore, so is the ability to deliver on them. If someone's idea doesn't inspire anyone to join them, that speaks for itself; but if people start poking at it and get interested in testing it out, they're welcome to join the team. Considering part of the process for inventing GORE-TEX was the result of an experimental accident, the company is all for going down new roads to see where they lead.

Invest in Building Psychological Safety

Building psychological safety is about sincere, consistent engagement and follow-through over time—those hundreds of little conversations held in meaningful ways. But as Jorrit van der Togt points out, psychological safety alone isn't enough. "It's important to feel safe," he said, "but that alone doesn't drive real progress. . . . Psychological safety is the ground tone, not the music." That's the growth mindset. When it comes to choosing the music, lead by example, demonstrating your own growth mindset in the face of personal or organizational adversity and make the most of opportunities for informed risk-taking.

As attorney, civil rights advocate, and PolicyLink founder Angela Glover Blackwell said when she worked with Jacqueline Novogratz at the Rockefeller Foundation, when we develop cultures that are not only comfortable with, but seek out, input from throughout the organization and community, we can invoke "minoritarian leadership," which can dramatically strengthen an organization. Blackwell explains, "Individuals in the dominant group assume that the rules work because they've always seemed fair to them. On the other hand, people who view themselves as outsiders have had to learn to navigate the dominant culture in order to be successful. Becoming attuned to how others function and make decisions is a critical skill set we need to inculcate in our next generation of leaders." That next generation of leaders could already be within your walls. By attending to psychological safety, you ensure that they can make powerful contributions, including helping your organization more effectively navigate risk and develop greater resilience. Later we'll explore how strong Cultures of Genius can disparately disadvantage people of color and destroy psychological safety. If you want to build a Culture of Growth, creating safe contexts for people to move toward their growth, rather than their fixed, mindset is key. The goal is to remove barriers and threats so that folks are free to deliver their best performance.

Look Elsewhere

Sometimes when we think of innovation, we focus only on new ideas, but innovation can also include new applications of existing ideas or taking inspiration from another industry and using it in a different way. A team of management researchers wanted to look at how people access and implement knowledge from adjacent fields. In one study, they recruited hundreds of carpenters, roofers, and in-line skaters and asked them all to give ideas about how to get folks in the other fields to wear safety gear. (Many spurned the gear, citing its lack of comfort.) They asked how the respirator masks recommended for carpenters, the safety belts roofers are supposed to wear, and skaters' knee pads could be redesigned to encourage use. They found that pretty much everyone was better at figuring out how to make innovative improvements to the other groups' equipment than to their own. Sometimes looking at adjacent and analogous fields can help us break down our mental barriers and shift into *Yeah, maybe* mode.

Financial and investing advice firm the Motley Fool, which is known for its irreverent and innovative culture, sends employees on a scavenger hunt for new ideas. During their Great Idea Hunt, employees split up into teams, with each team spending a few hours visiting an organization of their choosing (it can be any kind, from a business to a nonprofit) and bringing back at least one interesting idea they've discovered. When the Fools, as they call themselves, visited beverage company Honest Tea, most of whose staff worked remotely, they learned how the company streamlined company communications to give workers time and space to focus. Instead of shooting off separate emails or Slack-type updates, they compiled everything in a single daily newsletter called "Afternoon Tea," an idea the Fools considered adopting.

Take Note of Your Surprises

My colleague Kimberly Quinn recommends what she called "a surprise journal." When she or her students have a hypothesis about how something works, but they come across findings that seem strange or that surprise them in the lab, they write them down in a log. As they accrue these findings, patterns may emerge that enable them to revise their theory. What makes the surprise journal effective is that it busts through our tendency to engage in confirmation bias—that is, our tendency to expect ideas and people's behavior to be consistent with, well, what we expect. If we view one strategy as the obvious, well-tested, and acceptable one, we tend to automatically look for the ways that strategy is the most optimal. In this way, the confirmation bias moves us deeper into our fixed mindset. When a different strategy seems to have been successful, it surprises us. Instead of dismissing or glossing over occurrences where results don't comport with what we expect, we can note it in our surprise journal. This practice is one way Quinn fosters a Culture of Growth in her lab by helping her students keep track of new, often messy, findings so that they can see the innovative directions that those surprises point to.

CHAPTER 5

Risk-Taking and Resilience

"We want to talk about risk-taking."

I had heard some form of this request many times before. This time it came from Twitter. Vijaya Gadde, who at the time was Twitter's chief legal officer, and other executives had identified a challenge with their global legal team: Their attorneys were reluctant to take risks. It was understandable as lawyers are trained to be conservative decision-makers; often their job is to tell their client *no* to avoid potential legal risk. But in this case, erring on the side of caution was limiting Twitter's opportunities to be more innovative. Gadde wanted my help figuring out how to help the lawyers be less risk-averse, including identifying any cultural factors that might unintentionally be prompting them to overexercise such caution. Rather than asking themselves, "How can I keep Twitter safe from any risk that could open us up to legal challenges?" the executive team wanted them to ask, "How can I do my job responsibly while also helping the company become more innovative?"

I didn't know that when Gadde called me, then-CEO Jack Dorsey and the executive team were facing multiple high-stakes decisions about whether to label false speech on the platform and to intervene when the speech was determined to be inflammatory and potentially dangerous. It's not that the attorneys didn't want to do this, but making this decision would likely open up the organization to legal challenges. As the executives saw it, understanding legal's mindset microculture and agreeing on shared language and goals might help with measured risk-taking and innovation.

Twitter convened an all-hands retreat of the Global Legal, Policy, and Trust & Safety teams. Some 200 people flew to San Francisco and met at the company's headquarters, eager to discuss how Twitter could become more of a growth-minded organization. One moment stood out, when I asked the group, "What are your real fears around risk-taking? What scares you about moving farther toward the ledge—not falling off it, but inching more toward taking calculated risks?" Not surprisingly, their play-it-safe behavior wasn't due to some inherent aversion to risk-taking, or to a lack of intelligence or creative ability. These were smart, dedicated employees who wanted to do right by the company. "What if we're wrong and we expose Twitter to a lawsuit?" they replied. "And what if we get fired for making the wrong call?"

This type of fear is common in Cultures of Genius, typically due to anxiety over how managers and executives will respond to failure. Will it be deemed a personal shortcoming, evidence of bad judgment? Or even as a sign of low ability and competence? Will they be demoted or fired? In the case of the tweeps (as they call themselves), the attorneys worried about being too forward-thinking in their legal advice if, for example, they took action to label content as false and misleading. In so doing, they feared they could expose the company to legal risks and, by extension, put their own jobs on the line and potentially sour their chances for future employment elsewhere. When employees are triggered into their fixed mindsets in this way, they're (understandably) less likely to take risks.

In Cultures of Growth, risks are still risky—it's always uncertain how they will turn out—yet people understand that risk is essential to growth and innovation and necessary to reach one's goals. Risks are typically undertaken thoughtfully after careful planning, and there's likely to be a contingency plan (or several) in case the bet fails. When the outcome goes wrong in a growth-minded organization, people worry less about who to blame and more about how to solve the problem and learn from it. It's about asking, "What didn't go the way we'd planned and how can we do things differently?" rather than, "Which genius flubbed this one up?" When mistakes are made, employees need to know (and as soon as possible), but in Cultures of Growth, postmortems are aimed at learning, not at shaming and punishing the offenders. We saw this in the way Shell switched their safety incident response from one that was more focused on identifying who was to blame, to one that prioritized identifying the lessons that could be learned.

Risk-taking is the cousin of innovation. **If an organization wants to stay fresh and relevant, risk-taking is necessary behavior.** Cultures of Growth and Cultures of Genius differ in whether they support and encourage risk-taking, starting with how they perceive risk.

RE-CATEGORIZING RISK

Organizations categorize risk differently. Those with stronger Cultures of Genius, where one's reputation and livelihood are on the line, are more likely to view risk negatively. When people do take a chance, they're riddled with worry and anxiety because the personal and professional consequences of failure are so intense. In Cultures of Growth, risk-taking is perceived as an opportunity for learning, a strategy to help people reach their goals. And because they're less enamored of the status quo than Cultures of Genius, Cultures of Growth also tend to be more aware of the challenges and dangers of *not* changing or trying new things, like the willingness to label and take action against inflammatory language on a social platform.

If we're always geared toward learning and collaboration, people sometimes assume that the conversation will keep going indefinitely and we'll never make decisions or take risks. So, I asked my friend and research collaborator Ben Tauber—former CEO of the Esalen Institute, cofounder and former CEO of Silicon Valley execu-

tive coaching firm Velocity Group, and a former manager at Google
and Adobe—whether he sees times when it's helpful to lean on your
fixed mindset; in the various states of a startup, for instance. Ben recalled our research on whether it was beneficial for founders to be in
their fixed mindset during the fund-raising process. When it came
to getting investors and venture capitalists to take a risk on them,
being in a prove-and-perform mode seemed to pay off for founders such as Theranos's Elizabeth Holmes, Uber's Travis Kalanick,
and WeWork's Adam Neumann, who once boasted, "No one says *no*
to me." (Even after the colossal failures of WeWork, some investors
seem happy to take another chance on Neumann, funneling massive
investments into his follow-up venture, Flow.) However, our data
showed the opposite: Founders operating in their growth mindsets
during pitching were actually more likely to meet their fund-raising
goals than those in a fixed mindset.

"When you pitch at that early stage," Tauber said, "it's really
about the VC going, 'Do I believe this person is the person who can
figure it out?' Our initial hypothesis was that maybe founders in
their fixed mindsets would be more convincing. But now I would
make a distinction between belief and behavior. Mindset is a collection of beliefs. When I'm in my growth mindset, I'm here to learn.
But behavior is about how you communicate, and you can have a
learning mindset and still communicate with confidence." People
in their growth mindsets are more likely to have explored their idea
more thoroughly and learned as much as possible about how to
make it work, including the risks that may stand in their way. When
in our growth mindsets, our vision is broader and more accurate.
We're more open to seeing the challenges we face, and we have more
humility around our ideas, so we're more willing to stress test and
refine them. Therefore, when entrepreneurs go to pitch their idea,
they're backed by the benefits of knowledge and confidence afforded
by their growth mindset.

Silicon Valley is famous for its "fail fast" mantra. But we might be
better served by the mantra "learn fast." That would keep investors

focused on backing founders dedicated to creating growth mindset cultures and have a better chance at success. To assess how a founder might handle the complex decisions and shifts necessary to launch a business, the VC could look for clues that the founder is more likely to operate from their growth mindset most of the time—and that they will develop processes and norms that instill a Culture of Growth in their burgeoning organization. Investors should be wary of founders who emphasize their own inherent genius or the genius of their ideas over their ability to continuously improve.

"In the fixed mindset," Ben told me, "we can end up stuck, blaming the team or external factors if our plan isn't working. When we're in our growth mindset, we might iterate more. Say, 'If the difference between A, B, and C is only this much, how about we try A and if this isn't working in two weeks, we'll try B.'" As long as we're clear on the success metric, we can strategize, set targets, and be more flexible in our thoughts and actions.

When Satya Nadella took over at Microsoft, he had the challenge of reinventing a culture that had "killed collaboration" and "crippled innovation." By playing it too safe, Microsoft had come in late or missed out entirely on several waves of technology, such as smartphones. Then, a "wave of external competition crashed down on the firm, causing talent to jump ship," concluded a London Business School case study. Whereas the firm's former CEO, Steve Ballmer, was known for his risk aversion, Nadella has shown himself to be the opposite. He believed that mindset was at least partly to blame for the company verging on irrelevance within the tech world. "Each employee had to prove to everyone that he or she was the smartest in the room. Accountability—delivering on time and hitting numbers—trumped everything. . . . Hierarchy and pecking order had taken control, and spontaneity and creativity had suffered." After an extended listening and learning tour, Nadella shifted Microsoft to focus on mobile and cloud technologies and emphasized AI capabilities. He also noticed that employees were spending an inordinate amount of time poking at people's ideas (and in some cases, the people themselves) rather than approaching them with curiosity. He knew that the culture needed to change.

At today's Microsoft, people's contributions are largely focused on what does work about an idea, and on exploring what might help it work even better. Cultures of Growth, however, aren't short on critical thinking and candor—quite the opposite. As Nadella wrote in his book *Hit Refresh*, "Debate and argument are essential. Improving upon each other's ideas is crucial." Recall that growth mindset organizations have more psychological safety, a crucial element of candor. The focus is on people's ideas, not their inherent abilities. Rigorously analyzing an idea and figuring out how to improve upon it is different from abject naysaying that's aimed more at protecting one's own position within the organizational hierarchy than adding value. Incidentally, in *Hit Refresh*, Nadella noted that Microsoft employees desperately wanted "a roadmap to remove paralysis," or a way to get unstuck. The shift to a more growth-minded culture helped.

Nadella also encouraged Microsoft employees to start spending more time talking directly with customers to learn about what wasn't working and what would serve them better. This approach removes a layer of risk because you're more likely to build something that solves customers' problems. Kinney Zalesne, Microsoft's former general manager of corporate strategy, believes in this kind of collaboration not only for Microsoft, but for the world to solve complex problems. As Kinney told me, "I think there's nothing more important going forward in our society than the clash and intersection of ideas. If ideas are just rising in a little company or only in one sector, that's not what we need anymore. The problems we're facing globally are so big that we've got to find solutions that come at the intersection of different disciplines and different approaches, and I think growth mindset is the fundamental building block of even being able to get started having those conversations."

The goal isn't just to have happier employees and better results—though of course these are part of it. Kinney adds, "It's that problem-solving today and going forward is going to require interdisciplinary, bold, unorthodox thinking. That's what's got to be taught to everyone, and that's what's got to be valued by companies and governments."

No one person can be fully "interdisciplinary"; that requires pulling the best from a diverse array of people steeped in different sets of knowledge and experiences. If organizations and individuals believe it's too risky to share ideas and resources across groups and sectors, if employees are too focused on competing with one another to pool their knowledge and resources, and organizations hitch their wagons to a few stars instead of building their bench, we won't be able to think up and achieve the solutions necessary to rise to the level of the challenges we're facing.

Engaging people around data also helps Cultures of Growth determine what risks are worth taking, and how to take them.

DE-RISKING WITH DATA

When considering the two mindset cultures, I often ask myself, "Which is more risky?" Reflecting on our findings, and as a scholar, I'm more inclined toward data-informed decision-making. Sharing data widely turns out to be one of the most effective approaches Cultures of Growth use to make organizational change less risky. I discovered that in 2020 in collaboration with Microsoft and Keystone, a consulting firm, when we examined the data collection and data usage practices of a variety of companies.

In Cultures of Growth, we found that data were widely accessible. Everyone understood how to access and use data to inform their decision-making, not just those in IT and Analytics. Because of that, they had a shared context and understanding of the current state of affairs—and what the models predicted for the future. We also saw that leaders in Cultures of Growth were more confident in sharing their vision with their teams and inviting their team members into the process to make that vision a reality. When functioning in an environment with a clear vision, growth-oriented process, and relevant data review to assess whether they were headed in the right direction, teams in turn stepped up and often generated more creative solutions.

Meanwhile in Cultures of Genius, data were often siloed by strong gatekeepers. In some of the companies we interviewed, it could take months for IT to provide the data that people had requested—and often we saw data teams hoarding information and reluctantly sharing it only when a senior leader insisted on the information. Ironically, in Cultures of Genius we saw leaders more likely to rely on their gut and intuition rather than consult the numbers (when we know that optimal decision-making is a function of both data and intuition).

Data helped Louis Wool—with eventual support from other administrators, teachers, and school board members—transition an entire school district from a Culture of Genius to a Culture of Growth. When Wool became acting superintendent of the Harrison Central School District (HCSD) in Westchester County, roughly half an hour's drive north of New York City, he saw the story the numbers told—in terms of metrics such as student performance and resource allocation—and knew they could do better. Though it's considered a "low need" district overall, Harrison Central spans an economically diverse area—ranging from high-wealth sectors to working-class populations—and has a similarly diverse student body across schools. "I came to a community that looks to be extraordinarily wealthy," Wool told me, "but twenty-five percent of the community receives free and reduced fee lunch." Former board of education member David Singer described HCSD as a fixed-minded atmosphere replete with the "soft bigotry of low expectations." Throughout the community, among teachers, administrators, parents, and the school board, people largely didn't expect students from racially diverse and socioeconomically disadvantaged backgrounds to perform well. They took it as a foregone conclusion. But

Wool saw something different: a lack of equity that was blocking the path for some students while paving it for others. For example, schools in higher-income areas received more funding and students there had access to the latest textbooks, while in other areas, the textbooks weren't only outdated, there weren't enough to go around. When these groups of students then merged in junior high and high school, their outcomes varied, not due to raw ability, but because of differences in access and opportunity. Wool pored over the district's data, from budgets to performance metrics, and devised a plan to balance the division of both wealth and opportunity among the schools to provide greater equity for all students.

"Some of the evidence of disproportionate opportunity was embarrassingly evident," said Wool. "For example, there had never been, ever, a Hispanic child in an AP class in the history of the district. I could disaggregate the four elementary schools in the district completely blindly, by zip code, and tell which kids would end up getting what used to be called a Regents' Diploma, which was basically a college-level diploma, and which kids would not. I could tell by age ten, with one-hundred-percent accuracy, whether or not you'd end up in AP calculus. And nobody believed that was a problem. Nobody was crying out, 'Fix this.'"

Wool set about to change not just the policies and practices of the district, but its overall mindset culture. The fundamental goal was to achieve equity for all students. Shifts on the ground included major overhauls to school budgets, teacher evaluation systems, and measures of student progress. In the process, he faced massive opposition (which at times included physical threats) from teachers, school board members, and wealthy parents, the latter group asserting that some changes, such as doing away with the school's tracking system and allowing broad access to the high school's AP programs, would result in a less rigorous curriculum. When schools move to more equitable and inclusive curricula and practices, a common concern among parents and teachers is that these changes will "dumb down" the curriculum and hold back the "smarter, more gifted" students.

In other words, it will hold back the privileged—and in most cases White—stars. **In fact, research shows consistently that when implemented thoughtfully, modifications aimed at equity result in *all* students performing better.** In the case of HCSD, the organizational and culture changes were so successful to student outcomes that in 2009, Wool was named New York Superintendent of the Year, and performance rates for students have remained high.

The most dramatic shift Wool implemented that improved the district's culture was to take away all prerequisites to enter certain programs. "I don't believe in fixed traits or a singular assessment determining your destiny," he told me. The changes felt risky to everyone. "Everybody was losing something. Teachers losing their sense of efficacy. Some parents losing their sense of entitlement. The poor kids worried that it's just going to get worse. [To make change in a situation like that] you have to press in when everyone's telling you you're wrong." To be clear, this wasn't based on a hunch Wool had, or about making moves that would be bad for the district or the community—quite the opposite. Having conducted a rigorous analysis of the district's data and considered prior experiences he'd had improving outcomes in another underfunded school, Wool was making an evidence-based, informed push to do better by all students in the district. He says that maintaining humility and constantly checking and re-checking the plan and the progress were essential for driving change. And, as he told me, "[T]hat's where a growth mindset really comes in."

The results speak for themselves. Performance data show significantly improved outcomes for students overall, regardless of their backgrounds, throughout the district. For example, like many schools, HCSD used to track their middle school math program, so only some kids had access to higher-level classes like algebra. The last year that tracking system was in effect, only about 10 percent of students scored at mastery level on an algebra skills assessment test. Then Wool removed the tracking and made algebra available to all students and provided supports to help students be successful. As of

2023, nearly two decades since that shift, the average pass rate for algebra has risen to 90 percent, with 52 percent scoring at mastery level.

Wool explained, "One thing I would say that characterizes my behaviors as different from most is I'm not so driven by fear of conflict. I spend a lot of time coaching at this point in my life—young superintendents, young administrators—and they always err on the side of caution. They worry primarily about 'How do I maintain my job?' as opposed to 'How do I do the right work?'" The key is that conflict is issues-based, rather than interpersonal. It isn't about employees being competitive or arguing with one another, or the boss ruling with an iron fist. Instead, it's about being willing to dive in together to hash out the work, looking at agreed-upon metrics, feeling welcome and safe to express your opinion, respectfully, even if it differs with someone else's. Importantly, leadership sets the tone to emphasize that risks and conflict are okay, and even welcome, as long as they're well informed and aimed at improvement.

This is an important takeaway for those under the impression that Cultures of Growth are happy, easygoing places with little conflict. They are among the most rigorous and challenging environments to be in (which is why some will fight so hard to hang on to a Culture of Genius). Comfort has nothing to do with Cultures of Growth versus Genius. **Achieving greater equity, diversity, and inclusion are not about increasing people's comfort. Rather, they are about removing barriers and obstacles to opportunities that are present for some, so that success is available to all.** They are about removing *threats*, so that all students and employees can work to their true ability. When these barriers are removed, students can take on more rigorous curricula; within companies, employees are free to bring more of their resources to bear on the challenges of innovation, and to take the risks that go along with solving them.

Embracing risk is not about jumping into it blindly. Growth-minded teams lean heavily on data not only to navigate organizational change, but also to weigh whether a risk is worth taking.

They also use data to determine whether that decision, once made, is leading to success or needs to be reconsidered and adjusted. They are open to evidence that their decisions may (or may not) be contributing to the desired outcome. True Cultures of Growth use data to consider which risks to pursue, with regard to time, energy, and resources, and then continuously assess whether these risks are paying off.

Patagonia head of HR Dean Carter, who we met in Chapter 3, uses the data-driven model of regenerative agriculture to guide decision-making. When the company amended the standard work week so that corporate staff had every other Friday off, they surveyed employees before and after to "measure what we were putting in and taking out," says Carter. The other reason they surveyed employees is that they wanted to be sure that the schedule shift would provide the intended benefits and impact. They measured employees' levels of productivity, how much they were working, and their level of engagement. Carter calls those the "extractive" elements: "Is the company still getting out of people what we put in?" They also gauged what the company was putting into people's lives. "For example," he says, "did this [schedule shift] help with your relationship with your spouse? Did you have more quality time with your children? Were you able to prepare healthy meals? Were you able to have time to go to the doctor? Did this improve your relationship with and your ability to contribute to your community?" What they found was that across the board, these factors improved, along with employee engagement, while productivity and time spent working remained stable.

Following up to determine whether the changes they put in place have the outcomes they intend is the kind of rigorous, growth-minded approach that's essential to Patagonia's model of making decisions with the future in mind. "If I'm stewarding [these employees] as if I'm going to employ this population for the next hundred years then yes, I don't want them stressed," he explains. "I want [them] to take good care of their children because it's highly likely a hundred years from now that not only will I be employing their children, but I could be employing their grandchildren."

Incidentally, the company boasted a voluntary employee turnover rate of less than 4 percent during 2021, a time when the field averaged at least three times that, along with a shocking 100 percent retention rate of working mothers over a five-year span. During the Great Resignation, when companies struggled to hold on to employees, and when large numbers of women, especially, left the workplace, these figures point to a major competitive advantage. When companies overfocus on extraction and on what they can get out of employees in the short term, while largely ignoring what they put in or give back, they are poorly equipped for long-term success. Data help Cultures of Growth get a clear picture of what life is like for their employees, and how they can help them experience more balance—for the good of the people and the company.

FACTORS THAT INFLUENCE RISK-TAKING IN CULTURES OF GROWTH

Where do fixed mindset ideas around risk-taking originate within organizations? I went on the hunt for the source during my time with Twitter's legal team. For some, I found that it started with the interviewing and hiring process. Interviewers often asked about intellectual achievements and seemed to view the type of school people attended (fancy schools = smarter) and past employment (such as in-house experience) as best. This meant they would potentially be overlooking incredible candidates from lower-ranked schools or those with more diverse backgrounds that, while not an exact match for what they'd be doing at Twitter, could still prove valuable to the company. Questions about hypothetical scenarios seemed to have clearly right or wrong answers, which are not good predictors of actual performance since, in the course of a job, people are expected to research and learn about relevant contingencies rather than just respond on the spot with no information. Once hired, opportunities for learning and development—like the new-hire orientation—were usually limited to one day. Too often, people were inundated with information, then left largely on their own to figure things out. For many, this sink-or-swim mentality communicated a Culture of Genius more than one of Growth.

The tweeps wanted to change these processes to encourage a learning mindset right away. They thought examining candidates' quality—rather than quantity—of experience or school would be a better predictor of a willingness to develop. For example, "Tell me about a time that you faced a challenge and how you overcame it." And they thought it critical to hire based on relevant skills rather than hypotheticals. If a candidate is interviewing for the Trust & Safety team, you want to be sure they have ethical principles, so asking about times they found themselves challenged in this regard and how they handled it would be more telling than how they might handle a made-up situation.

The tweeps also recommended connecting potential employees with relevant affinity groups such as Twitter Women, Twitter Asia, and Blackbirds after their first interview. That way, the candidates could learn more about the company culture from these groups' perspectives, along with strategies for successfully navigating the larger organizational structure. They suggested either extending orientation or, better yet, weaving in chances for new hires to learn continuously together over the course of their first year on the job. They thought not only that this extended learning period could create a culture of camaraderie and connection across teams, but that the work itself might improve when people were sharing strategies and experiences across different business functions. They wanted more internal documentation, such as guides, tools, and how-tos, so that everyone had opportunities to learn, rather than having to piece it all together themselves.

These suggestions improved the hiring process, while also showing how employees experienced the culture at Twitter. But what impressed me most was how willing people were to work together to figure out ways to cultivate a stronger Culture of Growth. Their comfort in raising issues that might be barriers and in brainstorming ways to improve them demonstrated a strong sense of psychological safety.

Of course, as this book goes to print, Twitter (now called X) is undergoing a tectonic shift—and it's a good example of how fragile and leader-dependent organizational culture can be. Within two weeks of Elon Musk's purchase and assumption of the CEO role, he had dismantled all of the Twitter affinity groups, fired more than half of Twitter's workforce, and put an aggressive ultimatum to the remaining employees. His email to employees reads like a page out of the Culture of Genius manual. He wrote, "Going forward, to build a breakthrough Twitter 2.0 and succeed in an increasingly competitive world, we will need to be extremely hardcore. This will mean working long hours at high intensity. Only exceptional performance will constitute a passing grade." Employees had until five P.M. the next day to say whether they were "in" by clicking a survey link in the email. As you'd predict in a Culture of Genius where organizational trust and commitment are notoriously low (and especially when employees had previously worked hard to cultivate an inclusive Culture of Growth), more than half of the remaining employees jumped ship.

To build and maintain a Culture of Growth, leaders need to get people on board, as Shell, Microsoft, and Louis Wool did. Once on board, demonstrate that you've got changemakers' backs when they take calculated risks, encourage learning, and incorporate those lessons as you move forward. If you want folks to be innovative, risk-taking is a necessary element. Focus on ways you and your organization can create a context where people feel comfortable venturing into the uncomfortable territory of risk.

HOW YOUR ORGANIZATION CAN LEARN TO EMBRACE (SMART) RISKS AND BECOME MORE RESILIENT

Here are some tactics to help you instill and inspire a mindset that embraces calculated risk in your organization—more broadly, as well as one conversation at a time.

Seek Out Risks

Don't walk down dark alleys at night or order ghost peppers on your next burrito. But do seek out risks judiciously. In our growth mindset, we seek out thoughtful leaps in the direction where we want to go. As Wildfang cofounder Emma McIlroy observes, she learned as a competitive middle-distance runner that if she wasn't failing enough, she wasn't stretching herself enough—she was playing it safe by competing in a field that didn't hold enough challenge for her. If you haven't failed recently, you could be playing it too safe and too small to make real progress in your life—and the same could be true of your organization. (Incidentally, researchers point to a failure "sweet spot" of about 15 percent of your efforts coming up short.) If this is the case, identify a few areas where you can practice engaging your growth mindset around risk. Start out by identifying one to three places in work or life where you could take some measured risks. Maybe reach out to an admired peer to learn what they're doing well; take a risk and request more professional development so you can be ready for the next challenge that presents itself. Do your research, pack your parachute, and then jump!

Make Data Your Friend

Data put the "measure" in measured risk. Cozying up with data no matter where you are in your organization will help you feel more confident venturing into new territory, and will help you determine early on, and periodically throughout the process, whether the risk you're taking is moving you closer to your goal or farther from it. Data don't tell you whether you're right or wrong (that's a fixed mindset view), they tell you where you are in the moment, and what the trajectory from past to present and from present to future could look like. Set markers where you'll check in and reflect on the process. Reassess, try a new strategy, or pivot if you learn that the risk isn't paying off.

Take a Journey in the Wayback Machine

Before the Wayback Machine became the name of an internet archive, it was a time machine in the cartoon *The Rocky and Bullwinkle Show* that characters Mr. Peabody and Sherman used to visit important moments in history. You can use a version of the Wayback Machine to revisit your own history of risks that didn't quite work out as expected. We tend to shy away from our past failures because they can trigger us into our fixed mindsets: Those failures can lead us to create self-limiting beliefs about our own capabilities. But if we revisit those experiences with notepad and pen in hand, we can mine them for learning. Reflect and take notes on what you learned from those situations and how you handled them. Were you triggered into your fixed or growth mindset by the failure? Did you abandon ship, or grab the sheet, correct the luffing sails, and plow forward toward the horizon? What triggered or caused you to react either way? How did this experience inform your behavior going forward? How would your present-day growth mindset assess the usefulness of that risk, and if you encountered the same opportunity today, would you take the risk or not? Or would you take it, but approach the risk differently, and if so, how?

Pay Attention to the Messages You're Sending

As the tweeps and I discovered when reviewing the cultural messages their legal folks were communicating during the hiring processes, sometimes we can send fixed-minded messages unintentionally. Recruiting and hiring are two areas where this is particularly common. To infuse growth mindset in these areas, be consciously willing to invest in people who may not fit your genius prototype (especially because of their identity or background). Focus instead on those who are willing to bring their skills to the organization and to drive the company to reconsider its approaches. This might feel risky at first, but it's a powerful way to create a Culture of Growth.

Another way to support risk is to create an atmosphere where employees are not only encouraged to take chances, but see by watching others that it's safe to do so. If people see those around them get canned when they go out on a limb and it doesn't pay off, they're not likely to try something radically different. Instead, celebrate employee risk-taking at company events, on the website, or in employee communications. Point out successes, but also highlight failures and the useful insights they generated. Criticism aside, one of the things Amazon founder Jeff Bezos does particularly well is not only champion risk, but also embrace the failure that comes with it, as long as it's accompanied by learning. Bezos famously celebrates Amazon's failures because it means they're trying things, and for every Fire Phone, there are hopefully more Kindles, Fire Sticks, and Alexas. Admittedly, this is a complex example as Amazon has its challenges in other areas, but again, that illustrates the complexity of organizational culture. There can be growth-minded bubbles in some areas, even if other parts of the culture operate with more fixed-minded behaviors. It's a difficult endeavor to create and sustain a Culture of Growth across an organization, but it's worth the risk.

CHAPTER 6

Integrity and Ethical Behavior

If someone cheats or breaks the rules, they're unethical. That's the conclusion most of us jump to, that someone's behavior is determined by who they are as a person, rather than by situational factors. But it's the other way around: The situation we're in—and its culture—often play a stronger role in shaping our behavior than our character does.

This theory became reality for me when one of my own Stanford research assistants violated the standard I thought I had set for ethical behavior. Near the end of the quarter, when it looked like we might fall short of our target for recruiting students to participate in a study, one of my RAs started telling students to simply circle high numbers on our eligibility form to increase their chances of inclusion. When I learned about this after asking how we were getting so many new eligible participants, I had to stop the study altogether. We couldn't continue without knowing who actually qualified, versus those enticed to.

The student was embarrassed and devasted—after all, she had just wanted to help. I was obligated to report the situation to the university ethics board and the ensuing investigation endangered the student's chances of getting into medical school. Ultimately, we were able to repair the relationship and I found work that she could do in the lab while we rebuilt trust. But upon reflection about how we got there, I realized that it wasn't her fault alone.

Thinking about the Culture of Genius endemic at the university where students felt endless pressure to prove that they were smart enough made me reflect on the culture I'd created on my team that caused this student to think that corner-cutting would not just be acceptable but appreciated. As the leader of the lab, what had I said or done to make this student feel this way? I'd been so focused on making our numbers that I'd only stressed how important it was to get people into our study—without stopping to ask my RAs (tasked with making it happen) what they were seeing and learning on the ground. Was our target realistic? Did we need a backup plan? Were there different strategies we could be using to bring people in? I drove us toward the numbers without considering the pressure it put on students to prove and perform. It's perhaps not surprising that a dedicated student, not wanting to disappoint me, might do whatever it took to meet our goal. Had I re-created the university's Culture of Genius consciously and explicitly? Of course not. But my lack of pro-active attention to the culture I was forming locally meant that the dominant culture of the university in which we operated influenced us all, our thoughts, motivations, and behavior. From then on, I became much more intentional about the creation and maintenance of my lab's culture—taking time to check in and assess how it is perceived by those in the lab; how our policies, practices, and norms reflect the culture we aspire to; and regularly surfacing actionable steps we can take to continue to build and maintain it together as an inclusive Culture of Growth.

A lack of ethics and integrity isn't just about cheating or taking shortcuts. It encompasses a range of unscrupulous behaviors from information hoarding and subtle ways of subverting colleagues (*Oh, did I leave you off the meeting invitation?*) to covering up mistakes and out-and-out sabotage, deception, and fraud. These behaviors are more likely to happen in Cultures of Genius. **It's not that Cultures of Growth never experience ethical lapses, but when they do** occur, growth-minded organizations are more likely to demonstrate reflection and accountability and to act decisively to correct problems. They're also more likely to be proactively vigilant for violations, whereas Cultures of Genius are more apt to ignore them or attempt to cover them up.

When we're talking about the risk-taking that comes with innovation, we want to encourage metaphorical rule breaking, not actual rule breaking—to get people to think beyond what's been done and engage their creativity when solving problems. In this chapter, we're talking about the lines we *should not* cross. Ethical lapses erode the integrity of an institution and can result in people getting hurt.

Let's take a look at some examples of what ethics and integrity look like in Cultures of Growth and Cultures of Genius.

ETHICS AND INTEGRITY
THROUGH THE MINDSET LENS

In 2017, two months after leaving Uber, engineer Susan Fowler chronicled her experiences on her personal blog. On her first day on her new team, she wrote, "My new manager sent off a string of messages over company chat. He was in an open relationship, he said, and . . . he was looking for women to have sex with. It was clear that he was trying to get me to have sex with him, and it was so clearly out of line that I immediately took screenshots of these chat messages and reported him to HR." Uber's HR reps dismissed her complaints, telling Fowler the best they could do was give him "a warning and a stern talking to." Upper management's response was even more pointed, telling Fowler that the employee "'was a high performer' . . . and they wouldn't feel comfortable punishing him for what was probably just an innocent mistake on his part."

While "brilliant jerks"—a term used by former Uber board member Arianna Huffington in describing many of Uber's hires—can excel in Cultures of Genius (and in many cases they are the only ones who do), their achievement comes at a cost. Uber, Theranos, and WeWork are all prime examples of organizations that experienced major lapses in ethics and integrity, as is Goldman Sachs. Tagged as a major contributor to the 2008 financial crisis, Goldman continues to experience accusations of deep and ongoing ethics violations. A 2018 article in the *New York Times* describes former Goldman partner James Katzman's call to the company's whistleblower hotline, along with his accusations of multiple violations, including "repeated attempts to obtain and then share confidential client information." Reportedly, senior leadership urged Katzman to back off the claims. He refused and left the bank the next year, having signed a nondisclosure agreement that prohibited him from discussing the claims further. In her book *Bully Market*, former Goldman managing director Jamie Fiore Higgins describes a culture rife, behaviorally, with racism, sexism, and cutthroat competition; and procedurally, with policies and practices that encouraged these behaviors, such as stack ranking. According to Higgins, the culture is communicated long before prospective Goldman employees begin, with recruiters telling candidates they would be lucky to work for the bank. Once on board, they're told their status as Goldman employees makes them stars in the banking world, yet they're also warned that unless they consistently prove themselves, they will face pay cuts or termination.

That is not to say that Cultures of Growth should avoid high achievers when hiring. All companies want to hire smart, capable performers—and not all of them are brilliant jerks. As we saw with Twitter's global legal team, the way in which companies choose which smart, capable high performers to bring on board can have a big impact. The question is whether, once inside the company, employees are surrounded by a culture that will bring forward more of their fixed or growth mindset. At Uber, a few employees probably came on ready and willing to break the rules (and may have been hired expressly for this attitude), but for most others, it was likely the deep and powerful messages they received from their environment that encouraged their unethical behavior.

Is there anything a Culture of Genius can do to avoid cheating behavior?

Imagine if in your recruitment and hiring process, you proclaim that you only hire the "best and brightest" in your field or industry. When the person doing the hiring reaches out to offer a candidate the job, that candidate is told that they are clearly a star and welcomed aboard. Especially if your organization is a Culture of Genius, you may have just primed this employee for future lapses in integrity and ethics.

One organization working purposefully to avoid hiring "brilliant jerks" is the Good Food Institute (GFI). A science- and tech-heavy organization that wants to create a seismic shift in the global food industry, GFI is working to advance the science needed to create plant- and cell-based products. Instead of trying to create an Impossible Foods or Beyond Meat, GFI's founder Bruce Friedrich told me he set up the company as a nonprofit because "I think we can be thousands of times more effective in mission impact as a nonprofit." They didn't want their scientific discoveries sequestered behind intellectual property walls, so they work on an open-science model, funding research and sharing the results freely with other organizations.

GFI's hiring process underscores that candidates have to function well on teams and weeds out those who'd rather seek star status. Friedrich admits that every once in a while, the wrong picks do make it through the process, but in such a growth-minded atmosphere, they tend to reveal themselves pretty quickly. They're given support to course correct, but if they don't, they're let go.

Laura Braden, GFI's associate director of regulatory affairs, said in a personal interview that one of the things that distinguishes the company from anywhere else she's worked is GFI's rigorous adherence to their core organizational values: Believe change is possible, Do the most good we can, Share knowledge freely, Act on evidence, and Invite everyone to the table. As Braden said, "We are always evaluating and reevaluating our priorities within departments based on these values we use to center our work. My experience is that they're something we put conscious thought into as we're making decisions." She said they've been especially helpful for her department in deciding where to allocate resources—where GFI is uniquely positioned and where other organizations could do the work.

Braden's team has the considerable task of advocating, at the national and international levels, for fair and appropriate regulations for plant- and cell-based products. Not only are alternative proteins a relatively new market, regulations vary greatly across countries, and it's a thorny landscape, with traditional agriculture interests seeking to actively block new products and technologies from the market (such as barring alternative proteins from using words such as "milk" or "burgers" in advertising and on food labels). While Braden's team seeks to keep the doors wide open for alternative proteins, as part of their work, her team also assesses regulations for loopholes that would allow businesses to take shortcuts that could jeopardize product safety.

GFI applies its growth-minded approach in their partnerships as well. Their criteria for who to work with is whoever can help them make the most change in the industry. That's put them in the company of organizations and interests that might, at first, seem unlikely partners, like traditional meat producers JBS, Tyson, Smithfield, and Cargill. As Friedrich told me, "If you want to mainstream the idea of meat from plants or if you want to mainstream cultivating cell-based meats, having these kinds of companies launch their own plant- and cell-based products is one of the best ways to do that." It also helps to make collaborators out of competitors. As they grow their own stake in alternative meats, they also develop an interest in fair regulation for alternative proteins, and so more and more often, these large producers find themselves on the same side of the table as Braden. This is the kind of win-win collaborative innovation that Cultures of Growth seek to create, and it's the kind of big-picture, growth-minded thinking that Kinney Zalesne described as being essential to solve complex societal problems.

Now that we've seen some examples of how ethics and integrity play out in Cultures of Genius versus Cultures of Growth, let's look at some of the reasons behind this.

HOW ORGANIZATIONAL MINDSET SETS THE STAGE FOR ETHICAL VS UNETHICAL BEHAVIOR

In Cultures of Growth, which embrace learn-it-alls over know-it-alls, ethical lapses such as cheating simply aren't aligned with the core beliefs and goals of the culture because those kinds of behaviors thwart the possibility of learning. When you're cheating or gaming the metrics, you can't actually discern what works and what doesn't. In Cultures of Genius, a core belief is that it's more important to be among the star performers than pretty much anything else. If it takes unethical behavior to achieve or maintain that status, so be it. Again, this is often unintentional on the part of leadership. It's rare that I've come across an organization that wants its employees to behave this way, or even realizes this is the setup they've created, which is why it's important to be vigilant of the messages your culture is communicating.

Both Cultures of Genius and Cultures of Growth are concerned with success-seeking performance goals, but unlike more fixed-minded companies, growth-minded ones are also pursuing learning goals: Yes, we want to succeed, but are we also learning and growing in the process? And when we fail, are we learning there too, in ways that inform us so we can do better next time, or that show us when it's time to switch course?

One of the major factors that can encourage unethical behavior and sloppy shortcuts is the performance goals and incentives embedded in an organization.

Performance Goals and Incentives

The wrong goals and metrics can drastically impair an employee's ability to demonstrate or act in alignment with the organization's core values. For example, if an organization says it values safety, but its metrics are focused entirely on the speed at which an employee does their job or the volume they produce, these potentially competing priorities might put employees in a tough spot. They face the choice of falling short of their goals or taking shortcuts to get there.

One fail was Volkswagen's emissions scandal, in which engineers installed software—referred to as "cheat devices"—in roughly 11 million diesel cars. The devices fed false data to emissions testing computers to make it seem as though Volkswagen diesels spewed lower environmentally damaging emissions than they actually did. According to many in the business world, the root cause was VW's culture. Though the company purported to value the environment, sales were more important. Employees describe a "climate of fear" at VW, which, combined with former CEO Martin Winterkorn's goal of becoming the world's biggest car maker, primed the organization for a huge ethical lapse.

Cognitive scientist Susan Mackie described to me a disconnect she discovered between values and incentives in her work with a banking industry call center. Out of 104 calls in which customers had contacted the bank to close an account, there were only four in which a customer service representative made any effort to try to retain the customer. The problem was that the call center employees had been given task-directed instruction (how to close an account), and not goal-directed instruction (how to try to retain an account). Additionally, employee performance was being measured by metrics that supported task-directed behavior, such as the speed with which they processed calls. When the employees received a request to close an account, they knew that the fastest way to handle that request was simply to grant it. Then, they would pass the file to the customer recovery team, which would attempt to re-open the account. That's certainly not the outcome the bank was looking for, and yet that's what both the training and the performance metric were encouraging employees to do.

According to Mackie, "To unlock the potential of each customer interaction, organizations must develop team members who are goal-directed rather than task-directed. However, current approaches to developing customer service skills focus on building task-related competencies, such as opening and closing accounts and fixing billing errors. While these skills are essential to the staff member's ability to perform a rule," she explains, "they fail to teach the necessary skills required to identify the customer's goal, and how to achieve it." A growth-minded approach would recognize the complexity of customer interactions and would allow people to practice skills and develop competence in recognizing and responding appropriately over time. Organizations must focus on helping employees develop a core set of capabilities that can be applied dynamically to achieve an outcome that meets both the customer's and the organization's goal. Additionally, the metrics that measure employees' performance must reflect the organization's goals and encourage behavior that will meet them.

Working with Susan and her team, the organization switched their outcome metrics to how many accounts were saved, rather than the speed with which the representative handled the call or how many calls per day they fielded. Then they started getting the customer service–oriented results they wanted.

We also want to ensure that the compensation structure we create appropriately signals and supports the values we wish to cultivate within the organization. As Verne Harnish—founder of Scaling Up, an organization that advises entrepreneurs, and author of *Scaling Up Compensation*—told me, instead of just telling people you want 10-, 20-, or even 50× growth, it's about getting inside that growth and making it meaningful. In his experience, companies that set their sights on financial growth alone often collapse after several years. Organizations that grow through learning are more likely to last;

they can think bigger because they're operating on a longer timeline, and that means they're more likely to eventually hit that 50× goal.

In academic science, the obvious goal of learning is often undercut by two structural incentives: the pressures to "publish or perish" and to make results look flawless. They have prompted many researchers, whether purposefully or unconsciously, to engage in a series of questionable research practices (QRPs) to show their work in the best light. These include failing to mention every variable a study measured and dropping studies from the manuscript when the results didn't turn out "right," the way the scientists predicted—a practice known as *the file drawer problem*. Another QRP is stopping data collection once a team sees desirable results, thus excluding the possibility that additional data may paint a different picture. Hence the current replicability crisis across scientific disciplines, where it has become all too common for subsequent studies to fail to reproduce results reported by the original researchers. For science to advance, we need to know both what works and what doesn't. As University of Melbourne researcher Simine Vazire has put it, "Do we want to be credible or incredible?"

The lure of the incredible is what drove genetic researcher He Jiankui to violate the agreement of CRISPR pioneer Jennifer Doudna and fellow researchers to put the brakes on when, and even whether, the technology should be used on viable human embryos. Seeing an opportunity to make his mark as a genius, He Jiankui went rogue, using CRISPR to modify embryos that were implanted into two women who later gave birth to the world's first gene-edited babies. The scientist was put on trial in China, where he was sentenced to three years in prison and received a $430,000 fine and a lifetime ban on working in reproductive science. The court declared, "In order to pursue fame and profit, [he] deliberately violated the relevant national regulations and crossed the bottom lines of scientific and medical ethics."

Transforming an organization or the scientific research landscape into a Culture of Growth can happen in multiple ways. For example, encouraging and rewarding scientists to share information and collaborate is one place to start. The movement is being led largely by PLOS (for Public Library of Science), an Open Access publisher that operates as a nonprofit and was created to make peer-reviewed science more readily available. When I spoke with PLOS CEO Alison Mudditt, she said that focusing on a perception of scientific genius, in her view, is "fundamentally at odds with the core values of science. It's due to the imperatives of this pretty dysfunctional credit system in many ways. It's all about hoarding your data in case you get another grant on it, or a promotion on it, and it's about not sharing in case someone scoops your research." She observed that "scientists, like all of us, repeat behaviors that get rewarded. If you look at the currency in science, journal editors have tended to favor publishing papers that tell a nice, neat story. . . . But real data often are messy, so being transparent can open researchers up to critique." Mudditt underscored that the way funding is awarded also puts individual researchers in the spotlight rather than telling the story of the ten graduate students, postdocs, or research scientists who may have done much of the work. All of it creates and fuels a false narrative about how science is done.

"What we've been thinking at PLOS," Mudditt said, "is that there are two core challenges at the center of the system that's driving this. One is this incentive system that heavily favors novelty, along with publication in a small number of journals that are highly selective." I've known colleagues who were told that their job over the next several years was not to do the best, most impactful research they could, but to ensure they get published in one or two specified, top-ranked journals in order to secure promotion and tenure. In pretty much every university setting, faculty are judged on where they've published and how often, with a relative handful of journals being prized most. When that's the system, you can see why QRPs happen.

For its part, PLOS is working to tell more accurate stories, including to "publish rigorous, well-conducted, but ultimately null studies—so, studies that have failed." As Stuart Firestein, former chair of the Department of Biological Sciences at Columbia University, writes in his book *Failure: Why Science Is So Successful*, "Not appreciating failure sufficiently leads to distorted views of science." Failure, Firestein writes, is the pillar upon which all scientific advancement is built. In a Stanford University video celebrating her 2022 Nobel Prize in Chemistry, Carolyn Bertozzi said, "Science is sometimes thought of as being difficult and frustrating, because there is a high failure rate. Really, there are no failures. Rather, there are experiments whose outcomes you did not anticipate. This is your chance to learn something new." If we don't have a record of the results, how do we know what to try next? If we create an atmosphere in which failures are to be hidden and we share only what confirms what we already suspect to be true, we narrow the scope of scientific inquiry and slow the pace of discovery. And if we continue to worship the lone genius, the desire to achieve this status will continue to drive some scientists to commit significant ethical lapses as He Jiankui did.

Another way to foster Cultures of Growth and ethical behavior is to incentivize a more inclusive, collaborative approach to research. In 2020, I led a group of 28 researchers from diverse fields and backgrounds in examining two distinct ways of improving science across fields: the Movement for Reproducibility and the Movement for Open Science. Both movements are, in different ways, reacting to the prevalent Culture of Genius in Science (which we jokingly—or not—dubbed "King Science") that perpetuates the fixed mindset mythology of the lone genius, where a single well-resourced researcher (usually the principal investigator) is given most or all of the credit for the work of their team and hoards their resources, data, and materials until their group gets maximal benefit from them in the form of grants and publications. The Movement for Reproducibility has an interpersonally competitive edge to it and has, perhaps unintentionally, reproduced a Culture of Genius by focusing on identifying which findings are "right" by choosing studies to replicate and seeing which effects people within the movement can reproduce when they try to redo other people's work—essentially taking on the role of the critic who determines whose research and ideas are valid (or not) while embodying an "it's either true or false" fixed mindset dichotomy. The Movement for Open Science emphasizes a more interdependent and collaborative approach to sharing data, materials, and code, working to solve multidimensional problems such as addiction, climate change, or poverty with large, multidisciplinary teams. The goal of its adherents is to make the tools of science more readily accessible and available to everyone in order to speed discovery.

Our team found that across the fields of science, these two movements operate relatively independent of one another—taking two distinct cultural approaches. While both movements want to improve how science is done, they have vastly different ways to accomplish the goal. Interestingly, scientists from one camp tend to stick to that camp and rarely cross borders and publish as part of the other.

Not only did these movements differ in their mindset cultures, we also found that Open Science promotes greater equity and inclusion, attracting a broader cadre of scientists, including more women and people from diverse cultural backgrounds. How? By embodying the prosocial and communal (rather than independent and competitive) goals often valued by these groups. When applying a validated text dictionary to the abstracts of the thousands of papers in these literatures, we found that scientists in the Open Science movement used more interdependent and communal language to describe the science itself than did those in Reproducibility. And while women's participation in high-status authorship positions has been increasing over time in Open Science, it is decreasing over time within the Reproducibility movement. This not only impacts diversity within scientific research, but also shapes what research is conducted and how. Indeed, previous research has shown that women and people of color often choose to conduct research that has more socially oriented goals and seeks to improve society's health and well-being.

We don't see these kinds of mindset culture-related problems with ethics and integrity only in educational institutions or in scientific research. Across my research with both large companies and with startups, we asked participants the extent to which they agreed or disagreed with statements about their organization's behavioral norms regarding ethics and integrity, such as:

♦ In this company, people often hide information from others.
♦ In this company, when people make mistakes, they take full responsibility for them.
♦ In this company, there is a lot of cheating, taking shortcuts, and cutting corners.
♦ People are treated fairly in this company.
♦ People are trustworthy in this organization.
♦ Ethics are very important in this organization.

We also asked about their agreement with statements about management's approach to ethical behavior, such as:

♦ Management in this organization disciplines unethical behavior when it occurs.
♦ Penalties for unethical behavior are strictly enforced in this organization.
♦ The top managers in this organization adhere to high ethical standards.

In each case, one of the most consistent findings across our studies is that Cultures of Genius are associated with greater lapses in integrity and ethics, whereas in Cultures of Growth, employees are more likely to perceive their coworkers, managers, and the organization as having higher ethical standards and greater integrity.

Cultures of Growth value transparency and share information (rather than hoarding it to get ahead of others), and when people make mistakes in these organizations, they accept responsibility (instead of pointing fingers). Cultures of Genius have more backroom dealing and are less likely to enforce penalties or punishment when ethical breaches are discovered, turning a blind eye toward them or shrugging it off, especially when a high performer is at fault.

HOW INTERPERSONAL
COMPETITION IMPACTS ETHICS

Starting with getting into medical school, future doctors are groomed early on to be highly competitive. Yet the same competitive drive that can help someone successfully complete rigorous medical training may actually make them more prone to ethical lapses in their profession.

Dr. Jennifer (Jen) Danek, a board-certified physician at University of Washington Medicine and one of my research collaborators, has experienced this firsthand. She was fortunate to attend a medical school that functioned largely as a Culture of Growth, where students were supported to succeed rather than being encouraged by competitive tactics to continually prove they deserved to be there. "Everybody would fail an exam—maybe gastroenterology or endocrinology—at some point over the period. There was a policy that you could repeat one of your exams," Jen explains. "You just take it a second time and then you pass it. It was no big deal. A friend of mine failed an anatomy test two times, but it was in part because English wasn't her first language. The third time she took it, the professor stayed up until three A.M. to work with her, telling her, 'You are passing this exam. We are passing it together.' Basically, we were told from the very beginning, 'We've selected you, now you're ours, and you are going to succeed.'"

Jen experienced what students at many other medical schools do when, later in her education, she transferred so that she could be close to an ill family member. "I remember the first day they sat us down and gave us a set of rules and told us if we didn't follow the rules, we were out. I'm thinking, 'We're doctors and we're adults, and you're treating us like five-year-olds.' I just remember thinking I needed to get out of that place as soon as possible before it dumbed me down. I had the sense the culture wouldn't bring out the best in me if I stayed in it." This culture also contributed to secrecy and poor ethics. She recalled a resident who presented rounds based on money he'd been compensated by a drug company (which he didn't disclose). To Jen, it wasn't just the patients who were sick, it was also the culture.

The field of medicine in general operates as a Culture of Genius in which doctors—especially surgeons—are at the top of the pecking order. Many times, Jen says, she's had nurses call her for help in the middle of the night with a case for which she wasn't the primary physician. When she asked why they didn't call the patient's surgeon, they said they were afraid to wake the (usually male) surgeon up and get yelled at. Still, she says, she thinks medicine is making a shift toward a Culture of Growth in large part due to a focus on outcomes. When poor behavior contributes to illness, and even death, something has to be done.

One of these structural (and cultural) changes includes group rounds, during which everyone on a patient's care team convenes to discuss the care plan. When you just have a doctor doling out orders, you can miss things. "It's so complex that one human being can't do it all well," Jen says. "That has led to a shift to collaborative work that is more equalizing." There's still a hierarchy, Jen explains, and the doctor is still in charge, but in a group gathering, she receives information from a nurse who, because of their close interaction with the patient, may notice details the doctor might miss. Additionally, if the pharmacist is standing right there, they can point out that a medication being considered would interact negatively with another medication the patient is already taking and discuss another course of action.

Jen says that along with this shift, a more growth-minded approach means more error reporting, and that means more opportunities to correct mistakes and improve patient care, similar to what Amy Edmonson saw in her research on medical errors. "I feel relieved in that kind of system," Jen observes, "and I think everybody feels relieved because there's more sense of group ownership for the outcome." These changes in medicine seek to defuse competitiveness and boost learning and communication to improve outcomes. Cultures of Growth can also encourage some of the benefits of competition.

Just after World War II, Japan's economy was struggling, and the country focused on supporting a few key sectors that it believed could infuse much-needed cash into the nation's coffers, including the watchmaking industry. For years, Seiko had been a decent watch- maker, yet it struggled with reliability. If the company was going to try to take on the industry-leading Swiss, it would need to innovate, and fast. To that point, Seiko was primarily trying to replicate ele- ments of Swiss design, but it made a bold move to ditch this strategy, focusing instead on building its own technology from scratch.

To spur its efforts, Seiko sparked a fierce but friendly rivalry be- tween two of its factories—one in the bustling city of Tokyo and one in the countryside of Nagano. Like their geographic locations, the factories had distinct cultures, and Seiko's leadership figured that they would each take different creative approaches. They were right. Each time one factory solved a problem or created a superior tech- nology, Seiko challenged the other factory to beat it. But to keep the competition from turning ugly, Seiko's leadership instituted guide- lines. Seiko was a family, leadership told the factories, and a gain in one factory was a gain for the whole family. To reinforce this notion and to push innovation even farther, the factories were encouraged to reach out to one another if they hit any major roadblocks, and when one factory developed a new technology, they shared it with the other so they could both benefit. In a Culture of Genius, the factories would have been competing for individual glory (or to keep their jobs), and they may have resorted to underhanded means to get there. They certainly wouldn't have shared their learnings. But the culture and communication structures Seiko created kept the facto- ries from hoarding their work, and the strategy paid off.

By spurring one another on in this productive way, the factories made Seiko's watches more consistent, reliable, and visually appeal- ing, managing also to produce the company's first luxury watch. In 1964, Seiko became the first non-Swiss company to enter a renowned international watchmaking competition held in Switzerland. Each factory entered their own design, though each watch featured technological or manufactured components from both factories. By 1967, one of the factory's watches took fourth place at the competition. Then in late 1969, Seiko became the first company in the world to get a watch to market using quartz technology. Later that year, once again, they advanced their own technology and released a second quartz watch that outperformed offerings from Swiss manufacturers, who were still primarily focused on mechanical technology.

VIGILANCE FOR AND RESPONSES
TO ETHICAL LAPSES

Cultivating and tending a Culture of Growth is constant work. As Emma McIlroy says, organizations are organisms. They are constantly influenced by shifting internal and external dynamics such as changes in staffing, shifts in the marketplace, evolving regulatory structures, and ever-changing customer and employee expectations. (Imagine a complex sound board in a recording studio where a variety of levels have to be constantly monitored and adjusted as the music is made.) Because of their orientation to learning, Cultures of Growth are more likely to be attentive to their organizational culture and the behavioral norms within it, and to institute active monitoring systems to detect deviation from their values, standards, and progress toward their goals than are Cultures of Genius, which are more likely to keep an eye on individual performance and outcomes.

Even when an organization operates primarily from its growth mindset, lapses can occur. Humans are fallible, and the systems we build will reflect that fallibility. Most of us don't expect organizations to be perfect, but we do expect that when something goes wrong, they'll do their best to correct it, and to be transparent in the process, most certainly when lives are on the line. Two of the most dangerous product fails in history were when someone laced Johnson & Johnson's Tylenol capsules with cyanide, and when traces of benzene were detected in Perrier bottled water. In these examples, we see both Cultures of Growth and Cultures of Genius at play. Johnson & Johnson sought to affirm their commitment to consumer safety, taking products off the shelves and urging customers to stop using the capsules until the company could learn how and where the tampering had happened. Conversely, Perrier leadership leapt into prove-and-perform mode, recalling only a small number of bottles without accepting full responsibility. Remember, when a company shows itself to be in learning mode, consumers are more apt to trust them.

Throughout this chapter you've seen some of the ways Cultures of Growth engender trust, integrity, and ethical behavior. Let's look at some takeaways for your organization.

HOW TO ENCOURAGE ETHICAL BEHAVIOR AND HIGH INTEGRITY IN YOUR ORGANIZATION

Here are some strategies you can employ to encourage your organization to operate ethically and with integrity.

Use Measurement Systems for Identifying Opportunities for Development and Improvement

Ensure that the metrics by which you measure employee performance are robust and transparent. Make sure they are used to identify who may need more resources and support, and who may be good candidates to provide it. Look at which individuals and teams have an upward trajectory, and which have stagnated or are going backward (a sign that they could use new strategies and more support). Cultures of Growth value transparency: It not only helps employees understand clearly what they're aiming for and how they'll be evaluated, it also engenders psychological safety, trust, and commitment.

Recall Susan Mackie's experience with aligning call-center employee development and metrics to desired behavior and outcomes. The company she worked with had unintentionally trained and optimized for the opposite of what they wanted to achieve. Examine how you're instructing and developing employees and how you're measuring their performance: Are you conducting only task-based training, or are you helping employees develop a richer skillset? How are people engaging with the goals the company has set? Are there unintended consequences of any of the metrics? And while you're at it, it's a good idea to take a look at those targets and examine whether they're game-able. Are people doing their work in the best way they can, or working to make it look like they are?

In addition to making measurement transparent, make it rich. Augment standard performance targets (such as financial ones) with metrics that consider an employee's progress, challenges they've overcome, risks they've taken, their collaborative activities, what they've achieved by working across departments, and so on. As Susan describes it, "Layer in mastery goals that require employees to ask themselves questions such as, 'What do I need to learn to accomplish this goal?'" Additionally, include behavioral and values-oriented goals.

Combined, these types of goals will move you closer to the outcomes you really want to achieve and help individuals and your entire organization shift toward a Culture of Growth.

Hire for Integrity

In the interview process, look for red flags that could point to ethics issues. Do candidates talk about doing "whatever it takes" to meet targets or to beat the competition? Find out what they mean by that. Solicit stories about ethical challenges they've experienced in the past and how they've dealt with them.

In addition to paying attention to who you're hiring and what they value, you'll need to make sure that management is walking the talk, as well. If employees look to the top and see ethical issues, they'll be confused and perhaps they'll think it's okay (or even necessary) to backstab, hoard information, or cheat the system, like they're seeing leaders doing.

Integrate Ethics Everywhere

Organizations with the highest integrity do more than pay lip service to ethical standards. When federal guidelines required one government contractor in the Washington, DC, area to institute an ethics program, the company's response was to create a standard guide to ethical behavior that was distributed to employees (with no acknowledgment of cultural differences, even though the organization employed more than 1,500 people at diverse locations around the world). They also purchased a generic computer-based ethics training program where answering rather obvious questions earned the employee a certificate of completion. Finally, they created an ethics hotline monitored by a vice president who employees knew to be so overworked her voicemail was perpetually full. When the hotline never rang, they dubbed the program a success.

Ethics trainings like these, that check a box rather than provide useful, actionable information, are all too common. Marianne Jennings, a professor of business ethics at Arizona State University, writes in her book *The Seven Signs of Ethical Collapse*, "Employees should have specific examples of right and wrong, particular examples within their industry. Explaining lines employees should not cross in meeting [goals] and then providing them with examples of conduct that does and does not cross those lines gives employees a straight baseline. . . . Values determine what we will and will not do to get to the numbers."

Jacqueline Novogratz says that Acumen works to support an "ethos of truth telling, because I'd been in big institutions where you were rewarded for sounding smart. At Acumen, from the beginning, you had to be able to tell your story in a way that people could understand" rather than hiding behind complex linguistics and meaningless phrases. (Recall Frank founder Charlie Javice's description of her company as "Amazon for higher education.") Acumen reinforces this ethos every week. At every Acumen office around the world, there's a Monday morning meeting where employees are asked to highlight moments throughout the previous week that highlighted for them the company's values in action. "It's a time for storytelling," Novogratz told me. "For ritualizing and reinforcing things that we really care about. For instance, as CEO I might tell the other offices, 'There was a fraud situation in one of our regions, here's how the team handled it, and I'm so proud of them.'" As Novogratz noted, "A culture of public reflection is not a Culture of Genius."

Susan Mackie encourages the organizations she works with to normalize a *clarity pause*. Susan says that employees sometimes have "clarity-related fear, which says, 'What happens if I find something that means more work? What happens if I find something and I've got to share it and I look stupid? Or what happens if I find that we're doing something that's not accurate, or okay, or ethical—how do I raise that?'" Similar to the medical huddles Jen Danek described, the clarity pause is an opportunity for employees to check in with one another or with a supervisor. To "step back and test one another's assumptions. To test whether what you're about to go and do is the right thing." Marianne Jennings calls them "time-out cards," which can be literal checklists or symbolic phrases. She writes, "Time-out is a universal, diplomatic way for employees to go with their guts and ask for a pause in the march toward numbers and results." The key is to build this mechanism into your standard procedures so it defuses potential stigma that can come with identifying causes for concern.

As much as possible, Cultures of Growth weave ethics and integrity into everything they do, and they're explicit about their expectations. They have clear, accessible reporting systems where people are not only safe and encouraged to report problems, but they also know how to do so. After problems are reported, unlike Susan Fowler's experience at Uber, they're taken seriously. Additionally, don't think you have to passively wait and rely on employees to report issues on their own. Consider taking a proactive approach by including dimensions of ethics and integrity on employee pulse surveys and in regular conversations with teams and one-on-ones with managers.

Double Down on Collaboration to Cut Down on Unethical Competitive Behavior

Instituting policies and practices that show that working together—not sabotaging your peers—is the way to advance at your organization is one way to demonstrate your commitment to ethical behavior. Rather than pulling up the ladder once they're aboard or even shoving a colleague or two overboard, employees will see that your organization is more interested in group success. It's still possible for employees to distinguish themselves in these environments, but it becomes about the ways they've worked to develop their skillset and their willingness to partner with others for the larger cause that make them stand out.

When it comes to collaboration, don't just look in the same old places for potential partners, but rather at every level and across the organizational chart, and even outside the company. It's easy to think we have all the answers, but part of Cultures of Growth being learning organizations is that they're also *listening* organizations. Asking questions and listening to the responses (and then acting on what you learn) engenders trust—a critical component of integrity—and then spreads the learning throughout the organization. If organizational leaders, especially, are focused on issuing edicts, it's likely they're missing game-changing opportunities to listen and learn.

CHAPTER 7

Diversity, Equity, and Inclusion

Imagine this: You've just finished college and are deciding where to start your career. Two major companies are trying to recruit you, but as you scan their websites and the materials they've sent, you notice that most of the people pictured are White. And when you look at the bios of C-suite staff, everyone except the head of HR is male. As a Black woman, you question whether you'd be truly welcome in this environment.

Or, you're a male manager at an international banking organization. Your boss calls you into his office and tells you he's having a get-together for your team at his home on Friday evening to encourage team bonding. "It's a social event, so wives are welcome!" he smiles. You gulp. *But would my husband be welcome?* you wonder.

Or, you get the invite for the annual holiday party at a new location. You forward it to your HR rep. "This looks like a great place!" you write. "Is it wheelchair accessible?" A few minutes later you get a reply: "We're so excited about it! I'm not sure about accessibility, but I'll check and get back to you."

DEI encompasses much more than simply hiring a broadly representative workforce. While that's part of it, diversity, equity, and inclusion refer to three distinct organizational processes.

Diversity includes hiring and retaining people from diverse, structurally disadvantaged, and historically excluded groups. It's about numerical representation and underrepresentation.

Equity, on the other hand, comes down to how people are treated and the way resources and power are distributed in a company. Are people's different needs understood and provided for? Has the playing field been leveled? Or do the data show that people from certain social groups are systematically advantaged? Perhaps they tend to be more favorably evaluated, promoted, or trusted with opportunities. When an organization seeks to achieve equity, it takes into consideration everyone's starting point, provides people with the resources they need to succeed, and removes systemic obstacles that could limit advancement or access to opportunities. Importantly, equity is not the same as equality. While equality means that everyone is treated the same way, equity may require that some individuals or groups be given additional supports to ensure that everyone is empowered to succeed within the organization.

Inclusion addresses whether or not people feel as though they belong and are valued and respected in an organization. Inclusion is a subjective experience and the authorities on whether an organization is truly inclusive are those from structurally disadvantaged and historically excluded backgrounds. Their perceptions and experiences of whether their group is valued and respected are the metrics by which we assess an organization's inclusivity. Many organizations try to diversify their workforce, yet their work ends at hiring. Once employees are on board, many organizations do little or nothing to attend to equity and inclusion.

How do people come to know whether they are likely to be valued, respected, and included—or devalued, disrespected, and excluded— in a setting? Research I originally conducted with my graduate advisor, Claude Steele—and now extended by many others—supports what we termed the *cues hypothesis*. Essentially, people answer these questions for themselves by looking at the *situational cues* around them. In every environment, each of us is vigilant to cues, messages, and signals that tell us how our social identities might be seen and valued. For instance, we look around us to see who is typically included in high-visibility meetings or teams, or considered for high-profile projects or promotions. If none of them look like us—in any number of ways ranging from demographic characteristics to socioeconomic and education-based identities—we're less likely to believe that these opportunities will be available to us. If there are no women in the C-suite (or they're only in roles traditionally associated with women, such as HR), women are less likely to believe that they'll be encouraged and supported to rise to that level. The same holds for people in other groups. When mistakes are made, we notice who gets the benefit of the doubt and who doesn't. Who is afforded opportunities because someone higher up sees their "potential," and who seems to get routinely overlooked? These are all silent, but powerful, cues that tell us who is valued.

Over the last decade, my research has shown that an organization's mindset culture has significant consequences for diversity, equity, and inclusion. Cultures of Genius have strong and rigid prototypes by which they identify entire categories of people as likely to have it, or not. Those who don't fit these prototypes either don't get hired or, if they make it in the doors, are often overlooked when it comes to opportunities, resources, and promotions. Cultures of Growth value a diverse workforce not just for optics, but because they know it makes them better. It engenders broader thinking and more creativity, which leads to a better work product, including novel solutions to tough challenges. Cultures of Growth believe that good ideas come from everywhere and they value differences (cultural, economic, social). They acknowledge that diversity and inclusion are hard, but they take a learning orientation to cultivating them and they do the work to ensure that everyone gets what they need to succeed.

DEI IN CULTURES OF GENIUS

In Cultures of Genius, opportunities are usually afforded to a far narrower set of people than in Cultures of Growth. In American society, when we think of "genius," we are much more likely to conjure a White male than any other group (remember our Google search?)—and research shows we adopt this archetype as early as six years old. These images come from our society and the representations we observe in media and the stories and language we hear from birth. But it also means that many people are excluded by this genius prototype. It excludes Black, Latina/o, and Indigenous people, those who are differently abled, those who are neurodiverse, women, the LGBTQ+ community, those who are socioeconomically disadvantaged, people with a community college education (or no college degree at all), and so on. In many settings, these groups are negatively stereotyped along the dimensions of intelligence or competence, and those who belong to one or more of these groups are less likely to fit the prototype for success, especially in Cultures of Genius. Plus, we're more likely to be attuned to the situational cues that, to us at least, broadcast the misfit message loud and clear.

When we perceive cues and have interactions that suggest we could be negatively stereotyped because of our group membership, we're more likely to experience *stereotype threat*. We become concerned that we could be viewed and treated in terms of negative stereotypes associated with our social identity groups.

Everyone experiences stereotype threat in some form at different points in their lives. Even among groups considered to be privileged, White people are often concerned about being (and being perceived by others as) racist; men are often concerned about being (and being perceived as) sexist. Depending on what region or country you're from, or what your political or sexual orientation is, you might experience stereotype threat related to these group memberships. Yet not all social groups are negatively stereotyped specifically along the dimensions of intelligence, talent, and ability—and it is people from *these* groups who are most disadvantaged in Cultures of Genius.

Stereotype threat is compounded when a group is numerically underrepresented. In fact, numeric underrepresentation is one of the strongest cues to identity threat. For example, around the world women—especially women of color—are still typically, and often significantly, underrepresented in management roles.

Research shows that stereotype threat exacts cognitive, emotional, and physiological tolls that are experienced disproportionately by those in underrepresented groups. After all, it's stressful and exhausting to feel that you constantly have to pay attention to whether your own behavior could be seen as confirming negative stereotypes. In a vicious cycle, this burden may contribute to ongoing underrepresentation. Women in business experience this often when they work to make sure they are not perceived as too "soft" and emotional, or too manipulative and aggressive, or too distracted by parenting responsibilities, and so on—all on top of doing their job.

In a series of studies, my former graduate student Kathy Emerson and I found that an organization's mindset plays a role in cueing stereotype threat among women in business settings. We asked men and women to read a company's mission statement and website, both of which communicated the organization's mindset. Both women and men were less likely to trust the fixed-minded organization, but women significantly more so than men. Why? Because women *expected* to be stereotyped by management as less competent and capable. Men, on the other hand, assumed they'd be seen as equally competent and capable in either a Culture of Genius or a Culture of Growth. The reason men didn't trust the Culture of Genius wasn't because of stereotype threat, it was because they thought it was likely to be filled with competitiveness and interpersonal backbiting, which meant it would be an unpleasant environment for virtually everyone. Our studies found that organizational mindset is so powerful in this regard that when we adjusted the ratio of male to female employees in the sample companies so that there was an equal number of men and women, the Culture of Genius persisted in causing mistrust. So if you're thinking that simply hiring more women or people from any other group will—on its own—shift employees' perceptions, think again.

In another study, we told participants that after reviewing the company's materials, they'd meet with a representative of the organization, ostensibly to practice their interviewing skills. In preparation for their interview, they were asked to imagine that the interview went badly and to think about strategies they'd use to turn things around. Both men and women reported feeling more uncomfortable anticipating an interview with the fixed-minded organization. However, the organization's mindset also caused many of the women to disengage from the process. As they prepared for the interview with the Culture of Genius, women (but not men) were likely to say things like, "I didn't care about the interview anyway." First, the women experienced stereotype threat, as the company's Culture of Genius caused them to worry about being negatively stereotyped by the company's management—they simply didn't trust that the company would treat them fairly. Then, when they were told to imagine the interview wasn't going well, the combination of stereotype threat and mistrust caused them to disengage from the interview preparation process. This pattern didn't show up with the growth-minded organizations because stereotype threat wasn't present for women in those companies in the first place. **By the very nature of their core beliefs and assumptions, Cultures of Genius signal stereotype threat to women.**

We see similar impacts of mindset in entrepreneurial environments. In research with the Kauffman Foundation, we found that hundreds of entrepreneurs across industries universally perceived VCs and investors to be more likely to endorse fixed mindset compared to growth mindset beliefs about entrepreneurship. But those perceptions of investors did not affect everyone equally. Women entrepreneurs experienced more stereotype threat when pitching investors as they felt the VCs "would be surprised if someone like me were to be successful." (And in fact, that perception often plays out.) Investors' fixed mindsets didn't concern men as much because they are a closer fit to the prototype (stereotype) of a successful entrepreneur— so if anything, many felt they *benefited* from these assumptions.

Other research suggests these processes play out in similar ways for racial and ethnic minority individuals. In our study of an entire university's STEM faculty, we discovered that faculty's self-reported mindset beliefs predicted the size of the racialized achievement gaps in their classes. When faculty endorsed more fixed mindset beliefs, the racialized achievement gap between White students and racial-ethnic minority students in their class was *twice* as large. Growth-minded faculty not only had smaller achievement gaps in their classes, but their students also reported being more motivated and engaged, and they felt that the professor inspired them to do their best work.

Time and again we've seen that groups' mistrust of Cultures of Genius is not unfounded. Earlier, I mentioned that my research showed that women and people of color were less trusting of Cultures of Genius. In a study we conducted with a large multinational bank, women and ethnic minorities on fixed-minded teams experienced greater stereotype threat *and* actually received lower performance ratings on their performance reviews. And even for those who have not yet personally experienced these outcomes, simply perceiving that an organization is a Culture of Genius is cause for concern.

Yet how much does this matter when it comes to organizational performance? Is DEI just the latest initiative, destined to fall by the wayside when other business trends arise, or is it necessary for success?

WHY DEI?

As senior vice dean at Columbia Business School Katherine Phillips wrote, "[I]f you want to build teams or organizations capable of innovating, you need diversity. . . . Diversity can improve the bottom line of companies and lead to unfettered discoveries and break-through innovations. . . . When people are brought together to solve problems in groups, they bring different information, opinions and perspectives." As Phillips noted, one analysis of top companies in the Standard & Poor's Composite 1500 found that, on average, "female representation in top management leads to an increase of $42 million in firm value." And a survey from McKinsey showed that companies with the most racial and ethnic diversity were 35 percent more likely to best their competitors, while those with the most gender diversity were 15 percent more likely to do so. Admittedly, studies also show that diversity can be difficult at first. Clashes of ideas and behavior, norms, and styles of interaction can be challenging and create discomfort. Yet as we'll discuss shortly, Cultures of Growth, with their focus on learning from others, have multiple ways of helping everyone work through and learn from these friction points.

Cultures of Genius expect talent to come in a narrow set of identities—identities that Janice Bryant Howroyd, as a Black woman, does not share. Howroyd is the founder and CEO of ActOne Group, one of the largest personnel companies in the United States. Starting the company when she moved from North Carolina to California in 1978 with just $1,500, she rented a small office space in Beverly Hills, outfitted it with a fax machine and a phone, and then started cold calling. In 2020, ActOne reported a revenue of $2.8 billion and was number two on Black Enterprise's list of Black-owned businesses. Howroyd, herself, is the first Black woman to build and own a billion-dollar company.

As she was working to scale ActOne as a "minority" and "diverse" business, hers was often perceived to not have the capabilities of companies run by White men. But while she was getting roughly one tenth of the account work of other larger businesses, she still had to meet or beat those larger companies on price. Howroyd knew that to span that gap, she'd have to get creative and invoke the power of technology. So she hired a team of people to build technology that enabled detailed reporting for clients, which they couldn't get from other companies. The suite became so popular that ActOne began selling tech services in addition to staffing.

Howroyd says she's frequently encountered challenges being a Black woman in a White male–dominated industry. Early in Act-One's history, to address potential clients' fixed mindsets around race and gender, Howroyd would undertake the initial work to get her company in the door for the presentation, but when it came time to meet the client face to face, she'd ask her White male employees to take over. "I'm not proud of it," Howroyd recalls, but "there were times when I would gift my intelligence to other members of my team and have them go in and make a presentation so that the client wouldn't have to interact directly with me as an African American or as a female." In her experience, when Howroyd led the pitches, companies questioned whether ActOne was capable of doing the work. When the men took the lead, the companies assumed a level of capability, and asked the men to describe how they'd approach it.

Even though Howroyd experienced this issue decades ago, Black entrepreneur Courtney Blagrove, who founded Whipped-Urban Dessert Lab with her sister Zan B. R., says she experiences this type of discrimination today when she and Zan pitch to investors. The pair are routinely questioned as to when the founder will be arriving, assuming the founder is a *he* instead of two *shes*. The pair also face questions about whether they fully understand the science behind their tech-intense plant-based brand—even though Courtney holds a PhD in nutrition and metabolism; and they're grilled on whether they have their legal affairs in order—even though Zan is an attorney. They simply don't fit the genius prototype many investors have in mind.

Incidentally, we're now seeing that a lack of diversity in the tech sector can translate to actual product fails: The "smart" soap touchless dispenser that doesn't work on Black hands. Facial- and image-recognition software that either can't recognize or can't appropriately categorize Black faces. Speech-recognition software that can't understand people who are nonnative English speakers. When bias exists in engineers and systems, it exists in their products. As Erica Baker, an engineer and tech veteran who works as the chief technology officer for the Democratic Congressional Campaign Committee, explains, "Every time a manufacturer releases a facial-recognition feature in a camera, almost always it can't recognize Black people. The cause of that is that the people who are building these products are White people, and they're testing it on themselves. They don't think about it."

WHAT DEI LOOKS LIKE IN CULTURES OF GENIUS AND CULTURES OF GROWTH

Cultures of Genius must have their benefits, at least for the geniuses—right? As my research shows, not as much as you might think. For people who are *positively* stereotyped and fit the genius mold, they may benefit for a little while—as long as their proverbial star is rising. But of course, new stars are always being born. In Cultures of Genius, the drive to maintain and advance one's position in the hierarchy can sabotage individuals and organizations, and the fall from grace can be steep. With their restrictive models of success, fixed-minded cultures create a sort of mental, emotional, and performance-related straitjacket for positively stereotyped people as well.

I see these constraints frequently among leaders who want to break out from their company's Culture of Genius either because they know the company needs to change to remain competitive, or because they see an opportunity on the horizon that they don't want the organization to miss. The problem is that in a Culture of Genius, only a few ways exist to demonstrate your competence, and just one lapse can indicate that you've lost your edge, or worse, that you may never really have had it after all. Especially in times of uncertainty and change, Cultures of Genius can make even the golden ones feel boxed in.

George Aye is a former employee of IDEO, one of the world's foremost design firms, which had been crowned with the genius designation by several media outlets. In 2021, via an essay on *Medium*, Aye described how he, as a person of color, had been "bullied and humiliated" at the organization, where, he said, "[p]erfectionism, a perpetual sense of urgency, paternalism, power hoarding, fear of open conflict, and individualism were proudly on display." Aye writes that the tone was set on day one when a male colleague told him, "This place is sink or swim. If you don't make it here, it's 'cause you aren't cut out to be here." At first, Aye thought that didn't apply to him—after all, he'd been hired. Yet during his tenure he found himself working 60- to 80-hour weeks, terrified of falling below the invisible performance line.

Aye reports that this dynamic of being in a "perpetual interview" was especially hard on people of color at the firm. One employee described to Aye an incident where, even though his job was not related to the marketing and communications team, he was called on to review materials generated by the team for diversity and inclusion. Though he was uncomfortable, he agreed because it would give him more exposure to the leadership team. A woman of color recounted how she'd been "brought into the studio with great fanfare" owing to her experience and credentials, only to be told when she asked for more challenging assignments, "bide your time—be patient." She watched while White peers with lower levels of performance were given the assignments she wanted.

Cultures of Growth understand that maintaining strong DEI policies and practices is an essential component to becoming, and staying, a leader in their field. According to Jayshree Seth, 3M's chief science advocate, one of the reasons 3M has been so effective at creating such a diverse and innovative workforce is its broad view, typical of Cultures of Growth, about who can have a successful STEM career. Part of Seth's role in promoting science and science careers is to change our prototype of success in STEM: We have to change who we think about when we think about successful scientists and engineers. The company learned through their own survey that when people picture scientists, they mostly conjure a male genius laboring alone in a lab. "People don't see themselves in those lab coats and mixing those colored liquids if that's all the image of science they have. It leads to all sorts of misperceptions even [among] the youngest kids," Seth explains. "The kids see the image of a genius scientist or an evil scientist or a loner scientist or a maverick scientist, and if that's not what they want to be, then they disengage from science. So, the stereotypes and the bias and the gender issues and all of that gets rolled in there [and they think] 'That's not who I am' or 'That's not who I want to be.'"

Seth adds, "It's a disservice that we're doing to the science community by having those stereotypes, and we want to break down those barriers." As part of her role, Seth is working to encourage more interest in science, not only among children, but also among adults, and 3M is not just trying to get kids attracted to the idea of careers in science, but also to increase general science literacy across society. This illustrates a typical Culture of Growth method of tackling challenging issues: gathering the data, discovering that the dominant STEM culture is a Culture of Genius that disproportionately leaves certain groups out and holds others back, then developing initiatives that address this culture problem broadly and in novel ways, monitoring progress, and proactively looking for ways to do more.

When it comes to finding great talent, candidates who fall outside the genius model are not only less likely to want to apply to Cultures of Genius but also, when they do apply, they're less likely to perform well during common screening tests. At the start of the chapter, I described research that Kathy Emerson and I conducted showing the negative impacts of fixed mindset organizations on women's trust and motivation. In another study, we looked at performance on standardized IQ tests that are often used by companies in their hiring processes and found that, on average, everyone performed worse on these tests when they were applying to more fixed-minded companies. This was especially true for women and racial and ethnic minorities who expect to be stereotyped as less intelligent by these companies. When applying to companies with Cultures of Growth, however, these applicants performed as well as their White male counterparts, suggesting that the Culture of Genius was the problem.

The Pipeline Myth

When identifying and recruiting diverse talent, some organizations complain that there simply isn't a pipeline from which to hire. ("We'd love to hire more female engineers, but we just can't find any!") Judith Michelle Williams, SAP's head of people and sustainability and chief diversity and inclusion officer, calls foul on this myth. According to the U.S. Bureau of Labor Statistics, Black people compose approximately 5 to 6 percent of the labor force in the tech sector. As Williams told Diginomica, "I'm a data person, I always look at the numbers. If we are at three percent [of Black employees]—which we are—it means that we have not exhausted the pipeline. If we were sitting at six percent, I might say it's going to be a challenge to double that, but we're not. So any of those pipeline discussions, you have to make sure that you're actually getting the representation of the existing pipeline."

As I've seen in my research, mindset culture is both the cause and the consequence when it comes to a diverse workforce. Cultures of Genius tend to put out narrower job ads filled with the fixed traits they prize. These companies often proudly proclaim their mindset values in HR materials. Together, these cues cause mistrust among women, people of color, and other underrepresented groups who are wary of being devalued and disrespected in these cultures (a concern our data sadly confirms is valid). So, in some ways, fixed mindset companies are correct in that *their* companies' pipelines are dry because they simply don't attract the diverse talent that gravitates toward Cultures of Growth.

A lack of investment in people's development, along with less equitable environments, means Cultures of Genius are more likely to lose the diverse talent they have when a more growth-minded organization calls, so these companies are never really able to build their internal pipeline. Cultures of Growth, on the other hand, are more likely to do the hard work of analyzing the data to see where they need to improve their pipeline and their workplace environment, and to invest in development programs to ensure that everyone has their greatest chance of success. Let's look at some real-world examples.

Enlarging the Talent Pool

Similar to the pipeline problem, an issue that leaders frequently raise is not being able to find "hidden talent." Rather than just compete for what they perceive to be a handful of top performers from diverse backgrounds who often cycle from place to place as different organizations keep poaching these well-known stars, companies want to know how they can identify new talent that is otherwise hidden from view. Often, I work with companies through my organization, Equity Accelerator, to shift the company's mindset culture along with their policies and practices regarding talent search and development so that they recognize a more diverse workforce—and attract it with their Culture of Growth.

One of the ways Cultures of Growth are uncovering hidden talent is by ditching outdated and unnecessary restrictions on hiring people who are otherwise qualified, such as dropping requirements for a college education, or welcoming applications from people who were formerly incarcerated. Going on 40 years old, Greyston is a combination bakery and foundation that seeks to provide opportunities to a group of people who have much to offer the workforce, but are often overlooked: those who were formerly incarcerated. The company uses an innovative open hiring model that explicitly seeks out and welcomes "those who face rejection elsewhere." They've done away with background checks, résumés, drug testing, credit checks, and even interviews. Instead, would-be employees sign up on Greyston's job list and receive employment on a first-come, first-served basis. Such an approach flies in the face of the fixed mindset—how can we find the "best people" if we don't screen for special qualifications and weed out those who might not measure up? Sara Marcus, director of the Greyston Center for Open Hiring, says the primary qualification is a growth-minded one: being willing to learn. Everyone gets a chance, and once they're in the door, they're held accountable for their performance. If they're not able to meet expectations, despite the training, support, and opportunities to improve that they're given, then they're asked to leave. That said, Marcus says that Greyston has found "tremendous talent in the pools of folks who come to our doors. . . . We run a world-class manufacturing facility and serve world-class clients," among them Unilever, Ben & Jerry's, and Whole Foods.

While Greyston's specific approach may not work for many organizations, unlike Cultures of Genius, Cultures of Growth are willing to broaden their search for talent and to provide opportunities for growth and development once inside the organization.

Entrepreneur Karen Gross is a post-conviction restoration of rights attorney who founded Citizen Discourse, a training organization that provides curricula and restorative space for people to learn to engage in civil discourse, to develop more empathy, and to connect with one another across differences. When it comes to hiring, she says, "People deserve second chances, and we have this fixed mindset around people who are serving time or have a criminal history. We send people to prison or sentence them to probation and have them complete courses with the intent of rehabilitation so that they are ready to rejoin society. But we don't really treat them like they're rehabilitated. We don't treat them as people with potential. We don't make it easy for them to re-enter society and flourish. We make it really hard."

The growth mindset wants high-performing, dedicated people who are willing to apply themselves and continuously learn. It focuses on people's future and potential and the distance traveled over the course of their career. Because Cultures of Growth believe in people's abilities to develop, they provide their employees with concrete and widely accessible opportunities that help them realize their full potential. By doing this, they're not just supporting individuals or making a profit, they're also making an investment in society's collective future.

Now that we've seen what DEI can look like in Cultures of Genius and Cultures of Growth, let's examine what research shows about the role of mindset in supporting or squashing companies' DEI efforts.

SCIENTIFIC INSIGHTS INTO DEI AND ORGANIZATIONAL MINDSET

The link between organizational mindset and DEI occurs at the most basic level. Whether we're in our fixed or growth mindset determines whether or not we're drawn to diversity. My research collaborators Josh Clarkson, Josh Beck, and I demonstrated this in a series of studies. In the first fun but hunger-inducing experiments, we showed participants six types of candy bars and told them they could choose four to take home. They could pick four different candy bars, four of the same kind, three of one and one of another . . . You get the gist. When we prompted people's fixed mindset, they opted for less variety ("I'll take four of the same kind that I already know I like, please!") than those in their growth mindset ("Give me an assortment!"). We saw similar results when people were offered a "Select five, get the sixth free" deal on travel toothpastes; when they were asked to make a six-pack by choosing among six different branded sodas; and when they imagined a grocery run to pick up three kinds of fruits and three kinds of juices. In each case, those operating from their fixed mindset prioritized sameness, while those prompted toward their growth mindset chose diversity.

Mindset doesn't just affect us at the organization-wide or individual level, it influences whether interactions unfold equitably in small groups. Laura Kray, a leading scholar of equity, leadership, and management at the University of California, Berkeley, and her colleague, Michael Haselhuhn, conducted a series of studies that examined how people's mindset beliefs about negotiation ability (whether people, in general, can be natural-born, gifted negotiators, or whether negotiation is a skill that can be learned) affects the goals they pursue, the strategies they use, and their performance during negotiations. They found that teams who adopted more of a growth mindset prior to a negotiation task performed better than those who adopted more of a fixed mindset. In fact, these growth-minded teams were more likely to go beyond negotiators' stated positions, expand the pie, and construct deals that addressed the parties' underlying interests.

What does this have to do with DEI? In several studies, Kray and colleagues identified toxic, fixed-minded stereotypes about women that prevent them from reaching their potential in negotiations, and from being recognized as leaders in organizations. Specifically, that women are more cooperative and collaborative than men and that women are poor advocates for themselves. Cultures of Genius—with their greater likelihood to engage in heuristics and stereotyping— reinforce these views, while Cultures of Growth are more likely to challenge them. In fact, our study of the Fortune 500 reveals that companies with a stronger Culture of Growth have more women on their boards of directors. And it's not because they have larger boards on average, which is a tactic commonly used to increase board diversity by adding on extra seats for women and people of color. Cultures of Growth have similarly sized boards as Cultures of Genius, they're just more diverse.

Pursuing Organizational Transformation:
Creating Equitable Cultures of Growth

My most recent work founding the Equity Accelerator has focused on helping powerful people in organizations shift from a Culture of Genius toward a Culture of Growth—often motivated by the DEI benefits that Cultures of Growth experience. We've worked with more than 300 STEM faculty across six universities in the United States to create Cultures of Growth in their classrooms in what we called the Student Experience Project. College faculty engaged in workshops and consulted a library of practical, evidence-based tools and resources that we developed to help them evaluate and reshape their course policies and practices, their teaching strategies, and their interactions with students. For example, faculty learned how to describe prerequisites, how to experiment with new evaluation policies, and to provide opportunities for practice and feedback in their syllabi. They also experimented with "exam wrappers." These messages set the stage for what tests really mean beforehand (that is, stating that the test is an opportunity to assess where students are at that moment instead of a pronouncement of how smart or cut out for the subject they are) and help students make meaning of their performance afterward. Additionally, they offer strategies to improve on the next exam.

What happened when hundreds of faculty proactively turned their classrooms into more inclusive Cultures of Growth? Their approximately 30,000 students reported more belonging and identity safety (feeling valued and respected as a group member). These gains were even greater for students from backgrounds that were structurally disadvantaged in terms of gender, race-ethnicity, and socioeconomic status, along with transfer students and first-generation college students. It's nice to feel good, but these positive experiences also predicted students' end-of-term grades. In classrooms where professors created inclusive Cultures of Growth, students from underrepresented groups composed more of the A–B distribution (earning fewer Ds and Fs) and were less likely to withdraw from courses.

When it comes to creating systemic and institutional change, that's easier to do when you're building an intentional Culture of Growth, rather than functioning within a default Culture of Genius. The latter is highly prevalent in STEM, which is why these fields are a key area of focus for my team's research. When STEM professors created a Culture of Growth for themselves first by forming faculty learning communities (meeting regularly to share and discuss the strategies they were trying, the shifts they were seeing in class, and where they were getting stuck) their students were more likely to experience benefits. As student experience and performance rose, whole departments became interested in partnering with us. From there, growth-oriented approaches started appearing in university strategic plans and faculty union negotiations. It was growth mindset culture gone viral as these more inclusive practices spread outside the classroom and began to support other aspects of student success. (This is the kind of knock-on effect you can expect from real culture change.) University staff and administrators are now using these tools to redesign their messaging to students, their early alert systems, their probation policies, and their physical and virtual environments to encourage and enable student success.

College faculty—and especially those from research-intensive universities—are often stereotyped as set in their ways and uninterested in or disengaged from teaching and learning. But that has not been our experience. What started as a project to enhance equity, growth, and belonging among students in STEM classes became an intervention that changed and invigorated faculty—it transformed their relationships with their students, with their job, and with their institution.

Sanford "Sandy" Shugart had been trying to solve the learning puzzle for years when he took the helm as president (now retired) of Florida's Valencia College, a community college where racial-ethnic minority students compose more than 70 percent of the student body and more than 60 percent of students attend part-time because they are balancing school with work and family obligations. "I was really interested in why perfectly intelligent people learned and didn't learn sitting next to one another in the same class." When he arrived at Valencia in 2000, leaders and educators at the college were already asking, "Is this the best our students can do? Given that there's nothing defective with the students, what's going on here?" because the outcomes among students were so variable. They were determined to find a way to do better by everyone enrolled at the college. It was the start of a systematic overhaul that Shugart described as creating a *different anthropology* around the idea of learning—one centered around the belief that "anyone can learn anything under the right conditions." Shugart characterized it as a switch from higher education's *productivity culture*—where the focus is on cycling through as many students as possible—to a *learning culture*, where effectiveness is measured by student success. The new plan was to meet students where they were. It was similar to the plan with New York's Harrison Central School District: to take down any barrier educators could identify that would keep students from learning, not just on a systematic but on a case-by-case basis. With tens of thousands of students per year, that was a significant ask of educators, and therefore a huge risk that there would be pushback.

"No culture exists in isolation," Shugart noted. He wasn't trying to create a Culture of Growth out of nowhere. "Instead, you can use the existing culture to leverage your way to a new culture. We sat down with staff and educators and said, 'Okay, if we believe every student can learn, let's test every decision we make by two questions: How does this improve learning, and how do we know it does?' That's it. Then we just had hundreds of little conversations."

Shugart and his team were trying to create multiple Cultures of Growth layered on each other—one at the faculty level, encouraging faculty to adopt a growth mindset about themselves and what they were capable of, about the learning environment they could create for students, and about students and their capabilities. At the student level, Shugart had the idea that surrounding students with a Culture of Growth created by the faculty, staff, and administration would show them that they were valued and respected—and that the institution believed in their abilities to learn and develop. The idea was that in this kind of environment, students might shift toward their growth mindset more easily.

The educators had a solid handle on much of what was holding them back, and it turned out that it wasn't a barrier stemming from their students; it was constraints created by the college's structures and policies. "So we said, let's take the most difficult organizational behaviors that are undermining learning and let's change the organization." Shugart says it was the difference between telling faculty, "You need to teach differently" and assuring them, "I'm going to make it possible for you to teach differently." That included overhauling the tenure system to reward innovative, quality teaching; changing faculty onboarding and the college's professional development systems to help faculty learn as soon as they started at the college; and shifting teaching using the most updated evidence base available for effective pedagogy.

Valencia switched to a learning-centered model for faculty development and tenure in which professors design more of the curriculum themselves based on what they feel they need to learn to become an effective faculty member. Throughout their time at Valencia, and especially when coming up for tenure, faculty must demonstrate their own learning and development as teachers, and that includes showing how their teaching has benefited students.

One innovation was to do away with the traditional add/drop period at the start of each semester. Now, on day one, faculty know for sure which classes they'll be teaching; while before, classes that didn't make their numbers by the add/drop date were canceled. This certainty means faculty can come prepared to help students start learning right away knowing that the plug won't be pulled a week or two into the term—a benefit for both teachers and students.

The culture at Valencia is now faculty-driven, with educators collaborating to lend their expertise where they can make the greatest contributions. The change has not been fast, and years later they're still dedicated to it as the "little conversations" continue. Yet the mindset has now shifted significantly enough that as Amy Bosley, formerly Valencia's vice president of organizational development and human resources, said, it's essentially guaranteed that if something new is proposed, at least one faculty or staff will ask, "How will this affect students?" Educators and students are co-creating a learning environment.

One of Valencia's great successes is its "come as you are" message to make everyone feel welcome. They understand that when you spend energy worrying about how people will perceive you based on where you're from, or how you speak or look, you have less energy to dedicate to learning and teaching. By contrast, in Cultures of Genius, with narrow definitions of who fits and who doesn't, people may feel greater pressure to *code switch*—to present themselves in a way that's acceptable to the setting even if it's not who they fully are. As my research shows, when we bring fixed-minded restrictions to what people who work with us are supposed to be like, we erode their trust in the organization. Lanaya Irvin, a lesbian who dresses in styles traditionally associated with men, worked as a Wall Street financier, and as such, she was expected to look the part. "[Wall Street] is a fit culture, so there was a tremendous amount of covering on my part. I wore silk blouses and pearls. I wore the Wall Street uniform. I hyperfeminized so that the focus would be on my content and the words, and not focused on a masculine presentation." Eight years into her career at the firm, as she became more senior in the organization and had more flexibility, she decided that she would no longer do any speaking engagements for the bank "unless I could present the way I would like to present." Then she began to transition her outfits in the office. Ultimately, says Irvin, nothing changed for the clients. What did change was that she felt more comfortable when making presentations and delivering leadership messages in her "made-to-measure shirts and pocket squares. And it was an opportunity for me to signal to emerging talent that it's okay to actually live in your authenticity."

From these various examples and research findings, I'm sure you've intuited several ways you can help your organization become more of an inclusive Culture of Growth, but let's explore specific methods to transform into one.

HOW TO TUNE YOUR ORGANIZATION'S MINDSET TO SUPPORT DIVERSITY, EQUITY, AND INCLUSION

"Proceed intentionally." That's the advice that Lanaya Irvin gives companies when it comes to DEI. Irvin is now the CEO of Coqual, a think tank and advisory group that helps companies diversify their workplaces. Many well-meaning organizations end up taking a scattershot approach to their DEI efforts instead of engaging with an in-depth, long-term plan rooted in growth-minded culture. Here are some tactics to ensure that your organization is operating as an inclusive Culture of Growth that attracts and retains a wide range of talent.

Fine-Tune Your Cues Audit

Irvin says that it's important to have "organizational introspection" and diagnose your own cultural weaknesses when evaluating systems that could be producing bias. In Chapter 3, I described how to conduct a cues audit, which I highly recommend. Now that you've read about situational cues and how they shape some of the specific experiences people from a variety of groups have had at different companies, it's time to revisit your cues audit with a focus on DEI with these situational cues in mind. Explore your company through the eyes of some current, past, or prospective employees from different backgrounds or identities. What messages might they get based on who's on (and not on) your board of directors and in leadership positions? How about the language in your company's materials? Who is pictured (or not pictured) in those materials? What about accessibility issues? Would a person who uses a wheelchair or a person with dwarfism be challenged to access any aspect of your office environment? What kind of humor is considered acceptable? Is it okay to tease or flat-out make fun of people based on their identities, aspects of their background, or what they look like? What about your evaluation and promotion processes? Does everyone have equal access to mentors and sponsors?

When you conduct your audit, pay attention to policies that may be overlooked, such as dress codes and other rules around how people present themselves. Are they unnecessarily gendered? Could they unintentionally be communicating that success shows up in a narrow look or body, preventing folks from being their whole selves at work? Do they send a message that some parts of people's identities may not be welcome in your organization? It's not about not having fun; team bonding and cohesion are essential for high-performing teams. Instead, it's about creating an environment where everyone feels valued, respected, and inspired to do their best work together—and has equal access to the tools and resources that will help them get there.

Share Stories

Lanaya Irvin says, "As a Black, female-bodied LGBT leader on Wall Street, I know firsthand that at the intersections I'm going to be discounted in some of the spaces I occupy, despite the access and privilege I may have." Irvin says she's "never felt more seen" than when she had the opportunity to share some of these experiences with people in her organization. It's important for leaders and others throughout the organization to understand these types of dynamics so that everyone can watch out for biased practices and experiences. Creating opportunities for storytelling in your organization is a way to invite peer education and to cultivate deeper connection and identity safety.

Create Identity-Safe Containers for Challenging Conversations

An approach that doesn't rely on individual storytelling is to create regular, routine opportunities for people from underrepresented groups to speak with leadership. Too often, these kinds of listening sessions are only convened when there is an identity-based incident or emergency that has occurred. By making this a regular activity—instead of waiting for a company blow-up—trust and candor are cultivated over time so that when problems arise, a relationship and open communication already exist. Information gleaned in such experiences may even help to inform your cues audit.

Ellen Pao of Project Include says it's critical for companies to create routine safe structures in which to hold conversations around DEI. Irvin adds, "You don't have to have all the answers, just find a way to sit in the discomfort and know that it's better to show up imperfectly than not to show up at all. These conversations are an extremely important way to ensure that leaders maintain human connection, ensure people are heard." Just like shifting policies on how people dress or otherwise present themselves, these conversations don't only help people in underrepresented cohorts, they actually create a greater sense of trust and belonging for everyone.

At Karen Gross's Citizen Discourse, conversations are grounded in a Compassion Contract. At the outset, participants agree to hold a growth-minded standard of compassion for one another's ideas and experiences and to express themselves in a manner that's respectful of others. People are encouraged to get curious when engaging in conversation across differences. Instead of trying to show you know how to have these kinds of conversations in a "fake-it-'til-you-make-it" approach, adopt a learning orientation. Research shows that having learning goals defuses the tension that often exists in intergroup interactions.

Re-evaluate All HR Processes through a Growth Mindset Lens

Whether it's writing job ads, creating hiring protocols, conducting interviews, onboarding new employees, or evaluating and promoting current ones, your organization's mindset will shape who you seek, whether you are able to retain talented employees from diverse backgrounds already in your organization, and whether employees are motivated and willing to fully bring their skills and talents to work. Explicitly consider which skills are required at the outset and which can be developed over time. In many cases, employers find it beneficial to train and develop their employees so that the employer's approach and "organizational DNA" is suffused throughout the organization—but training and resources need to be robust. It's not a growth-minded approach to hire people and then throw them into the deep end to sink or swim with no guidance and support.

Consider making your candidate pool even broader. As Sara Marcus from Greyston says, you don't have to make the leap to open hiring—you can start by simply removing background checks, getting rid of the credit check and automatic disqualification of anyone who's been incarcerated, or just reconsidering whether someone really needs a college or even high school diploma to perform a particular job well. (Consider that more and more schools are putting their curricula online, many for free. Nearly all of MIT's undergraduate and graduate courses are available online at no cost, so the way we become educated—and educate ourselves—is changing.) Review your hiring, evaluation, and promotion models and consider what arbitrary criteria or unnecessary hurdles you may be creating that keep you from truly accessing and retaining the best, most diverse talent available.

It's not easy, and it's going to take time and dedicated effort and resources, but you're ready to take the first steps to make your organization and team into an inclusive Culture of Growth. Without a doubt, transforming your organization into a Culture of Growth is a journey far more than it is a destination, as is identifying our mindset triggers and continuously adjusting our own mindset set points.

Now that we've looked at how mindset culture is created and reinforced at an organizational level, let's examine how it works at the more micro, interpersonal level. As part of this exploration, we'll examine the four most common cues that prompt each of us into our fixed or growth mindset and learn strategies for when we find ourselves unwittingly headed toward our fixed mindset, to switch gears and move toward growth. Not only that, we'll see how understanding the power of these mindset moments can help us build microcultures of growth in our teams and in our interpersonal interactions where everyone has agency and influence.

PART THREE

Identifying Your Mindset Triggers

CHAPTER 8

Mindset Microcultures

Mindset isn't only in your head; its influences are all around us. Now that we've explored the impact of an organization's wider mindset culture, we'll drill down to examine the influence of microcultures we experience in different interpersonal situations. Within a Culture of Genius or Culture of Growth, we can experience mindset microcultures that can be similar to or different from our organization's overarching mindset orientation. I've worked with several Fortune 100 companies in which the organization seemed to embody a Culture of Genius, but when we measured the mindset culture, there were smaller microcultures—a division or two, a department, or a handful of teams—that seemed to cultivate a Culture of Growth within the group. They had formed their own local culture.

These anomalous microcultures are important because, as an organization undertakes the effortful task of culture change, they are a good place to start. Something about these teams has afforded a different culture from the larger one surrounding it. Understanding how these microcultures came to be and how they sustain themselves gives clues as to how organizational culture change can happen in a company—plus, these microcultures are homegrown. Rather than using outside examples (which can be helpful at times), these microcultures inside an organization offer important insights as these groups have the company's DNA and can model what's possible within it.

In the next few chapters, we'll view these microcultures through the lens of *mindset triggers*, including the four most common inter-personal situations where research shows people are likely to move toward their fixed or growth mindset.

THE FOUR MINDSET TRIGGERS

In 2016, a large multinational bank approached my team and me requesting that we create a mindset assessment to use in growing and developing their employees. Even though their intentions were positive, as I've discussed, evaluating an employee's mindset in a one-and-done assessment is simply not the best way to predict how someone will behave in the "real world." Yet we saw an opportunity in this request to test a hunch we'd been investigating.

After reviewing reams of data and the literature, my team isolated four situations that seemed most likely to move people along the fixed-growth continuum. Now, it was time to test our hypothesis. We examined how thousands of the bank's employees responded to these four situations and how they related to their performance, with the data converging on these four triggers as predictors of employees' motivation, behavior, and performance. Employees found it useful to know about their mindset triggers and were eager to learn how to navigate them. Managers found it useful to know which cues shifted their direct reports toward fixed and growth mindsets and were able to use this information to tailor developmental feedback and opportunities to help employees move toward growth mindset more of the time at work.

Buoyed by these findings, we went on to do a deeper investigation with managers at different companies to see whether these four cues applied to other organizations in different industries. We went next to Shell, and then in a series of focus groups and workshops in companies large and small we did the same, with similar results.

Each time we shared these insights, we were met with something surprising: relief. People found freedom in finally being able to discuss when their fixed mindset emerged. Explaining the mindset continuum—and showing how we all have both—normalized the fixed mindset as something we could all relate to. Learning that mindset isn't static, and instead is often situation-dependent, freed people from the moralization and judgment they were used to. They felt liberated by the discovery that how they respond to these four challenging situations isn't just about them—and that their responses are changeable! Every person's response is the result of a complex interaction between their personal beliefs, experiences, and history, and the organization's culture (as communicated by its policies, practices, and behavior).

So, as we move forward with our exploration of mindset, keep in mind that understanding these four triggers and how to navigate them is essential not only for individuals themselves, but also for those charged with their performance and development, and anyone who influences the organization's culture. Why? Because culture is made by individuals in interaction with each other and people are both influencers of and influenced by these triggers. Knowing how your group responds to them reveals tangible ways to shape these situations and interpersonal interactions that, together, make up mindset culture.

1. Evaluative Situations

Whether you're an employee preparing an important presentation, a manager anticipating your 360-review results, or a CEO getting ready to deliver a speech about a new corporate policy, you naturally anticipate how you'll be evaluated by others. These situations can push us into a prove-and-perform mode, where we focus on how we come across, *or* they can flip us into learning mode, where we undertake growth-oriented behaviors.

2. High-Effort Situations

Often, we find ourselves in situations requiring extra attention and energy. This happens routinely at companies like Google, for example, where teams get reformed every six to eight weeks, requiring people to learn a new workflow, product, or service very quickly. When people are triggered toward their fixed mindset by these high-effort situations, they can be so worried about failing that they refuse valuable transfers or promotions that will help them move ahead; however, when these same high-effort situations trigger people toward their growth mindset, they believe that the best way to improve and advance is to put forth the effort and challenge themselves.

3. Critical Feedback

Different from when we *anticipate* being evaluated by others, these are the situations where we receive negative feedback. Through a fixed mindset lens, critical feedback can be especially threatening, reflecting not just on whether we are good or bad at a task, but whether we are a good or bad person. When we are in our fixed mindset, we believe that underneath the criticism of our work is a negative pronouncement on who we are as an individual; we didn't display the shortcomings only in our skillset, but in our self and our ability to do better. Thus, employees operating in their fixed mindset avoid asking for critical feedback, which stunts their growth, creating a self-perpetuating cycle. When people can approach critical feedback from their growth mindset, they're far more likely to learn and develop. In fact, we see many people, when moved toward their growth mindset, actively seek critical feedback. That doesn't mean it feels great to fall short, but they embrace the opportunity to know and improve.

4. Success of Others

Situations when a peer achieves some level of success, such as a promotion or award, can influence our behavior as we witness it from the sidelines. When others' success triggers us toward our fixed mindset, we can easily become demotivated: "I'll never be as good as Yen, so why should I try?" In our growth mindset, we are more likely to be inspired by the success of others and to view it as an opportunity to learn new strategies that will help us achieve our own success: "Yen really nailed that project. Maybe she can give me some tips."

As I mentioned in the last chapter, situational cues signal how likely we are to experience positive or negative treatment: Will we be listened to? Will our opinions matter? Will we be included and treated respectfully? Situational cues tell us what experiences we're likely to have based on our social identity, but we also monitor the people, norms, and interactions in our surroundings to figure out whether our *local environment* values fixed- or growth-minded beliefs and behavior.

My research shows that different people are more (or less) attuned to different mindset triggers, and the effects of these situations on people's mindsets can vary. For example, one person might find high-effort situations threatening when they first start a new job but tend to view critical feedback as an opportunity to improve. Someone else may tend to struggle more with evaluative situations but have no trouble celebrating and learning from the success of others. Throughout Part Three, our investigation of these mindset triggers will help you discover your hot buttons right now, knowing that these can change over time. (And if it's all four, don't worry—you're not alone.) You'll also learn strategies to help gear your response toward growth, even if the culture around you celebrates genius.

For all of this, it's helpful to understand what it actually *feels* like to be in your growth or fixed mindset. So, let's start there.

WHAT MINDSET FEELS LIKE

Think about a time when you've engaged a new idea or cultivated a hobby simply because it brings you delight. When you felt voracious, wanting to learn everything you could about it and do it as much as possible, watching videos and reading books and listening to podcasts. You were eager to jump in and do, open to learning and improving as you went, and you experienced that most delicious of states: flow. This is what operating in your growth mindset can feel like. It doesn't mean that what you're pursuing is easy—in fact, that's rarely the case. As research shows, flow states frequently come when we are operating at the edge of our ability—in other words, the space where we're challenged, but with some effort can meet that challenge. When you're geared toward growth, there's a magnetic quality associated with what you're pursuing. You are deeply engaged not just to check a box, but for the sake of mastery or enjoyment. Sure, when it comes to work you may be checking a box, too, but you engage with the task or project from your growth mindset, not because you have to, but because you want to.

Once, while on sabbatical, I was walking along the street in San Francisco on a beautiful spring day when I turned a corner and saw a gorgeous six-foot mural with decorative writing and flourishes that read: "Become Who You Are Meant to Be." In a moment of inspiration, I thought: *I wonder if I could make art like that?* Now, my penmanship has always left something to be desired (just ask my students when I turn back scribbled comments on their dissertations), and I am not that artsy or creative (shhh, fixed mindset!). I've always said that my brilliant sister, Maureen, got the creative gifts in our family and I can't draw a stick figure to save my life. Yet, back at home, I found myself ordering pens, falling down the YouTube hand-lettering hole (it's deep!), buying workbooks, and feeling energized and excited to learn something new—just for the fun of it. Of course, at first I was terrible at it (and I'm still working on it), but it didn't matter. I was learning something new and it felt great. And that drive to learn prompted me out of my fixed mindset around the idea that I didn't have the inherent talent to be creative. I was prompted into my growth mindset.

But that was a hobby, for fun. What about when it comes to our work or the craft that pays the bills? For that, let's look at Daniel "Rudy" Ruettiger, who inspired the movie *Rudy*. He was so passionate about wanting to play football for Notre Dame that he did absolutely everything in his power on and off the field to become part of the team. This included starting out at a community college where he worked hard to complete the classes and earn the grades that would qualify him for admittance to Notre Dame. Then, he had to earn a spot on the football team as a walk-on—no easy task for Ruettiger, who, though he was a good football player, at 5 feet 6 inches tall and only 165 pounds, lacked the size to be competitive at that level. But he was dedicated to improving. Eventually, Ruettiger secured a spot on the scout team, which helped the varsity team prepare for games. During practice, Ruettiger gave everything he had to help his teammates improve, encouraging them and pushing them to work harder. In many ways, Ruettiger became the heart of the team. In the last home game for which Ruettiger was eligible to play, he was instructed to dress, and he got to realize his dream, taking the field for three plays. In the final play, he sacked Georgia Tech's quarterback—his first and only official Notre Dame stat—after which his teammates carried him off the field. He was the first Notre Dame player ever given this honor. Ruettiger created a microculture of growth for himself amid all kinds of structural and institutional messages that he wasn't cut out for the team. His initial rejections, coupled with his undeterred dedication, moved him toward his growth mindset. He in turn cultivated that mindset within the team, and the rest is history. Additional examples include coders who solve problems and share their solutions for fun, simply to make contributions to the knowledge base. Or that student who's compelled to learn more about a topic than what's required by the curriculum.

That's the growth mindset in action—where learning feels rewarding. Instead of chasing external awards or accolades, our progress is its own reward; it's internally motivated, and we just want to discover more. In our growth mindset, it doesn't feel like another "to do" list item to learn more. That's not to say it feels easy or that we're suddenly, magically good at something because we'd like to be or we're in the "right" mindset. In fact, brain studies reveal that while we are developing new skills, we often experience a fair bit of agitation as we engage the learning process. When we're operating from our growth mindset, however, we're motivated to keep working at it. Over time, we develop new skills and knowledge and notice that our understanding is getting deeper.

At the other end of the continuum, we become less engrossed in what we're doing, and more concerned about how we're perceived by others. Are we coming across as smart and competent? If we're worried that we're not, our bodies can fill with tension and anxiety. Rather than focus on how we might approach a task in a way that can maximize our learning, we fixate on how we can showcase ourselves in the best light. These types of thoughts and feelings are indications that we are in our fixed mindset or moving toward it.

One of my friends says that she knows she's moved into her fixed mindset when she can't laugh appreciatively at her own mistakes, and her body feels "like a cage for [her] anxiety." In these moments, there's nothing to feel awful about—we all embody our fixed mindsets sometimes. The most growth-oriented response is to simply learn to recognize when it happens and invoke the strategies that will help us shift back toward growth.

What I've just shared celebrates the growth mindset, but I want to be careful that you're not left with the impression that growth is good and fixed is bad—a common misperception. Mindset simply is. It is generally more advantageous to operate from your growth mindset, but that isn't an absolute, and remember: We fluctuate between them. Let's take a minute to examine our much-maligned fixed mindset in more detail.

UNDERSTANDING OUR FIXED MINDSET

People often ask me whether it's ever good to "have" a fixed mindset (or more accurately, to be in your fixed mindset, since we all have it). Certainly, I can think of instances to which the answer is some approximation of yes. When we're interacting with someone in their fixed mindset, it can be useful to be able to take their perspective— embodying our own fixed mindset for a moment to see the world through their eyes. Understanding their mindset triggers or the concerns they have that stem from their fixed mindset beliefs might help us understand how to help them see things in a different way. Also, being familiar with our fixed mindset can help us strategically navigate fixed-minded Cultures of Genius, as we've seen in my research. When we recognize the fixed mindset culture of an organization, we can see what the company wants from us and we can choose to adaptively respond to get our foot in the door and later to reap the rewards of the context. Indeed, these Cultures of Genius are likely more prevalent in industries where safety and strong priors about how things should be done are based on what's been done in the past. These include industries such as law, medicine, and accounting and roles such as data entry, quality control, or auditing. However, even here, as we have seen in Candy Duncan's auditing work at KPMG or with Shell's safety-focused Goal Zero, the growth mindset can still be important for innovation and success in these industries.

Really, I think asking if a fixed mindset is ever good isn't the right question. Perhaps the question is whether it's advantageous to lean toward your fixed mindset most of the time. The answer to that is no, because it unnecessarily restricts who we believe ourselves to be and what we are capable of doing. Another more apt question could be whether embodying our fixed mindset is ever functional, to which I would say sure.

You might be surprised to know that many people I like and work with tend to embody the fixed mindset as their default belief system. When presented with something that will require that they stretch, for instance, their immediate reaction is often to view it as an obstacle rather than an opportunity. Is that immediate internal reaction in and of itself bad? No. Is it functional? Perhaps. It depends on how we use what comes from our fixed mindset. For example, in our fixed mindset, our immediate response may be to forecast the problems we foresee in meeting the challenge or identify what *won't* work. These types of responses can actually help us frame the parameters of potential solutions. Where the fixed response would hold someone back is if they stayed there and focused *only* on what won't work. As it is, my friends and colleagues who are highly successful have learned to recognize when they're in their fixed mindset. They view the situation through that lens and then nudge themselves toward growth by asking questions such as, "Okay, so if those approaches won't work, then what could?"

Each of these concepts will be easier to grasp as we explore examples of people dealing with the four most common mindset triggers that shape our personal mindset beliefs in a given situation. The first of these is: evaluative situations.

CHAPTER 9

Evaluative Situations

I'm going to be testing you on the material in this book, so make sure you read and understand it thoroughly. Moreover, how well you recall and understand what you've read will tell me a lot about how smart and capable you are—and how successful you'll be in the future.

Now, stop and notice what you're thinking and feeling. Are you anxious and apprehensive, or are you excited and ready to dive in? Does your body feel tense and constricted, or poised for action?

Of course, you're not actually going to be tested. Yet how you reacted to the idea that you would can provide a clue to how you respond to the first of the four mindset triggers—evaluative situations.

Evaluative situations are situations where we *anticipate* being assessed or evaluated by others. Perhaps it's a routine meeting where you know you'll be asked to give an account of your team's work. Maybe you're about to give an important presentation. Or perhaps you're preparing for your annual performance review. Whatever the situation, you know that others will be responding to your work and likely evaluating you on the basis of it.

In simply reading those examples, your body may have offered further clues. If you felt anxious, or your muscles tensed and your heart fluttered, it's likely that evaluative situations trigger you toward your fixed mindset (at least in your current environment). Conversely, if you felt excitement rather than anxiety, these situations may spark your growth mindset. If you think about similar situations you've experienced, can you remember what you felt like as you prepared? Did the situation prompt anxiety or excitement? Did it feel more like an obligation where you were required to prove and perform, or like an opportunity to learn? For each of us as individuals, regardless of setting, evaluative situations tend to cue us to lean (or all-out sprint) toward our fixed or our growth mindset.

This variation in responses is exactly what I found in one of my executive education classes at the Stanford Graduate School of Business. The participants were a group of about 15 Dutch CEOs who were in town for a week-long intensive. I was teaching them about the situations that prompt us toward our fixed and growth mindsets and how to identify their responses. After describing the mindset triggers, I asked the executives to split into pairs for a sharing exercise. "Okay," I instructed, "I want you to go through these four situations and discuss which you see in your own experiences, either in the past when you were coming up in your career, or as something you experience now—knowing they can trigger different responses at different points of our lives."

One of the things I enjoyed about the group was the direct, explicit communication style common among them. As I listened to some of the exchanges, I heard a fair amount of brusque, but healthy, in-your-face debate. When I reconvened the group and asked for volunteers to share what they had uncovered, though, the room went silent. To be fair, sharing—especially going first—requires some vulnerability, which some might view as weakness. Finally, a tentative hand went up. "Great," I encouraged, "let's hear what you came up with."

"Well . . ." he cleared his throat. "It's just that with evaluative situations, I feel like I have been burned too often when I've put forward proposals that I know will be controversial within the company. I find myself more and more wanting to delegate the preparation of these because it puts me in such an anxiety kind of focus. So, I ask those who work for me—the next level of executive leadership—to put together my slides or speech. I might edit them lightly, but I realize that the reason I do this is because in some way it protects me from the response people might have. So, I'm anticipating how people are going to respond, and I'm delegating this work to others so that it doesn't take away my focus."

Around the small room, heads began to nod and voices began to mutter. "Oh yeah. Yeah, I can see that." Then another hand went up.

"Well, you know," the next CEO ventured, "I have a lot of these fixed mindset triggers, but I actually think that evaluative situations are maybe my growth cue."

"Really?" the others asked.

"Yeah! I love to sit there and strategize about the best ways that we can ask our employees questions. How we can structure feedback loops so that we can actually get information to improve the company. And when I am in that mindset it just feels like everything is possible. I don't know that I anticipate getting much positive feedback, I just love that feeling of being able to plan in advance how to get the most helpful information back from the clients we interact with." In fact, he added, at his meetings, he often spends more time listening than talking. "Sometimes I get dinged for that," he said, "but it's just the way that I feel like I make the best decisions is to open myself up for learning as much as possible."

You can see the contrast in these responses. When evaluative situations cue us toward our fixed mindset, we emphasize our personal performance. We wonder, "How can I show myself in the best light?" As we prepare a report, presentation, or speech, we focus on exhibiting our intelligence and competence. We source and present material in ways we hope will feature our brilliance. And when it comes to reflecting on our process, we'll often avoid discussing the challenges and setbacks we have faced for fear that these struggles may make us look weak or diminish our reputation.

From our fixed mindset, we adopt a narrow performance-oriented goal—to prove our worth. We see the work product as a test we have to pass by showcasing our intellect. On the surface, this might not seem problematic—after all, we want high-achieving, motivated employees, right? However, this mindset is limiting because the goal is an individual one (the product must reflect the employee's brilliance) rather than a team or organizational one (the product should contribute to the advancement of the organization). It's also limiting because when an employee is overly focused on performance, typically they are under-focused on learning, and that inhibits their ability to gather the data and evidence that will spur their growth and development, and by extension the product's and organization's as well.

EVALUATIVE SITUATIONS ON THE FIXED AND GROWTH CONTINUUM

FIXED ←————————————→ GROWTH

Goals

Look smart at all costs.	Learn at all costs.

How it sounds

"The main thing I want when I do my work is to show how good I am at it."	"It's much more important for me to learn do things in my work than it is to get the best evaluations."

How it shapes our responses

Defensive: "They don't know what they're talking about."	Receptive: "That's so helpful! I understand better now."

Conversely, the view from a growth mindset is more expansive: We are likely to adopt learning goals such as, "How can I use this to improve my ideas?" As we prepare our work, we focus on ways to seek feedback from others (creating a microculture of growth around us) to refine the idea we're creating. When we present our work, we might feature our successes to date, but we also might share some of the challenges and struggles we've faced along the way, and the strategies we're using to overcome them. This allows others to learn from our experiences (again, cultivating that microculture around us) and invites them to offer insights to help us navigate our current dilemmas.

Theranos founder Elizabeth Holmes presents a modern cautionary tale of fixed mindset behavior in the face of evaluative situations. As the *Wall Street Journal*'s John Carreyrou reported, from an early age, Holmes was labeled an exceptional child. During her first year at Stanford, she devised an idea to create an adhesive patch that could monitor people's blood counts. Holmes took the idea to Phyllis Gardner, a professor of medicine. "I kept saying to her, 'It's not feasible,'" Gardner told another reporter, but Holmes wouldn't listen. Instead, she managed to win support from another professor at Stanford, who called her a genius and compared her to Beethoven. In 2003, at age 19, she dropped out of school to found Theranos, where her patch idea morphed into plans for a personal computer-sized device—which Holmes dubbed "Edison"—that would perform more than two hundred tests on a tiny sample of blood attainable through a finger prick.

Quickly, Holmes became a darling of the tech world and found herself in a high-stakes evaluative situation: She had to make good on hundreds of millions of dollars in venture funding and substantiate her company's $9 billion valuation. To grow her company, Holmes needed to produce a device that worked. Only she couldn't. Engineers could not solve the challenges of having such a small device perform such varied testing, and the impossibly small blood samples had to be diluted to perform even half of the promised tests, making results drastically unreliable. Yet instead of coming clean or asking her prestigious board or mentors for help, Holmes lied to investors, employees, the Theranos board, and federal regulators. Workers falsified test results or sent blood samples to standard blood testing labs for analysis, then pretended the samples had been analyzed by Theranos machines. At one point, Holmes told the head of engineering to have his staff work around the clock to fix the problems with the Edison. When he refused, saying staff were already overworked, she hired a competing team of engineers and set the two teams against one another; the winners could keep their jobs.

What might Holmes's journey have looked like had she been able to shift toward her growth mindset in the face of these high-stakes evaluative situations? For one, she might have listened to what her employees were telling her about why the Edison didn't work and the challenges they faced. She could have turned to her extensive network, including her board, which included some of the brightest minds in technology and some of the most celebrated military and political leaders of recent times, to request help. Had Holmes shifted to a learning approach, Theranos might have eventually made good on its promise—or pivoted to a more feasible technology-based solution. Gathering enough data and learning from others helps people in their growth mindset pivot to new strategies when it is clear that new directions are needed to move forward. Instead, in 2018 the company was dissolved and in 2022, Holmes was convicted on four counts of fraud and former COO Ramesh "Sunny" Balwani was found guilty on 12 counts.

If Elizabeth Holmes serves as a model for the extremes of fixed-minded behavior in the face of evaluative situations, Katrina Lake—cofounder and former CEO of Stitch Fix (a role she has resumed as interim as of the writing of this book)—could be her antithesis. Like Holmes, Lake attended Stanford, after which she spent two years at a consultancy, where she devised a plan to transform retail by marrying personal shopping with technology. In her model, shoppers would enter a warehouse-like facility where they could peruse options and wave a wand over what they liked. When they were ready, all of the clothes, in their sizes and desired colors, would be available in a fitting room, along with several selections by one of the store's personal shoppers. Colleagues pointed out significant problems with Lake's idea, so after some consideration, she jettisoned her plan. But after a stint at a venture capital firm, she felt the enduring tug to start her own company.

Before going to VCs for startup capital, Lake decided to hold back; she wanted to develop a strong model with lots of supporting data that would be as close to a sure thing for potential investors as possible. She enrolled in Harvard Business School, figuring that in addition to learning more about business and venture capital, she would buy herself time to test her idea. During this time, Lake devised the idea of Stitch Fix—a subscription service that provided personal shopping for the masses. Lake (along with cofounder Erin Morrison Flynn, who later left the company) tested the idea thoroughly, all the while recording and tracking data. Finally, she set out with her spreadsheets to raise money . . . and was rejected.

Unlike Holmes, who doubled down on her prove-and-perform tactics, Lake continued to refine her idea, incorporating the viable feedback she'd received from the more than 50 VCs who turned her down. To continue Stitch Fix's growth trajectory, Lake hired people she says were "far smarter and far more talented," including a former COO of Walmart and a former head of algorithms for Netflix. Stitch Fix continued to grow and picked up a few more investors.

When Lake and her team prepared for their biggest evaluative situation yet—taking the company public—they again struggled with financial support. Two days before the IPO, one of Lake's advisors told her she had the option of waiting 18 months and trying again, but this time, Lake declined. Even if investors had cold feet, with all her team had learned and created to that point, Lake was now confident in how the ultimate evaluators—the consumers— would respond. "If we go low today," Lake said, "we'll prove ourselves. We've been underestimated before." In 2017, Lake became the youngest woman ever to take a company public, and she is now counted among Silicon Valley's most successful founders/CEOs.

Now that we've identified some of the potential pitfalls of a prove-and-perform mindset, let's investigate how we can encourage a shift toward our growth mindset when we (and those we interact with) encounter our own evaluative situations.

FOSTERING A GROWTH MINDSET
IN EVALUATIVE SITUATIONS

Here are five ways we can approach evaluative situations, based on research and case studies, so that they are more likely to cue us toward adaptive, growth-minded behaviors.

Set the Context

When a leader recognizes an evaluative situation, they can *set the context* to encourage a collaborative- and learning-oriented mindset. In our work with leaders, we help them present the situation or task using language designed to defuse competitive tension and encourage collaboration and creativity in ways that feel authentic to their style. They can set the stakes transparently, letting employees know how they will be evaluated and helping them anticipate the situation in a way that frames it as an opportunity for learning rather than one in which they're expected to prove their competence.

In an interview with entrepreneur and author Dave Asprey, author and motivational speaker Simon Sinek described a meeting he held with his team during the first months after the COVID-19 pandemic struck, drastically impacting his mostly in-person business model of presentations and workshops. Sinek told his team they each had 48 hours to come up with 15 ideas of how they could shift the company's business model so they could stay engaged and relevant. He knew 15 was a high bar, but he wanted them to stretch creatively, which he explained to them.

Before the team presented their ideas, Sinek set the context away from a prove-and-perform microculture to a share-and-support one. "This is not about competition, this is about contribution," he said. "I am fully aware that there are some people on this team that are going to have six amazing ideas and some people on this team that are going to have zero, and I'm okay with that. . . . Because what I also recognize is that the people who are having the ideas probably are not the best people to execute on those ideas. . . . If anything, the thing that this will reveal is where our strengths are and how we're going to work together." In framing the meeting this way, Sinek defused what could have been an evaluation-related fixed mindset trigger by recognizing people's different inputs and acknowledging that having a "great" idea was just one of the elements needed for the organization to be successful. Sinek said that at the meeting the team discussed the top ideas and further shaped them together, and so in the end, the entire team owned the ideas, not just one or two people. While not everyone "got a trophy" in terms of having one of their ideas selected, everyone did shift toward their growth mindset during the process and had different opportunities to contribute to the team's overall success.

How you frame the work is important. Then, it's equally critical to allow people to execute that work in the way that's most effective for them.

OVERDETERMINATION Some companies create an atmosphere of *overdetermination*, where employees face an excess of evaluative situations that undermine people's autonomy and expertise. When an organization or manager requires continual proof of performance—such as near-constant check-ins or production of superfluous deliverables—it suggests to employees that the organization is unsure whether they can do the work required of them. This ongoing evaluation can make employees feel as if they are under a microscope and is likely to trigger them toward their fixed mindset. As culture writer Anne Helen Petersen notes in her book *Can't Even: How Millennials Became the Burnout Generation*, such atmospheres require employees—especially those working remotely—to LARP (live-action role play) their jobs. In some cases, they spend more time assuring managers and coworkers that they are present and performing than actually getting meaningful work done. And the additional effort that requires and the frustration it creates, writes Petersen, can contribute significantly to job-related burnout. But what creates the setup for overdetermination?

In 2020, I engaged in a brief project with Tom Kudrle, Ellora Sarkar, and their team at Keystone examining fixed- and growth-mindset behaviors in companies' data cultures. We wanted to know how companies that take a more fixed- or growth-minded approach to data and their use might be related to other organizational outcomes like innovation and adaptability. One thing we saw clearly was that companies with a Culture of Genius around data (who can collect them, what they're good for, who can access them) also had overdetermination problems. We found that overdetermination often crops up when a company lacks a clear vision or goal and they don't provide employees with the latitude to be creative and innovative. When the corporate vision is fuzzy, employees often struggle to articulate where the company is headed and why they, in their roles, do what they do. Because of this lack of clarity, managers tend to monitor groups and employees more tightly and put more constraints around their work. Employees feel the constant pressure of proving themselves in every evaluative situation because they are, in fact, overcontrolled. To be fair to managers, in such environments, they are doing their best to make order from chaos. In a company that lacks a clear vision, people can set out in multiple directions because there is no unifying direction for employee effort and engagement, so managers overevaluate them.

THE "I KNOW!" KID . . . OR ADULT This next insight comes from my collaborator Stephanie Fryberg, who took time off from her professor job to work inside her child's school district in her family's Native tribal community to transform it into an inclusive Culture of Growth. You might be familiar with the "I Know!" Kid, whether you have a child of your own like this, or you've noticed this behavior in your family or peer group. The "I Know!" Kid is the one who, when offered advice or instruction, fires back with, "I know!" instead of listening. Now, granted, a few "I know!" kids may be reacting to hovering or over-instructive parents (a possible response to overdetermination), but in most cases, this is an indicator that the child is being triggered toward their fixed mindset by what feels like, to them, an evaluative situation. When a child retorts, "I know, I know, I know! Don't help me!" what they are often saying is, "I don't want you to think I'm stupid," or, "I don't want you to think I can't do it." They are anticipating an evaluative situation, and they are afraid that through either their effort or its outcome, you will see them as lacking.

Many of us have sympathy for the "I Know!" Kid, especially when that kid is our own child; but we tend to have less compassion for the "I Know!" Adult. Still, the situational mindset cue is the same—a concern about being perceived as incompetent, incapable, or unintelligent. The "I Know!" Adult's refrain is similar: "Don't tell me how to do it—I know. Don't tell me when it's due, I've got it."

To encourage both children and adults toward their growth mindset, set the context by addressing their underlying concerns about how you might perceive their ability. Tell them that you believe they are competent and capable. Instead of saying, "This is what I'd like you to do and this is how you should do it," you might say, "This is what I'd like you to do. Now, I know you've never tried this, or some aspects of this, before, and it can be challenging, so I wanted to give you some ideas for how you might approach it." Or you might say, "Hey, you did a great job doing it this way last time," acknowledging their skill and abilities, then adding, "Now I'd like to help you expand your skillset, or do it faster or more efficiently, by trying it this way." Another approach involves destigmatizing struggle. "This is often a challenging task for people, but it's a great learning opportunity." It can also be helpful to underscore that you're invested in their advancement. "You're already doing a great job, and I want to make sure you're exposed to projects and experiences where you're challenged so that you can keep stretching and growing. I'd like to offer you some ideas that I think will help you along the way." This can defuse any fear or anxiety about any judgments of their performance.

Focus on Growth

Another way to encourage a growth mindset in evaluative situations is to bake growth and learning behaviors directly into the activity. Some organizations have responded to the challenge of shifting people toward their growth mindset during meetings by implementing a "thorns and roses" component. At the beginning of weekly meetings, for example, attendees are encouraged to spend some time talking about what they are most excited about or what they view as a big success for the week. Those are the roses. They're also asked to reflect on some of the thorny issues they're dealing with or the hurdles they anticipate (that's where the potential for learning comes in). The speaker can then request ideas or strategies from the group as to how they might navigate those more challenging issues. Again, struggle and asking for help are destigmatized and become central to the regular norms of meetings.

John Mackey, cofounder and former CEO of Whole Foods Market, describes a "challenge and support" approach to bring the best out in teams. He writes in the book *Conscious Leadership*, "The *challenge* side often involves pushing and pressing team members . . . to put in the extra effort necessary to achieve the organization's higher purpose . . . while the *support* side of this equation is anchored in patience, providing strategies, and nurturing care for team members and their needs." In such an atmosphere, employees are encouraged to view evaluative situations as opportunities to develop and learn, and they receive the resources and guidance necessary to do so.

Get Support

What if you're the only one? What if you are a mostly growth-oriented person functioning within an organization or with a manager that largely operates from their fixed mindset? Once again, we can take a lesson from the COVID-19 pandemic. Feeling alone and isolated because of safety guidelines, many people created pandemic pods—groups of families or friends with whom they socialized—while some even created pod-based mini home schools for their kids. Or take a tip from Bozoma Saint John and her squad. Saint John, along with Issa Rae, Luvvie Ajayi, and Cynthia Erivo, compose a pod of powerhouse professional women. The group, who've adopted the nickname West African Voltron, share personal and professional support along with encouragement and, as the name implies, laughter. Creating these microcultures of Growth in otherwise larger Cultures of Genius is something we can all do within and outside organizations.

When facing an evaluative situation, such as preparing a presentation, you can create your own small team to ensure that you get the diverse insights and feedback to help you meet your growth-oriented learning goals (and, of course, create a stronger product). If you don't already know similarly growth-minded people in your organization, pay attention at meetings and in other situations where people's mindsets are on display. Notice who's asking insightful questions and providing constructive, meaningful feedback.

Still, pod-worthy people may be in short supply, in which case you can look beyond your organization to create your pod. Many CEOs prefer to have a cohort of peers outside their companies to compare notes with because the view from the top can be different from other places throughout the company. While feedback from all levels is important to being an effective leader, when it comes to some issues, they need the perspective of people who know what it's like to be the boss.

Guide and Release

To guard against overdetermination, leaders can provide a clear understanding of the company's mission and how employees' work fits within it. This, of course, means that an organization needs to have a clear vision to begin with.

Beyond an understanding of the vision and their role, employees must be enabled and empowered to support that vision. This involves thoughtful training and dialogue, so that employees understand the strategies that can help them do their job. They also need awareness of and easy access to resources to support them along the way. And then? Let them execute. If you've tasked someone with carrying out an employee survey, you've talked with them about how they might approach it and let them know who and what is available to help them design it, let them go do it. Don't hover or ask them for constant updates, which will communicate that you don't trust them or their abilities.

This of course doesn't mean check out. But if the environment has been tuned to growth and if employees are well trained, managers can trust that employees can function well independently and will check in as needed with both challenges and successes. (And if that doesn't happen, it's up to managers to discern what's needed to support employee success, whether it's more training, a clearer articulation of some element necessary for the employee's understanding and success, or something else.)

Another benefit of the guide and release method is that if an organization has truly cultivated a learning-oriented Culture of Growth and entrusts employees to carry out their work, employees will be vigilant for new, innovative ways to contribute. Not only will they hone their own work, but they'll also look for potential changes to help the organization get closer to its goals.

Model a Growth Mindset

If you're a leader, you have an opportunity to *model* a growth mindset in the face of evaluative situations. Not only does this provide you with the opportunity to learn and grow yourself—as in the example of our Dutch executive—it also serves as a visible example of the behavior you want to encourage in others and throughout the organization.

This strategy mirrors something Mark Zuckerberg and Sheryl

Sandberg have done since the early days at Facebook (now Meta) with their Friday "all hands" meetings. Whether separately or together, the two convene large-scale Q&A sessions in which they take the first few minutes to fill employees in on some of the company's newest initiatives. Then, they open up the floor for questions or suggestions about anything. In a fixed mindset mentality, presenters are known to do the opposite, filling up the time with their own talk and leaving little or no time at the end so that negative feedback or challenging topics don't have a chance to surface.

When we learn to employ these strategies at all levels of an organization, we can transform evaluative situations from those that induce fear and a defensive prove-and-perform mentality to opportunities that expand our capabilities and our capacity together.

QUESTIONS FOR REFLECTION

♦ Recall a time when your "I Know!" Adult reared its head. What concerns did you have about the way you were being perceived that caused you to have that reaction? What can you do to reassure and bolster that "I Know!" Adult so that you can shift away from the prove-and-defend mindset to your learn-and-develop mindset the next time the I-Know-It-All shows up?

♦ If you're a leader, how can you set up evaluative situations for those you lead so that they can be nudged toward their growth mindset? What language and practices can you build in that will set up these situations to facilitate people's development?

♦ In the next evaluative situation you encounter, how can you notice the physical tension and defensiveness that are a hallmark of the fixed mindset, acknowledge it, and transition toward your growth mindset? Remember that recognizing it is the first step toward shifting it. How can you approach your next evaluative situation at work with a "how can I learn the most from this" mindset? What would that feel like? Look like? Sound like?

CHAPTER 10

High-Effort Situations

The blank page. Few prompts are more inspiring, or anxiety-inducing, than a fresh piece of paper or a screen waiting to be populated. Most writers agree that creating something novel (including an actual novel) requires work, sustained focus, and a willingness to try and try again. Whether the thought of an empty canvas—and the sheer amount of work that the project will require—inspires fear or excitement can be a clue as to how you tend to respond to the second mindset trigger: high-effort situations.

A high-effort situation is one where success is contingent on applying more effort, time, or mental resources and attention than you've had to in the past. Sometimes, it involves being in a new context, such as starting a new job or class, or transferring to a new team where the work requires learning new skills or applying your skills in a new way. High-effort situations arise when you can no longer lean on prior knowledge, or when approaches that worked in the past may no longer apply.

While some of us avoid high-effort situations—which by their very nature essentially guarantee some degree of failure—others, like Ramona Hood, seek them out. Hood is the president and CEO of FedEx Custom Critical and the first Black woman to lead a FedEx company. Hood started as a receptionist at age 19. A single mother, she was looking to get out of retail and into a more stable schedule that would allow her to balance the demands of work, motherhood, and college. Hood quickly advanced to a job in the safety and contractor relations department. After several years, although she was comfortable there and performing well, an opportunity arose in operations and, wanting to diversify her experiences, Hood went for it. From there, she went on to sales and marketing, then to leading a business unit within a company FedEx had just acquired, and finally back to FedEx Custom Critical and a new operations role. In January 2020, she took over as CEO. Again and again in her career, Hood not only rose to meet challenges, but sought them out for herself. As she told theSkimm in 2020, "I think it could have been easy for me to get into a leadership role and never leave the operational area. I was good at it. I had strong skills and competencies that were demonstrated in the results. But I felt that it was important to be comfortable with the uncomfortable of learning something new—taking some risks as well as having some failure to be able to grow."

As Hood's attitude illustrates, when high-effort situations spark us toward our growth mindset, it's due to a belief that the way to improve and succeed is to challenge ourselves and find the strategies that will help us pursue our goals. We seek opportunities to develop our skills and often feel dissatisfied or bored by easy, effortless tasks (or at least too many of them) because we know that when we're not being challenged, we are not learning and growing. Conversely, when we're prompted toward our fixed mindset by high-effort situations, it's often due to an underlying belief that effort and ability are negatively correlated—that if we find ourselves working hard on a project that feels difficult, it must mean we don't have what it takes. High-effort situations make us vulnerable because they place us in new territory. If we worry that we may be "found out" and deemed not up to snuff, we may respond by staying in our comfort zone. A founder I once worked with reported his own high level of irritation when his first two or three attempts at solving a problem didn't work. Fearing negative feedback from others, and already having doled out a fair bit to himself, he found himself shifting toward his fixed mindset and contracting out the task or just plain giving up.

Highly visible examples of top athletes or professionals cued toward their fixed mindsets by high-effort situations are hard to come by because those people often quit when faced with the amount of effort required to make it to the top of their fields. Or perhaps they were that athlete, artist, or manager who purposefully stayed at a more middling role in their field because once they met the edge of their natural talent, a fixed-minded response kept them from pushing beyond it. Most of us recall a high school athletic star or valedictorian who appeared to come by their success so effortlessly that they seemed destined to take the world by storm. Instead, their glow dimmed once they found themselves in the company of other stars—ones who were willing to put in the work, seek help, and find new strategies to keep rising.

Turning back to the blank page, we find the story of one writer you may have heard of. He nearly quit a high-effort project, but instead learned to move into his growth mindset with legendary results. Stephen King had been writing for years and had experienced some modest success selling short stories to men's magazines, when he took on a job as a high school English teacher to pay the bills. He started writing *Carrie*, then threw his efforts into the trash. It was going to be too difficult to write—the story needed to be a novella to work, and King wasn't a novelist. Plus, as he told his wife, Tabitha, when she confronted him with the draft pages she had fished out of the trash, he'd never been a teenage girl. How could he write one? King was burning up most of his brain power teaching all day anyway; he had little left to pen a whole novel. Tabitha replied that she could help him with the teenage girl part, and that he should keep going with the story because what he'd started had merit. So, he picked it up again, and *Carrie* became the novel that made Stephen King a household name.

As King says, the lesson he learned from *Carrie* was that "stopping a piece of work just because it's hard, either emotionally or imaginatively, is a bad idea." King has written more than 60 books and developed a reputation for a legendary work ethic, writing his 2,000 words per day, holidays and all. He says it's a misconception

of his process to think that regularity breeds ease; he's simply programmed himself to embrace the struggle. In his book *On Writing*
King declares, "You can approach the act of writing with nervous-
ness, excitement, hopefulness, or even despair—the sense that you
can never completely put on the page what's in your mind and heart.
You can come to the act with your fists clenched and your eyes narrowed, ready to kick ass and take down names. . . . Come to it any
way but lightly."

So how do we become more like a King or a Hood, shifting toward
our growth mindset in the face of high-effort situations? It starts
with addressing that underlying belief about the correlation between
effort and ability. Research shows that those who lean toward their
fixed mindset tend to see the two as being negatively correlated; that,
if I have to try hard at something, it means I must not be good at it.
At work, it can make us think, *This work is so challenging—maybe
this isn't the job for me.* Or after being promoted to a managerial role
from a contributor position and, for the first time, taking on challenges such as forming new relationships with colleagues who had
formerly been peers and keeping tabs on others' work products and
needs, we might think, *Maybe I'm not cut out for leadership after all.*
In classrooms, it can prompt a student to think, *I'm struggling with
these math problems, so I must not be good at math.*

When we believe there is a *positive correlation* between effort and
ability, we're more likely to see problems as solvable with the right
tools. We see consistent hard work as a price worth paying to grow.
And as the science shows, this is true not only at the psychological
level, but also at the cellular level.

CHALLENGE GROWS THE BRAIN

Just like a muscle, our brain gets stronger through hard work. The idea
sounds catchy, but is it true? After all, our brain isn't a muscle—it's
far more complex. Hoping to answer this question, a group of re-

searchers placed study participants in an fMRI machine, then monitored their brain activity while they listened to two tones. Their task was to press a button to indicate whether the second tone was longer or shorter in duration than the first. In the "easy" portion of the test, the tones were more clearly differentiated, whereas in the "difficult" portion, the second tone was more like the first. As the researchers dialed up the difficulty, the participants' brains began to light up: The more challenging the task was and the more effort it required, the more areas of the brain were recruited to help. Not only was there more activity and connectivity among different parts of the brain during the challenging task, one of the areas that came online during the hard part was the dorsolateral prefrontal cortex. This part is associated with higher-level executive functions such as our working memory, ability to switch between multiple concepts, and abstract reasoning. The more we're challenged, the more parts of the brain we call on to help us and that, in essence, increases our overall abilities to meet the goal.

Research also shows that it's not just any effort that makes us grow new neural cells and pathways, but effort expended in the process of learning—something we call *effective effort*. Scientists compared the brains of two groups of "gym rats," which were put on different physical exercise regimens, with a control group of "cage potato" rats and a group of "acro-rats" who learned to navigate an elevated obstacle course—a task that was mentally, but not physically, challenging. Though both groups of gym rats developed a higher density of blood vessels in their brains than the cage potatoes, the acro-rats developed more synapses per nerve cell than all three other groups. When we're working hard *and* learning something new, we develop more connections among different parts of our brain, and that helps us complete tasks more quickly and easily in the future.

The neural pathways we don't use die off over time. What makes our brains hold on to these pathways—and create more—is not simply repeating the same things we've learned over and over again, but continually taking on difficult problems. Just like exercising our muscles or our cardiovascular system, once we've got something down so well that we can perform it with little effort, it may boost our ego, but it won't boost our performance. We've got to keep dialing up the level of challenge. If you've heard the advice that the way to keep your brain sharp is to tackle Sudoku or the *New York Times* crossword puzzle, those activities may serve you up to a point, but only so long as they remain challenging. Spending an afternoon with a Rubik's cube would make my brain grow (and make me grow plenty frustrated), but not so for mathematician and data scientist Cathy O'Neil, who's been solving them since she was 14. Neuroscientist David Eagleman says that in order to keep his brain healthy, he constantly invests in challenging activities, such as learning new software programs and wrestling with Mandarin.

Yet if multiple avenues of scientific exploration tell us that it's only by engaging in challenging tasks that we develop and grow, why does the belief that *having to apply more effort means less ability* persist? What's keeping it going?

FUELING FALSE BELIEFS ABOUT EFFORT AND ABILITY

Fitbit may be one of the hottest fitness-related companies out there. (As of 2023, more than 31 million people around the world used a Fitbit at least once a week.) Yet while wearable tech is commonplace now, in 2007, when cofounders James Park and Eric Friedman set out to put a data-gathering sensor in a device small enough that someone wouldn't mind wearing it all day, they struggled to create a prototype that worked. Finally, in 2015, Fitbit went public, yet shortly after, they started to lose money. By 2017, employees handed Park what amounted to a no-confidence vote. Some even wrote to the board of directors asking that he be removed as CEO. As devastated as Park was, instead of leaving, he committed to learning from his mistakes and doing better. As he told interviewer Guy Raz, "My primary focus [after the employee survey] was, 'How do I get things back on track?'" Park drilled down on his management shortcomings, while also investigating where the company had missed out, and he realized that because they had been late to diversify, they were getting clobbered by the competition. In addition to broadening the product line, Park pushed to change Fitbit's positioning from a maker of a fitness device to a "healthcare data analysis company." Instead of just reporting stats to users, Fitbit began to provide coaching and other support to help people change their numbers. When asked how Park hung in and kept pressing forward when the company was in serious jeopardy of going under, he recalls his parents.

In their native Korea, Park's father had been an electrical engineer and his mother had worked as a nurse. After they emigrated to the United States (when James was four years old), as with many immigrants, they had trouble finding the same level of employment, so they decided to become small business owners. Park says the pair ran a wig shop, a dry cleaner, a fish market, and an ice cream shop. "They could switch from one genre or one type of business to another and really not skip a beat," says Park. Park says his parents' staunch determination and work ethic contributed to his own mindset of resilience—the idea that hard work is the price of advancement. In a story that echoes those of many children of immigrants who went on to achieve success in their fields, struggle and challenge were normalized.

Certainly, this advice is not only born from some innate knowing of the value of hard work, but it stems from an awareness of the often very real necessity to prove oneself to combat negative stereotypes about immigrants. Yet the lingering effect for many seems to be that, as with Park, high-effort situations shift them toward their growth mindset. Like the Marquis de Lafayette and Alexander Hamilton sing in one of the most powerful lyrics in the musical *Hamilton*: "Immigrants . . . we get the job done." Regardless of our backgrounds, our parents' beliefs and behaviors regarding effort and ability tend to make a deep impression on us.

Researcher Julia Leonard and colleagues launched a series of studies to determine how parents' "taking-over" behaviors affect children's persistence on difficult tasks. The results showed that parents who tended to take over for their children when they struggled (rather than encouraging or coaching them on what methods they might try next) were more likely to describe their children as less persistent.

In a subsequent study involving four- and five-year-olds, researchers assigned children to one of three groups. In the first, after a ten-second interval, the researcher interrupted the child's attempted puzzle solving, saying, "Hmm . . . this is hard. Why don't I just do it for you?" In the second group, the researcher used a variety of teaching interventions to support the child's attempts, and in the third group, they didn't intervene at all. Afterward, the experimenters presented the students with a wooden box toy that they encouraged the children to try to open, but it was an impossible task as the toy was glued shut. The children for whom the experimenter had taken over in the initial puzzle-solving task gave up faster than the children in the other two groups. As the researchers concluded, "When adults take over and solve hard problems for children, children persist less." Then there's the influence of the culture we're surrounded by outside our homes.

You might be familiar with some version of the widely acknowledged Stanford Duck Syndrome—something I experienced personally in grad school. To be successful in the elite, high-pressure educational environment of Stanford, you were expected to glide gracefully across the water, though, beneath the surface, you were kicking like crazy to keep up. Hardship and struggle were expected to simply roll off your back. In the day-to-day, undergrads, in particular, could be seen lounging around the student union or coffee shops, listening to music or socializing as if they hadn't a care in the world. No one seemed to have to try hard to make it. By evening, they would begin to hit the books, sometimes studying alone in their rooms through the night in an effort to, well, hide their effort.

The price they paid to align themselves with the cultural value of genius was a high one: Exhaustion and psychological distress were common.

Fellow researchers and I saw something similar at Cornell University. Personnel in the Cornell Health Counseling and Psychological Services (CAPS) group shared with us that students there were contending with enormous levels of anxiety and depression. (Cornell has been dubbed a "suicide school" due to perceived high rates of death by suicide among students, though the data show that rates of depression and suicidal thinking are on par with students nationwide.) During the 2016–17 school year, 21 percent of Cornell students sought assistance from CAPs, up from 13 percent in 2005–06. Some of this was due to a concerted effort by the school to destigmatize seeking mental health assistance. But CAPS staff also wanted to mitigate potential cultural influences and norms that could be driving anxiety and depression.

Through a series of focus groups with students, CAPS counselors identified an unusual and disturbing trend. As is typical at many colleges and universities, companies selling a variety of dorm room posters—everything from puppies to popular bands—would come on campus to peddle their wares. During the most challenging times of the semester, such as during midterm and final exams, the most popular poster was one that was supposed to be motivational. It read, essentially, *While you're sleeping, someone else is getting ahead.* One could argue that the posters simply encouraged the students to dig in and work hard. When such "motivation" links to a cultural belief system where hard work is thought to signal low ability or talent, it can fuel mental health issues.

Again, these beliefs tend to start young. Kindergarten through sixth-grade teachers attending our summer institute often describe how difficult it is to counter children's perceptions that if they have to try hard at something, it means they're not good at it. The teachers, themselves, sometimes harbor these same beliefs. One of the ways we see this is when teachers take our baseline evaluation survey and they give an affirmative response to statements such as, *I hate to see my students struggle*; *Seeing my students struggle makes me uncomfortable*; and *I am likely to assist right away when I notice my students struggling*. But as we've seen, struggle is a critical element of the learning process.

As researchers Elizabeth and Robert Bjork found, when we create learning conditions where our performance increases rapidly (where we "get it" quickly), our long-term learning may suffer. If learning feels more challenging and comes more slowly, we generally retain what we've learned longer and are better able to apply that learning more broadly. That doesn't mean we have to be pounding our head against the desk at all times, but if we want to learn and retain that learning, we do need to be challenging ourselves. But wouldn't this kind of effort eventually lead to burnout? As cognitive psychologist Nate Kornell says, "What you want is to make it easy to make it hard." If we can find delightful ways to invite mistakes and challenges in, and to persist and play with them, struggle is more sustainable. Instead, what happens more often in classrooms, at least in the United States, is that when we bump into struggle, we release the pressure too soon through hint giving and allowing students to simply guess at correct results without reflecting on whether true understanding has been achieved. Conversely, in China and Japan, for example, students are more often encouraged to stay with the struggle as teachers help them chart a path to learning that includes multiple wrong turns and dead ends. Researchers Harold Stevenson and James Stigler have found that Chinese and Japanese parents and teachers place far less importance on intelligence scores and other static assessments. Instead, they underscore the value of effective effort in achievement. Students in these countries are encouraged to share their mistakes so that the group can dissect and learn from them. In this way, failure is an expected encounter on the path of learning.

As Kornell and his colleagues have discovered, the idea of *errorless* learning—the perception that fewer errors on tests means better learning—leads one to assume that getting answers wrong would have a negative impact on learning. In fact, the opposite is true; when we get a question wrong, we're actually more likely to get it right in the future if we take the time to struggle with it afterward. Struggle enhances learning and recall. This could be more true for those who have a growth-minded response to challenging tasks, given that they are more likely to pay attention to their mistakes than those in their fixed mindset.

Still, we don't want to blindly encourage all struggle, but instead emphasize strategies that enable effective effort. It's critical that we praise effort in the right direction. Research further clarifies that the effectiveness of what we refer to as *effort praise* is tied to our beliefs about effort and ability. Among students who believe that effort is an important way to increase their ability, having their effort praised boosted their views of themselves and their levels of intrinsic motivation. The stronger their belief, the bigger the boost.

As we've seen, beliefs about the inverse relationship between ability and effort begin early. Then, as we start to think about careers, countless counselors and coaches encourage us to look to our natural abilities, reinforcing the idea that there are talents we're gifted with, and those that simply pass us by.

HOW AN OVERFOCUS ON STRENGTHS FAILS US

A young man enrolled in seminary school. While he frequently scored high marks in theology, he was not particularly gifted in public speaking, receiving some of his worst grades there. That student was Martin Luther King Jr. Though we refer to him as one of history's most gifted and talented public speakers, he was not born with a strength for public speaking but developed it.

Given what you've read to this point, if I were to tell you that you have certain innate talents and strengths and should focus almost exclusively on maximizing those, that advice would likely give you pause. Yet much of the career development and personal fulfillment narratives these days say exactly that.

The general approach to maximizing your strengths starts with a static assessment, which is a slippery slope. The idea of assessing and then leaning heavily on our strengths has several implicit assumptions that are problematic when viewed in the light of broader psychological research. One assumption is that at the time you take the test, you have some strengths and some weaknesses. While that may be true on some level, it's highly contextual and depends on a host of factors, including the group with which you're comparing yourself. There will always be those with superior or inferior levels of skills, experiences, or strengths. In that light, what it means to be good at something becomes both relative and tough to measure. In sports, for instance, even among top professional athletes, where data points abound, there is still a huge amount of disagreement over what individual athlete, or team, is the GOAT (of course it's Serena Williams).

Next, while it's true that we may display certain "talents" from our early days, we tend to fall into a trap of overemphasizing the value of what comes easily to us. Once we have this snapshot of what we're already good at, we set about hacking our lives or our jobs, arranging everything from everyday tasks to our very career paths so that we can do more of those things. That may create success in the short term or in settings that don't require or encourage you to stretch yourself, innovate, or try new things. But it's not the formula for continued personal growth or for success in organizations that prioritize ongoing development or novel approaches. Especially given the current pace of innovation, most organizations are interested in candidates with a demonstrated history and desire to learn and grow—people like Ramona Hood. They don't just want effortless high performers; in most areas they want high performers with multiple capabilities—and with a growth mindset about those capabilities.

When I talk with executives about the problems with the "play to your strengths" model, I often end up needing to clarify that ability and mindset are distinct characteristics—and that they are orthogonal to each other. I usually take out a marker and draw on the whiteboard a two-dimensional space with mindset on the horizontal axis, going from fixed to growth, and ability on the vertical axis, from low ability at the bottom to high ability at the top (like the image below). Now, if you're an executive at a company, you want high-ability people—people who are above the horizontal axis on the graph. The question is: Do you want those people to operate from their fixed mindset regarding their high abilities (on the left) or their growth mindset about their abilities (on the right)? The strengths model doubles down on the upper-left quadrant. It says, here are my two or three strengths and abilities and I've got to focus on those because they can't be changed. So, it's best to find situations where I can just play to those strengths. Too many people like that in a company and you'll soon find yourself in an out-prove/out-perform, interpersonally competitive, backbiting Culture of Genius. Whereas

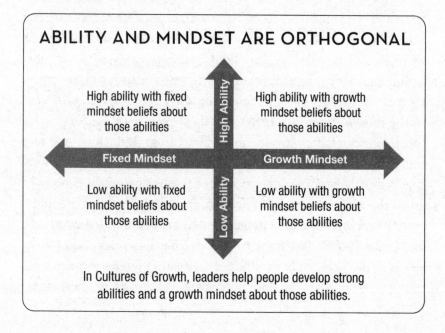

ABILITY AND MINDSET ARE ORTHOGONAL

High ability with fixed mindset beliefs about those abilities

High Ability

High ability with growth mindset beliefs about those abilities

Fixed Mindset — **Growth Mindset**

Low ability with fixed mindset beliefs about those abilities

Low Ability

Low ability with growth mindset beliefs about those abilities

In Cultures of Growth, leaders help people develop strong abilities and a growth mindset about those abilities.

the people who are more likely to succeed—and among whom Cultures of Growth are more likely to flourish—are those who adopt a growth mindset about what they're capable of. Not only are ability and mindset unrelated, but mindset also trumps ability over the long haul because mindset helps people take the actions needed to grow their abilities.

This story around playing to one's strengths links to another problematic narrative, one about passion. As the meme goes, each of us was born with a passion, and discovering it is the key to success. Like strengths and talents, passion can be seen as something that's innate and fixed rather than developed. In a series of five studies, Yale University's social psychologist Paul O'Keefe, along with Carol Dweck and fellow Stanford professor Greg Walton, examined how we're affected by fixed- or growth-mindset beliefs about passion—specifically, whether we subscribe to the view that our interests are innate or something we develop. The research revealed that those with a fixed belief perceived that once they discovered their passions, they would experience boundless motivation to pursue them and would encounter few difficulties. This belief prompted them to give up sooner when they did encounter inevitable challenges. In other words, "Urging people to find their passion may lead them to put all their eggs in one basket but then to drop that basket when it becomes too difficult to carry." Conversely, a growth mindset around passion "may help sustain interest in the face of frustration or difficulty."

Sapna Cheryan, a professor at the University of Washington and one of my old grad school buddies from Stanford, studies gender gaps in STEM fields, including computer science. Sapna says that, typically, young women are not *socialized* to feel passionate about computers or coding and so are unlikely to seek out these types of experiences for exploration. Simply look at our media portrayals: From fictional hacker Alec Hardison of TV's *Leverage* and Jimmy Fallon's irritating IT guy on *Saturday Night Live* to real-life portrayals of tech icons Steve Jobs, Bill Gates, and Mark Zuckerberg, the computer whizzes we see are almost always male. Women who do make their way into computer science often start their journeys by accident: They get into gaming, discover that coding is one way to solve a problem they care about, or computer science turns out to be a required course that sparks their interest.

The overarching narrative around discovering rather than developing passions may be contributing to the gender gap in computer science. If girls and young women buy into the fixed mindset view, they may expect to feel a natural inclination or passion toward a field that's a good fit for them, and as we've seen, the social cards are stacked against them. Couple that with the research from O'Keefe and we see that when these women finally give computing a shot, if they have to work hard to be successful, a negative effort–ability belief could derail them. Yet if they believe—and our media, leaders, parents, and teachers communicate—that passions are in fact developed *and* society as a whole does more to provide girls and women with opportunities to try computer science, we are more likely to bridge the gap. Fixed mindset views of things like strength, talent, and passion can have disparate impact on those not encouraged by their parents, peers, and society—either because of prescribed social roles or cultural stereotypes—to develop these strengths and passions early on.

Another place we commonly find stereotypes mingled with unhelpful beliefs about talent and effort is the realm of entrepreneurship.

THE FALSE LORE OF THE ENTREPRENEUR

It's easy to look at a Steve Jobs or Emma McIlroy and think they did it alone. Previously we touched on the mythology of the lone genius scientist who suddenly and single-handedly makes a breakthrough discovery. In my work with the Kauffman Foundation around entrepreneurs' fixed- versus growth-mindset triggers, I came across similar lore—a hoodie-clad frontiersman (usually male, usually young, usually White) hacking his way through the digital brush, grinding it out until he sells or takes his startup public. But wait, that's a growth mindset in action, right—displaying grit and gumption in the face of one long, grueling high-effort situation? The problem is that all of this entrepreneurial grinding doesn't always constitute effective effort.

We don't want to "just apply our grit"; we need to apply it in meaningful ways that actually move us closer to our goals. A growth mindset isn't just about putting in sheer effort; it's far more discerning than that, and it's also far more expansive. When we're in our growth mindset, we find ways to invite challenge in and to play with the struggle it brings. We focus on possibilities, try new strategies, and experiment. And we do it in a conscious, thoughtful way.

Also, almost no one does it alone. There are always cofounders, mentors, or others who contribute significantly to a startup's success. Perpetuating the idea of the solopreneur as someone who literally did it by *him*self may be discouraging a broader range of people, with interdependent and communal values, who thrive from partnership and teaming. According to data my team and I gathered, when we describe entrepreneurs as a community dedicated to tackling some of the world's biggest problems rather than a collection of gritty geniuses, we attract more women and people of color, who feel more at home in a Culture of Growth as part of a community of innovators.

Another barrier to women and people of color in entrepreneurship is a perception of bias. It's the idea that almost all White, almost all male VCs don't see women or people of color (or transgender people, or essentially anyone who doesn't fit the stereotypical mold of "success") as naturally talented entrepreneurs. They think that people from more structurally disadvantaged groups have to try much harder to make it. Ironically, those people often do—but only because of structural disadvantages and documented gender and racial biases in access to funding, not because of any inherent lack of ability. And that's where the effort–ability belief becomes pernicious. If people from these groups have to try harder to make it, it confirms the idea that they're less "naturally suited" to entrepreneurship (or any occupation) compared to their White, male, middle- to upper-class peers. As *TechCrunch* reports, in 2022 only 1.9 percent of venture capital dollars went to female founders, despite the fact that, as *PitchBook* states, "female founders had lower median burn rates, greater valuation growth at the early stage and lower valuation declines at the late stage compared to all-male founded companies year-over-year." In the same year, Black founders received only 1 percent of VC dollars.

My own research shows that a significant portion of entrepreneurs who are women and people of color experience stereotype threat—a concern that they will be reduced, in the eyes of VCs, to negative ability stereotypes about their groups. All of this adds up to a net loss of women and people of color attempting to become entrepreneurs or receiving support for entrepreneurial ventures when they do try. And this is where a growth mindset in the midst of such exceptionally high-effort situations such as starting a business can be not only helpful, but critical. Katrina Lake and Calendly founder Tope Awotona each struggled to raise money, and such was the case for Robin McBride and Andréa McBride John, who set out to disrupt the wine industry, where people of color are often excluded.

The McBride sisters started their entrepreneurial journey importing high-end New Zealand wines into the United States with a goal of making great wine accessible to all. First, they sought to distribute them with major grocery store chains, when a buyer at Kroger asked a pivotal question: "Why aren't you making your own wine?" The buyer was prepared to put in a major order for March. The problem was, it was September, which left them four months to make 25,000 cases of wine and ship it to Kroger distribution centers for winter arrival. When interviewer Guy Raz of the *How I Built This* podcast commented in a subsequent interview that the prospect sounded absolutely terrifying, Robin corrected him, saying

"Exciting!" "Thrilling!" Andréa added. And it was in large part that growth mindset in the face of repeated high-effort situations that helped the sisters meet the Kroger deadline. It's also made the Mc-Bride Sisters Collection the largest Black-owned wine company in the United States.

But let's hit rewind for a moment and look at how it was that the sisters met that Kroger buyer in the first place: It was through a direct introduction from a supplier diversity director at a different grocery chain. He was impressed by the sisters' motivation and gave them several suggestions for how they could be successful in large chains, even introducing them to buyers at other companies. Then, the sisters faced the prospect of filling the initial Kroger order and creating four varieties of wine from scratch with no investors and almost no cash. As Robin pointed out to Guy Raz, "Black women are the least funded of all entrepreneurs, so there was still a perception of risk [around us]." Their strategy was to trade on their knowledge of wine and their relationships, asking grape producers and wine-makers in New Zealand and California to trust them. They took an inclusive approach, creating a community around their winemaking process, which is something we often see from organizations created by founders from diverse backgrounds.

So, how do we nurture the kind of can-do, growth mindset the McBride sisters displayed when they were confronted with multiple high-effort situations? Several strategies exist, including one with parents and educators.

HELPING STUDENTS (AND TEACHERS) TACKLE HIGH-EFFORT SITUATIONS

Superstar climber Alex Megos had notched a number of first ascents of some highly challenging routes, and yet, as he admits, none of those routes stretched him to his limits. He was known for his style of climbing hard routes fast. Megos told a film crew, "I've never really tried anything that took me longer than ten days." Though Megos was hailed as a genius climber—and perhaps because of it—he was afraid to take on a route that would require a new level of effort. "I slowly realized it will take time if I want to climb my limit," Megos said. In 2020, Megos knocked off his biggest accomplishment yet—a free-climbing first ascent of a route that he worked on for roughly sixty days over a three-year span. As the climber said, it was a totally different experience to tackle a problem he didn't actually know if he could solve. Just as Megos had to train himself to see high-effort challenges through his growth mindset, leaders need to do the same for others.

One of the most powerful ways we help teachers in our summer institute encourage growth-minded beliefs and behaviors about high-effort situations is to not focus exclusively on individual student behavior but to attend to the mindset culture they create. On the first day of school or very early in the year, teachers of these age groups (kindergarten through sixth grade) typically set up *classroom agreements*—a system whereby teachers sit down with students and brainstorm a set of agreements that become the organizing principles of the classroom's culture for the year. At the institute, we share with teachers some language that can help build Cultures of Growth, such as agreements that we're going to "dedicate ourselves to growing our brain eight hours a day," "work hard at learning," "make mistakes and help each other figure them out," and "not leave anyone behind in their learning."

In its daily execution, this can manifest in several ways. One is teachers apologizing to students when an exercise or problem is too easy. "Wow, I overestimated how hard that problem would be for you—that didn't grow your brain. Let's see if we can find one that's more challenging that will actually help you learn." They not only demonstrate that they are responsible for ensuring that each student is sufficiently challenged, they also perpetuate and normalize the idea that what it takes to "grow your brain" is difficulty and having to puzzle over it.

Admittedly, especially in large classes and ones with a wide range of skill levels, it can be difficult to provide the kind of individualized attention this approach requires. One tactic that can help with this is something we call *back-pocket problems*. When teachers make the rounds of the classroom while students work on math equations or science problems, they have with them a variety of more challenging problems they can easily dole out to students who arrive at solutions easily. So no matter where a student is on the continuum of learning, they have the opportunity to apply themselves consistently.

In true growth mindset fashion, many teachers devise their own insightful methods to create a Culture of Growth in class. When we checked in with some graduates of our institute, we were amazed and delighted by what we saw. One teacher posted on the wall work that showed where students had been with their math problems in week one, and where they were three months later. This helped students see how they'd improved, and underscored progress as a core value of that classroom. These are the types of efforts that get to the root of the negative effort–ability belief and reprogram it to the positive.

To address teachers' common challenge watching students struggle, we start by sharing stories about people arriving at a solution because of—not in spite of—struggle. We also encourage them to reflect on and share their own similar stories. They can then use this same story-sharing approach with their students. Alex Megos's story would make a great illustration because it showcases first the reluctance to and then the benefits of challenging yourself to something you weren't quite sure you could figure out.

If you're now itching to tackle a new high-effort problem or return to one you've left unsolved, you may have already been clued in to the fact that this storytelling strategy can be an effective one for all of us.

FOSTERING A GROWTH MINDSET
IN HIGH-EFFORT SITUATIONS

Here are five practical ways to reprogram the negative effort–ability belief and encourage a growth-minded response to high-effort situations.

Break It into Manageable Pieces

In her bestselling book *Bird by Bird*, writer Anne Lamott describes an incident where her brother put off a large school assignment until its due date. Overwhelmed by the enormity of the task that confronted him—which involved cataloging birds—he had no idea how he might possibly complete it. Well, her father advised, you'll just have to take it bird by bird. And that's something we can learn to do, too.

Both rock climbers and inventors use the language of "solving problems," and they take similar approaches to effort: breaking the larger challenge down into smaller pieces, addressing one at a time. Though this advice might seem pedestrian or obvious, when you're prompted into your fixed mindset by the prospect of a high-effort situation, your vision contracts as your anxiety and self-focus expand. This can cause you to forget the basic tactic of one step at a time. One of the reasons stories like those of Megos and the McBride sisters are effective at gearing us toward growth is that we see how others broke down a major accomplishment into manageable chunks. To countless others, the prospect of making and shipping 25,000 cases of wine in just a few months would have been a nonstarter, but the sisters were successful because they didn't try to make and ship 25,000 cases. Instead, they focused on what needed to be done next—on choosing grapes and constructing the varietals, on getting the applications filed and the labels printed. Each of those tasks was doable. We each can cultivate this ability to isolate our next one or two steps and start there. And if we have trouble doing this, we can ask trusted advisors, like peers, managers, or mentors.

The same advice applies to managers making high-effort assign-ments: Don't toss people in the deep end. To encourage employees into their growth mindsets, dial up the challenge and struggle in-crementally. A good tennis coach doesn't hand you a racket and say, "Good luck!" Instead, they show you how to hold the racquet, then how to hit a forehand. When you've had some success, they teach you the backhand, and so on. If you give an employee too much too fast, they are more likely to become overwhelmed by the percep-tion that they don't have the strategies or resources required to be successful. By exposing them to incremental levels of challenge, you help them build the skills they need to progress bird by bird.

Self-Affirmation

Another tactic we can deploy at the individual level comes from one of my PhD mentors, Claude Steele, and another of his students, Geoff Cohen, called self-affirmation. The core tenet behind the idea of self-affirmation is that most of us want to see ourselves as good at something—competent, moral, and effective. When we encounter a high-effort situation and we have an underlying belief that if we have to try hard, we're not good at it, effort undermines our ability to see ourselves in these positive ways. High-effort situations become an indictment of who we are and challenge our core beliefs about ourselves. When these situations occur at work, we feel even more threatened. So many of us tie a chunk of our identities to our work (according to Gallup, 55 percent of Americans get a sense of iden-tity from their work, and of those with a college degree the number is 70 percent) that when our ability to do our work well becomes threatened, it makes us question who we are.

The process of self-affirmation broadens our sense of ourselves so that we are less affected by the fear and doubt that a high-effort situation can incite. The first step is to list out every identity and group membership and role that you have as an individual that is important to you. (And you need to actually write them out, not just list them out loud or in your mind.) So, you might write, *I'm a sister, a mother, a Texan, I'm a friend, a dog lover*, and so on. Once you have the list, rank the identities from most to least important. Then, strike out the one that is threatened at the moment, such as *employee*. Next, spend 15 to 20 minutes writing about your three highest traits or characteristics (or next highest, if the one you just crossed out ranks among the top three). Focus your writing on how important those roles are to you and others, and the positive impact that role has in your life or the lives of others.

According to Steele, and to several researchers who expanded on his initial work, this helps you see yourself more broadly. When one aspect of your identity comes into question because you are at the precipice of a high-effort situation that you just aren't sure you can accomplish, you're less threatened by it because you have a broader sense of who you are than just that one role. And not only are we less threatened when we practice self-affirmation, we're also more engaged, and so we're more likely to triumph in those high-effort situations.

Reprogram Your Core Beliefs

One of the most powerful ways to shift to our growth mindset is to reprogram our beliefs about the relationship between effort and ability. Again, storytelling is one of the most effective ways to do this. In addition to the earlier examples, there's rapper and business executive Shawn Carter (more commonly known as Jay-Z), who was turned down by every major record label he approached. This rejection led him to become a producer himself and start Roc-A-Fella Records. The list goes on (and could make a great research project for students to help create a classroom culture that shifts everyone toward growth). And sometimes the example could be you. Sharing your own story of struggle is not only a powerful learning tool for others, but also helps you see your own experience as a story that's still being told.

Remember the Stanford Duck Syndrome? To counter this, my own PhD cohort decided to opt out of the pond. Once a week, we had a happy hour where, in addition to just having fun, we talked about our challenges and struggles and how much work we were putting in. We also agreed as a group to help and support one another. Rather than compete with one another, we would take a team approach and put in the required work together. The work was still hard and required lots of effort, but much of it came to be enjoyable, and we felt like we could be challenged *and* learn *and* be successful. And better yet, we could do it together. In an attempt to decrease anxiety and depression among coeds there, Cornell's CAPS staff also worked to normalize struggle.

As a leader, you can engage in and encourage storytelling in a similar way. One of the most impactful stories you can share with employees is your own. Share your struggle stories. By helping employees understand that the way you get better is through meaningful, sustained effort, you can release some of the pressure and fear around being judged as lacking (or decrease the inclination to self-judge). Also, let them know that you *want* them to feel adequately challenged so they will continue to grow and remain excited and engaged but that you're also there to provide the resources and support they need to be successful.

Call on the Community

One of the reasons high-effort situations can be so daunting is that we often think we need to go it alone. By leaning on one another, my Stanford cohort increased our collective and individual capacity. We wanted to learn and grow as individuals, but that didn't mean we had to do it by ourselves. One simple but powerful question can play a major role here: "What are my resources?" When we ask ourselves that question (or mentor our employees to ask it), we teach ourselves how to identify the people who can assist us.

Key to achieving success as an individual is learning how to identify, engage, and learn from the skills of others. We can say the same about organizations—that learning to look outside our own walls, to be open and honest about the challenges facing us, and to actively engage others in supporting us makes high-effort tasks more achievable. There is power in teams that create their own microcultures of growth around them.

Tune the Environment to Growth

Just like our teachers and their classroom agreements, leaders can set team and organizational agreements that tune the environment to growth. As I mentioned earlier, some organizations such as Google re-form teams frequently, thereby putting employees in repeat high-effort situations. In such situations, it's essential to surround employees with a Culture of Growth focused on collaboration over competition, where they feel safe making mistakes and helping one another improve over time. By working with different people in different parts of the business, employees have ongoing opportunities to learn, and to share their own knowledge and ideas beyond what a typical static structure would enable. Yet this ideal only becomes reality when the culture supports it.

Consider how you might have the equivalent of back-pocket problems ready for your employees or yourself when you're not feeling challenged. According to 2022 data from Gallup, only 21 percent of employees report feeling engaged at work. As any HR exec will tell you, lack of engagement is a major challenge to employee retention, so keeping employees on a growth trajectory isn't just good for their careers, it's also good for the bottom line. For individuals, those back-pocket problems can look like putting yourself on your manager's radar for stretch assignments and flat-out asking for new challenges. Maybe your manager has a task on their plate that's become easy for them that they'd be happy to offload to you. This gives you a chance to grow and provides your manager more bandwidth to take on novel opportunities of their own.

QUESTIONS FOR REFLECTION

♦ Think of a time in the past when you found yourself drifting toward your fixed mindset in the face of a high-effort situation— it could be a work situation, a family situation, or something else. How did it feel to find yourself slipping toward your fixed mindset? What did you tell yourself? What did you do? What would you tell your former self now that would have been useful to hear? How would you mentor yourself toward your growth mindset?

♦ What's your growth mindset story around high-effort situations? When have you found yourself responding from your growth mindset? What did you tell yourself? What did you do? What was the outcome? Can you share this story with your peers or direct reports and encourage them to share their own?

♦ Thinking about strengths through a growth mindset lens, what are the strengths you'd like to *develop* in your life (even if developing those strengths might require a lot of effort)? What is one step you can take today to move you closer to developing a new strength in your life?

♦ Where is there an effortful situation in your life right now? What can you do to remind yourself that effort is for building ability (rather than a sign that you lack it)? When I got a Peloton, I established a goal of riding it four to five times a week—but it was hard! (I had never cycled and the seat hurt . . . a lot!) I put a sticky note on my screen that read, "Just 20 minutes a day"—because that's all I needed to build ability. How can you remind yourself about the positive correlation between effort and ability?

♦ Finally, how can you track whether the effort you're putting in is *effective effort*? What are the small, measurable signs you're making progress, however incremental, toward your goal? (Remember, incremental is good, sustainable, and better for people in the long term.)

CHAPTER 11

Critical Feedback

You just received an email from your boss: "Let's schedule a catch-up this week. I'd like to give you some feedback." Or perhaps as you were heading out to work this morning your spouse said, "Let's make some time this weekend to talk about us." When you know feedback is coming, how do you feel? Do you dread it and find yourself bracing for impact? Or do you get excited and find yourself looking forward to hearing what they have to say? Sometimes critical feedback stokes anxiety and sometimes it heralds opportunity. Sometimes it's a mixture of both. And that's why critical feedback is our third mindset trigger.

As a quote commonly attributed to Aristotle goes, "Criticism is something we can avoid easily by saying nothing, doing nothing, and being nothing." Whether it's a performance evaluation, an exam score, or a Yelp review, we're all destined to receive critical feedback. (No offense to Aristotle, but saying and doing nothing can prompt criticism, as well.) Different from evaluative situations—where people are in preparation mode and *anticipate* the possibility of a positive or negative assessment—with the critical feedback trigger, people actually receive some kind of evaluation. When we are triggered into our fixed mindset by critical feedback, we tend to respond defensively when it arrives, often discounting the validity of the assessment or the knowledge or skills of the person offering it, or simply not seeing or processing the criticism at all.

When viewed through the lens of our fixed mindset, we perceive critical feedback as a pronouncement on whether we are good or bad at our job or at a particular skill or task—or, at the more extreme end, whether we are a good or bad person. Our attention narrows and we zoom in on ourselves, believing that the critique is about us as a person rather than our work or our behavior. When we overfocus on ourselves, we often miss the opportunities that critical feedback can offer: Rather than seeing possibility, we see a pronouncement. Our fixed mindset tells us that people either have natural abilities or lack them. That's why so-called negative feedback can be particularly threatening. We hear it and think, "I guess I'm just not good at that," and believe we have no recourse for improvement.

At other times, critical feedback may prompt us toward our growth mindset. Through this lens, we experience critical feedback as an opportunity that provides insights about where our work or approach could use improvement—information that's essential if we wish to strengthen our work or expand our capabilities. Actionable criticism has the potential to help us assess where we are so we can plot a course to where we want to be. When viewed from our growth mindset, we not only perceive critical feedback as a chance to learn and grow, but we may also feel annoyed or frustrated when others shy away from providing it, or when the feedback they offer is vague or not useful.

When we first encounter critical feedback, it's common for our internal voice to say, "Ouch!" Remember that when Barre3 cofounder and CEO Sadie Lincoln received blistering feedback through that anonymous employee survey, she was not immediately triggered into her growth mindset. When the results pointed the finger at her as the source of the company's woes, she said, "It was earth shattering." Her immediate response was to go on the defensive. In her own mind and to a few close confidants, she dismissed the criticism as unfair, criticized the criticizers, and even contemplated selling the company.

Once the immediate sting started to wear off, Lincoln turned to a circle of peers—all founders of companies—for advice. After soothing Lincoln with Tater Tots, the group helped shift into her growth mindset. Before we get into the specifics of how, first we'll zoom in on a simple but critical step Lincoln took that enabled her to shift from the initial pain to a willingness to hear and accept the feedback that was worthwhile. She paused, and in that pause she was able to defuse her emotions. The classic theory of emotions holds that (unless we're a Vulcan), emotions are something we can't control: Something happens to us, we feel an emotion, and then that emotion stimulates a bodily response. We jump up and cheer, cry, or call a friend for empathy as indicated. Neuroscientist Lisa Feldman Barrett says the data tell a different story: that we don't react to emotions, we create them. When our brain receives sensory information, it runs a series of simulations to try to answer the question, "What is this new sensory input most similar to?" In Feldman Barrett's *theory of constructed emotion*, the brain uses what she calls emotion concepts based on our past experiences, upbringing, and culture to both guide our actions and give meaning to sensations. Essentially, the brain searches through its historic database and when it matches the combination of sensations we're experiencing to an emotion concept it has on file, it constructs that emotion. This all happens so quickly that it *seems* automatic, when in reality, our brains are just that fast and good at making use of this system of matching and prediction. Sometimes, though, the match that comes back doesn't accurately describe our experience. For instance, when we feel a racing heart and sweaty palms, the brain might hastily dial up a fear response. But, we're not actually terrified because we're about to give a big presentation to our peers, we're excited. Fortunately, with some awareness, we can correct for such errors. In other words, we have far more choice than we realized about how we feel. And in that gap between stimulus and response, we have the opportunity to consciously engage our growth mindset.

Something else that aided Lincoln's shift was turning down her defensiveness so that her logical brain could engage, as well. (As research shows, our brains have a harder time hearing negative feedback when our self-protective responses are engaged.) As it turned out, someone in her peer group had expertise in research, and she encouraged Lincoln not to push the feedback away, but to dive deeper in. "She helped me process it from a data perspective and helped me get the emotion out," says Lincoln. As they stepped back to analyze the feedback, they excluded "the things that were not productive"— mostly unactionable personal comments about Lincoln. Then they tuned in to the professional insights that had been hard for Lincoln to see. Finally, another of the group shared her own experience of having learned and grown by owning tough critical feedback. "The combination of those two factors changed me," Lincoln reflects.

Especially when it's out of line with our expectations, critical feedback can be initially painful; that discomfort is something that, regardless of our mindset set point, most of us experience. However, we can exacerbate that pain when we become entrenched in our fixed mindset and let it threaten our identity as a good, competent person. As Lincoln notes, prior to Barre3's employee survey, "I was so identified with being a beloved leader [whose] worth was attached to being successful." When critical feedback showed her that her self-assessment was out of line with how others saw her, she was both hurt and upset.

When we're in our fixed mindset, we derive our self-esteem from being at the top (versus developing and learning). Feedback that says otherwise can feel disorienting, as if we're getting knocked down a peg. In response, we become like "Fragile Frankie" Merman on the show *Seinfeld* who, when faced with critical feedback, would run into the woods and sit in a ditch, or like Jack Nicholson's Colonel Nathan Jessup in *A Few Good Men*, exploding in outrage when his tactics were questioned. In the work world, this can look like simply dismissing critical feedback (or those who provide it) and even discouraging the practice of giving and receiving feedback entirely. It can also look like backing off from difficult or high-visibility assignments that, while somewhat riskier, could provide opportunities to grow. When we're in our fixed mindset, we tend to hide or play it

safe to avoid the negative feedback that could result if we stepped up
to a challenge. Instead, we can respond more like Sadie Lincoln and
move from our initial discomfort into a space where we prioritize
growth.

The Backpack Kid (and Adult)

Earlier, I described the "I Know!" Kid—the child who is unwilling
to receive advice or instruction for fear that they will be perceived
as incompetent or incapable. If the "I Know!" Kid has a comrade in
critical feedback, it is the Backpack Kid.

At our summer institute for teachers, we illustrate the fixed
mindset response to critical feedback with an all-too-common example that teachers recognize: the student who receives a graded
assignment, glances at the score, then shoves it to the bottom of their
backpack. If there is a class-wide postmortem in which the teacher
and students review a test along with the solutions and strategies
that could have been employed, the Backpack Kid often tunes out.
(Of course, this kind of behavior may not only be the result of mindset. For example, a student who receives a low grade may engage in
this behavior because they know that poor performance is likely to
garner harsh treatment at home. Here, when I'm discussing individual mindset cues, I am describing behavior and beliefs that an
individual holds about their own performance.)

We see a similar response in the workplace when employees who
receive feedback from a manager, such as an annual 360 or quarterly review, scan for their bottom-line score (and perhaps whether
they will receive a raise), and then close the document or slip it in a
drawer, rather than actually reading and reflecting on the content
of the feedback itself. And that can happen whether we receive high
marks or low; when we are in our fixed mindset, the only question
we ask is: Did I measure up or not? If the feedback indicates we have
one or more areas in which we could improve—as we'd expect it to
if the manager is operating from their growth mindset—we may slip

into defensive mode. We may seek the companionship of colleagues who we know to be below-grade performers, dismiss the manager (*They don't know what I'm actually doing!*), or make other excuses (*I'm on a weak team!*). In any event, the opportunity to learn is lost.

Before we look at how to shift to our growth mindset in the face of others' assessments (or encourage employees to do so), first we'll explore the research about how our mindsets influence our desire and ability to receive, interpret, and leverage critical feedback.

HOW MINDSET INFLUENCES THE WAYS WE FILTER FEEDBACK

Do you want to be *better, or* feel *better*? That's the question that confronts us when we're presented with critical feedback. At the heart of the matter lies self-esteem.

When feedback runs counter to the way we view ourselves, what determines whether we'll tackle the issue head-on, through direct action, or whether we'll become defensive? To answer that question, my grad school friend David Nussbaum and Carol Dweck ran a series of studies. In each, university students were divided into two groups and shifted toward their fixed or growth mindset by a short, scientific-style article that they were asked to read. One article proclaimed that "current research shows that almost all of a person's intelligence is either inherited or determined at a very young age"—a fixed mindset view; while the other article stated, "current research shows that intelligence can be increased substantially"—a growth mindset perspective. Next, to challenge their self-esteem, the researchers gave participants just four minutes to read a dense, lengthy, rather confusing excerpt from Freud's *The Interpretation of Dreams*. Participants then took an eight-question reading comprehension quiz.

After supposedly scoring their test, researchers told participants that their performance had landed them in the thirty-seventh percentile of students at the university—a score they expected would shock and dismay the participants. At this point in the study, the participants were presented with the critical measure: As they prepared to undergo a speed-reading challenge, they were shown a list with the scores of eight past study participants, which ranged from the fourteenth to the ninety-eighth percentile, and told they were welcome to click on past participants to see the strategies they had employed when they completed the same task. Participants who had been shifted toward their fixed mindset tended to respond defensively by choosing to review strategies of prior participants who had performed *worse* than they did. This let them feel better about themselves in the moment (*Ha! Look at what that guy did wrong!*), but it didn't give them any insight as to how to improve in the next round. However, those who were shifted toward their growth mindset largely opted to view the strategies of those who had done *better* than they had, putting themselves in a position to learn new or different strategies before the next test.

Nussbaum and Dweck's research studied conscious behavior in the face of explicit negative feedback. However, neuroscience indicates that when we occupy our fixed mindset, it's possible that we may not even notice critical feedback. Using electroencephalographic technology (EEG scans), researchers evaluated brain activity among groups of students when they were asked questions. In one study, college students were asked to complete a general knowledge task (answering questions such as, "What is the capital of Australia?"). Following each question, they were first shown whether their answer was correct or incorrect, and, if incorrect, they were shown the correct answer. By dividing the feedback into two portions, the researchers could monitor what happened in participants' brains when they were first given an overall indication of performance, and then what happened when they were provided with a learning/corrective opportunity.

Regardless of the participants' mindset set points, the scans showed that they all had similar brain activity when they initially viewed the performance feedback: Getting things wrong felt bad to everyone. However, when they were provided with the corrective feedback, participants in their growth mindset showed far more activity in an area of the brain associated with error correction. It's important to underscore that this was *preconscious* neural activity—they didn't have to think about it, their brains were literally geared toward growth. Subsequently, participants in their growth mindset performed better on a surprise re-test of the material. Additional studies support the theory that when we're in our growth mindset, our brain *automatically* attends to our mistakes and looks for ways to correct them, making it easier for us to engage in better responses in the future. This suggests that our beliefs about the fixedness or malleability of intelligence can actually bias our brain toward rendering those beliefs a self-fulfilling prophecy. Research also shows that our mindsets have a significant impact on the accuracy of our self-assessments, especially in the face of failure.

In a 2020 edition of her *Dare to Lead* podcast, research professor and author Brené Brown interviewed Harvard professor and author Sarah Lewis. In the interview, Lewis describes a space she calls *blankness*, which she says is how it feels when "the feedback you receive forces you to have to wipe clean your field of possibility and reimagine yourself anew." Brown replies: "There's a part of me in the midst of failure that is excited and passionate about the blankness; about the starting over." Brown then proposes that shame is the enemy of blankness. "[Y]ou can't seize the opportunity of blankness if you are belittling yourself about the failure."

Lewis agrees, as do I, and research supports Brown's idea. When we feel shame because of critical feedback, we often are taking the feedback personally—as an assessment of us as an individual, which is an indicator that we are in our fixed mindset. As we've just seen, our fixed mindset also may, at the neuronal level, render us less able to "seize the opportunity of blankness." It's harder to reimagine ourselves and recalibrate our self-assessments if we're focused on our inherent lack of ability or worth instead—or on disproving or discrediting the feedback.

We have these types of reactions to interpersonal and societal situations too. If, for example, one is confronted with an accusation of having said or done something racist, our fixed mindset takes over all too easily. Our immediate response is often defensive, such as offering excuses for the behavior—*That wasn't my intent*, or, *I didn't mean it like that!* These kinds of accusations, too, are a form of critical feedback. When someone points to questionable or flat-out unacceptable behavior, in our fixed mindset we feel like we're a bad person, and research shows that we tend to lash out—labeling the person who highlighted our behavior as too sensitive or as a complainer, even though they might have been trying to help us. Sadly, in our fixed mindset, we tend to discredit the feedback rather than trying to learn from it. Some of the research I've done with my collaborators Aneeta Rattan, Katie Kroeper, Rachel Arnett, and Xanni Brown shows that in our growth mindset, we become less defensive in response to even this type of critical feedback and, importantly, we are more willing to believe that confronting racism (sexism, and so on) is a viable way to help others improve as well.

If, like Brown, we are triggered into our growth mindset by critical feedback, information about where we came up short and how we could do better is more salient to us. Research reveals that this enhanced salience actually makes us better able to filter the quality of feedback we receive to determine what's relevant and helpful for our growth, and what we can discard—mirroring the process Sadie Lincoln went through when analyzing the employee feedback with her peer group.

When we're in our growth mindset, our learning and development are priorities, so we are constantly attending to where we are and recalibrating our perceptions and expectations, fine-tuning our self-awareness in these areas. We're able to engage in a more subtle discernment process when faced with critical feedback than when we're in our fixed mindset. When we do receive feedback that doesn't comport with where we believe we are, we are better equipped to evaluate its usefulness.

The Dunning-Kruger effect is a type of cognitive bias in which we tend to overestimate our knowledge or our abilities in defined areas. The concept comes from research in which social psychologists David Dunning and Justin Kruger tested participants on a variety of factors, including logic and sense of humor. As it turned out, many of those who performed the worst rated themselves as having above-average skills. The researchers concluded that such gaps in self-awareness are the result of a *dual burden*: Our lesser ability actually keeps us from realizing that we have lesser ability. It's hard to know what we don't know.

In subsequent work, Joyce Ehrlinger, along with Ainsley Mitchum and Carol Dweck, looked at how mindset influences our tendency to fall prey to the better-than-average bias of the Dunning-Kruger effect. Their studies showed that those who tend to operate in their growth mindset are more likely to offer better-calibrated, more accurate self-evaluations—again, because they are motivated to improve. To improve, you first have to know where you stand. Thus, people operating from their growth mindset tend to engage in more self-assessment (not less) to determine where they are on their own path and what they need to do to move forward. In our fixed mindset, because we're not fully and accurately perceiving our mistakes and missteps, we're not as well calibrated and end up with a lower degree of accurate self-awareness. We take on the easy tasks, excel at them, and ultimately end up thinking more highly of our abilities. When the tasks become more challenging, we're likely to stumble on the high-effort trigger or the critical feedback trigger, or both.

Some of us are so chronically oriented toward growth that we shift quickly to learning mode, as Brené Brown touched on when she said that part of her was excited at the prospect of a canvas wiped clean by a failure. Yet for many (perhaps most) of us, we experience at least an initial loss when we receive a less-than-stellar assessment. And that reaction can of course be amplified by the language in which the feedback is given or the manner in which it's delivered. Later, I'll describe strategies for delivering useful feedback that sparks people toward their growth mindset, but first let's look at how we can move into our growth mindset when we receive feedback and how we can filter feedback for maximum learning and development.

RECEIVING FEEDBACK: FLIPPING FROM FIXED TO GROWTH

As the first Black ballerina to be promoted to principal dancer in the American Ballet Theatre's 75-year history, Misty Copeland is accustomed to receiving a litany of criticism—some of it productive and helpful, some decidedly not. When a dancer is preparing a part, critical feedback is detailed and ongoing. Yet while that feedback is essential for improvement, every dancer's body and sensibilities are different and to an extent it is up to them to discern what will help them grow as a dancer, and what could lead to a career-ending injury—often a difficult distinction. In an interview with theSkimm, Copeland said that learning to filter critical feedback has been an essential tool for her success. "My body reacted to what I knew was right for it before my mind could," Copeland says. "[Learning how to listen to my body] allowed me to respectfully sift through what I took in." This points to a high degree of both physical and mental self-awareness.

Copeland has received another brand of feedback, as well: criticism focused on her body type and skin color. As she says, frequent comments that she "doesn't have the body" for dance or that her "muscles are too large" are "code words that Black dancers have experienced since the beginning of time." That it's an acceptable way of saying, "You don't have the right skin color for ballet." For some time, such feedback nearly sidetracked her; she developed unhealthy eating habits and questioned whether she indeed had what it took to achieve her goals of becoming a top dancer. (As cultural historian and author Brenda Dixon-Gottschild notes, in ballet there is a focus on assimilation and uniformity that works against Black ballerinas.

As I will describe in more detail below, identity-based criticism, or the perception of it, can act as a powerful mindset trigger.)

Copeland says she's learned that while it's important to listen to what others have to say, it's equally important to "not get lost in other people's words." In some cases, Copeland confronts race-based criticism by speaking out in interviews and re-posting some of the criticism on her own social media platform. In one post deriding her performance in *Swan Lake*, Copeland noted the race-based elements, yet also took care to acknowledge potentially valid (if subjective) points as they related to her dancing: "I am happy this has been shared because I will forever be a work in progress and will never stop learning."

Recounting the criticism she received in design school, award-winning designer and author Jessica Hische says, "At school, twenty people are happy to sh*t on your work all day long and that's actually helpful, because I don't get that kind of criticism anymore." When asked why her feelings weren't hurt by criticism, Hische explains that she's almost always been able to "take criticism as a whole package, thinking about the person that's delivering the criticism as well as the criticism itself." If a peer evaluating her work didn't attempt the same approaches or techniques in their work for which they were criticizing Hische, she placed less weight on their feedback. Instead, she emphasized the feedback of teachers who had a high standard and who had shown through their own careers that they really knew their stuff. In other words, consider the source along with what's spoken.

Let's start with how we think of critical assessments and praise. Rather than describe feedback as "good/bad" or "positive/negative," when we are in our growth mindsets, we characterize feedback by its usefulness in helping us improve or develop. When we are in our fixed mindset, the comment "This report stinks" is categorized as negative, while "This report is great" is seen as positive. Yet from our growth mindset, neither of these simplified evaluations is satisfactory. When our primary goal is learning and development, the value of the feedback we receive relates more to whether we can use it—and often critical feedback is more useful than an empty pat on the back.

Criticism and praise that contribute to growth and development are both *specific* and *actionable*. Otherwise, there is no path forward. In the example above, the feedback does contain information—that the report either missed or hit the mark—but in neither case is the information actionable. Saying "This report stinks" lacks the detail necessary to correct lesser-quality work; and saying "This report is great" provides no idea how to duplicate or even expand on our success next time.

When critical feedback shifts us toward our fixed mindset, we become overly focused on ourselves and see the assessment as a judgment of who we are. When we orient toward growth, instead of fixating on ourselves, our attention is on our larger goals and the path to attain them. Instead of thinking, "I missed the mark—I'm a failure," our response is, "I missed the mark—what do I need to do differently so that I hit it next time?"

Former Whole Foods Market CEO John Mackey writes in *Conscious Leadership* that Whole Foods is devoted to "constantly evolving [their] team," which he thinks has been crucial to their success promoting from within. Part of this effort to provide ongoing development is the company's "recycle" program, which takes leaders who were promoted too soon and, instead of firing them, backtracks them to a point at which they were successful, then provides them with detailed coaching and support to do better the next time around. Mark Dixon was once recycled: In 1988, Dixon was promoted to store team leader for a location in Dallas. As Mackey notes, the store was a stretch for the company because it was in an area with very little awareness of natural or organic foods, and Dixon struggled from the start. After two years, sales volume was low and morale among the store's team was flagging. Mackey and colleagues made the call to bring in a new store leader, yet instead of firing Dixon, they demoted him to his prior role and provided support, including additional leadership training, to help him grow in the areas where he'd been unsuccessful. Dixon went on to lead three other stores successfully, was promoted to regional vice president, then headed the entire southwest region for more than a decade. When he retired in 2020, Dixon was inducted into the Whole Foods Hall of Fame.

Without a doubt, critical feedback can make us vulnerable. It's unlikely Dixon received the news of his demotion with a cheer, yet when the leadership at Whole Foods worked with him to identify a way forward, he was able to engage his growth mindset to take on the task. In a moment, we'll learn some specific tactics we can employ to open ourselves to the opportunities feedback has to offer. First, let's look at some potential pitfalls for those giving feedback, and how to avoid them.

GIVING WORTHWHILE FEEDBACK: HOW TO AVOID SHIFTING OTHERS TOWARD THEIR FIXED MINDSET

How we deliver feedback can influence whether someone is prompted toward their fixed or growth mindset. Helping to nudge someone toward growth starts with shifting into our own growth mindset *before* we begin the evaluation process. If we tend to be triggered into our fixed mindset by feedback, we likely struggle giving growth-minded feedback to others. Making the shift starts with how we think about the goals of feedback. Do we think of feedback as an indictment or an opportunity? Do we see the task of giving feedback and evaluating others' work as the downside of managing people, or do we view it as an essential component to spur their development? Once we've minded our own mindset around critical feedback, we're more likely to be able to give growth-minded feedback to others.

Just as feedback is not helpful if it's vague, it's also not helpful if it focuses on perceived innate talents ("You're a genius!"). Most of us enjoy a pat on the back, yet at times **nonspecific praise that is**

untethered to our actual work and behavior can trigger us into our fixed mindsets, prompting us to engage in more conservative, risk-averse behavior in the future.

Imagine this: You spend weeks preparing a presentation and after you finally deliver it, your boss says, "Nice job on that presentation!" and is off to the next meeting. Initially, that feels great, but as the compliment fades, you're left to wonder, "What did they like about it? And how do I do that again?" You know *something* worked, but without a clear line of sight on what, when it comes time to prepare the next presentation, you're likely to try to blindly repeat the formula for your past success for fear of losing "great presenter" status—without knowing what that formula really is. You're also unlikely to try to build on what worked (How could you without knowing what it was?) or to innovate further.

Now picture instead: Your boss says, "That was a great presentation! It was concise, the story from the field you shared was impactful, and the data you cited clearly and powerfully supported your insights. Next time, I'd also love to see you offer one or two potential solutions, even if they seem like moon shots. If you leave more time for Q&A, we can discuss the ideas there." Now you not only know what worked and are feeling good from the praise, you also gained some insight into how you can make your next presentation even better. Also, it's clear that your boss is invested in your development; they welcome your ideas, and the unspoken implication is that you have a future at this company, all of which contributes to your psychological safety.

Ideally, critical feedback is ongoing rather than limited to a single annual evaluation dictated by HR. When managers normalize feedback as a routine and expected part of interactions, they lessen the likelihood that employees fear that a bomb will be dropped every time their boss pulls them aside; instead, employees grow accustomed to continuously receiving insights meant to guide their growth. In the example above, the boss offered encouragement and guidance to aim for a few moon shots when offering possible solutions. This further contributes to psychological safety because it communicates support in stretching and taking risks.

In offering growth-minded critical feedback aimed at corrective action (so-called "negative" feedback), we want to target it toward exactly what people need to improve. We want to give actionable information and strategies on how people can anticipate and overcome difficulties and achieve their goals. And we want to focus on behaviors, choices, and processes that people can control. Conversely, fixed-minded feedback usually includes a focus on innate talents or skills (*It's okay, this might just not be one of your strengths.*), or external situations out of their control (such as critiquing data in a presentation that was provided by another division), which may leave people feeling powerless.

When it comes to praise (or "positive feedback") to shift people toward their growth mindset, highlight their effective effort, the process they used, and their persistence instead of how smart or talented they are or how effortless the performance seemed, all of which moves people toward their fixed mindset. Growth-minded praise is specific about what people are doing well so that the recipient isn't left with the feeling that their work somehow succeeded through a magical, mystical process they may be hard-pressed to re-create.

CRITICAL FEEDBACK ON THE FIXED AND GROWTH CONTINUUM

FIXED ←——————————→ GROWTH	
Vague	Specific and targeted
Focuses on innate talents or skills, or external situations beyond people's control	Focuses on behaviors, choices, and processes people can control
Praises intelligence and perfection	Praises effective effort, process, and persistence

When we lay out these elements of growth-minded feedback, they're all relatively straightforward and, with some examples and practice, easy to grasp. Yet there's another layer to feedback that can be far more challenging: bias. Bias can, for example, be gendered, or invoke stereotype threat, and because it is largely unintentional, in many cases it can be exceptionally challenging to spot unless you know what you're looking for.

An example of feedback laced with unintentional bias came up during my meeting with Facebook (now Meta) staff. (To be clear, I'm not picking on Meta—as you're about to see, bias crops up everywhere and staff there recognized that this kind of feedback was problematic, if common; hence, their desire to work on it.) Now that I've primed you, see if you can you spot the unconscious bias in this feedback: "I've noticed that you aren't really participating in meetings. I'd love for you to find your voice."

That's not so bad, right? Our manager wants us to speak up; they must value what we have to say. And yet, if I asked you to guess the gender of the people to whom this feedback was most often provided, what would you say? Would you associate the phrase "find your voice" with one gender more than others? In reality, there are many reasons why someone might not speak up in a meeting. They may be more focused on listening and gathering information, and may have insights to offer at a later time. Perhaps there isn't space for them to speak up, and they're not someone who is willing to interrupt or talk over others to be heard. Then there is the known double-bind that some groups face in workplace settings: Being too quiet or too nice means you aren't assertive enough—not leadership material—but being assertive can be read as not getting along well with others. The assumption that someone is quiet during a meeting because they lack the confidence to speak up is typically applied to women, as it was in this example. When we encourage a woman to "find her voice," it conjures stereotypes about women's agency and assertiveness. (Of course, people of any gender may lack the confidence to speak up, but as I will describe later, their reasons could become apparent in a *feedback conversation* that also looks at structural factors and norms.)

Again, as managers, when we are in our fixed mindset around assessment, it's not only likely to color how we give feedback, but also whether we give it at all. We may choose to provide feedback only to star performers and largely ignore the rest. Or perhaps we are unsure of how to offer productive feedback, and instead of seeking instruction, we avoid it. As I mentioned previously, this can be particularly frustrating for employees in their growth mindset who see feedback as essential for their learning and development. Not providing feedback can actually backfire, making these people feel threatened, unseen, and as if you don't believe in their abilities to make progress. At best, growth-minded employees will press you for feedback, seek it from other managers or peers, or even seek to change teams. At worst, they may become disengaged or quit.

Bias—or, more precisely, fears about being perceived by others as biased—is another reason some managers withhold feedback. Claude Steele provides an instructive illustration of this type of situation. An elementary school teacher is hosting seasonal parent–teacher conferences. Two parents arrive, smiling and ready to hear how their son is doing. The teacher, Mrs. Williams, provides detailed praise, enumerating the areas in which he's doing well: He participates, he seems to have good relationships with his classmates, and he is well-liked. Yet she is reluctant to share her concerns about the boy's lagging academic progress. In this scenario, the student in question is Black and Mrs. Williams is White. She is well aware of negative cultural stereotypes prevalent in American society about Black people and intelligence, and is nervous that by raising her concerns about the boy's academic struggles, she will be seen as reinforcing these stereotypes. In other words, she's afraid the parents will think she's racist. Yet if she withholds this feedback from the boy's parents and, perhaps more importantly, from the boy himself, he will lose out on the opportunity to improve.

In the workplace, women, people of color, and especially women of color are more likely to experience certain forms of feedback bias from managers afraid of seeming racist, sexist, or both. Female leaders may withhold corrective feedback for fear of being seen as "catty" or mean, thereby confirming negative stereotypes about female leaders.

Yet feedback is an essential tool for self-awareness and to accurately track the progress we're making toward our goals. I referred earlier to Joyce Ehrlinger's work on accurate self-perception. Her research also revealed that inaccurate assessments of our skills can actually differ by group because leaders dole out critical feedback differentially by group. If all you ever receive are surface-level comments such as, "Good job," because your boss is worried about being judged as racist or sexist, you may come to believe there's nothing to work on. Thus, people from underrepresented groups can have more inaccurate self-perceptions when their supervisor is worried about being seen through the lens of these cultural stereotypes.

Steele and his colleagues Geoff Cohen and Lee Ross use the term *mentor's dilemma* to describe situations where people from majority groups—typically White people and men—who are in higher-status mentoring or supervisory roles are faced with the question: *Do I offer critical feedback that's going to help someone grow and develop and risk the perception that I am giving this assessment because I am racist or sexist, or do I withhold the feedback and decrease the likelihood of their succeeding?* Fortunately, their research shows that there are some surprisingly simple but effective ways to resolve the mentor's dilemma.

Wise feedback describes a series of strategies that are attuned to the ways people see themselves and make sense of the world around them. Specifically, wise interventions address three needs: our need to understand our social world so we can make appropriate decisions about our behavior; our need to see ourselves as having self-integrity (a combination of being "good," competent, and able to adapt); and our need to belong. Critical feedback can threaten any one of these in terms of our self-perception, so wise interventions seek to defuse any potential threat to these three areas. One intervention is pretty astonishing in its effectiveness given its simplicity.

Through prior research, we know that one reason Black students tend to receive lower grades than their peers is due to an element of mistrust for the school system and/or their teachers' stereotypical judgments. David Yeager and colleagues were interested in looking at interventions that could overcome these perceptions and bolster success among Black students. They recruited Black and White seventh graders who were earning Bs and Cs and asked them to write an essay about a personal hero of theirs. When the students received feedback on the essays, they were randomly assigned to one of two groups. Students in the *standard condition* group got their papers back with a note attached that read: "I'm giving you these comments so that you'll have feedback on your paper." In other words, a comment that essentially said nothing. Students in the *wise criticism condition* group received a note that read: "I'm giving you these comments because I have very high expectations and I know that you can reach them."

Of the Black students in the standard feedback group, 27 percent opted to revise their essays. Of those in the wise criticism group, more than twice as many Black students opted to try again. There was no significant difference between the two groups of White students in terms of who opted to revise their essays: The content of feedback had little effect. Why was this? The authors argue that Black students are skeptical about negative feedback regarding their intellectual abilities, given societal stereotypes that impugn their abilities—especially when it comes from a White teacher. This makes a lot of sense. At the very least, *why* the teacher is giving critical feedback is ambiguous. The feedback could be because the student legitimately needs to work on their writing skills, but it also could be because the teacher thinks Black students have inferior abilities. That's what makes the wise criticism so powerful. The feedback itself reassures Black students that the teacher believes in their ability to meet the high standards of the teacher. White students, on the other hand, generally don't have these same concerns: There is no racial stereotype that impugns their intellectual abilities. Therefore, they don't have to contend with the same ambiguity; they can just take critical feedback as a sign that they need to improve their skills.

When we receive an assessment from a boss, how we receive it and the mindset we're triggered into can be influenced by how we think our boss perceives our abilities—that is, by what we think *they* think of us, or, in the case of stereotypes, of people in our identity group. Journalist Kara Swisher says for years she edited herself at work, carefully monitoring her presentation over concern of how managers and coworkers might stereotype her if they knew she was a lesbian. (Incidentally, now Swisher says she sees more explicit biases as an indication that she's winning her argument because her conversation partner is disengaging from the facts of the discussion. "When someone tries to shut me down by calling me bossy or outspoken, that's when I go full in.") It matters whether we think that our boss has a fixed or growth mindset about our abilities, whether they think we're capable of performing at a high level. If we perceive that our manager doesn't think we can cut it—either because of bias or for some other reason—we're less likely to process their feedback with our growth mindset engaged and more likely to tune out or discount the feedback. Yet if our manager takes our perspective and precedes critical feedback with the assurance that the reason they are providing it is because they have high standards and believe we can meet them, we're far more likely to take on the challenge.

Developing genuine relationships with those to whom we're giving feedback makes what we have to say more relevant, especially when we're offering it across gender, race, or culture lines. If you don't truly know an employee and you criticize their work, it's not going to mean the same thing as if you've developed a relationship of trust and psychological safety. In the latter circumstance, people are far more likely to take the feedback to heart and act upon it.

We've already reviewed several potential pitfalls when providing feedback, along with ways to provide growth-minded feedback.

Here are a few more concrete strategies that can help you give and receive feedback more effectively.

FOSTERING A GROWTH MINDSET IN THE FACE OF CRITICAL FEEDBACK

Embedded in this chapter were a few hidden gems—hints at additional ways you can support a growth mindset around feedback. Here we unearth them, along with a few others.

Normalize Feedback

One of the most effective ways to stop critical feedback from triggering people into their fixed mindset is to normalize it. As I discussed in Part Two, organizations with strong Cultures of Growth include multiple avenues and opportunities for feedback. At Pixar, for example, animators are accustomed to daily feedback sessions in which each shows pieces of scenes they're working on and their peers provide detailed criticism. Feedback is delivered thoughtfully, constructively, and regularly. In this way, it's ingrained in the artists and everyone else working on the film that feedback isn't personal (it's just Pixar).

When feedback is a routine part of a company or team culture, it's easier to receive it to help us improve. While feedback still needs to be specific and actionable, it doesn't always have to be formal, and it definitely does not have to wait for an annual evaluation. Providing feedback in a timely manner—such as asking an employee to stay for a few minutes after a meeting—can help them course correct more quickly or repeat positive actions sooner and more reliably. Opportunities to learn and grow should be clear and consistent, not just annual. Additionally, workplaces and classrooms that are psychologically safe encourage feedback in all directions. On growth-minded teams and in growth-minded organizations, feedback is not only welcome from every source, it is viewed as an essential tool for identifying what's working and what's not at all levels.

Storytelling is another helpful tool for normalizing feedback. When we see that others have rebounded from tough criticism and when we learn about their strategies for doing so, it can help us stay oriented toward learning. For example, when Sadie Lincoln turned to her peer group for advice, one of them shared her own story of receiving difficult feedback. We can offer this. We can also seek out others' stories as a way of reaffirming that difficult feedback doesn't mean the end of the road and may be pointing to a new, more effective way forward.

Leaders can also model feedback. When James Park of Fitbit received a dismal evaluation on an employee survey, he didn't ignore it or fire back an angry retort. He considered it thoughtfully, came up with a plan of action that acknowledged the aspects of the feedback that he believed (and that the data showed) were on the mark, and shared it with his team. And for her part, by sharing it in public spaces, Misty Copeland is challenging biased feedback.

Have a Feedback Conversation

Good feedback doesn't have to be positive, as I explained at the start of the chapter, but it does have to be clear, specific, and actionable, otherwise employees have no way forward. Feedback should also be sincere, not rote. If you're giving wise feedback, for instance, you don't want to use the same introductory phrase every time or your sincerity will quickly become suspect. Similarly, beware the *feedback sandwich*. You know the one—where positive remarks form the bun around a criticism-burger. Most of us are savvy to this tactic, with the result that many view the initial positive remarks as simply a preamble meant to disarm us before the *real* feedback—the bad stuff.

One effective approach to being sincere in providing feedback is to make it a conversation rather than a presentation. Managers can ask the employee about their goals and their perceptions about how they're progressing with an emphasis on understanding what has contributed to their successes and challenges, including barriers like institutional structures or policies that could be disparately disadvantaging some employees. This allows insights and context that the manager may not have been aware of—and helps managers to see the extent to which the employee's goals align with the role or organization's goals. The manager can take actions to eliminate structural barriers and make specific suggestions as to how the employee can move forward while also eliciting ideas from the employee based on what they think might work. This not only energizes and engages employees who are already more growth-minded, but also those who might otherwise be Backpack Adults. When critical feedback is normalized and made part of a conversation rather than a decree, it's less likely to be viewed as a periodic judgment and more as a tool for ongoing development.

USEFUL FEEDBACK . . .

- Identifies specific and targeted issues
- Focuses on behaviors, choices, and processes that people can control, not innate talents or things that are otherwise out of people's control
- Acknowledges employees' efforts
- Focuses on progress and development and helps employees chart their progress
- Discusses multiple strategies and approaches to improve even further

Seek Growth-Minded Feedback

In research my team undertook in 2020, we videotaped 60 STEM faculty teaching their classes over the course of the semester. Using an app we had developed, we polled students periodically throughout the course asking them what their professors were doing and what they thought the mindset beliefs of their professors were. (We then compared these with the professors' actual beliefs, which we'd obtained through self-reports.) A big takeaway from the study was that one thing instructors can do to demonstrate a growth mindset to students is to *ask for critical feedback of themselves*. For students, how faculty handled feedback opportunities such as course evaluations was a clear indicator of the teachers' mindset. Instructors who more chronically embodied their fixed mindset saw feedback forms as a required but largely inconsequential bureaucratic hassle. Those who gravitated toward a growth mindset took them more seriously and encouraged students to complete them—often leaving time in class for students to do so. For example, in addition to the required numerical ratings, they included open-ended questions such as, "What areas did you struggle with in class and how might I have supported your learning more effectively?," "How do you think I can improve as an instructor?," and "What supports do you think would be useful for me to put in place for next year's class?"

We want to maximize the benefits of critical feedback, so why wait until the end of term to ask for it? When I was part of the Faculty Success Program—a national institute for faculty of color—we were given the advice to offer a mid-term evaluation asking simple questions such as, "What are some things you are struggling with in this course, and what might I change that could help?" Often at that point in the semester, students would express feeling overwhelmed with coursework. This gave the instructor the opportunity to take away an assignment or otherwise relieve some of the pressure on students. It didn't have to be big, but the gesture helped students feel heard and supported, and this practice communicated our interest in students' feedback. We can do this in the workplace, as well, requesting feedback from our employees or holding check-ins where we ask for feedback and assess how we're each making progress toward our goals and how we might assist each other (or if they're ahead of where they thought they'd be, offer concrete praise about what they've done well and a back-pocket challenge as a stretch goal).

As employees, if we have a manager who is triggered into their fixed mindset by critical feedback, they may be reluctant to provide it. When we receive little or no feedback, or when feedback seems vague or insincere, we can increase our chances of getting necessary information by directly asking for it, using the same guidelines as above for giving useful feedback. We can request specific feedback on our work and on how we're progressing, ask for strategies and insights on how we might improve further, and so on. I haven't studied this strategy, but you might even try something akin to wise feedback on your boss. "I have high standards for my own performance. It's important to me that I keep developing and growing, and I know that you can provide insight and guidance that will help me do that." (And let me know how that works!)

Next, we'll explore our last mindset trigger: the success of others. But first, some reflection.

QUESTIONS FOR REFLECTION

♦ Remember the last time you received critical feedback that shifted you to your growth mindset and helped you take action to improve. What did the person offering it say, and how did they say it? Reach out and thank the person. Consider acknowledging how vulnerable it can be to give critical feedback and how grateful you are for how they helped you receive it in the spirit in which it was intended.

♦ The next time you find yourself giving someone else critical feedback, consider making your belief about their ability to change explicit. How can you more explicitly communicate that you're providing this feedback because you believe in the person and their ability to change or improve?

♦ When critical feedback triggers us toward our fixed mindset, remember that it often causes us to turn inward, and the self-focus leaves us feeling lonely and isolated. With your trusted

Culture of Growth partner or pod, role play giving and receiving critical feedback. What strategies work best to shift you—as giver and receiver—toward growth?

♦ Have you noticed that you're not really getting much critical feedback from others? Ask yourself why. In the past, have you received feedback in a way that makes it less likely that people will give you critical feedback in the future? Make a few notes about how you can ask for some next week. Remember to be specific about the feedback you're looking for. Instead of asking broad questions like, "What did you think of my presentation?" consider asking questions that can motivate action. "Did my presentation make you feel interested? Curious? Wanting to learn more? Next time, how do you think I could make the work more engaging to the client?"

CHAPTER 12

Success of Others

You open your alumnae newsletter to find that a classmate in your field has just been promoted. Your company's been working for months to solve a problem and though you're sure you're close to a solution, your coworker cracks the code first. Are you inspired, or dejected? Do you offer a high five, or toss darts at their photo? Do you double down on your efforts, or give up? Your answer indicates how you tend to respond to the fourth common mindset trigger: the success of others.

Using someone else as a yardstick is neither good nor bad. When someone's accomplishments inspire us to identify the gaps in our own performance or the steps we may need to take to realize similar accomplishments, then the success of others prompts us into our growth mindset. But when that person becomes a frenemy or nemesis and their success makes us want to give up or, alternatively, take them down because we perceive this office isn't big enough for the both of us, we've engaged our fixed mindset.

When we observe others' achievements through our fixed mindsets we slip into zero-sum territory, perceiving a scarcity in which there is now less opportunity for us. It's another form of extreme self-focus. When we see someone succeed, we think things like, "She's so good—I'll never achieve at that level. Why even try?" or "They've got some special talent that I don't." One of the downsides of shifting into our fixed mindset when others are successful is that it deprives us of the opportunity to understand potential strategies and pathways. (And it deprives them of recognition, along with sincere connection from colleagues.) We don't take the time to dig deeper because it's so self-threatening that we don't look further into what the person actually did to become successful. And if we think their success must be due to some inherent talent we don't possess, it feeds our fixed mindset: We see success as out of our control, and so we don't attempt to puzzle out how we might achieve it.

Yet, it's possible that these same situations can nudge us toward our growth mindset, where we get curious about what we can learn from others' success. Our path likely won't look exactly the same, and indeed, we may not have the same privileges or resources as others, but identifying core elements of what worked can help us along our way. For instance, someone may have had a leg up because their parent was able to make some key introductions for them in the industry. We may not have that kind of backdoor access, but we can look at that and understand that if we want to have similar opportunities, we're going to need to build our network. We can be creative and authentic in how we approach that, including looking to others who've done it and seeking insight and support from our pod. In *Every Other Thursday: Stories and Strategies from Successful Women Scientists*, Ellen Daniell writes about how as women, when many in her network of women STEM professors saw others in their field highlighting and taking credit for their achievements, they initially viewed it as somehow wrong, embarrassing, or distasteful. When they shifted to their growth mindset, they were able to recognize that as women, they'd been socially programmed to downplay their accomplishments. From that point they worked with one another to practice engaging both pride and humility in accepting compliments and owning their professional achievements.

One of the biggest challenges in addressing this mindset trigger is acknowledging it. Inevitably, when I ask workshop participants how many people identify success of others as one of their fixed mindset triggers, silence often ensues. But later, it's the one that almost everyone wants to discuss privately with me. It's understandable. While owning up to any type of situation that engages our fixed mindset requires some degree of vulnerability, there is perhaps none more vulnerable than the success of others. It's likely that people are reluctant to share because when we're open about who we're comparing ourselves to—or the fact that we're comparing ourselves at all—in a way, it gives the other person power over us. If Anthony in Accounting admits that when his colleague, Jacquie, was awarded a spot that he'd been working toward, it clues Jacquie in to the fact that Anthony is, at least to some extent, measuring his success against hers. Also, we don't want to appear selfish or withholding to others, even if that's how we feel inside.

But hey, there's nothing wrong with engaging a little "friendly competition" to get people motivated, right? As we've seen, interpersonal competition can create a very fine line that can bring out the best or the worst in us (depending on our mindset in the moment)— one so fine as to perhaps not be worth the risk. In spite of corporate leaders' affinity for competitive sports analogies, there are other ways to encourage folks to give it their all than to set them up to vie with one another for finite resources. Yet even in the sports world, where competition seems fundamental to advancement, plenty of examples exist of athletes triggered into their growth mindset by the success of others.

Rivalries make for some of the most memorable sports moments. Frazier–Ali. Palmer–Nicklaus. Johnson–Bird. Yet without a doubt, one of the most memorable and longest running was the 15-year rivalry between tennis legends Chris Evert and Martina Navratilova. The pair were so dominant in the sport that, for more than a decade, one or the other of them was always the top-ranked player of the year. For perspective, Joe Frazier and Muhammad Ali fought three times, while Evert and Navratilova battled it out in more than 80 matches. Evert chalked up 125 straight tournament victories on clay. Navratilova garnered a staggering 354 titles across singles, doubles, and mixed doubles.

In the course of the Evert–Navratilova rivalry, it wasn't bitterness that developed, but deep respect and even friendship. And more important for their careers, each says the presence of the other helped them raise their game. For Navratilova, facing off against Evert was like confronting "an impenetrable wall," and she says Evert's mental fortitude motivated her to become tougher. Evert was nicknamed the "Ice Maiden" for her relentless stoicism on court, and yet she confesses to envying Navratilova's ability to let out her emotions. Countering Evert's emotional strength was Navratilova's physical power, which forced Evert to the gym. "I tried to follow [Martina's] example," she recalls. And that's an essential indicator that the qualities responsible for each player's success shifted both Evert and Navratilova into their growth mindsets. As the two traded victories, they looked to the other for indications as to what they could improve about their own game. As Evert says, when she lost to Navratilova, "it propelled me to work harder and be more determined . . ." That's why they were able to be friends: They looked to each other for inspiration and information, but never made the game all about the other.

The pair even practiced with one another from time to time and warmed up together before matches in which they were set to compete. It's an illustration of something my colleagues and I found in our research, which is that when we base our sense of success on our own progress rather than on outperforming others, we are more likely to offer help to others and master what we are working on by teaching them. Had either seen the other as a threat to their success, they likely never would have become friends, and for their careers, they also might never have become legends. We see examples of competitive collaboration in the running world, as well.

When Des Linden took to the streets of Boston for the city's 2018 marathon, the weather was miserable. She already hadn't been feeling right, and after a few miles of cold rain and gusty wind, Linden decided that it just wasn't going to be her day. Mentally, she dropped out, opting to save the push for another day, but instead of stepping off to the sidelines, she made an unheard-of offer to fellow runner and marathon legend Shalane Flanagan. "Hey," Linden told Flanagan, "if you need help with anything along the way, I'm happy to run through the wind for you and just kind of be a block or whatever you might need." Flanagan was the competition, but instead of being prompted into her fixed mindset by Flanagan's potential victory, Linden switched to team mode, opting to gut it out in support of her countrywoman. Flanagan herself has earned a reputation for generosity, supporting and mentoring young runners to an extent that's exceedingly rare in the ultracompetitive sport. Yet as it turned out, that day in Boston wasn't to be Flanagan's, either. Once she dropped off, Linden paced for another runner, Molly Huddle, hoping to help her reach the finish line. But, when Huddle also fell off the lead pack, Linden found that she still had steam to go. "Just one more mile," she told herself over and over again, all the way to first place.

It's easy to confuse a growth mindset in sports with just pushing harder and getting more competitive, but as studies we've reviewed show, interpersonal competitiveness actually limits our options and creativity by narrowing our strategies. Without the burden of having to prove herself, Des Linden was able to stay flexible and open to options as the minutes unfolded. She was able to constantly assess where her effort could best be directed—toward her own race, then her teammates, then back to herself. Early on, had she been turned off by the idea of one of her American rivals winning, she would have simply ended her race and left them to fend for themselves. Instead, Linden tried to do a teammate a good turn, and ended up with her first Boston victory. Linden was not unaware that helping someone else could also help her. In the running world, they call it the Shalane Effect: supporting the careers of those around you, while using that momentum to slingshot yourself forward, as well. It's the kind of win-win that directly opposes the zero-sum mentality of the fixed mindset.

Thomas Edison would likely have scoffed at the Shalane Effect. One of the world's most celebrated and prolific inventors, Edison applied for his first patent at age 21 and by the time his career was complete, he had received 1,093 patents for his inventions. Or rather, for his *team's* inventions. Though Edison was an intellectual giant in his own right, his ego was reportedly equally large, and he routinely diminished or erased the importance of the significant contributions made by his highly engaged squad of Menlo Park engineers. Though Edison is still widely hailed as a visionary to be admired, less discussed is his decidedly fixed mindset behavior when faced with the success of others (along with the fact that Edison is known to have flat-out taken credit for others' work).

Interestingly, though Edison is praised as someone who "had enough genius to see the genius in others," when it came to identifying the genius of one of his employees—a young man from Serbia named Nikola Tesla—Edison shifted straight to his fixed mindset, with disastrous consequences. At the time, Edison had declared that through a system of direct current (DC), his company would soon power homes and industry across the country. Though he and his team had succeeded in creating dynamos and power stations, they struggled to deliver the DC current more than a mile from the station. Inspired by the challenge, Tesla created a design for a dynamo that would work using alternating current (AC). Edison dismissed the design as impractical and dangerous; he had already announced to the world that DC was the way to go. Frustrated, Tesla quit. Eventually, he pitched his plan to one of Edison's chief rivals in the power business, George Westinghouse.

"Edison's great weakness [was] his inability to shift his mindset as the industry changes," says Paul Israel, director and general editor of the Thomas A. Edison Papers project. "He was invested both financially and [with] his personal reputation." During some of his darkest days, Edison partnered with an unscrupulous disciple and authorized torturous experiments on stray dogs, horses, and other animals aimed at proving that AC was deadly. He also embarked on a smear campaign that included lobbying officials to use AC current for the first electric chair so that AC would be thought of as "the death current."

At one point, Westinghouse offered to partner with Edison to end the current war and speed adoption of AC, but Edison refused. In the end, Edison lost the confidence of his own board, who consolidated his company and left him with just 10 percent of the company's stock.

It's natural to measure ourselves against others. As those in our field achieve greater recognition, it moves the goal for everyone. We attend to these advances because we care about our position—in our field, in the social and professional hierarchy, in our work. And when others achieve success, we may find ourselves in our fixed mindset. Yet we can learn to transition to an attitude of learning. Historians speculate that if at any point Edison had opted to incorporate AC, his massive operation could have overtaken Westinghouse; but to him, it was a matter of reputation. For Edison, it was personal, but sometimes, our fixed mindset is shaped by the structural and institutional factors that surround us. Everything from collaboration and innovation to creativity suffers when people are pitted against one another by a system designed for limited recognition and resources. Unfortunately, organizations often institutionalize such competition.

SCARCITY FROM THE TOP

When the zero-sum belief is instituted into an organization's policies and procedures, it can move everyone toward their fixed mindset. In these cases, the Culture of Genius comes from the top.

Perhaps no other practice illustrates the zero-sum mentality and activates the success-of-others fixed mindset trigger more than stack ranking—a system I described earlier in which employees are routinely evaluated, then placed into brackets, with those at the top rewarded and those at the bottom replaced. The practice, colloquially known as *rank and yank*, was popularized in the early 1980s by Jack Welch, then-CEO of GE. The company created three tiers:

employees in the top 20 percent, those in the middle 70 percent, and those in the bottom 10 percent, who were likely to be let go. In an article published in 2018, Welch (who died in 2020) still defended the system, saying it's not about purges, but about consistency, transparency, and candor, along with "making sure all employees know where they stand." He also claimed it should include intensive counseling and mentoring for those in the bottom tier so that they could either improve or find their way to the door. Welch wrote, "Yes, I realize that some believe the bell-curve aspect of differentiation is 'cruel.' That always strikes me as odd. We grade children in school, often as young as 9 or 10, and no one calls that cruel. But somehow adults can't take it? Explain that one to me." As it happens, forced ranking doesn't work particularly well in classrooms, either, as I'll explain in a moment. (And there's reason to question ranking of all kinds. As business journalist Arwa Mahdawi has highlighted, a fair number of those who've landed on Forbes's "30 Under 30" and similar lists have wound up facing criminal charges. Singling out stars can dramatically increase pressure to prove and perform.)

Critics of stack ranking underscore that pitting employees against one another erodes teamwork, to which Welch counters that if an organization wants teamwork to be a value, it need only identify it as such, then "evaluate and reward people accordingly." Yet these mixed messages create a confusing conflagration of priorities in the minds of employees: Should we team, or should we compete? (Incidentally, the opposite of schadenfreude—when we experience glee from others' misfortunes—is *freudenfreude*, where we revel in and celebrate others' accomplishments.) When companies try to shoehorn the value of teamwork into an environment that ranks and yanks, employees will perceive a large value–implementation gap. The company might say it values teamwork, but the ultimate valuation is determined by everyone in competition. This breeds cynicism and distrust—not just of each other, but of the company as well.

For those who say, "But those ninety percent who aren't in the bottom tier don't have anything to worry about," that's simply not true. Pushed toward their fixed mindset by the structural features of ranking-based reward and punishment systems, they fear loss of status—of doing something that could cause them to fall below the line. Those in the top tier are forced to always defend their position, which means they're less likely to share resources and help colleagues for fear that they may be overtaken in the rankings. Additionally, they end up dedicating more energy to watching others to keep an eye on their competition than focusing on how and where they can keep growing. And for those who advocate competition as a means of encouraging folks to shape up or ship out, the challenge of competition is that, again, it's a fine line. Competition, itself, may be neither inherently good nor bad (in fact, soccer legend Abby Wambach says that it is the uncertain outcome that makes competition fun for her), but given that our brain is vigilant to anything that could negatively impact our chances of survival, when we're in our fixed mindset we experience it as a threat. Stack ranking systems make the perceived threat a reality, applying dire consequences that can impair performance—and, at worst, spark unethical behavior.

In a now-famous scandal, front-line employees at Wells Fargo felt forced to create false accounts as a means of meeting quotas and keeping their jobs. Fierce competition for limited jobs was the major reason employees at the erstwhile *News of the World* and several other of Rupert Murdoch's papers say they committed illegal acts ranging from phone hacking and police bribery to flat-out fabrication of stories. And according to former managing director Jamie Fiore Higgins, relentless competition and frequent firings at Goldman Sachs often prompted employees to try to make one another look like poor performers to secure their own status. Once a Culture of Genius, Microsoft learned firsthand how interpersonal competition can negatively impact business outcomes.

A "decade littered with errors, missed opportunities, and the devolution of one of the industry's innovators . . ." This was how Kurt Eichenwald characterized Microsoft's prior ten years in a 2012 *Vanity Fair* article. Eichenwald interviewed dozens of the company's past and current executives. He wrote, "Every current and former Microsoft employee I interviewed—every one—cited stack ranking as the most destructive process inside of Microsoft, something that drove out untold numbers of employees." A software developer told the reporter, "If you were on a team of ten people, you walked in the first day knowing that, no matter how good everyone was, two people were going to get a great review, seven were going to get mediocre reviews, and one was going to get a terrible review. It leads to employees focusing on competing with each other rather than competing with other companies." To describe the situation at Microsoft when he became CEO, Satya Nadella pointed to a well-known cartoon with a mock organizational chart showing guns pointing in every direction.

Eichenwald wrote, "Supposing Microsoft had managed to hire technology's top players into a single unit before they made their names elsewhere—Steve Jobs of Apple, Mark Zuckerberg of Facebook, Larry Page of Google, Larry Ellison of Oracle, and Jeff Bezos of Amazon—regardless of performance, under one of the iterations of stack ranking, two of them would have to be rated as below average, with one deemed disastrous." As it happens, one of the casualties of Welch's rank-and-yank system was David Cote, who went on to become the CEO of Honeywell. (Ironically, when Cote took the reins at Honeywell, his first task was to rescue it from ruin thanks to a botched merger with GE.)

At Microsoft, for an employee in such a Culture of Genius, even achieving your goals didn't guarantee safety because it was always possible that a colleague could achieve them better. Employees became more focused on suppressing their colleagues than on innovating. As one engineer told Eichenwald, "One of the most valuable things I learned was to give the appearance of being courteous while withholding just enough information from colleagues to ensure they didn't get ahead of me on the rankings." When it came time to rank employees, as many as 30 supervisors gathered in a closed-door meeting, haggling over who should fall where, all the while keeping a laser focus on their own best interests.

As Margaret Heffernan emphasizes in a TED Talk, most organizations have spent the past fifty years or more adhering to pecking orders in which "success is achieved by picking the superstars—the brightest men, or occasionally women, in the room—and then giving them all the resources and all the power. And the result has been ... aggression, dysfunction, and waste. If the only way the most productive can be successful is by suppressing the productivity of the rest, then we badly need to find a better way to work and a richer way to live."

Suppressing Diversity and Innovation

The uber- (or Uber-) competitive, brilliant-jerks atmosphere of the Culture of Genius has more losers than winners. One of the biggest losers is the company when employees who are either not in the spotlight or not attracted to an atmosphere of fierce individualism leave. Research indicates that this is more likely to happen with women and people of color, who, on average, are motivated more by communal goals than by cutthroat interpersonal competition. Many years ago, Microsoft's hypercompetitive culture nearly cost it one of its rising stars. Yet instead of quitting, Melinda French decided to give Microsoft one more chance, on her own terms. To that point, she'd been doing her best to mimic her male colleagues and play by the unspoken rules of the bro culture that surrounded her. Rather than quit, she decided to take a huge risk: being herself. She would lead her team the way she wanted to, focusing on teamwork and inclusivity. (In her TED Talk, Harvard Business School professor Frances Frei identifies authenticity as a necessary element of engendering trust.) Before long, the former Microsoft exec, now Melinda French Gates, says, other team leaders were wondering how it was she was attracting so many of the company's best employees to her team. As it turned out, while these employees still wanted to be part of a high-performance culture, many were more interested in achieving those goals together. In this way, French Gates was successful in navigating a notorious Culture of Genius by creating her own Culture of Growth—and it attracted some of the best talent in the company.

People (usually management) often mistakenly believe that the prestige of the Culture of Genius, embodied by norms of interpersonal competition, will keep people sharp, keep them innovating, and keep them at the top of their game. This is simply not true. **In dozens of studies, we find that when given the choice between organizations with a Culture of Growth or a Culture of Genius, everyone—and *especially* the highest performers—prefers the Culture of Growth.** The Culture of Genius requires a vigilance to one's position and status that interferes with work and is emotionally and cognitively taxing.

In organizations I've worked with where innovation is essential, people who were part of research and development (R&D) teams that exemplified the Culture of Growth were more creative and consistently higher performing than the Culture of Genius teams. When I asked employees why they thought these performance differences emerged (even though the teams were working on very similar projects), they said that the culture their team had created allowed them to take risks and develop together. Not even financial incentives or raises could draw these folks away from their microcultures of growth and toward the more fixed-minded ones.

Working together enables greater problem-solving. A group of researchers from MIT was interested in uncovering whether there were any predictors of what makes some teams more successful than others at resolving tough challenges. Looking at 699 people working in small teams composed of two to five members, the researchers found three factors that linked reliably to group success and to what they termed high *collective intelligence*: (1) the group members had strong social skills; (2) instead of being dominated by a few, conversation included input and ideas from all members; and (3) there were women on the team. What was also interesting was what the researchers did *not* find: The collective intelligence of the group did not correlate with the average intelligence of its members or with the intelligence of its smartest member. Groups where everyone's input is solicited and valued foster the kind of psychological safety necessary for innovation. At Cultures of Growth such as Pixar, conflict isn't born of competition, but is framed as engaged and respectful friction that makes ideas better. Conversely, stack ranking promotes self-protection and mistrust, and, as research points out, in such systems women—who emerged as key drivers of the most highly productive teams—are less likely to rise to the top.

As researchers on gender and leadership Linda Carli and Alice Eagly note, in the workplace men typically display more *negative assertion*, "which involves threat, aggression, hostility, or control of others," while women tend to display more *positive assertion*, "which balances self-expression with respect for the rights of others." Because stack ranking encourages competition over mutual support and respect, organizations that make use of it inherently favor male employees. Additionally, Carli and Eagly report that when women engage in negative assertion to further their careers, it actually tends to reduce their chances of advancing, placing them in a "double bind."

According to behavioral and data scientist Paola Cecchi-Dimeglio, the very performance reviews used to create such rankings typically shortchange women. A content analysis of individual performance reviews showed that "women were 1.4 times more likely to receive critical subjective feedback (as opposed to either positive feedback or critical objective feedback)." Cecchi-Dimeglio writes that the subjectivity of reviews "opens the door" to both gender and confirmation bias, which "can lead to double standards, in that a situation can get a positive or a negative spin, depending on gender." She offers an example of a double standard on display in one manager's reviews: "[The manager noted,] 'Heidi seems to shrink when she's around others, and especially around clients, she needs to be more self-confident. But a similar problem—confidence in working with clients—was given a positive spin when a man was struggling with it: 'Jim needs to develop his natural ability to work with people.' In another case, the reviewer described a woman's 'analysis paralysis,' while the same behavior in a male colleague was seen as careful thoughtfulness."

Fewer women and people of color rising to the top tier within such systems also means less diversity at the leadership level, which may deter women and people of color from wanting to be part of these organizations in the first place. After Uber's culture challenges came to light, one of the fixers brought on board to help save the company was Bozoma Saint John, a highly regarded executive who'd been a brand manager at PepsiCo and had most recently served as Apple Music's head of consumer marketing. Saint John departed her role as Uber's chief brand officer after just one year, explaining, "When I got to Uber I was honest in my desire to go and change essentially what I thought was a challenging environment, especially for women and for people of color. At some point it became too overwhelming for me," she concluded. As we saw in Chapter 7, when competition is institutionalized, it has a disproportionate effect on marginalized groups, and it can not only turn DEI efforts into an uphill battle but can also make them appear downright hypocritical to employees.

Stack ranking isn't the only structural element within Cultures of Genius that inhibits the progression of women and people of color. In a system with few prestige roles for a handful of superstars, people's fixed mindset reactions to the success of others do, in fact, indicate some degree of lack of opportunity for them. Knowing that, on balance, there tend to be fewer roles for women and people of color can amplify this as a mindset trigger in Cultures of Genius. Institutionalized scarcity can become internalized, leading to unfortunate incidents such as women sabotaging other women, including supervisors hampering the careers of female subordinates who they deem to be a threat to their own positions. Managers can support such behavior when they—through their individual words or behaviors, or through formal company policy—pit employees against one another. In the worst cases, fixed mindset approaches can support massive ethical breaches.

As Carol Dweck and I had shown in our research, newcomers to a field look to the mindset beliefs of prominent figures to determine what characteristics are valued in that field. Subsequently, my team's analysis showed that when students perceive that their STEM professors endorse more fixed mindset beliefs, they are less likely to show interest in pursuing STEM careers. When they perceive that professors endorse growth mindset beliefs, they are more likely to believe that a career in STEM will allow them to meet goals that serve them individually, as well as society as a whole. Cultures of Growth have policies, practices, and norms that communicate that employees can meet a much wider range of their goals, from communal (helping, prosocial, and relatedness) goals to more independent and agentic goals. Connection and belonging are drives shared by all. Cultures of Genius, where leaders typically lead from their fixed mindset, are likely to be less attractive not only to women and people of color, but to all applicants with communal goals.

Competition is not the only way to spark motivation, growth, and achievement. When it comes to the success of others, we can encourage ourselves and those around us into our growth mindset by making one person's success the group's success, and vice versa. When Pierre Johnson, Max Madhere, and Joseph Semien arrived at Xavier University in New Orleans roughly two decades ago, they were strangers with two things in common: They wanted to become doctors, and they were Black. They also knew that in some ways, the latter would make the former harder to achieve. As we've seen earlier, academic medicine is a notorious Culture of Genius, and these men knew that their professors would not likely see them as matching the prototype of pre-med success. In fact, few do. According to the Association of American Medical Colleges (AAMC), in 2018 only 5 percent of practicing physicians were Black. Not only were they up against biases inherent in the culture of academic medicine, more immediately they had to contend with their own traumatic backgrounds that stemmed from their previous experiences. As Johnson says, "When we found each other, we were all clinically depressed." As he characterizes it, at first the three started talking about basketball, but quickly they recognized something in one another. "We looked at each other and saw just a look of determination . . . and even though we were doing poorly at that time, we knew that we had the drive. . . . We were young men that had a dream and a vision to do something bigger than ourselves." From that point, they made a pact. "We said, 'We don't know what tomorrow's going to bring, but we know we can push together." They encouraged and advised one another, all the way through undergrad and separate medical schools, and on to becoming practicing doctors.

As this powerful story further shows, when we find people who help us shift into growth mindset, we not only don't mind when others succeed, we *want* them to succeed. It's a version of the Shalane Effect. These three successful doctors are now investing in the careers of future doctors, dedicating part of their salaries to fund scholarships. Semien recalls sitting in his office one day looking at the wall where all of his degrees were posted, wondering why he didn't feel as happy as he'd expected he would at that point given all of his accomplishments. "It was because I needed to share something with someone else, to push someone not to achieve my goals, but even do better, to go beyond what I had done." Theirs is a beautiful illustration of both group and individual goals at work, showing how creating a pod with a Culture of Growth can help push through the fixed mindset messages that come from a biased system (though the system should be held accountable to change, as well). It's also an example of how a peer group can create a microculture of growth with strong psychological safety. Competition undermines psychological safety, especially in places where we need it most, like schools.

COMPETITION IN THE CLASSROOM

There is hardly a more effective way for a teacher to signal a Culture of Genius in the classroom than to seat students in order of IQ score, yet that's what happened to Carol Dweck when she was in elementary school. In a form of stack ranking, from day one students were moved immediately into their fixed mindsets as no one wanted the shame of being relegated to the back of the classroom.

While this behavior may seem extreme, we routinely expose students to a variety of highly visible ranking systems, from openly displaying class ranks and GPAs to tracking. Pressure to test into gifted and talented programs as early as kindergarten has initiated a dramatic rise in the number of tutoring companies focused on helping youngsters beat out the competition at red light, green light (a game that one school uses as part of its admissions test). Anxious parents who are privileged enough to have the resources will invest loads of energy and money into efforts to get their kids tracked toward the best colleges as early as possible.

Having experienced the zero-sum mentality as far back as elementary school, it's no wonder so many Cornell students were hanging posters over their bed admonishing themselves for sleeping while "someone else is getting ahead." By that time, social comparison could be so deeply ingrained that it's difficult to see the world any other way. Such posters and an attitude of competition may be viewed by some as a healthy form of motivation. Yet when there's a belief system that's been triggered that says that achievement is a zero-sum proposition, it can have consequences ranging from unfortunate to tragic—from hoarding knowledge and resources to suicide.

Cornell launched a massive campaign involving CAPS and their world-renowned health communication department, along with other faculty and students, aimed at helping students re-set their mindsets around, among other things, competition and achievement. Included in the campaign is education about the necessity and benefits of sufficient sleep and the importance of minding mental health, along with destigmatizing reaching out for help. Cornell has successfully created viral moments around community-oriented school-wide campaigns that encourage social connectedness over social comparison. These programs shift students toward their growth mindset and away from the narrowness that stems from a fixed mindset view of what it means to be a successful student.

Certainly, mental health issues aren't just a Cornell problem. According to data from the National Alliance on Mental Illness, 80 percent of students feel overwhelmed by college responsibilities, 50 percent describe their mental health as poor or below average, and 40 percent fail to seek help. Additionally, Reuters reports that from 2013 to 2018, the number of college students with severe depression rose from 9.4 percent to 21.1 percent. Though there are many factors behind these figures, the overlay of a Culture of Genius with its narrowed perception of who can be successful coupled with the self-focus it activates no doubt plays a significant role. When speaking of social comparison, especially among young people, it would be remiss to ignore the role of influences that operate well beyond campus borders.

Perhaps no tool stokes the fire of social comparison more than social media, which is found on every campus and probably close to every classroom and dorm room around the world. More than half of the world's population uses social media, to the tune of an average of two hours and 22 minutes per day as of 2023. As the documentary *The Social Dilemma* frighteningly illustrates, the drive for comparison can become an addiction where we no longer have a clear sense of who we are, except in terms of how we measure up against others. Ironically, we're not actually measuring ourselves against reality, but against highly curated presentations—we're gauging our own success and value against who others want us to think they are. It's similar to the Stanford ducks: performative, disorienting, and exhausting. Research shows that while, theoretically, scholars believed that social comparison could improve self-esteem (as long as you perceive yourself coming out on top), frequent comparison actually induces feelings of envy, guilt, regret, and defensiveness. It is also associated with increased lying and blaming of others.

As my team's research on professors' mindsets demonstrates, teachers can have an outsized impact on students' mindsets and performance because the teachers are the culture creators of their classroom. Campus-wide campaigns are a great idea in that they help to set and communicate an institution's mindset culture, but just as with managers in a company, more direct and perhaps in some cases more impactful interventions can occur at the interpersonal level, within classrooms. As we think back to the culture cycle, change at any level—at the societal, institutional, interpersonal, and individual levels—will impact others, creating a more effective mindset culture.

Classical music is a notoriously competitive field, and yet one of the greatest violinists of all time seeks to buck the dominant mindset culture among the students he teaches. In the biopic *Itzhak*, Itzhak Perlman says that he and his wife, Toby, who together run the Perlman Music Program, are often asked by media to watch as he teaches one of his "best students." Says Itzhak, "We never do that because we feel that there's no such thing as the best student." Toby adds, "Every child develops at his or her own pace. They come to us out of these competitive situations and we're exactly the opposite." Toby founded the Perlman Music Program, for which Itzhak is the faculty leader, with the goal of creating an alternative to the "competitive and isolating environment that exceptional young artists often grapple with in pursuit of their craft." The program seeks to nurture students in an environment that "emphasizes connection over competition."

Itzhak describes the early years of his own musical education as "the triangle of hell," with his teacher pressuring his parents, his parents pressuring him, and his teacher pressuring him, as well. His parents frequently compared him with other young musicians, saying he wasn't driven enough, and his teacher would tell him, "Do what I tell you and you'll play very well." When he got to Juilliard, Itzhak was shocked when his teacher Dorothy DeLay would ask him, "What did you think about that?" of his own performance, encouraging a more open and self-reflective learning process. At first, the style made him uncomfortable; he wanted to be told what to do. Now it's DeLay's style he uses as a teacher. For example, he rarely demonstrates during his master classes because he knows so many students have such great ears they'll simply set out to imitate him. "I want whenever they do something to be their own because they figured it out," he says. While playing a concerto might seem like something you get right or wrong, two violinists may have vastly different interpretations of the same piece, including different fingerings and bowings. There's a lot of room for creativity, and that's what the Perlmans want to foster: learning from others, while advancing and developing in your own way.

When we lose focus on our own goals and instead find ourselves prompted into our fixed mindset by the success of others, we fixate on the idea that someone else's accomplishments diminish our own chances at success. The stakes become higher and can feel out of our control. And this isn't only a mental function; as research shows, our bodies can both reflect and magnify this state.

CHALLENGE VS. THREAT

Social psychophysiologists Jim Blascovich and Wendy Berry Mendes have studied how we evaluate stressors in our environment. As they explain, states of challenge and threat represent a complex interplay of not only cognitive and emotional processes, but also physiological ones: Threat and challenge aren't just mental or feeling states, they are also body states.

Threat and challenge states come to play a role when we are in a situation where we expect to perform and be evaluated (including self-evaluations), and where the performance is relevant to our goals. In other words, when we believe our performance matters and that we will be judged on it. In these situations, we appraise ourselves and the situation in ways we may or may not be aware of. In this appraisal process, we assess the situation's demands and our resources to cope with those demands—the danger, uncertainty, or required effort involved versus the resources, knowledge, and skills we possess to perform in the face of it. Essentially, it's a two-tiered evaluation: What's the demand here, and do I have the resources to effectively meet this demand? When we surmise that we have enough resources—even if we have to stretch a bit—to meet the demand and perform well, we enter a *challenge state*. If the demands seem to us to exceed our ability to meet them, we enter a *threat state*. In our fixed mindset, we are much more likely to enter into the threat state.

When we experience the success of others, we can experience challenge or threat responses. If we believe we can accomplish something similar and even learn from that person's success, we land in a challenge state. We may have to stretch ourselves, but it's a demand we believe we can meet. In our fixed mindset, when we think someone else's success makes it harder or impossible for us, or believe they have some innate skill and talent that we don't and that we can't develop, we land in a threat state. Fortunately, we can invoke some tools to rise to the challenge.

HOW TO ENCOURAGE INSPIRATION INSTEAD OF AGGRAVATION WHEN OTHERS SUCCEED

When our frenemy gets the award, our initial response might be a clench-jawed, "Well done," while our hands ball into fists. The good news is we don't have stay in that state, and with some practice, we can start to shift more reliably to our growth mindset, from which we can thoughtfully formulate our next steps.

Recall the Largeness of You

You're bigger than your smallest response to the success of others, and reminding yourself of that can help you move toward your growth mindset. Previously, I described the exercise of self-affirmation. That activity is helpful in switching from a threat to a challenge state, by reminding ourselves just how large and multifaceted we are and how many interpersonal resources we have. I am not only a scientist, or a wife, or a dog mom, or a fun aunt, or a lover of Tex-Mex, I am all of these things, and you too are incredibly multifaceted. Panning back on just how broad we are—how many valued identities we have—helps to lower the percentage of our self under threat when someone else succeeds. If I identify nearly exclusively with my role as an academic and my next grant gets rejected, it can feel as if 90 percent of me is under threat. When I widen the lens and take in all of my various roles, that percentage shrinks substantially, giving me much-needed breathing room where I can reevaluate the situation. While I'm at it, I can also remind myself that challenge, and stretching beyond my comfort zone, grows my brain.

We may get an additional boost by noticing resources we have marshaled in the past that could be useful under the threat of the fixed mindset. And our pod could lend some help. When researcher Ellen Daniell was denied tenure—a move that effectively terminated her employment at the university—she was devastated. Fortunately for Daniell, she had six other women scientists in her group, who walked her through a self-affirmation process where she acknowledged other roles she played and looked to the skills and learning they could offer her in dealing with the present situation. Daniell didn't magically feel great after the gathering, but she felt resourced, which enabled her to shift from threat to challenge.

Self-affirmation can also look like a little healthy pushing back. Bozoma Saint John made a splash at Pepsi when she talked the company into signing an up-and-comer named Beyoncé Knowles (you may have heard of her) to be their brand ambassador. She then worked with the singer on her "culture-defining" 2013 Super Bowl halftime show. Yet later that year, in Saint John's performance review, her boss told her she "wasn't hitting enough home runs." (I don't know about you, but if those two acts don't constitute home runs, I'm not sure what it would take to be positively evaluated by that manager.) In the face of what would have been a bubble-bursting moment for most of us, Saint John went out and bought a baseball bat—not to bash in the windows of her supervisor's car, but as a means of self-affirmation. "I bought myself a Louisville Slugger. I wanted to keep it in my office to remind me that I do hit home runs. [And when I do,] I'm gonna cheer for myself." When our performance is unfairly compared to that of others, we can advocate for ourselves, vocally or symbolically.

Recognize the Actor-Observer Effect

When we see someone else achieve, it's like we're the audience in the theater while they take main stage. In our fixed mindset, we tell ourselves that they must have been born with special skills and that there's an element of magic and mystery to their success. In social psychology, that's an attributional bias called the *actor–observer asymmetry.* When we're the actor—when we're the one who has succeeded—we have a good sense of the path we took to get there. We know about the many people and circumstances that influenced us, who helped us along the way, what decisions we made, the challenges we overcame, and the effort we put in. In most cases, that journey is not available to the observer—who only sees the end result. The actor's success seems magical or otherwise inaccessible to us when we are in the observer role.

One way we can flip this is, instead of focusing on the outcome, zeroing in on the path the actor took to get there—particularly their challenges, as these are most likely to impart insight. The concept of the theatrical or mythological origin story can be helpful here. It's one thing to think, "She has mythical powers bestowed on her by the ancestors—she was born special." It's another to see her journey.

"Oh, she actually trained her entire life for that role, and then she had to demonstrate her learning in several contexts and even fight for her position, and she lost and then had to win it back! How did she have the fortitude to do that? What tools did she use?" Every successful person has their own origin story, and many of them are instructive of how we can be successful, too, especially when those stories involve challenge and struggle.

While it's great for individuals to take initiative in mining these stories, we don't want to put the onus solely on employees. We're better served building this kind of perspective into workplace culture. For example, we might invite people to give lunch-and-learns where they describe their path and even answer questions. Atlassian uses corporate storytelling in a podcast they've launched, called *Teamistry*, to share examples of how great teams achieved success, including the challenges they experienced and what they didn't do well along the way. Itzhak Perlman routinely asks his students what they're struggling with—not *whether* anything is challenging them, but *what* is—thus normalizing struggle. He then shares some of his own struggle stories, including how he resolved the challenges (and what challenges him still), and he coaches the students to come up with their own solutions. All of this underscores something critical: that other people's successes have value for us, as well.

Another way for companies to normalize sharing the journey is through mentoring or otherwise thoughtfully grouping people for the purpose of skill sharing. In my work with Shell, our data analysis revealed a team that had created an incredible Culture of Growth among themselves. Surprisingly, they turned out to be a team composed entirely of project managers who each served other teams. Because the group had no material overlap other than their roles, there was no competition and they felt especially free to share their challenges, along with solutions that had worked for them in the past.

Recognize the Value of Others' Success

As Simon Sinek defines it, a worthy rival is someone who not only inspires you to up your game (not someone you want to crush at all costs), but also someone who *helps you do so* because they are stronger in your less developed areas. Like Evert and Navratilova did for one another, a worthy rival helps you identify areas where you can improve, along with how to do it. Notice, again, that while this idea of worthy rivals has the air of competition, at the heart it's not about outperforming the other person, it's about doing better, yourself.

I've had my own share of worthy rivals in my work, many of whom are dear friends—as we've seen, the two don't have to be mutually exclusive. Back in grad school, however, I struggled with this a bit, as do many (perhaps most) in academia. When you're emerging from your studies and toward your professional career, the awareness of the limited number of jobs in the academy can cast a pall over relationships. I see this today among the graduate students I work with. I've taken to the practice of taking on two to three postdocs at a time so that they have a small cohort they can collaborate with, and inevitably, many of them become close friends. Yet when they're about to go on the market, their fixed mindsets can start to encroach and tensions appear as they each need letters of recommendation, sometimes for the same position.

Fortunately, I get it, and now that I've been doing this for a while, I can lend some perspective to nudge them toward their growth mindset. In these cases, I encourage them to talk about the awkwardness with each other to normalize these feelings and to broaden their perspective. We discuss the long-term benefits of having friends and close colleagues in the field. You can't really have a successful career in academia if you're the only one studying something. If you're in such a small niche that no one else's work relates to it, you're in trouble. You want your ideas to be picked up by others because they will have more reach to improve society and will be built out and expanded on in directions you would never have imagined. Also, if we let a threat assessment poison our relationships early on, we won't have productive and collegial relationships later; this not only makes it harder for us to succeed, it also negatively impacts our quality of life. While reassuring others, you might even tell the story of Des Linden and the Shalane Effect as a further illustration that success is available for all of us, and that when we act from that growth mindset, we're more likely to experience it.

Recognize When It's Your Success That's Triggering Others Toward Their Fixed Mindset

Maybe it's happened to you: A friend or colleague became weirdly distant after you were promoted. Sometimes it's our success that's triggering for others. To build the best and most effective teams and outcomes, we should remember it involves collaboration, and collaboration is based on relationships. So what do we do when our success is the catalyst that sends others into their fixed mindsets? What you don't want to do is downplay your accomplishment. Women, in particular, experience social pressure to do this, and it has a negative impact on advancement.

What we can do when we're the source of envy is to consider the actor–observer effect: Remember that others haven't seen our journey, and so they likely have inaccurate perceptions about what it took for us to get where we are. We can remedy that by sharing our experiences, either formally or informally. We can offer to advise or mentor a colleague. We can offer a talk. If we're highly visible, we can speak to our journey in interviews. In more informal settings, we can remind others of where we stumbled. "Remember when I was passed up for tenure? Back then I was so glad that others could help me identify my resources and how I might regroup and move forward strategically. If I hadn't done that, I don't think I'd have made the move to private industry and I never would have become a vice president." This not only defuses the trigger, but helps to elevate others, much as the three doctors I mentioned earlier in the chapter are reaching back into their communities to help other aspiring doctors discern a path to success.

QUESTIONS FOR REFLECTION

♦ The next time you feel that tightness in your body when your worthy rival is lauded and you notice yourself moving into that zero-sum, scarcity mindset, start to catalog all the ways this person, and people like them, have helped you in ways large and small to become who you are today. Feel the tension release and the gratitude grow. With your feelings of connection restored, can you tell them how they've inspired you? Can you spend some time getting to know them better, as a whole person? By doing so, you reverse engineer the disconnect that the fixed mindset engenders.

♦ Do a cues audit focused on your own and your team's praise practices. Could they unintentionally be cueing people toward their fixed mindset? What can be done to shift folks toward growth? How can the learning and strategies that led to success be highlighted so they can empower everyone?

♦ Another thing you can do with your Culture of Growth pod is to collect and share stories of folks whose success inspires you. Pick one, study the example together (preferably while sharing tasty snacks), and spend some time discussing how they got there. Are there some strategies you can use to pursue your goals?

Conclusion

We've made it! In terms of this book, our journey has ended. Yet when it comes to the work of mindset culture, it's just beginning. Fortunately, as I've tried to impress upon you, this work doesn't have to be done alone, nor can it really. When it comes to truly realizing the potential of mindset to change how we live and work together, it's a group effort. But it can start with you and extend outward to the teams and the organizations that you're a part of—from workplaces to schools to athletic teams, spiritual communities, families, and more.

"Come on," you might say. "How likely is that to actually happen?"

Well, let's look at an example. In the 1950s, a group of scientists wanted to observe how learned behavior among monkeys spread and became normative within a cultural group. They looked to a remote subtropical island in Japan where monkeys had lived for generations with little human contact. There, the scientists left potatoes (a novel treat!) on the beach. But the monkeys didn't hang out on the beach very often, preferring the jungle next to the sea. When the monkeys finally did venture seaside and discovered the potatoes, they deemed the goodies to be inedible because they were covered with sand. One day, though, a monkey who the researchers eventually named Imo (Japanese for "potato") discovered a solution. She picked up a potato and dipped it into the ocean. She began to rub it and, once the potato was sand-free, happily chomped away. The young monkeys watched Imo with curiosity (and I imagine more than a little jealousy, given the tasty treats she was munching). After observing her for a while, they began to imitate her behavior, cleaning then devouring their own potatoes. Finally, even the older, more reluctant monkeys followed suit. In a matter of months, not only had this group of monkeys all learned how to wash potatoes, but the behavior had extended to the adjacent colonies of monkeys, as well. It was the monkey equivalent of a TikTok dance going viral.

This is how innovation can travel in Cultures of Growth. Of course, monkeys don't necessarily believe in the growth mindset—at least, not in the way that humans do. But they also don't saddle themselves with the limiting beliefs of the fixed mindset. Cultures of Growth naturally contain opportunities for learning and functional adaptiveness, and that openness to change allows strategies to travel through the culture and better the whole. I don't mean to imply that in Cultures of Growth change is easy—it's not—it's simply more accessible. It's easier to consider other ways of being when you have a fundamental belief that learning and growth are possible in the first place. That the ability to develop and expand our capabilities is something inherent to all of us.

A postscript on Imo, by the way. Throughout her life, she went on to pioneer other discoveries and innovations for her crew, such as discovering that when wheat was submerged into the water, it would float to the surface similarly sand-free. This system was adopted by the other colonies on the island too. Unfettered by the fixed mindset, the innovation cycle continued.

Organizational mindset is powerful because it shapes how we interpret and make sense of the world around us. It has the power to align our goals, beliefs, and behaviors. That's why it has such vast and consistent effects across so many different behaviors and outcomes in such a wide variety of "organizations." Again, wherever two or more people are gathered in a group, mindset culture is at work. To shift culture, therefore, requires interrogating it at the root. We must look to the policies and practices, the messages provided by leadership, and so on, examining them through the lens of mindset culture. If we want to transform our organizations to be more cohesive, successful, innovative, and diverse, to create a broad and lasting impact, culture change must be at the heart of the work.

Again, this is not easy. Growth mindset as a concept is relatively simple but putting it into practice and infusing it throughout an organization is demanding, and it may require partnering with culture change experts. If you find yourself in more of a Culture of Genius, don't feel defeated; the beauty of culture is that it is always evolving and changing; shifting mindset culture is doable. Start with some of the strategies I've offered here. And, if you find yourself in a strong Culture of Growth (congratulations!), remember that sustaining and tending culture is a continuous journey, not a final destination. In fact, the organizational examples I provide throughout this book are snapshots of these cultures as they exist at the time of this writing; it doesn't mean that exemplars of Cultures of Growth (or Genius) will stay that way. To build and maintain strong Cultures of Growth takes attention, resources, and years of consistent effort, and then requires an ongoing commitment to attending to the culture as it evolves.

Yet by any measure—especially those that consider the value of maximizing not only human potential to produce, but more importantly, human potential to derive a sense of meaning and purpose from life—it is worth it.

Every single one of us is a *culture creator*. You have the power to shape your own mindset, and to help others shape theirs. To identify what moves you and those you interact with toward your fixed or growth mindsets, and to employ strategies to inhabit your growth mindsets more often. And in so doing, you become a modern, human version of Imo, showing others how it's done. Making it possible for all of us to shine. Recall, too, that you can have the opposite impact. (And I'm especially speaking to you here, leaders.) By embodying your fixed mindset much of the time in your interactions with others, you encourage that way of thinking and behaving. Each of us has the power to strike a tone, and it's up to us to be mindful of the one we're sounding.

By engaging others and setting up more opportunities to embody growth, you amplify that tone. So, find your pod, work as a team, and create your own microcultures of growth. Then, lead by example and watch them spread. Remember that just one small move, one innovation, can create powerful momentum toward a Culture of Growth.

I hope this book has inspired you to commit to this journey and that you'll return to the stories, tools, and resources in these pages to support you along the way. Please consider me a member of your pod and let me know how it's going! In growth mindset fashion, I look forward to your feedback and the opportunities it will provide to further refine these ideas and my team's work.

Join me in this worthwhile journey of creating inclusive Cultures of Growth so that, together, we can create the conditions necessary for equity, belonging, development, and success for everyone.

Acknowledgments

Writing this book was my pandemic project. I'd never written a book before. Could I do it? Where would I start? Talk about a potential fixed mindset trigger! But I took my own advice and I cultivated a Culture of Growth pod who, luckily for me, were game to take the journey together. Science doesn't happen in a vacuum—and, it turns out, neither does writing a science-based book. It takes a village, and I am so grateful for mine.

First, there would be no *Cultures of Growth* without my partner through all of it, the uber-talented and passionately dedicated Kelly Madrone. My literary agent, Jim Levine, matched us when I signed my book contract (thanks, Jim!), and the rest is history. Kelly's wisdom, deep knowledge, and steadfast commitment gave me the confidence I needed to make it through. She was basically my book doula. She held my hand through the drafts and interviews and made sure I kept breathing and pushing. If you loved the stories and examples in this book, you probably have Kelly to thank for them. She not only understood the phenomenon, she was every bit as geeked about the research as she was about the examples of it out in the world. Thank you, Kelly, for believing in this. Thank you for the hours and hours of research and editing. And, most of all, thank you for helping me find my voice. I am so grateful to you.

Next, there would also be no *Cultures of Growth* without Jim Levine. I met with many agents, referred by friends, and Jim was special. He immediately got the idea for the book—sending me loads of rich examples before I even signed. He could see the contribution and how these ideas might help people in the world. He helped me craft a compelling book proposal, he played matchmaker with me and Kelly, and he intensely advocated for me throughout the process. Jim is a true believer and his confidence inspired my own. Anytime I had a question, Jim had a good answer. I can't believe how fortunate I was to partner with him. Jim, I am deeply grateful to you.

Then, there's Stephanie Frerich. I immediately felt a connection with Stephanie when I spoke with her and Jon Karp at Simon and Schuster. She also got the ideas right away and she asked great questions. I knew that if she could ask these types of questions without even knowing much about the work, I could only imagine what she could do when we dove in! Stephanie's advice and wisdom have been essential to the book you're reading today. She knew where to cut, when to add, and when I needed to *not* say "practices, policies, norms, and interactions" yet again! Stephanie, the work of an editor is not easy—it requires grace and balance, and you showed up to this project with both in spades. Thank you for being Team Growth!

Of course, there would be no research to share without my mentors, collaborators, and students. I have never published a solo-written research article because that's not the way our science works. We do team science. Claude Steele inspired me from the first day of graduate school and taught me over the years to ask big questions about how to make the world a more equitable place. Claude's guidance and advice have never led me astray. He made me feel and believe that I belonged, and I am eternally grateful for his mentorship and friendship. In my last year of graduate school, there was that fateful meeting with Carol Dweck, who had just arrived at Stanford. It feels auspicious that we didn't miss each other. Little did I know that that meeting would signal the beginning of a beautiful collaboration and friendship that would continue for decades. I am so grateful that Carol took a growth mindset to my pronouncement about mindset culture—and that we've worked together ever since to bring it into the world. I'm also grateful for the mentorship and friendship of Jennifer Richeson, who supported me as a postdoc at Northwestern, helping me become the scholar I am today. My grad school buddies and I formed our own Culture of Growth to support each other through the PhD and beyond. Valerie Jones Taylor, Sapna Cheryan, Nic Anderson, Julie Heiser, Natalia Mislavsky Khilko, Nick Davidenko, Dave Nussbaum, Paul Hamilton, Chris Bryan, Kelly Wilson, Jennifer Wagner, Hal Hershfield, Valerie Purdie Greenaway, Phil Solomon, Paul Davies, Joyce Ehrlinger, and Kali Trzesniewski—I am so grateful for the laughs we've shared. My collaborators and coauthors who've been on the front lines of the studies and experiments we've run and who've shared in the many journal and grant rejections as well as the sweet victory of acceptances. There are too many to list, but special thanks to Sabrina Zirkel, Julie Garcia, Daryl Wout, Stephanie Fryberg, Laura Brady, Megan Bang, Amanda Diekman, Greg Walton, David Yeager, Nick Bowman, Ken Fujita, Laura Wallace, Aneeta Rattan, Josh Clarkson, Ben Tauber, and Chris Samsa. Extra special thanks to my work spouse, Christine Logel, who has collaborated on this work, shared in the running of our lab, and reminded me to rest, eat, and go to the spa. Thanks as well to Tiffany Han, who has guided and supported me these last five years, and to Shaylee Correll, who makes my life manageable by exquisitely playing offense and defense with my schedule. I am grateful to Margaret Levi, the Class of 2015–16, and the staff at the Center for Advanced Study in the Behavioral Sciences at Stanford University, where I spent an incredible year in warm fellowship, thinking and writing about these ideas and beginning this book.

My students, postdocs, and lab managers deserve their own thanks since their brilliance and dedication have enriched these ideas; much of the work I report here was done in collaboration with these dedicated scientists. Sylvia Perry, Kathy Emerson, Evelyn Carter, Katie Kroeper, Elise Ozier, Heidi Williams, Caitlyn Jones, Katie Boucher, Elizabeth Canning, Katie Muenks, Dorainne Green, Jennifer LaCosse, Stephanie Reeves, Wen Bu, Asha Ganesan, Nedim Yel, Shahana Ansari, Julian Rucker, Trisha Dehrone, Tiffany Estep, Ben Oistad, thank you for working with me across these past 16 years. I am proud of the difference you are making in the world.

I also want to thank the team at Equity Accelerator, past and present, for bringing this Culture of Growth work to thousands of people in schools and companies throughout the world. Steve Bernardini, Jen Coakley, Kathy Emerson, Cassie Hartzog, Sophie Kuchynka, Katie Mathias, Krysti Ryan, Stephanie Schacht, Samantha Stevens, Chris Smith, Chaghig Walker, and Sara Woodruff, thank you for your innovation and dedication to creating more equitable learning and working environments and thank you for cocreating and sustaining a Culture of Growth in our organization.

I am grateful for my colleagues at the University of Illinois, Chicago and at Indiana University, who have given feedback on this work across the years, read grants, and supported me and my students. Courtney Bonam, Bette Bottoms, Dan Cervone, Jim Larson, Linda Skitka, Sabine French-Rolnick at UIC and Amanda Diekman, Dorainne Green, Ed Hirt, Kurt Hugenberg, Anne Krendl, John Kruschke, BJ Rydell, Jim Sherman, Rich Shiffrin, and Eliot Smith at IU—thank you for making our work better. I am grateful to the funders who have supported this work over the years including the National Science Foundation, the Raikes Foundation, Character Lab, the Bill & Melinda Gates Foundation, the Spencer Foundation, the Russell Sage Foundation, the Alfred P. Sloan Foundation, the Kern Family Foundation, the Ewing Marion Kauffman Foundation, and the Student Experience Research Network. Special thanks to Lisa Quay, Dina Blum, and Zoe Stemm-Calderon, who have offered guidance and support throughout the years.

Thank you to everyone who sat for personal interviews and shared their stories: Alison Mudditt, Amanda Arrington, Amy Bosley, Becki Cohn-Vargas, Ben Tauber, Bill Strickland, Bruce Friedrich, Candy Duncan, Carol Dweck, Cassie Roma, Claude Steele, Dina Blum, Jacqueline Novogratz, Jennifer Danek, Jorrit van der Togt, Karen Gross, Kathleen Boyle Dalen, Wendy Torrance, Kinney Zalesne, Laura Braden, Lou Wool, Sandy Shugart, Susan Mackie, Tom Kudrle, and Verne Harnish. I regret that due to space limitations, I wasn't able to use them all, but my gratitude remains.

Thank you to Adam Grant, Angela Duckworth, Dave Nussbaum, Dolly Chugh, Eli Finkel, Emily Balcetis, Elizabeth Dunn, Jennifer Eberhardt, Katherine Howe, Katy Milkman, Kerry Ann Rockquemore, Michele Gelfand, and Tim Wilson, who gave me advice about the book writing process and introduced me to others who could help.

Finally, I am so grateful to my family, especially Mom (Bertie), Dad (Richard), Dad (Tom), Patrick, Maureen, Yen, and the entire Esquivel tribe, who have always held me up and made it possible to have the life and career I do. I am especially grateful that, on that first meeting, Victor Quintanilla insisted on dancing together at our friends' wedding—and that we haven't stopped since. Thank you, Victor, for doing life with me; it is more meaningful, more joyful, and more delightful because you are my partner in it all.

Notes

INTRODUCTION

xiv *Throughout this book, I'll explain*: Ashley Stewart and Shana Lebowitz, "Satya Nadella Employed a 'Growth Mindset' to Overhaul Microsoft's Cutthroat Culture and Turn it Into a Trillion-Dollar Company—Here's How He Did It," *Business Insider*, March 7, 2020, https://www.businessinsider.com/microsoft-ceo-satya-nadella-company-culture-change-growth-mindset.

xiv *In 2014, when Nadella took over*: Eric Jackson, "Steve Ballmer Deserves His Due as a Great CEO," CNBC, January 17, 2018, https://www.cnbc.com/2018/01/17/steve-ballmer-deserves-his-due-as-a-great-ceo.html.

xiv *In November 2021*: "Microsoft Corp," Barchart, accessed May 5, 2023, https://www.barchart.com/stocks/quotes/MSFT/performance.

xiv *Microsoft shifted from its heavy dependence*: Will Feuer, "Microsoft Becomes Second US Company to Reach $2 Trillion Valuation," *New York Post*, June 23, 2021, https://nypost.com/2021/06/23/microsoft-second-us-company-to-reach-2-trillion-valuation/.

xv *In the wake of some cringeworthy stumbles*: Amy Kraft, "Microsoft Shuts Down AI Chatbot After It Turned into a Nazi," CBS News, March 25, 2016, https://www.cbsnews.com/news/microsoft-shuts-down-ai-chatbot-after-it-turned-into-racist-nazi/.

xv *(and more recently, Bing)*: Kif Leswing, "Microsoft's Bing A.I. Made Several Factual Errors in Last Week's Launch Demo," CNBC, February 14, 2023, https://www.cnbc.com/2023/02/14/microsoft-bing-ai-made-several-errors-in-launch-demo-last-week-.html.

xv *It's worth noting that*: Anthony Colannino, "Celtics' Brad Stevens Discusses a Growth Mindset," *Mindset Works*, August 10, 2016, https://blog.mindsetworks.com/entry/celtics-brad-stevens-discusses-a-growth-mindset-1; Kevin Ding, "This LeBron Season Exemplifies His Lifelong Mindset," *The Point*, March 30, 2020, https://www.nba.com/lakers/the-point-lebron-season-exemplifies-his-lifelong-mindset; Lee Jenkins, "From 'The Dungeon' to the Top: Erik Spoelstra's Rise with the Heat," https://www.si.com/nba/2014/09/24/erik-spoelstra-miami-heat.

xviii *First, Theranos CEO Elizabeth Holmes*: Avery Hartmans, Sarah Jackson, and Azmi Haroun, "The Rise and Fall of Elizabeth Holmes, the Former Theranos CEO Found Guilty of Wire Fraud and Conspiracy—Who Just Managed to Delay Her Prison Reporting Date," *Business Insider*, April 26, 2023, https://www.businessinsider.com/theranos-founder-ceo-elizabeth-holmes-life-story-bio-2018-4.

xviii *Then there is Arif Naqvi*: David Smith, "A Financial Fairytale: How One Man Fooled the Global Elite," *Guardian*, July 14, 2021, https://www.theguardian.com /books/2021/jul/14/the-key-man-simon-clark-will-louch-private-equity.

xviii *We also have Charlie Javice*: Arwa Mahdawi, "30 Under 30-Year Sentences: Why So Many of Forbes' Young Heroes Face Jail," *Guardian*, April 7, 2023, https://www .theguardian.com/business/2023/apr/06/forbes-30-under-30-tech-finance-prison.

xviii *so people who apply for jobs in these organizations often feature*: Mary C. Murphy and Carol S. Dweck, "A Culture of Genius: How an Organization's Lay Theory Shapes People's Cognition, Affect, and Behavior," *Personality and Social Psychology Bulletin* 36, no. 3 (October 2009): 283–96, https://doi.org/10.1177 /0146167209347380.

CHAPTER 1: THE MINDSET CONTINUUM

3 *Mindset exists on a continuum*: Mary C. Murphy and Stephanie L. Reeves, "Personal and Organizational Mindsets at Work," *Research in Organizational Behavior* 39 (2019), https://doi.org/10.1016/j.riob.2020.100121.

4 *Since Carol Dweck first introduced*: Carol S. Dweck and Ellen L. Leggett, "A Social -Cognitive Approach to Motivation and Personality," *Psychological Review* 95, no. 2 (1988): 256–73, https://doi.org/10.1037/0033-295X.95.2.256; Carol S. Dweck, *Self-Theories: Their Role in Motivation, Personality, and Development* (Philadelphia: Psychology Press, 2000); Carol Dweck, *Mindset: The New Psychology of Success* (New York: Ballantine Books, 2007).

4 *we've seen the following illustration*: Murphy and Reeves, "Personal and Organizational Mindsets at Work"; graphic by Reid Wilson, Wayfaring Path, www.wayfar ingpath.com.

5 *Although, as we will see, people and cultures*: Carol Dweck, "What Having a 'Growth Mindset' Actually Means," *Harvard Business Review*, January 13, 2016, https://hbr.org/2016/01/what-having-a-growth-mindset-actually-means; Carol Dweck, "Carol Dweck Revisits the 'Growth Mindset'," *Education Week*, September 22, 2015, https://www.edweek.org/leadership/opinion-carol-dweck -revisits-the-growth-mindset/2015/09?print=1; Carol Dweck, "Recognizing and Overcoming False Growth Mindset," *Edutopia*, January 11, 2016, https://www .edutopia.org/blog/recognizing-overcoming-false-growth-mindset-carol-dweck; Christine Gross-Loh, "How Praise Became a Consolation Prize," *Atlantic*, December 16, 2016, https://www.theatlantic.com/education/archive/2016/12/how-praise -became-a-consolation-prize/510845/.

5 *In the teacher training institute*: Mary Murphy, Stephanie Fryberg, Laura Brady, Elizabeth Canning, and Cameron Hecht, "Global Mindset Initiative Paper 1: Growth Mindset Cultures and Teacher Practices," *Growth Mindset Cultures and Practices* (August 27, 2021), http://dx.doi.org/10.2139/ssrn.3911594; K. Morman, L. Brady, C. Wang, M. C. Murphy, M. Bang, and S. Fryberg, "Creating Identity Safe Classrooms: A Cultural Educational Psychology Approach to Teacher Interventions," paper presented at the American Educational Research Association Annual Meeting, Chicago, IL (April 2023).

6 *"It's okay, not everyone*: Aneeta Rattan, Catherine Good, and Carol Dweck, "'It's

Ok—Not Everyone Can Be Good at Math': Instructors with an Entity Theory
Comfort (and Demotivate) Students," *Journal of Experimental Social Psychology*
48, no. 3 (May 2012): 731–37, https://doi.org/10.1016/j.jesp.2011.12.012.

6 *Instead of simply having a fixed or growth mindset*: Murphy and Reeves, "Personal
and Organizational Mindsets at Work"; Dweck, "What Having a 'Growth Mindset' Actually Means."

6 *Understanding our mindset set point*: Dweck, *Mindset*; Peter A. Heslin, Lauren A.
Keating, and Susan J. Ashford, "How Being in Learning Mode May Enable a Sustainable Career Across the Lifespan," *Journal of Vocational Behavior* 117 (March
2020), https://doi.org/10.1016/j.jvb.2019.103324.

6 *In fact, one of the most surprising findings*: Murphy and Reeves, "Personal and
Organizational Mindsets at Work"; L. S. Blackwell, K. H. Trzesniewski, and C. S.
Dweck, "Implicit Theories of Intelligence Predict Achievement Across an Adoles-
cent Transition: A Longitudinal Study and an Intervention," *Child Development*
78, no. 1 (2007): 246–63, http://dx.doi.org/10.1111/j.1467-8624.2007.00995.x;
Y. Hong, C. Chiu, C. S. Dweck, D. M.-S. Lin, and W. Wan, "Implicit Theories, At-
tributions, and Coping: A Meaning System Approach," *Journal of Personality and
Social Psychology* 77 (1999): 588–99, https://doi.org/10.1037/0022-3514.77.3.588;
A. David Nussbaum and Carol S. Dweck, "Defensiveness Versus Remediation:
Self-Theories and Modes of Self-Esteem Maintenance," *Personality and Social
Psychology Bulletin* 34, no. 5 (March 5, 2008): 599–612, https://doi.org/10.1177
/0146167207312960; Dweck and Leggett, "A Social-Cognitive Approach to Moti-
vation and Personality"; Heslin, Keating, and Ashford, "How Being in Learning
Mode May Enable a Sustainable Career Across the Lifespan."

7 *The culture surrounding us*: Murphy and Reeves, "Personal and Organizational
Mindsets at Work"; Mary C. Murphy and Carol S. Dweck, "A Culture of Genius:
How an Organization's Lay Theory Shapes People's Cognition, Affect, and Behavior," *Personality and Social Psychology Bulletin* 36, no. 3 (October 2009): 283–96,
https://doi.org/10.1177/0146167209347380; Murphy et al., "Global Mindset Initiative Paper 1"; Katherine T. U. Emerson and Mary C. Murphy, "Identity Threat
at Work: How Social Identity Threat and Situational Cues Contribute to Racial
and Ethnic Disparities in the Workplace," *Cultural Diversity and Ethnic Minority
Psychology* 20, no. 4 (October 2014): 508–20, https://doi.org/10.1037/a0035403;
Elizabeth A. Canning, Mary C. Murphy, Katherine T. U. Emerson, Jennifer A.
Chatman, Carol S. Dweck, and Laura J. Kray, "Cultures of Genius at Work: Organizational Mindsets Predict Cultural Norms, Trust, and Commitment," *Personality and Social Psychology Bulletin* 46, no. 4 (2020): 626–42.

7 *Mindset culture is so powerful*: Murphy and Reeves, "Personal and Organizational
Mindsets at Work"; Murphy and Dweck, "A Culture of Genius"; Elizabeth A.
Canning, Katherine Muenks, Dorainne J. Green, and Mary C. Murphy, "STEM
Faculty Who Believe Ability Is Fixed Have Larger Racial Achievement Gaps and
Inspire Less Student Motivation in Their Classes," *Science Advances* 5, no. 2 (Feb-
ruary 15, 2019), https://doi.org/10.1126/sciadv.aau4734; Mary C. Murphy and
Carol S. Dweck, "Mindsets Shape Consumer Behavior," *Journal of Consumer Psy-
chology* 26, no. 1 (2016): 127–36, http://dx.doi.org/10.1016/j.jcps.2015.06.005; K.
Muenks, E. A. Canning, J. LaCosse, D. J. Green, S. Zirkel, and J. A. Garcia, "Does

My Professor Think My Ability Can Change? Students' Perceptions of Their STEM Professors' Mindset Beliefs Predict Their Psychological Vulnerability, Engagement, and Performance in Class," *Journal of Experimental Psychology: General* 149, no. 11 (2020): 2119–44, https://doi.org/10.1037/xge0000763; Canning et al., "Cultures of Genius at Work"; David S. Yeager, Jamie M. Carroll, Jenny Buontempo, Andrei Cimpian, Spencer Woody, Robert Crosnoe, Chandra Muller, Jared Murray, Pratik Mhatre, Nicole Kersting, Christopher Hulleman, Molly Kudym, Mary Murphy, Angela Lee Duckworth, Gregory M. Walton, and Carol S. Dweck, "Teacher Mindsets Help Explain Where a Growth-Mindset Intervention Does and Doesn't Work," *Psychological Science* 33, no. 1 (2022): 18–32, https://doi.org /10.1177/09567976211028984; Elizabeth A. Canning, Elise Ozier, Heidi E. Williams, Rashed AlRasheed, and Mary C. Murphy, "Professors Who Signal a Fixed Mindset about Ability Undermine Women's Performance in STEM," *Social Psychological and Personality Science* 13, no. 5 (2022): 927–37, https://doi.org/10.1177 /19485506211030398; Cameron A. Hecht, David S. Yeager, Carol S. Dweck, and Mary C. Murphy, "Beliefs, Affordances, and Adolescent Development: Lessons from a Decade of Growth Mindset Interventions," *Advances in Child Development and Behavior* 61 (2021): 169–197, https://doi.org/10.1016/bs.acdb.2021.04.004; Cameron A. Hecht, Carol S. Dweck, Mary C. Murphy, Kathryn M. Kroeper, and David S. Yeager, "Efficiently Exploring the Causal Role of Contextual Moderators in Behavioral Science," *Proceedings of the National Academy of Sciences* 120, no. 1 (2023): https://doi.org/10.1073/pnas.2216315120.

7   *For example, Barre3 CEO Sadie Lincoln*: Megan DiTrolio, "Being a Female CEO Is Not My Identity," *Marie Claire*, July 3, 2019, https://www.marieclaire.com/career -advice/a28243947/sadie-lincoln-barre-3/; "Sadie Lincoln Is Rewriting the Fitness Story: Thoughts on Movement, Community, Risk & Vulnerability, Episode 501," interview by Rich Roll, *Rich Roll Podcast*, February 24, 2020, https://www.richroll .com/podcast/sadie-lincoln-501/.

7   *"I lost team members*: DiTrolio, "Being a Female CEO Is Not My Identity."

8   *And as Lincoln told Guy Raz*: "How I Built Resilience: Live with Sadie Lincoln," interview by Guy Raz, *How I Built This*, June 20, 2020, https://www.npr.org/2020 /06/18/880460529/how-i-built-resilience-live-with-sadie-lincoln.

8   *In response to the Black Lives Matter Movement*: "How I Built Resilience: Live with Sadie Lincoln," interview by Guy Raz.

8   *The company has been working with*: "Diversity, Equity, and Inclusion Update at Barre3: An Update," *Barre3 Magazine*, February 4, 2021, https://blog.barre3.com /diversity-equity-inclusion-update/.

8   *Organizational mindset refers to the shared beliefs*: Murphy and Reeves, "Personal and Organizational Mindsets at Work"; Murphy and Dweck, "A Culture of Genius"; Katherine T. U. Emerson and Mary C. Murphy, "A Company I Can Trust? Organizational Lay Theories Moderate Stereotype Threat for Women," *Personality and Social Psychology Bulletin* 41, no. 2 (February 1, 2015): 295–307, https://doi .org/10.1177/01461672145649; Canning et al., "Cultures of Genius at Work."

9   *Organizational mindsets also exist*: Ibid.

9   *Organizational mindset beliefs*: Ibid.

9   *Fixed mindset organizations—or Cultures of Genius*: Ibid.

10 *As Harvard professor Marjorie Garber*: Marjorie Garber, "Our Genius Problem: Why This Obsession with the Word, with the Idea, and with the People on Whom We've Bestowed the Designation?" *Atlantic*, December 2002, https://www.theat lantic.com/magazine/archive/2002/12/our-genius-problem/308435/.

10 *When I asked Carol Dweck*: Carol Dweck, interview by Mary Murphy, June 23, 2021.

10 *Stanford psychology professor Claude Steele*: Claude Steele, interview by Mary Murphy, July 9, 2021.

11 *Consistent with these analyses*: Murphy and Reeves, "Personal and Organizational Mindsets at Work;" Canning et al., "Professors Who Signal a Fixed Mindset"; Murphy et al., "Global Mindset Initiative Paper 1"; Canning et al., "STEM Faculty Who Believe Ability Is Fixed"; L. Bian, S. Leslie, M. C. Murphy, and A. Cimpian, "Messages about Brilliance Undermine Women's Interest in Educational and Professional Opportunities," *Journal of Experimental Social Psychology* 76 (May 2018): 404–20, https://doi.org/10.1016/j.jesp.2017.11.006; Lile Jia, Chun Hui Lim, Ismaharif Ismail, and Yia Chin Tan, "Stunted Upward Mobility in Learning Environment Reduces the Academic Benefits of Growth Mindset," *Proceedings of the National Academy of Sciences* 118, no. 10 (March 1, 2021): https://doi.org/10.1073 /pnas.20118321. See also: D. Storage, T. E. S. Charlesworth, M. R. Banaji, and A. Cimpian, "Adults and Children Implicitly Associate Brilliance with Men More than Women," *Journal of Experimental Social Psychology* 90 (2020), https://doi.org /10.1016/j.jesp.2020.104020; L. Bian, S. J. Leslie, and A. Cimpian, "Evidence of Bias Against Girls and Women in Contexts that Emphasize Intellectual Ability," *American Psychologist* 73, no. 9 (2018): 1139–53, https://doi.org/10.1037/amp0000427; E. K. Chestnut, R. F. Lei, S. J. Leslie, and A. Cimpian, "The Myth that Only Brilliant People are Good at Math and Its Implications for Diversity," *Education Sciences* 8, no. 2 (2018): 65, https://doi.org/10.3390/educsci8020065; Andrei Cimpian and Sarah-Jane Leslie, "The Brilliance Paradox: What Really Keeps Women and Minorities from Excelling in Academia," *Scientific American*, September 1, 2017, https://www.scientificamerican.com/article/the-brilliance-paradox-what -really-keeps-women-and-minorities-from-excelling-in-academia/; D. Storage, Z. Horne, A. Cimpian, and S. J. Leslie, "The Frequency of 'Brilliant' and 'Genius' in Teaching Evaluations Predicts the Representation of Women and African Americans Across Fields," *PLOS ONE* 11, no. 3, (March 3, 2016), https://doi .org/10.1371/journal.pone.0150194; and S. J. Leslie, A. Cimpian, M. Meyer, and E. Freeland, "Expectations of Brilliance Underlie Gender Distributions Across Academic Disciplines," *Science* 347, no. 6219, (2015): 262–65, https://doi.org/10.1126 /science.1261375.

11 *But this flies in the face of my research*: Canning et al., "STEM Faculty Who Believe Ability Is Fixed"; Yeager et al., "Teacher Mindsets"; K. M. Kroeper, A. Fried, and M. C. Murphy, "Toward Fostering Growth Mindset Classrooms: Identifying Teaching Behaviors that Signal Instructors' Fixed and Growth Mindset Beliefs to Students," *Social Psychology of Education* 25 (2022): 371–98, https://doi .org/10.1007/s11218-022-09689-4; K. M. Kroeper, K. Muenks, E. A. Canning, and M. C. Murphy, "An Exploratory Study of the Behaviors that Communicate Perceived Instructor Mindset Beliefs in College STEM Classrooms," *Teaching and*

Teacher Education 114 (2022), https://doi.org/10.1016/j.tate.2022.103717; Muenks et al., "Does My Professor Think My Ability Can Change?"; J. LaCosse, M. C. Murphy, J. A. Garcia, and S. Zirkel, "The Role of STEM Professors' Mindset Beliefs on Students' Anticipated Psychological Experiences and Course Interest," *Journal of Educational Psychology* 113 (2021): 949–71, https://doi.org/10.1037/edu0000620; K. L. Boucher, M. A. Fuesting, A. Diekman, and M. C. Murphy, "Can I Work With and Help Others in the Field? How Communal Goals Influence Interest and Participation in STEM Fields," *Frontiers in Psychology* 8 (2017), https://doi.org /10.3389/fpsyg.2017.00901; Melissa A. Fuesting, Amanda B. Diekman, Kathryn L. Boucher, Mary C. Murphy, Dana L. Manson, and Brianne L. Safer, "Growing STEM: Perceived Faculty Mindset as an Indicator of Communal Affordances in STEM," *Journal of Personality and Social Psychology* 117, no. 2 (2019): 260–81, https://doi.org/10.1037/pspa0000154; K. Boucher, M. C. Murphy, D. Bartel, J. Smail, C. Logel, and J. Danek, "Centering the Student Experience: What Faculty and Institutions Can Do to Advance Equity," *Change: The Magazine of Higher Learning* 53 (2021): 42–50, https://doi.org/10.1080/00091383.2021.1987804.

12 *My research shows that an organization's*: Murphy and Reeves, "Personal and Organizational Mindsets at Work"; Murphy and Dweck, "A Culture of Genius"; Emerson and Murphy, "A Company I Can Trust?"; Canning et al., "Cultures of Genius at Work."

13 *An organization's mindset may rest*: Ibid.

13 *As with personal mindset*: Ibid.

13 *You and others may have triggers*: Murphy and Reeves, "Personal and Organizational Mindsets at Work."

CHAPTER 2: ORGANIZATIONAL MINDSETS

15 *William James, often credited*: William James, *The Principles of Psychology* (New York: Henry Holt, 1890), 294.

17 *A large body of research had shown*: Carol Dweck, *Mindset: The New Psychology of Success* (New York: Ballantine Books, 2007); H. Grant and C. S. Dweck, "Clarifying Achievement Goals and their Impact," *Journal of Personality and Social Psychology* 85 (2003): 541–53, https://doi.org/10.1037/0022-3514.85.3.541; Y. Hong, C. Chiu, C. S. Dweck, D. M.-S. Lin, and W. Wan, "Implicit Theories, Attributions, and Coping: A Meaning System Approach," *Journal of Personality and Social Psychology* 77 (1999): 588–99, https://doi.org/10.1037/0022-3514.77.3.588; D. C. Molden and C. S. Dweck, "Finding 'Meaning' in Psychology: A Lay Theories Approach to Self-Regulation, Social Perception, and Social Development," *American Psychologist*, 61 (2006): 192–203, https://doi.org/10.1037/0003-066X.61.3.192; Dweck and Leggett, "A Social-Cognitive Approach to Motivation and Personality"; David Nussbaum and Carol S. Dweck, "Defensiveness Versus Remediation: Self-Theories and Modes of Self-Esteem Maintenance," *Personality and Social Psychology Bulletin* 34, no. 5 (March 5, 2008): 599–612, https://doi.org/10.1177/0146167207312960; J. S. Moser, H. S. Schroder, C. Heeter, T. P. Moran, and Y.-H. Lee, "Mind Your Errors: Evidence for a Neural Mechanism Linking Growth Mind-Set to Adaptive Posterror Adjustments," *Psychological Science* 22 (2011): 1484–89, https://doi.org

/10.1177/0956797611419520; J. A. Mangels, B. Butterfield, J. Lamb, C. Good, and C. S. Dweck, "Why Do Beliefs about Intelligence Influence Learning Success? A Social Cognitive Neuroscience Model," *Social Cognitive and Affective Neuroscience* 1 (2006): 75–86; https://doi.org/10.1093/scan/nsl013; L. S. Blackwell, K. H. Trzesniewski, and C. S. Dweck, "Implicit Theories of Intelligence Predict Achievement Across an Adolescent Transition: A Longitudinal Study and an Intervention," *Child Development* 78, no. 1 (2007): 246–63, http://dx.doi.org/10.1111 /j.1467-8624.2007.00995.x; C. S. Dweck, C. Chiu, and Y. Hong, "Implicit Theories and Their Role in Judgments and Reactions: A World from Two Perspectives," *Psychological Inquiry* 6, (1995): 267–85, https://doi.org/10.1207/s15327965pli0604_1; S. R. Levy, J. E. Plaks, Y. Hong, C. Chiu, and C. S. Dweck, "Static Versus Dynamic Theories and the Perception of Groups: Different Routes to Different Destinations," *Personality and Social Psychology Review* 5 (2001): 156–68, https://doi.org /10.1207/S15327957PSPR0502_6; C. Chiu, Y. Hong, and C. S. Dweck, "Lay Dispositionism and Implicit Theories of Personality," *Journal of Personality and Social Psychology* 73 (1997): 19–30, https://doi.org/10.1037/0022-3514.73.1.19; C. A. Erdley and C. S. Dweck, "Children's Implicit Personality Theories as Predictors of their Social Judgments," *Child Development* 64 (1993): 863–78, https://doi.org /10.2307/1131223; S. R. Levy, S. J. Stroessner, and C. S. Dweck, "Stereotype Formation and Endorsement: The Role of Implicit Theories," *Journal of Personality and Social Psychology* 74 (1998): 1421–36, https://doi.org/10.1037/0022-3514.74.6.1421; J. E. Plaks, S. J. Stroessner, C. S. Dweck, and J. W. Sherman, "Person Theories and Attention Allocation: Preferences for Stereotypic Versus Counterstereotypic Information," *Journal of Personality and Social Psychology* 80 (2001): 876–93, https:// doi.org/10.1037/0022-3514.80.6.876; J. E. Plaks, "Implicit Theories: Assumptions that Shape Social and Moral Cognition," in *Advances in Experimental Social Psychology* 56, ed. J. M. Olson (New York: Academic Press, 2017), 259–310.

17 *One of the ways my team evaluates*: Mary C. Murphy and Stephanie L. Reeves, "Personal and Organizational Mindsets at Work," *Research in Organizational Behavior* 39 (2019), https://doi.org/10.1016/j.riob.2020.100121; Mary C. Murphy and Carol S. Dweck, "A Culture of Genius: How an Organization's Lay Theory Shapes People's Cognition, Affect, and Behavior," *Personality and Social Psychology Bulletin* 36, no. 3 (October 2009): 283–96, https://doi.org/10.1177/0146167209347380; Katherine T. U. Emerson and Mary C. Murphy, "A Company I Can Trust? Organizational Lay Theories Moderate Stereotype Threat for Women," *Personality and Social Psychology Bulletin* 41, no. 2 (February 1, 2015): 295–307, https://doi .org/10.1177/01461672145649; Elizabeth A. Canning, Mary C. Murphy, Katherine T. U. Emerson, Jennifer A. Chatman, Carol S. Dweck, and Laura J. Kray, "Cultures of Genius at Work: Organizational Mindsets Predict Cultural Norms, Trust, and Commitment," *Personality and Social Psychology Bulletin* 46, no. 4 (2020): 626–42.

18 *My research shows that organizations*: Murphy and Reeves, "Personal and Organizational Mindsets at Work"; Canning et al., "Cultures of Genius at Work."

18 *The following are characteristics*: Murphy and Reeves, "Personal and Organizational Mindsets at Work"; Emerson and Murphy, "A Company I Can Trust?"; Canning et al., "Cultures of Genius at Work."

19 *This brilliance heuristic*: Benjamin Frimodig, "Heuristics: Definition, Examples, and How They Work," *Simply Psychology*, February 14, 2023, https://www.simply psychology.org/what-is-a-heuristic.html; L. Bian, S. J. Leslie, and A. Cimpian, "Gender Stereotypes About Intellectual Ability Emerge Early and Influence Children's Interests," *Science* 355 (2017): 389–91, https://doi.org/10.1126/science.aah6524; M. Bennett, "Men's and Women's Self-Estimates of Intelligence," *Journal of Social Psychology* 136 (1996): 411–12, https://doi.org/10.1080/00224545.1996.9714021; M. Bennett, "Self-Estimates of Ability in Men and Women," *Journal of Social Psychology* 137 (1997): 540–41, https://doi.org/10.1080/00224549709595475; K. C. Elmore and M. Luna-Lucero, "Light Bulbs or Seeds? How Metaphors for Ideas Influence Judgments about Genius," *Social Psychological and Personality Science* 8 (2017): 200–8, https://doi.org/10.1177/1948550616667611; B. Kirkcaldy, P. Noack, A. Furnham, and G. Siefen, "Parental Estimates of Their Own and Their Children's Intelligence," *European Psychologist* 12 (2007): 173–80, https://doi .org/10.1027/1016-9040.12.3.173; A. Lecklider, *Inventing the Egghead: The Battle over Brainpower in American Culture* (Philadelphia: University of Pennsylvania Press, 2013); Seth Stephens-Davidowitz, "Google, Tell Me. Is My Son a Genius?" *New York Times*, January 18, 2014, http://www.nytimes.com/2014/01/19/opinion /sunday/google-tell-me-is-my-son-a-genius.html; J. Tiedemann, "Gender-Related Beliefs of Teachers in Elementary School Mathematics," *Educational Studies in Mathematics* 41 (2000): 191–207, https://doi.org/10.1023/A:1003953801526; Sandra Upson and Lauren F. Friedman, "Where are all the Female Geniuses?" *Scientific American Mind*, November 1, 2012, https://www.scientificamerican.com /article/where-are-all-the-female-geniuses/.

20 *Just for kicks*: "What Does Genius Look Like?" Google search, accessed May 6, 2023, https://www.google.com/search?q=what+does+a+genius+look+like&tbm =isch&ved=2ahUKEwj9h5Obi-H-AhUTLN4AHXhZAQIQ2-cCegQIABAA&oq =what+does+a+genius+look+like&gs_lcp=CgNpbWcQAzIECCMQJzIG CAAQBxAeMgYIABAIEB5Q9gJYoAlgpQpoAXAAeACAAZMBiAHxAZI BAzEuMZgBAKABAAoBC2d3cyl3aXotaW1nwAEB&sclient=img&ei=53xWZ L34I5PY-LYP-LKFEA.

20 *In Cultures of Genius*: L. Bian, S. Leslie, M. C. Murphy, and A. Cimpian, "Messages about Brilliance Undermine Women's Interest in Educational and Professional Opportunities," *Journal of Experimental Social Psychology* 76 (May 2018): 404–20; https://doi.org/10.1016/j.jesp.2017.11.006.

20 *gives rise to behavioral norms*: Canning et al., "Cultures of Genius at Work."

21 *Edgar Schein, professor emeritus at MIT*: Edgar H. Schein, *Organizational Culture and Leadership*, 4th ed. (San Francisco: Jossey-Bass, 2010).

21 *mindset is one of those core beliefs about human behavior*: Murphy and Reeves, "Personal and Organizational Mindsets at Work"; Canning et al., "Cultures of Genius at Work."

22 *Depending on what we perceive*: Murphy and Reeves, "Personal and Organizational Mindsets at Work."

22 *In my lab's research, we found that*: Murphy and Reeves, "Personal and Organizational Mindsets at Work"; Murphy and Dweck, "A Culture of Genius."

22 *Employees have less trust*: Murphy and Reeves, "Personal and Organizational Mindsets at Work"; Murphy and Dweck, "A Culture of Genius"; Emerson and Murphy, "A Company I Can Trust?"; Canning et al., "Cultures of Genius at Work."

23 *My colleagues and I found that*: Canning et al., "Cultures of Genius at Work."

24 *As our analysis showed, in stronger Cultures of Genius*: Emerson and Murphy, "A Company I Can Trust?"; Canning et al., "Cultures of Genius at Work."

25 *Next, we were curious how managers' perceptions*: Canning et al., "Cultures of Genius at Work." See also: P. A. Heslin, "'Potential' in the Eye of the Beholder: The Role of Managers Who Spot Rising Stars," *Industrial and Organizational Psychology: Perspectives on Science and Practice* 2, no. 4 (2009): 420–24, https://doi.org/10.1111/j.1754-9434.2009.01166.x

27 *Consistent with the Fortune 500 results*: Mary C. Murphy, "Mindsets in Entrepreneurship: Measurement and Validation Results," report to the G2 Advisory Group and the Kauffman Foundation (April 2020).

CHAPTER 3: COLLABORATION

33 *Our studies show that Cultures of Growth*: Mary C. Murphy and Stephanie L. Reeves, "Personal and Organizational Mindsets at Work," *Research in Organizational Behavior* 39 (2019), https://doi.org/10.1016/j.riob.2020.100121; Mary C. Murphy and Carol S. Dweck, "A Culture of Genius: How an Organization's Lay Theory Shapes People's Cognition, Affect, and Behavior," *Personality and Social Psychology Bulletin* 36, no. 3 (October 2009): 283–96, https://doi.org/10.1177/0146167209347380; Elizabeth A. Canning, Mary C. Murphy, Katherine T. U. Emerson, Jennifer A. Chatman, Carol S. Dweck, and Laura J. Kray, "Cultures of Genius at Work: Organizational Mindsets Predict Cultural Norms, Trust, and Commitment," *Personality and Social Psychology Bulletin* 46, no. 4 (2020): 626–42; M. C. Murphy, B. Tauber, C. Samsa, and C. S. Dweck, "Founders' Mindsets Predict Company Culture and Organizational Success in Early Stage Startups" (working paper); Mary C. Murphy, "Mindsets in Entrepreneurship: Measurement and Validation Results," report to the G2 Advisory Group and the Kauffman Foundation (April 2020). Note: The work with the Kauffman Foundation was conducted in collaboration with Wendy Torrance and Kathleen Boyle Dalen.

34 *Adam Neumann claimed that WeWork*: WeWork: Or the Making and Breaking of a $47 Billion Unicorn, directed by Jed Rothstein, Campfire/Forbes Entertainment/Olive Hill Media, 2021.

34 *This process, called stack ranking*: Steve Bates, "Forced Ranking," *HR Magazine*, June 1, 2003, https://www.shrm.org/hr-today/news/hr-magazine/pages/0603bates.aspx.

34 *referred to at WeWork as "Jen-ocides,"*: Reeves Wiedeman, *Billion Dollar Loser: The Epic Rise and Fall of WeWork* (London: Hodder & Stoughton, 2020).

35 *According to data from the Center for American Progress*: "There Are Significant Business Costs to Replacing Employees," Center for American Progress, November 16, 2012, https://www.americanprogress.org/article/there-are-significant-business-costs-to-replacing-employees/.

35 *Gallup estimates that churn*: Amy Adkins, "Millennials: The Job-Hopping Generation," Gallup, accessed May 6, 2023, https://www.gallup.com/workplace/231587/millennials-job-hopping-generation.aspx.

35 *Among their top priorities*: Lauren Vesty, "Millennials Want Purpose Over Paychecks. So Why Can't We Find It at Work?" *Guardian*, September 14, 2016, https://www.theguardian.com/sustainable-business/2016/sep/14/millennials-work-purpose-linkedin-survey.

35 *As our study of Glassdoor data revealed*: Canning et al., "Cultures of Genius at Work."

35 *When 2021's unprecedented*: "Quits: Total Nonfarm," Federal Reserve Bank of St. Louis, accessed May 6, 2023, https://fred.stlouisfed.org/series/JTSQUL?utm_source=npr_newsletter&utm_medium=email&utm_content=20220122&utm_term=6236291&utm_campaign=money&utm_id=1253516&orgid=278&utm_att1=nprnews.

35 *organizational behavior experts noted*: Donald Sull, Charles Sull, and Ben Zweig, "Toxic Culture Is Driving the Great Resignation," *MIT Sloan Management Review*, January 11, 2022, https://sloanreview.mit.edu/article/toxic-culture-is-driving-the-great-resignation/.

35 *One of the most powerful influences*: Murphy and Reeves, "Personal and Organizational Mindsets at Work"; Katherine T. U. Emerson and Mary C. Murphy, "A Company I Can Trust? Organizational Lay Theories Moderate Stereotype Threat for Women," *Personality and Social Psychology Bulletin* 41, no. 2 (February 1, 2015): 295–307, https://doi.org/10.1177/01461672145649; Canning et al., "Cultures of Genius at Work"; P. A. Heslin, "'Potential' in the Eye of the Beholder: The Role of Managers Who Spot Rising Stars," *Industrial and Organizational Psychology: Perspectives on Science and Practice* 2, no. 4 (2009): 420–24, https://doi.org/10.1111/j.1754-9434.2009.01166.x; Heslin, Keating, and Ashford, "How Being in Learning Mode May Enable a Sustainable Career Across the Lifespan."

35 *Only when Neumann's former assistant*: WeWork: Or the Making and Breaking of a $47 Billion Unicorn.

36 *Yet as our research has revealed*: Murphy and Reeves, "Personal and Organizational Mindsets at Work"; Emerson and Murphy, "A Company I Can Trust?"; Canning et al., "Cultures of Genius at Work."

36 *Ironically, WeWork sold itself*: WeWork: Or the Making and Breaking of a $47 Billion Unicorn.

36 *Neumann was eventually ousted*: Samantha Subin, "Outsted WeWork CEO Says $47 Billion Valuation Went to His Head Before Botched IPO," CNBC, November 9, 2021, https://www.cnbc.com/2021/11/09/ousted-wework-ceo-adam-neumann-47-billion-valuation-went-to-his-head.html; Wiedeman, *Billion Dollar Loser*.

36 *modern examples such as WeWork*: Wiedeman, *Billion Dollar Loser*.

36 *and Theranos*: John Carreyrou, *Bad Blood: Secrets and Lies in a Silicon Valley Startup* (New York: Knopf, 2018); *The Inventor: Out for Blood in Silicon Valley*, directed by Alex Gibney, HBO Documentary Films/Jigsaw Productions, 2019.

36 *Wells Fargo*: Chris Prentice and Pete Schroeder, "Former Wells Fargo Exec Faces Prison, Will Pay $17 Million Fine Over Fake Accounts Scandal," Reuters, March 15,

2023, https://www.reuters.com/legal/former-wells-fargo-executive-pleads-guilty
-obstructing-bank-examination-fined-17-2023-03-15/.

36 *and Enron*: Bethany McLean and Peter Elkind, *Smartest Guys in the Room: The Amazing Rise and Scandalous Fall of Enron* (New York: Portfolio, 2003).

36 *And disconcertingly, stack ranking*: A. J. Hess, "Ranking Workers Can Hurt Morale and Productivity. Tech Companies Are Doing It Anyway," *Fast Company*, February 16, 2023, https://www.fastcompany.com/90850190/stack-ranking-workers -hurt-morale-productivity-tech-companies?utm_source=newsletters&utm _medium=email&utm_campaign=FC%20-%20Compass%20Newsletter.Newslet ter%20-%20FC%20-%20Compass%202-17-23&leadId=7181911.

36 *Instead, it can follow directly*: Murphy and Reeves, "Personal and Organizational Mindsets at Work"; Emerson and Murphy, "A Company I Can Trust?"; Canning et al., "Cultures of Genius at Work."

37 *In my research with Fortune 500 companies*: Canning et al., "Cultures of Genius at Work."

38 *As CEO, entrepreneur, and business professor*: Margaret Heffernan, *A Bigger Prize: How We Can Do Better than the Competition* (Philadelphia: PublicAffairs, 2014).

39 *As it happens, a team of researchers*: Omri Gillath, Christian S. Crandall, Daniel L. Wann, and Mark H. White II, "Buying and Building Success: Perceptions of Organizational Strategies for Improvement," *Journal of Applied Psychology* 51, no. 5 (May 2021): 534–46, https://doi.org/10.1111/jasp.12755.

39 *For example, design candidates*: "How to Nail Your Design Interview: What to Expect and What We Look For," Atlassian, accessed May 6, 2023, https://www .atlassian.com/company/careers/resources/interviewing/how-to-nail-your -design-interview.

40 *There's separate information*: "Breaking the Glass Ceiling in Tech: Advice from Three Atlassian Engineering Managers," Atlassian, accessed May 6, 2023, https:// www.atlassian.com/company/careers/resources/career-growth/breaking-the -glass-ceiling-in-tech.

40 *Another page offers a Q&A*: "Common Challenges of Interns and Grads and the Solutions to Them," Atlassian, accessed May 6, 2023, https://www.atlassian.com /company/careers/resources/career-growth/common-challenges-of-interns-and -grads.

40 *Atlassian's philosophy*: "Employee Development Templates," Atlassian, accessed May 6, 2023, https://www.atlassian.com/software/confluence/templates/collec tions/employee-development.

40 *Atlassian also shares the journeys*: "From New Grads to Engineering Managers: Three Atlassian[s] on their Journeys, Constant Learning, and Support Along the Way," Atlassian, accessed May 6, 2023, https://www.atlassian.com/company/ca reers/resources/career-growth/from-new-grads-to-engineering-managers.

40 *They also seek to learn*: Sarah Larson, "The Employee Attrition Spike is Here: How to Hang on to Your Best People," Atlassian, June 22, 2021, https://www.atlassian .com/blog/leadership/attrition-spike.

41 *According to Glassdoor data from 2023*: "Atlassian," Glassdoor, accessed May 6, 2023, https://www.glassdoor.com/Reviews/Atlassian-Reviews-E115699.htm.

41 *And for those concerned*: "Atlassian," MarketCap, accessed May 6, 2023, https://companiesmarketcap.com/atlassian/marketcap/.

41 *The Yerkes-Dodson law*: Ronald A. Cohen, "Yerkes-Dodson Law," *Encyclopedia of Clinical Neuropsychology*, accessed May 6, 2023, https://link.springer.com/referenceworkentry/10.1007/978-0-387-79948-3_1340.

41 *And again, our research has shown*: Canning et al., "Cultures of Genius at Work"; Murphy and Reeves, "Personal and Organizational Mindsets at Work"; Emerson and Murphy, "A Company I Can Trust?"

42 *As a young girl, Jennifer Doudna*: Walter Isaacson, *The Code Breaker: Jennifer Doudna, Gene Editing, and the Future of the Human Race* (New York, Simon & Schuster, 2021).

43 *She also put aside*: Walter Isaacson, "CRISPR Rivals Put Patents Aside to Help in Fight Against Covid-19," *STAT*, March 3, 2021, https://www.statnews.com/2021/03/03/crispr-rivals-put-patents-aside-fight-against-covid-19/.

43 *The result was a CRISPR-based*: "STATus List 2022: Jennifer Doudna," *STAT*, accessed May 6, 2023, https://www.statnews.com/status-list/2022/jennifer-doudna/.

43 *For Doudna, maintaining*: Walter Isaacson, *The Code Breaker*.

44 *From the outset Yvon Chouinard*: Yvon Chouinard, *Let My People Go Surfing: The Education of a Reluctant Businessman—Including 10 More Years of Business Unusual* (New York: Penguin, 2016).

46 *Langer is chair of neurosurgery*: "Overview," Lenox Hill Hospital, accessed May 6, 2023, https://lenoxhill.northwell.edu/about.

46 *"If you don't have collaboration,"*: *Lenox Hill*, season 1, episode 1, "Growth Hurts." Netflix, 2020.

48 *Running coach Steve Magness*: "Steve Magness: How to Do Hard Things and the Surprising Science of Resilience, Episode 686," interview by Rich Roll, *Rich Roll Podcast*, June 13, 2022, https://www.richroll.com/podcast/steve-magness-686/.

48 *On the sitcom* Friends: *Friends*, season 5, episode 5.13, "The One with Joey's Bag," NBC, February 4, 1999.

49 *Tech company DigitalOcean*: Lisa Bodell, "Reward Programs that Actually Boost Collaboration," *Forbes*, November 30, 2019, https://www.forbes.com/sites/lisabodell/2019/11/30/reward-programs-that-actually-boost-collaboration/?sh=706c797871ee.

49 *In 2013, Microsoft threw out*: Stephen Miller, "'Stack Ranking' Ends at Microsoft, Generating Heated Debate," SHRM, November 20, 2013, https://www.shrm.org/resourcesandtools/hr-topics/compensation/pages/stack-ranking-microsoft.aspx.

49 *Dean Carter, head of human resources*: "Can Patagonia Change the World? With CHRO Dean Carter and Dr. David Rock," interview by Chris Weller, *Your Brain at Work*, August 5, 2019, https://neuroleadership.com/podcast/planting-seeds-at-patagonia-with-dean-carter.

51 *As part of its Talent Assessment Program*: "Talent Assessment Program," GitLab, accessed May 6, 2023, https://about.gitlab.com/handbook/people-group/talent-assessment/#measuring-growth-potential.

CHAPTER 4: INNOVATION AND CREATIVITY

52 *We don't know how fast*: Jorrit van der Togt, interview by Mary Murphy, July 8, 2021.

53 *Set in 2007, Goal Zero*: "Safety: Our Approach," Shell, accessed May 6, 2023, https://www.shell.com/sustainability/safety/our-approach.html.

55 *Duncan said in a personal interview*: Candace Duncan, interview by Kelly Madrone, December 2, 2020.

55 *Leading by example has been*: Crystal L. Hoyt, Jeni L. Burnette, and Audrey N. Innella, "I Can Do That: The Impact of Implicit Theories on Leadership Role Model Effectiveness," *Personality and Social Psychology Bulletin* 38, no. 2 (December 5, 2011) https://doi.org/10.1177/0146167211427922.

56 *In the case of the ride-sharing app Uber*: Mike Isaac, *Super Pumped: The Battle for Uber* (New York: W. W. Norton & Company, 2019).

57 *At KPMG*: Candace Duncan, interview by Kelly Madrone, December 2, 2020.

57 *At Uber*: Mike Isaac, *Super Pumped*.

58 *Frei implemented a massive increase*: Frances Frei, "How to Build (and Rebuild) Trust," TED2018, April 2018, https://www.ted.com/talks/frances_frei_how_to _build_and_rebuild_trust#t-848544.

58 *Incidentally, Uber's new CEO*: Kara Swisher, "Here's One of Uber CEO Dara Khosrowshahi's New Rules of the Road: 'We Do the Right Thing. Period.,'" *Vox*, November 7, 2017, https://www.vox.com/2017/11/7/16617340/read-uber-dara -khosrowshahi-new-rule-values-meeting.

58 *When we're in prove-and-perform mode*: Marie Crouzevialle and Fabrizio Butera, "Performance-Approach Goals Deplete Working Memory and Impair Cognitive Performance," *Journal of Experimental Psychology* 142, no. 3 (August 2013): 666–78, https://doi.org/10.1037/a0029632.

59 *Conversely, a different set of studies*: Nujaree Intasao and Ning Hao, "Beliefs about Creativity Influence Creative Performance: The Mediation Effects of Flexibility and Positive Affect," *Frontiers in Psychology* 9 (September 24, 2018), https://doi .org/10.3389/fpsyg.2018.01810.s

59 *Researchers ran a study to measure*: Alexander J. O'Connor, Charlan J. Nemeth, and Satoshi Akutsu, "Consequences of Beliefs about the Malleability of Creativity," *Creativity Research Journal* 25, no. 2 (May 17, 2013): 155–62, https://doi.org /10.1080/10400419.2013.783739.

59 *In another study, researchers measured convergent*: Ibid.

60 *As a quote frequently attributed to Charles Darwin*: "It Is Not the Strongest of the Species that Survives but the Most Adaptable," Quote Investigator, accessed May 8, 2023, https://quoteinvestigator.com/2014/05/04/adapt/.

60 *Yet companies are often faced*: Charles A. O'Reilly and Michael L. Tushman, *Lead and Disrupt: How to Solve the Innovator's Dilemma* (Redwood City, CA: Stanford Business Books, 2016).

60 *Research shows that individuals and organizations*: Elizabeth A. Canning, Mary C. Murphy, Katherine T. U. Emerson, Jennifer A. Chatman, Carol S. Dweck, and Laura J. Kray, "Cultures of Genius at Work: Organizational Mindsets Predict Cultural Norms, Trust, and Commitment," *Personality and Social Psychology Bulletin* 46,

no. 4 (2020): 626–42; Don Vandenwalle, "A Growth and Fixed Mindset Exposition of the Value of Conceptual Clarity," *Industrial and Organizational Psychology* 5, no. 3 (January 7, 2015): 301–05, https://doi.org/10.1111/j/1754-9434.2012.01450.x.

60 *Jacqueline Novogratz was excelling*: Jacqueline Novogratz, *The Blue Sweater: Bridging the Gap Between Rich and Poor in an Interconnected World* (New York: Rodale, 2009); Jacqueline Novogratz, *Manifesto for a Moral Revolution: Practices to Build a Better World* (New York: Henry Holt, 2020); Jacqueline Novogratz, interview by Mary Murphy, March 16, 2023.

62 *By 2023, d.light had helped*: "1,400,000 Lives. Transformed." d.light, accessed May 8, 2023, https://www.dlight.com/.

62 *According to Novogratz*: Jacqueline Novogratz, *Manifesto for a Moral Revolution*.

62 *When I spoke with Jacqueline Novogratz*: Jacqueline Novogratz, interview by Mary Murphy, March 16, 2023.

63 *Yes, according to multiple studies*: Mary C. Murphy and Carol S. Dweck, "Mindsets Shape Consumer Behavior," *Journal of Consumer Psychology* 26, no. 1 (2016): 127–36, http://dx.doi.org/10.1016/j.jcps.2015.06.005.

63 *University of Cincinnati researcher Josh Clarkson*: Cammy Crolic, Joshua J. Clarkson, Ashley S. Otto, and Mary C. Murphy, "Motivated Knowledge Acquisition: Implicit Self-Theories and the Preference for Knowledge Breadth or Depth," *Personality and Social Psychology Bulletin* (forthcoming, 2024).

64 *People operating from their fixed*: Carol S. Dweck and Ellen L. Leggett, "A Social-Cognitive Approach to Motivation and Personality," *Psychological Review* 95, no. 2 (1988): 256–73, https://doi.org/10.1037/0033-295X.95.2.256.

64 *How products are marketed*: Murphy and Dweck, "Mindsets Shape Consumer Behavior"; Mary C. Murphy and Carol S. Dweck, "Mindsets and Consumer Psychology: A Response," *Journal of Consumer Psychology* 26 (2015): 165–66, https://doi.org/10.1016/j.jcps.2015.06.006.

64 *Additionally, organizational behavior studies*: Murphy and Dweck, "Mindsets Shape Consumer Behavior"; J. K. Park, and D. R. John, "Got to Get You Into My Life: Do Brand Personalities Rub Off on Consumers?," *Journal of Consumer Research* 37 (2010): 655–669, https://doi.org/10.1086/655807; J. K. Park and D. R. John, "Capitalizing on Brand Personalities in Advertising: The Influence of Implicit Self-Theories on Ad Appeal Effectiveness," *Journal of Consumer Psychology* 22 (2012): 424–32, https://doi.org/10.1016/j.jcps.2011.05.004.

65 *People often perceive fixed-minded organizations*: Murphy and Dweck, "Mindsets Shape Consumer Behavior"; Emerson and Murphy, "A Company I Can Trust?"; Mary C. Murphy and Carol S. Dweck, "A Culture of Genius: How an Organization's Lay Theory Shapes People's Cognition, Affect, and Behavior," *Personality and Social Psychology Bulletin* 36, no. 3 (October 2009): 283–96, https://doi.org/10.1177/0146167209347380.

65 *This is also one of the reasons*: Seth Stevenson, "We're No. 2! We're No. 2! How a Mad Men–Era Ad Firm Discovered the Perks of Being an Underdog," Slate, August 12, 2013, https://slate.com/business/2013/08/hertz-vs-avis-advertising-wars-how-an-ad-firm-made-a-virtue-out-of-second-place.html; Murphy and Dweck, "Mindsets Shape Consumer Behavior."

65 *A Meta survey of Millennials*: "Millennials + Money: The Unfiltered Journey,"

Meta, September 25, 2016, https://www.facebook.com/business/news/insights/millennials-money-the-unfiltered-journey.

66 *That was the message consumers*: Christopher Klein, "Why Coca-Cola's 'New Coke' Flopped," History, March 13, 2020, https://www.history.com/news/why-coca-cola-new-coke-flopped; Murphy and Dweck, "Mindsets Shape Consumer Behavior."

66 *Another example is a ketchup*: Sandie Glass, "What Were They Thinking? The Day Ketchup Crossed the Line from Perfect to Purple," *Fast Company*, September 14, 2011, https://www.fastcompany.com/1779591/what-were-they-thinking-day-ketchup-crossed-line-perfect-purple.

66 *These brands prompt a growth mindset*: Murphy and Dweck, "Mindsets Shape Consumer Behavior"; E. A. Yorkston, J. C. Nunes, and S. Matta, "The Malleable Brand: The Role of Implicit Theories in Evaluating Brand Extensions," *Journal of Marketing* 74 (2010): 80–93, https://doi.org/10.1509/jmkg.74.1.80; P. Mathur, S. P. Jain, and D. Maheswaran, "Consumers' Implicit Theories about Personality Influence Their Brand Personality Judgments," *Journal of Consumer Psychology* 22 (2012): 545–57, https://doi.org/10.1016/j.jcps.2012.01.005.

66 *Organizational mindset also plays a role*: Murphy and Dweck, "Mindsets Shape Consumer Behavior."

66 *Intergroup mindsets refer to*: E. Halperin, A. Russell, K. Trzesniewski, J. J. Gross, and C. S. Dweck, "Promoting the Middle East Peace Process by Changing Beliefs about Group Malleability," *Science* 333, no. 6050 (2011): 1767–69, https://doi.org/10.1126/science.1202925; R. J. Rydell, K. Hugenberg, D. Ray, and D. M. Mackie, "Implicit Theories about Groups and Stereotyping: The Role of Group Entitativity," *Personality and Social Psychology Bulletin* 33 (2007): 549–58, https://doi.org/10.1177/0146167206296956.

67 *An example is when Taco Bell*: Mark Stevenson, "Taco Bell's Fare Baffles Mexicans," *Seattle Times*, October 10, 2007, https://www.seattletimes.com/business/taco-bells-fare-baffles-mexicans/; Murphy and Dweck, "Mindsets Shape Consumer Behavior."

67 *McDonald's has done a far better*: Murphy and Dweck, "Mindsets Shape Consumer Behavior"; D. Daszkowski, "How American Fast Food Franchises Expanded Abroad," About.com, accessed May 15, 2023, http://franchises.about.com.

67 *"Fear inhibits learning."*: Amy Edmonson, *The Fearless Organization: Creating Psychological Safety in the Workplace for Learning, Innovation, and Growth* (New York: Wiley, 2018).

69 *As Jacqueline Novogratz observed*: Novogratz, *The Blue Sweater*.

70 *"If you have middle management"*: Jorrit van der Togt, interview by Mary Murphy, July 8, 2021.

72 *In 2020, Shell took a huge step*: Jorrit van der Togt, interview by Mary Murphy, July 8, 2021; "Oil and Gas Extraction," U.S. Bureau of Labor Statistics, accessed May 15, 2023, https://www.bls.gov/iag/tgs/iag211.htm; "Oil Mining and Gas Extraction," U. S. Bureau of Labor Statistics, accessed May 15, 2023, https://data.bls.gov/pdq/SurveyOutputServlet.

73 *Patagonia's philosophy is that*: Chouinard, *Let My People Go Surfing*.

73 *Pixar employs many strategies*: Ed Catmull with Amy Wallace, *Creativity, Inc.*:

Overcoming the Unseen Forces that Stand in the Way of True Inspiration (New York: Random House, 2014).

74　*Emma McIlroy, cofounder of Wildfang*: "The Wildfang Way: Emma McIlroy," interview by Jonathan Fields, *The Good Life Podcast*, August 7, 2019, https://www.goodlifeproject.com/podcast/emma-mcilroy-wildfang/.

75　*Visa cofounder Dee Hock once said*: "Dee Hock," Quotes, accessed May 8, 2023, https://www.quotes.net/quote/41629.

76　*Atlassian combines these norms*: "ShipIt," Atlassian, accessed May 8, 2023, https://www.atlassian.com/company/shipit.

76　*Many other organizations have similar*: Kaomi Goetz, "How 3M Gave Everyone Days Off and Created an Innovation Dynamo," *Fast Company*, February 1, 2011, https://www.fastcompany.com/1663137/how-3m-gave-everyone-days-off-and-created-an-innovation-dynamo.

77　*Google allows employees*: Bill Murphy Jr., "Google Says It Still Uses '20 Percent Rule' and You Should Totally Copy It," *Inc.*, November 11, 2020, https://www.inc.com/bill-murphy-jr/google-says-it-still-uses-20-percent-rule-you-should-totally-copy-it.html.

77　*At manufacturer W. L. Gore*: Heffernan, *A Bigger Prize*; Jay Rao, "W. L. Gore: Culture of Innovation," Babson College, April 2012, http://www.elmayorportaldegerencia.com/Documentos/Innovacion/%5bPD%5d%20Documentos%20-%20Culture%20of%20innovation.pdf.

77　*But as Jorrit van der Togt*: Jorrit van der Togt, interview by Mary Murphy, July 8, 2021.

78　*As attorney, civil rights advocate*: Novogratz, *The Blue Sweater*.

78　*A team of management researchers*: Nikolaus Franke, Marion K. Poetz, and Martin Schreier, "Integrating Problem Solvers from Analogous Markets in New Product Ideation," *Management Science* 60, no. 4 (November 26, 2013): 805–1081, https://doi.org/10.1287/mnsc.2013.1805.

79　*Financial and investing advice firm*: John Mackey, Steve McIntosh, and Carter Phipps, *Conscious Leadership: Elevating Humanity Through Business* (New York: Portfolio, 2020).

79　*My colleague Kimberly Quinn*: @kimberlyquinn, "Have you heard of a surprise journal? When people do something that surprised you, write it down. If you analyze it and figure out why it was surprising, you can learn about what your implicit default expectations are—which can suggest interesting hypotheses." March, 8, 2021, 1:50pm, https://twitter.com/kimberlyquinn/status/1369012627217788928.

CHAPTER 5: RISK-TAKING AND RESILIENCE

81　*I didn't know that when*: David Smith, "Is Donald Trump's Love-Hate Relationship with Twitter on the Rocks?" *Guardian*, May 31, 2020, https://www.theguardian.com/us-news/2020/may/31/donald-trump-twitter-love-hate-relationship.

83　*So, I asked my friend*: Ben Tauber, interview by Mary Murphy, June 30, 2021.

84　*Adam Neumann, who once boasted*: Reeves Wiedeman, *Billion Dollar Loser: The Epic Rise and Fall of WeWork* (London: Hodder & Stoughton, 2020).

84　*Even after the colossal failures*: Clint Rainey, "Adam Neumann Talked About Flow for a Full Hour and We Still Don't Know What It Is," *Fast Company*, February 8, 2023, https://www.fastcompany.com/90847220/adam-neumann-a16z-flow-startup -real-estate-explained.

84 *"When you pitch at that early stage,"*: Ben Tauber, interview by Mary Murphy, June 30, 2021.

84 *Silicon Valley is famous for*: Rob Asghar, "Why Silicon Valley's 'Fail Fast' Mantra is Just Hype," *Forbes*, July 14, 2014, https://www.forbes.com/sites/robasghar/2014 /07/14/why-silicon-valleys-fail-fast-mantra-is-just-hype/?sh=3f54c7d724bc.

85 *"In the fixed mindset,"*: Ben Tauber, interview by Mary Murphy, June 30, 2021.

85 *When Satya Nadella took over*: Herminia Ibarra, Aneeta Rattan, and Anna John- ston, "Satya Nadella at Microsoft: Instilling a Growth Mindset," London Business School, 2018, https://hbsp.harvard.edu/product/LBS128-PDF-ENG.

86 *As Nadella wrote in his book*: Satya Nadella, *Hit Refresh: The Quest to Rediscover Microsoft's Soul and Imagine a Better Future for Everyone* (New York: Harper Busi- ness, 2017).

86 *Kinney Zalesne, Microsoft's former*: Kinney Zalesne, interview by Mary Murphy, June 29, 2021.

87 *In Cultures of Growth, we found that data*: Catherine Poirier, Carina Cheng, Ellora Sarkar, Henry Silva, and Tom Kudrle, "The Culture of Data Leaders," Keystone, February 2, 2021, https://www.keystone.ai/news-publications/whitepaper-the -culture-of-data-leaders/.

88 *Data helped Louis Wool*: Louis Wool, interview by Mary Murphy, September 29, 2020.

88 *Former board of education member*: David A. Singer, "Harrison School's Louis N. Wool Named New York Superintendent of the Year," *HuffPost*, December 11, 2009, https://www.huffpost.com/entry/harrison-schools-louis-n_b_389177.

88 *Throughout the community*: Louis Wool, interview by Mary Murphy, September 29, 2020.

90 *In fact, research shows consistently*: Amy Stuart Wells, Lauren Fox, and Diana Cordova-Cobo, "How Racially Diverse Schools and Classrooms Can Benefit All Students," Century Foundation, February 9, 2016, https://tcf.org/content /report/how-racially-diverse-schools-and-classrooms-can-benefit-all-students /?agreed=1. See also: Aaliyah Samuel, "Why an Equitable Curriculum Matters," NWEA, September 19, 2019, https://www.nwea.org/blog/2019/why-an-equitable -curriculum-matters/.

90 *Wool was named New York Superintendent of the Year*: Singer, "Harrison School's Louis N. Wool Named New York Superintendent of the Year."

90 *and performance rates for students*: Louis Wool, interview by Mary Murphy, Sep- tember 29, 2020. Mastery-oriented goals not only help move students toward their growth mindset, but also may increase grit. As research from Angela Duckworth and her team showed, "students who perceived their schools as more mastery goal-oriented were grittier and earned higher report card grades. In contrast, stu- dents who perceived their schools as more performance goal-oriented were less gritty and earned lower report card grades." Daeun Park, Alisa Yu, Rebecca N. Baelen, Eli Tsukayama, and Angela L. Duckworth, "Fostering Grit: Perceived School Goal-Structure Predicts Growth in Grit and Grades," *Contemporary Ed-*

ucational Psychology 55 (October 2018): 120–28, https://doi.org/10.1016/j.ced psych.2018.09.007.

90 *As of 2023, nearly two decades*: Louis Wool, correspondence with Mary Murphy, May 3, 2023.

91 *Wool explained, "One thing"*: Louis Wool, interview by Mary Murphy, September 29, 2020.

92 *Patagonia head of HR Dean Carter*: Chris Weller, "Patagonia and the Regenerative Approach to Performance Management," NeuroLeadership Institute, August 15, 2019, https://neuroleadership.com/your-brain-at-work/patagonia-your-brain-at-work-podcast; "Can Patagonia Change the World? With CHRO Dean Carter and Dr. David Rock," interview by Chris Weller, *Your Brain at Work*, August 5, 2019, https://neurole adership.com/podcast/planting-seeds-at-patagonia-with-dean-carter.

93 *Incidentally, the company boasted*: Ash Jurberg, "Patagonia Has Provided a Business Blueprint in How to Avoid the Great Resignation," Entrepreneur's Handbook, November 26, 2021, https://medium.com/entrepreneur-s-handbook/patagonia -has-provided-a-business-blueprint-in-how-to-avoid-the-great-resignation -6dcd6ea6f668.

95 *Within two weeks of Elon Musk's*: John Corrigan, "Elon Musk Gives Remaining Twitter Employees an Ultimatum," November 16, 2022, https://www.hcamag.com /us/specialization/employee-engagement/elon-musk-gives-remaining-twitter -employees-an-ultimatum/427677.

96 *As Wildfang cofounder*: "The Wildfang Way: Emma McIlroy," interview by Jonathan Fields, *The Good Life Podcast*, August 7, 2019, https://www.goodlifeproject .com/podcast/emma-mcilroy-wildfang/.

96 *Incidentally, researchers point to*: Robert C. Wilson, Amitai Shenhav, Mark Straccia, and Jonathan D. Cohen, "The Eighty Five Percent Rule for Optimal Learning," *Nature Communications* 10, no. 1 (November 5, 2019), https://doi.org/10.1038 /s41467-019-12552-4.

98 *Criticism aside, one of the things*: Taylor Soper, "'Failure and Innovation are Inseparable Twins': Amazon Founder Jeff Bezos Offers 7 Leadership Principles," *Geek-Wire*, October 28, 2016, https://www.geekwire.com/2016/amazon-founder-jeff -bezos-offers-6-leadership-principles-change-mind-lot-embrace-failure-ditch -powerpoints/.

CHAPTER 6: INTEGRITY AND ETHICAL BEHAVIOR

100 *It's not that Cultures of Growth*: Mary C. Murphy and Stephanie L. Reeves, "Personal and Organizational Mindsets at Work," *Research in Organizational Behavior* 39 (2019), https://doi.org/10.1016/j.riob.2020.100121; Mary C. Murphy and Carol S. Dweck, "Mindsets Shape Consumer Behavior," *Journal of Consumer Psychology* 26, no. 1 (2016): 127–36, http://dx.doi.org/10.1016/j.jcps.2015.06.005.

101 *In 2017, two months after*: Susan Fowler, "Reflecting on One Very, Very Strange Year at Uber," Susan Fowler blog, February 19, 2017, https://www.susanjfowler .com/blog/2017/2/19/reflecting-on-one-very-strange-year-at-uber.

101 *While "brilliant jerks"*: Mike Isaac, *Super Pumped: The Battle for Uber* (New York: W. W. Norton & Company, 2019).

102   *Theranos*: John Carreyrou, *Bad Blood: Secrets and Lies in a Silicon Valley Startup* (New York: Knopf, 2018).

102   *WeWork*: Reeves Wiedeman, *Billion Dollar Loser: The Epic Rise and Fall of WeWork* (London: Hodder & Stoughton, 2020).

102   *as is Goldman Sachs*: Emily Flitter, Kate Kelly, and David Enrich, "A Top Goldman Banker Raised Ethics Concerns. Then He Was Gone," *New York Times*, September 11, 2018, https://www.nytimes.com/2018/09/11/business/goldman-sachs-whistleblower.html.

102   *In her book* Bully Market: Jamie Fiore Higgins, *Bully Market: My Story of Money and Misogyny at Goldman Sachs* (New York: Simon & Schuster, 2022).

103   *Instead of trying to create*: Bruce Friedrich, interview by Mary Murphy, July 8, 2021.

103   *Laura Braden, GFI's associate director*: Laura Braden, interview by Kelly Madrone, October 10, 2022.

104   *GFI applies its growth-minded approach*: Bruce Friedrich, interview by Mary Murphy, July 8, 2021.

106   *One fail was Volkswagen's*: Robert Glazer, "The Biggest Lesson from Volkswagen: Culture Dictates Behavior," *Entrepreneur*, January 8, 2016, https://www.entrepreneur.com/leadership/the-biggest-lesson-from-volkswagen-culture-dictates/254178.

106   *Cognitive scientist Susan Mackie described*: Susan Mackie, interview by Mary Murphy, July 13, 2021; Susan Mackie, correspondence with Mary Murphy, May 8, 2023. Susan noted that there are three key strategies that will transform customer experience programs: 1. Developing goal-directed customer conversations as opposed to task-based ones; 2. Creating performance management and reward systems that perpetuate a goal orientation; and 3. Developing a growth mindset to encourage goal pursuit and goal-directed conversations in customer-facing staff. Transitioning from task to goal orientation requires that organizations go beyond giving people basic skills to perform a basic job and develop their capacity to think, engage, and solve problems. They must distinguish training from learning. Whereas the former is designed to address routine and basic elements of the role, learning teaches the employee to seek out solutions to loosely defined problems. For instance, an employee in their fixed mindset—as encouraged by organizational culture—might take a customer call and think, "I know I should try and save this account, but my stats will look bad if I spend too much time with them." Whereas an employee in their growth mindset—who is supported by a Culture of Growth—might say to the customer, "That's interesting that you don't feel this product suits your needs. Can I ask you to explain to me what your needs are so that perhaps I can help you find a product that works better for you?" Developing employees in this way of course requires more work—after all, it's generally easier to capture and measure task-related performance metrics and to teach task-oriented behavior than to teach and help people cultivate more complex skills. Yet a Culture of Growth looks more at the long-term value of saving accounts, and the follow-on benefits of both positive customer relationships and having employees with higher self-efficacy.

107   *As Verne Harnish*: Verne Harnish, interview by Mary Murphy, July 14, 2021.

108 *As University of Melbourne*: Simine Vazire, "Do We Want to Be Credible or Incredible?" Association for Psychological Science, December 23, 2019, https://www.psychologicalscience.org/observer/do-we-want-to-be-credible-or-incredible.

108 *The lure of the incredible*: Walter Isaacson, *The Code Breaker: Jennifer Doudna, Gene Editing, and the Future of the Human Race* (New York, Simon & Schuster, 2021).

108 *The scientist was put on trial*: Antonio Regalado, "The Creator of the CRISPR Babies has been Released from a Chinese Prison," *MIT Technology Review*, April 4, 2022, https://www.technologyreview.com/2022/04/04/1048829/he-jiankui-prison-free-crispr-babies/. Also, as Regalado notes in an earlier article, even if Hu acted on his own, he was encouraged by peers: "While responsibility for the experiment fell on He and other Chinese team members, many other scientists knew of the project and encouraged it. These include Michael Deem, a former professor at Rice University who participated in the experiment, and John Zhang, head of a large IVF clinic in New York who had plans to commercialize the technology." Antonio Regalado, "Disgraced CRISPR Scientist had Plans to Start a Designer-Baby Business," *MIT Technology Review*, August 1, 2019, https://www.technologyreview.com/2019/08/01/133932/crispr-baby-maker-explored-starting-a-business-in-designer-baby-tourism/.

109 *When I spoke with PLOS CEO*: Alison Mudditt, interview by Mary Murphy, September 30, 2020.

109 *As Stuart Firestein*: Stuart Firestein, *Failure: Why Science Is So Successful* (Oxford: Oxford University Press, 2015).

110 *Carolyn Bertozzi*: @Stanford, "I understand the gravity of being a woman and now a #Nobel laureate in the sciences. There aren't that many of us—yet." Prof. @CarolynBertozzi on chemistry, mentorship and representation, October 5, 2022, 10:45pm, https://twitter.com/Stanford/status/1577882613293146113.

110 *In 2020, I led a group of 28 researchers*: Mary C. Murphy, Amanda F. Mejia, Jorge Mejia, Xiaoran Yan, Sapna Cheryan, Nilanjana Dasgupta, Mesmin Destin, Stephanie A. Fryberg, Julie A. Garcia, Elizabeth L. Haines, Judith M. Harackiewicz, Alison Ledgerwood, Corinne A. Moss-Racusin, Lora E. Park, Sylvia P. Perry, Kate A. Ratliff, Aneeta Rattan, Diana T. Sanchez, Krishna Savani, Denise Sekaquaptewa, Jessi L. Smith, Valerie Jones Taylor, Dustin B. Thoman, Daryl A. Wout, Patricia L. Mabry, Susanne Ressl, Amanda B. Diekman, and Franco Pestilli, "Open Science, Communal Culture, and Women's Participation in the Movement to Improve Science," *Proceedings of the National Academy of Sciences*, 117, no. 39 (September 29, 2020): 24154–64, https://doi.org/10.1073/pnas.1921320117.

111 *Across my research with both*: Murphy and Reeves, "Personal and Organizational Mindsets at Work"; Elizabeth A. Canning, Mary C. Murphy, Katherine T. U. Emerson, Jennifer A. Chatman, Carol S. Dweck, and Laura J. Kray, "Cultures of Genius at Work: Organizational Mindsets Predict Cultural Norms, Trust, and Commitment," *Personality and Social Psychology Bulletin* 46, no. 4 (2020): 626–42; M. C. Murphy, B. Tauber, C. Samsa, and C. S. Dweck, "Founders' Mindsets Predict Company Culture and Organizational Success in Early Stage Startups" (working paper); Mary C. Murphy, "Mindsets in Entrepreneurship: Measurement and Validation Results," report to the G2 Advisory Group and the Kauffman Foundation (April, 2020).

112 *In each case, one of the most*: Ibid.

113 *Dr. Jennifer (Jen) Danek*: Jennifer Danek, interview by Mary Murphy, July 2, 2021.

114 *similar to what Amy Edmonson*: Amy Edmonson, *The Fearless Organization: Creating Psychological Safety in the Workplace for Learning, Innovation, and Growth* (New York: Wiley, 2018).

114 *"I feel relieved*: Jennifer Danek, interview by Mary Murphy, July 2, 2021.

115 *Just after World War II*: "Seiko's Duelling Factories," *Teamistry Podcast*, season 2, episode 1, September 20, 2020, https://www.atlassian.com/blog/podcast/teamistry/season/season-2/seiko-duelling-factories.

116 *As Emma McIlroy says*: "The Wildfang Way: Emma McIlroy," interview by Jonathan Fields, *The Good Life Podcast*, August 7, 2019, https://www.goodlifeproject.com/podcast/emma-mcilroy-wildfang/.

116 *Two of the most dangerous*: Murphy and Dweck, "Mindsets Shape Consumer Behavior."

118 *Recall Susan Mackie's*: Susan Mackie, interview by Mary Murphy, July 13, 2021.

119 *Marianne Jennings, a professor*: Marianne Jennings, *The Seven Signs of Ethical Collapse: How to Spot Moral Meltdowns in Companies . . . Before It's Too Late* (New York: St. Martin's Press, 2006).

119 *Jacqueline Novogratz says*: Jacqueline Novogratz, interview by Mary Murphy, March 16, 2023.

120 *Recall Frank founder Charlie Javice's*: Arwa Mahdawi, "30 Under 30-Year Sentences: Why So Many of Forbes' Young Heroes Face Jail," *Guardian*, April 7, 2023, https://www.theguardian.com/business/2023/apr/06/forbes-30-under-30-tech-finance-prison.

120 *At every Acumen office*: Jacqueline Novogratz, interview by Mary Murphy, March 16, 2023.

120 *Susan Mackie encourages*: Susan Mackie, interview by Mary Murphy, July 13, 2021.

120 *Similar to the medical huddles*: Jennifer Danek, interview by Mary Murphy, July 2, 2021.

120 *the clarity pause*: Susan Mackie, interview by Mary Murphy, July 13, 2021.

120 *Marianne Jennings calls them*: Jennings, *The Seven Signs of Ethical Collapse*.

CHAPTER 7: DIVERSITY, EQUITY, AND INCLUSION

123 *Research I originally conducted with*: Mary C. Murphy, Claude M. Steele, and James J. Gross, "Signaling Threat: How Situational Cues Affect Women in Math, Science, and Engineering Settings," *Psychological Science*, 18, no. 10 (October 2007): 879–85, https://doi.org/10.1111/j.1467-9280.2007.01995.x; Kathryn M. Kroeper, Heidi E. Williams, and Mary C. Murphy, "Counterfeit Diversity: How Strategically Misrepresenting Gender Diversity Dampens Organizations' Perceived Sincerity and Elevates Women's Identity Threat Concerns," *Journal of Personality and Social Psychology* 122, no. 3 (2022): 399–426, https://doi.org/10.1037/pspi0000348; M. C. Murphy and V. J. Taylor, "The Role of Situational Cues in Signaling and Maintaining Stereotype Threat," in *Stereotype Threat: Theory, Process, and Applications*, ed. M. Inzlicht and T. Schmader (Oxford: Oxford University

Press, 2012), 17–33; K. L. Boucher and M. C. Murphy, "Why So Few? The Role of Social Identity and Situational Cues in Understanding the Underrepresentation of Women in STEM Fields," in *Self and Social Identity in Educational Contexts*, ed. K. I. Mavor, M. Platow, and B. Bizumic (Philadelphia: Routledge/Taylor & Francis, 2017), 93–111; M. C. Murphy, K. M. Kroeper, and E. Ozier, "Prejudiced Places: How Contexts Shape Inequality and How We Can Change Them," *Policy Insights from the Behavioral and Brain Sciences* 5 (2018): 66–74, https://doi.org/10.1177/2372732217748671; Katherine T. U. Emerson and Mary C. Murphy, "Identity Threat at Work: How Social Identity Threat and Situational Cues Contribute to Racial and Ethnic Disparities in the Workplace," *Cultural Diversity and Ethnic Minority Psychology* 20, no. 4 (October 2014): 508–20, https://doi.org/10.1037/a0035403; G. M. Walton, M. C. Murphy, and A. M. Ryan, "Stereotype Threat in Organizations: Implications for Equity and Performance," *Annual Review of Organizational Psychology and Organizational Behavior* 2 (2015): 523–50, https://doi.org/10.1146/annurev-orgpsych-032414-111322.

124 *Over the last decade, my research*: Mary C. Murphy and Stephanie L. Reeves, "Personal and Organizational Mindsets at Work," *Research in Organizational Behavior* 39 (2019), https://doi.org/10.1016/j.riob.2020.100121; Mary C. Murphy and Carol S. Dweck, "A Culture of Genius: How an Organization's Lay Theory Shapes People's Cognition, Affect, and Behavior," *Personality and Social Psychology Bulletin* 36, no. 3 (October 2009): 283–96, https://doi.org/10.1177/0146167209347380; Elizabeth A. Canning, Katherine Muenks, Dorainne J. Green, and Mary C. Murphy, "STEM Faculty Who Believe Ability Is Fixed Have Larger Racial Achievement Gaps and Inspire Less Student Motivation in Their Classes," *Science Advances* 5, no. 2 (February 15, 2019), https://doi.org/10.1126/sciadv.aau4734; K. Muenks, E. A. Canning, J. LaCosse, D. J. Green, S. Zirkel, and J. A. Garcia, "Does My Professor Think My Ability Can Change? Students' Perceptions of Their STEM Professors' Mindset Beliefs Predict Their Psychological Vulnerability, Engagement, and Performance in Class," *Journal of Experimental Psychology: General* 149, no. 11 (2020): 2119–44, https://doi.org/10.1037/xge0000763; David S. Yeager, Jamie M. Carroll, Jenny Buontempo, Andrei Cimpian, Spencer Woody, Robert Crosnoe, Chandra Muller, Jared Murray, Pratik Mhatre, Nicole Kersting, Christopher Hulleman, Molly Kudym, Mary Murphy, Angela Lee Duckworth, Gregory M. Walton, and Carol S. Dweck, "Teacher Mindsets Help Explain Where a Growth-Mindset Intervention Does and Doesn't Work," *Psychological Science* 33, no. 1 (2022): 18–32, https://doi.org/10.1177/09567976211028984; Elizabeth A. Canning, Elise Ozier, Heidi E. Williams, Rashed AlRasheed, and Mary C. Murphy, "Professors Who Signal a Fixed Mindset about Ability Undermine Women's Performance in STEM," *Social Psychological and Personality Science* 13, no. 5 (2022): 927–37, https://doi.org/10.1177/19485506211030398; M. C. Murphy and G. M. Walton, "From Prejudiced People to Prejudiced Places: A Social-Contextual Approach to Prejudice," in *Frontiers in Social Psychology Series: Stereotyping and Prejudice*, eds. C. Stangor and C. Crandall (New York: Psychology Press, 2013), 181–203; Emerson and Murphy, "Identity Threat at Work"; Katherine T. U. Emerson and Mary C. Murphy, "A Company I Can Trust? Organizational Lay Theories Moderate Stereotype Threat for Women," *Personality and Social Psychology Bulletin* 41, no. 2 (February 1, 2015): 295–307, https://

doi.org/10.1177/01461672145649; Walton, Murphy, and Ryan, "Stereotype Threat in Organizations"; Boucher and Murphy, "Why So Few?"; L. Bian, S. Leslie, M. C. Murphy, and A. Cimpian, "Messages about Brilliance Undermine Women's Interest in Educational and Professional Opportunities," *Journal of Experimental Social Psychology* 76 (May 2018): 404–20, https://doi.org/10.1016/j.jesp.2017.11.006; Melissa A. Fuesting, Amanda B. Diekman, Kathryn L. Boucher, Mary C. Murphy, Dana L. Manson, and Brianne L. Safer, "Growing STEM: Perceived Faculty Mindset as an Indicator of Communal Affordances in STEM," *Journal of Personality and Social Psychology* 117, no. 2 (2019): 260–81, https://doi.org/10.1037/pspa0000154; L. A. Murdock-Perriera, K. L. Boucher, E. R. Carter, and M. C. Murphy, "Belonging and Campus Climate: Belonging Interventions and Institutional Synergies to Support Student Success in Higher Education," in *Higher Education Handbook of Theory and Research*, vol. 34, ed. M. Paulsen (New York: Springer, 2019), 291–323; Murphy et al., "Open Science, Communal Culture, and Women's Participation in the Movement to Improve Science," *Proceedings of the National Academy of Sciences*, 117, no. 39 (September 29, 2020): 24154–64, https://doi.org/10.1073/pnas.1921320117; K. Boucher, M. C. Murphy, D. Bartel, J. Smail, C. Logel, and J. Danek, "Centering the Student Experience: What Faculty and Institutions Can Do to Advance Equity," *Change: The Magazine of Higher Learning* 53 (2021): 42–50, https://doi.org/10.1080 /00091383.2021.1987804; Canning et al., "Professors Who Signal a Fixed Mindset"; D. J. Green, D. A. Wout, and M. C. Murphy, "Learning Goals Mitigate Identity Threat for Black Individuals in Threatening Interracial Interactions," *Cultural Diversity and Ethnic Minority Psychology* 27 (2021): 201–13, https://doi.org/10.1037 /cdp0000331; J. LaCosse, M. C. Murphy, J. A. Garcia, and S. Zirkel, "The Role of STEM Professors' Mindset Beliefs on Students' Anticipated Psychological Experiences and Course Interest," *Journal of Educational Psychology* 113 (2021): 949–71, https://doi.org/10.1037/edu0000620; Mary Murphy, Stephanie Fryberg, Laura Brady, Elizabeth Canning, and Cameron Hecht, "Global Mindset Initiative Paper 1: Growth Mindset Cultures and Teacher Practices," *Growth Mindset Cultures and Practices* (August 27, 2021), http://dx.doi.org/10.2139/ssrn.3911594.

125 *In American society*: Jilana Jaxon, Ryan F. Lei, Reut Shachnai, Eleanor K. Chestnut, and Andrei Cimpian, "The Acquisition of Gender Stereotypes and Intellectual Ability: Intersections with Race," *Journal of Social Issues* 75, no. 4 (December 2019): 1192–1215, https://doi.org/10.1111/josi.12352.

125 *In many settings, these groups are negatively stereotyped*: Murphy and Reeves, "Personal and Organizational Mindsets at Work"; Canning et al., "STEM Faculty Who Believe Ability Is Fixed"; Canning et al., "Professors Who Signal a Fixed Mindset"; Murphy and Walton, "From Prejudiced People to Prejudiced Places"; Emerson and Murphy, "A Company I Can Trust?"; Walton, Murphy, and Ryan, "Stereotype Threat in Organizations"; Boucher and Murphy, "Why So Few?"; Bian et al., "Messages about Brilliance"; Canning at al., "Professors Who Signal a Fixed Mindset"; La-Cosse et al., "The Role of STEM Professors' Mindset Beliefs"; Murphy et al., "Global Mindset Initiative Paper 1"; M. C. Murphy and S. Zirkel, "Race and Belonging in School: How Anticipated and Experienced Belonging Affect Choice, Persistence, and Performance," *Teacher's College Record* 117 (2015): 1–40, https://doi.org/10.1177 /016146811511701204; Murphy and Taylor, "The Role of Situational Cues."

125 *When we perceive*: Murphy, Steele, and Gross, "Signaling Threat: How Situational Cues Affect Women in Math, Science, and Engineering Settings"; Murphy and Taylor, "The Role of Situational Cues"; Boucher and Murphy, "Why So Few?"; Murphy, Kroeper, and Ozier, "Prejudiced Places: How Contexts Shape Inequality and How We Can Change Them"; Emerson and Murphy, "Identity Threat at Work"; Walton, Murphy, and Ryan, "Stereotype Threat in Organizations"; Claude M. Steele and Joshua Aronson, "Stereotype Threat and the Intellectual Test Performance of African Americans," *Journal of Personality and Social Psychology* 69, no. 5 (1995): 797–811, https://doi.org/10.1037/0022-3514.69.5.797; Claude M. Steele, Steven J. Spencer, and Joshua Aronson, "Contending with Group Image: The Psychology of Stereotype and Social Identity Threat," in *Advances in Experimental Social Psychology*, vol. 34, ed. M. P. Zanna (New York: Academic Press: 2002), https://doi.org/10.1016/S0065-2601(02)80009-0; Claude M. Steele, "A Threat in the Air: How Stereotypes Shape Intellectual Identity and Performance," *American Psychologist* 52, no. 6 (1997): 613–29, https://doi.org/10.1037/0003 -066X.52.6.613; Claude Steele, *Whistling Vivaldi: How Stereotypes Affect Us and What We Can Do* (New York: W. W. Norton & Company, 2010); Steven J. Spencer, Christine Logel, and Paul G. Davies, "Stereotype Threat," *Annual Review of Psychology* 67 (2015): 415–37, https://doi.org/10.1146/annurev-psych-0731150103235; Geoffrey L. Cohen and Julio Garcia, "Identity, Belonging, and Achievement: A Model, Interventions, Implications," *Current Directions in Psychological Science* 17, no. 6 (2008): https://doi.org/10.1111/j.1467-8721.2008.00607.x.

126 *Stereotype threat is compounded*: Murphy, Steele, and Gross, "Signaling Threat: How Situational Cues Affect Women in Math, Science, and Engineering Settings"; Murphy and Taylor, "The Role of Situational Cues"; Boucher and Murphy, "Why So Few?"; Emerson and Murphy, "Identity Threat at Work"; Walton, Murphy, and Ryan, "Stereotype Threat in Organizations"; Steele, Spencer, and Aronson, "Contending with Group Image"; Spencer, Logel, and Davies, "Stereotype Threat"; D. Sekaquaptewa and M. Thompson, "Solo Status, Stereotype Threat, and Performance Expectancies: Their Effects on Women's Performance," *Journal of Experimental Social Psychology* 39, no. 1 (2003): 68–74, https://doi.org/10.1016/S0022 -1031(02)00508-5; Nicholas A. Bowman, Christine Logel, Jennifer LaCosse, Lindsay Jarratt, Elizabeth A. Canning, Katherine T. U. Emerson, and Mary C. Murphy, "Gender Representation and Academic Achievement Among STEM-Interested Students in College STEM Courses," *Journal of Research in Science Teaching*, 59, no. 10 (2022): 1876-1900, https://doi.org/10.1002/tea.21778.

126 *For example, around the world women*: In 2021, the number of women filling senior management roles globally was 31 percent. Africa topped worldwide regions at 39 percent, followed by Southeast Asia at 38 percent, and North American and the Asia Pacific regions trailed at 33 percent and 28 percent, respectively. "Women in Management (Quick Take)," Catalyst, March 1, 2022, https://www.catalyst.org /research/women-in-management/. Among the Fortune 500, in 2022 only about 15 percent of companies were headed by women. Katharina Buchholz, "How Has the Number of Female CEOs in Fortune 500 Companies Changed Over the Last 20 Years?" World Economic Forum, March 10, 2022, https://www.weforum.org /agenda/2022/03/ceos-fortune-500-companies-female. And, of course, those

percentages are far smaller for women of color. In 2021, only two Fortune 500 companies were led by Black women. Beth Kowitt, "Roz Brewer on What It Feels Like to Be 1 of 2 Black Female CEOs in the Fortune 500," *Fortune*, October 4, 2021, https://fortune.com/longform/roz-brewer-ceo-walgreens-boots-alliance -interview-fortune-500-black-female-ceos/.

126 *Research shows that stereotype threat*: M. Johns, M. Inzlicht, and T. Schmader, "Stereotype Threat and Executive Resource Depletion: Examining the Influence of Emotion Regulation," *Journal of Experimental Psychology: General* 137, no. 4 (2008): 691–705, https://doi.org/10.1037/a0013834; W. B. Mendes and J. Jamieson, "Embodied Stereotype Threat: Exploring Brain and Body Mechanisms Under-lying Performance Impairment," in *Stereotype Threat: Theory, Process, and Application*, ed. M. Inzlicht and T. Schmader, 51–68; R. J. Rydell and K. L. Boucher, "Stereotype Threat and Learning," in *Advances in Experimental Social Psychology* (New York: Elsevier Academic Press, 2017): 81–129, https://doi.org/10.1016 /bs.aesp.2017.02.002; R. J. Rydell, A. R. McConnell, and S. L. Beilock, "Multiple Social Identities and Stereotype Threat: Imbalance, Accessibility, and Working Memory," *Journal of Personality and Social Psychology* 96, no. 5 (2009): 949–66, https://doi.org/10.1037/a0014846; T. Schmader and S. Beilock, "An Integration of Processes that Underlie Stereotype Threat," in *Stereotype Threat: Theory, Process, and Application*, ed. M. Inzlicht and T. Schmader, 34–50; T. Schmader, C. E. Forbes, S. Zhang, and W. B. Mendes, "A Metacognitive Perspective on the Cognitive Deficits Experienced in Intellectually Threatening Environments," *Personality and Social Psychology Bulletin* 35, no. 5 (2009): 584–96, https://doi.org /10.1177/0146167208330450; T. Schmader and M. Johns, "Converging Evidence that Stereotype Threat Reduces Working Memory Capacity," *Journal of Personality and Social Psychology* 85 no. 3 (2003): 440–52, https://doi.org/10.1037/0022 -3514.85.3.440; Spencer, Logel, and Davies, "Stereotype Threat"; Murphy, Steele, and Gross, "Signaling Threat: How Situational Cues Affect Women in Math, Science, and Engineering Settings"; C. Logel, G. M. Walton, S. J. Spencer, E. C. Iserman, W. von Hippel, and A. E. Bell, "Interacting with Sexist Men Triggers Social Identity Threat Among Female Engineers," *Journal of Personality and Social Psychology* 96 no. 6 (2009): 1089–1103, https://doi.org/10.1037/a0015703.

126 *In a series of studies, my former*: Emerson and Murphy, "Identity Threat at Work"; Emerson and Murphy, "A Company I Can Trust?"

127 *In another study, we told*: Ibid.

127 *In research with the Kauffman Foundation*: Murphy, "Mindsets in Entrepreneurship: Measurement and Validation Results."

128 *In our study of an entire university's*: Canning et al., "STEM Faculty Who Believe Ability Is Fixed."

128 *Earlier, I mentioned that my research*: Murphy and Reeves, "Personal and Organizational Mindsets at Work"; Murphy and Dweck, "A Culture of Genius"; Canning et al., "STEM Faculty Who Believe Ability Is Fixed"; Muenks et al., "Does My Professor Think My Ability Can Change?"; Elizabeth A. Canning, Mary C. Murphy, Katherine T. U. Emerson, Jennifer A. Chatman, Carol S. Dweck, and Laura J. Kray, "Cultures of Genius at Work: Organizational Mindsets Predict Cultural Norms, Trust, and Commitment," *Personality and Social Psychology Bulletin* 46, no. 4

(2020): 626–42; Canning et al., "Professors Who Signal a Fixed Mindset"; Emerson and Murphy, "Identity Threat at Work"; Emerson and Murphy, "A Company I Can Trust?"; Walton, Murphy, and Ryan, "Stereotype Threat in Organizations"; Green et al., "Learning Goals Mitigate Identity Threat for Black Individuals in Threatening Interracial Interactions"; LaCosse et al., "The Role of STEM Professors' Mindset Beliefs"; Murphy et al., "Global Mindset Initiative Paper 1."

128   *As senior vice dean*: Katherine W. Phillips, "How Diversity Makes Us Smarter: Being Around People Who are Different from Us Makes Us More Creative, More Diligent and Harder-Working," *Scientific American*, October 1, 2014, https://www .scientificamerican.com/article/how-diversity-makes-us-smarter/. Also of note: An international analysis of 2,360 companies showed greater returns and better growth when there is at least one woman on the board (though I'll discuss my research on the "one woman" phenomenon later in the chapter). Among a survey of 177 U.S. national banks, of those focused on innovation, racial diversity predicted better financial performance.

129   *And a survey from McKinsey*: Dame Vivian Hunt, Dennis Layton, and Sara Prince, "Why Diversity Matters," McKinsey & Company, January 1, 2015, https:// www.mckinsey.com/capabilities/people-and-organizational-performance/our -insights/why-diversity-matters.

129   *Admittedly, studies also show that diversity*: J. A. Richeson and J. N. Shelton, "Negotiating Interracial Interactions: Costs, Consequences, and Possibilities," *Current Directions in Psychological Science* 16, no. 6 (2007): 316–20, https://doi.org/10.1111 /j.1467-8721.2007.00528.x; Sophie Trawalter, Jennifer A. Richeson, and J. Nicole Shelton, "Predicting Behavior During Interracial Interactions: A Stress and Coping Approach," *Personality and Social Psychology Review* 13, no. 4 (2009), https:// doi.org/10.1177/1088868309345850; A. D. Galinsky, A. R. Todd, A. C. Homan, K. W. Phillips, E. P. Apfelbaum, S. J. Sasaki, J. A. Richeson, J. B. Olayon, and W. W. Maddux, "Maximizing the Gains and Minimizing the Pains of Diversity: A Policy Perspective," *Perspectives on Psychological Science*, 10 (2015): 742–48, https://doi .org/10.1177/1745691615598513; D. van Knippenberg, C. K. W. De Dreu, and A. C. Homan, "Work Group Diversity and Group Performance: An Integrative Model and Research Agenda," *Journal of Applied Psychology*, 89 (2004): 1008–22, https:// doi.org/10.1037/0021-9010.89.6.1008; John F. Dovidio, Samuel L. Gaertner, and Kerry Kawakami, "Intergroup Contact: The Past, the Present, and the Future," *Group Processes and Intergroup Relations*, 6, no. 1 (2003), https://doi.org/10.1177 /1368430203006001009; J. F. Dovidio, S. E. Gaertner, K. Kawakami, and G. Hodson, "Why Can't We Just Get Along? Interpersonal Biases and Interracial Distrust," *Cultural Diversity and Ethnic Minority Psychology* 8, no. 2 (2002): 88–102, https://doi.org/10.1037/1099-9809.8.2.88.

129   *Howroyd is the founder and CEO*: Samantha Goddiess, "The 10 Largest Recruiting Firms in the United States," Zippia, April 12, 2022, https://www.zippia.com /advice/largest-recruiting-firms/.

129   *Starting the company when*: "Act One Group: Janice Bryant Howroyd (2018)," interview by Guy Raz, *How I Built This*, December 28, 2020, https://www.npr.org /2020/12/22/949258732/actone-group-janice-bryant-howroyd-2018; "Janice Bry-

ant Howroyd and Family," *Forbes*, accessed May 11, 2023, https://www.forbes.com/profile/janice-bryant-howroyd/?sh=244962786da8.

130 *Even though Howroyd experienced*: "Being an Underrepresented Founder with Courtney Blagrove," interview by Jenny Stojkovic, *VWS Pathfinders Podcast*, Spotify, May 3, 2021, https://podcasters.spotify.com/pod/pod/show/vegan womensummit/episodes/Being-an-Underrepresented-Founder-with-Courtney -Blagrove--Co-founder-of-Whipped--on-the-VWS-Pathfinders-Podcast-with -Jenny-Stojkovic-e10668i.

130 *Incidentally, we're now seeing*: Ray Douglas, "Lack of Diversity Increases Risk of Tech Product Failures," *Financial Times*, November 13, 2018, https://www.ft.com/content/0ef656a8-cd8a-11e8-8d0b-a6539b949662.

130 *Facial- and image-recognition software*: Shane Ferro, "Here's Why Facial Recognition Tech Can't Figure Out Black People," *HuffPost*, March 2, 2016, https://www.huffpost.com/entry/heres-why-facial-recognition-tech-cant-figure-out-black -people_n_56d5c2b1e4b0bf0dab3371eb.

131 *As Erica Baker*: Ibid.

132 *George Aye is a former employee*: George Aye, "Surviving IDEO," Medium, May 23, 2021, https://medium.com/surviving-ideo/surviving-ideo-4568d51bcfb6. Aye goes on to write that one woman was fired while on legally protected maternity leave. Reportedly, the same manager who fired her had previously complained to her about "having to pay for an entire year of maternity" for a different employee "only to have them not return." Several people recounted to Aye an incident in which staff were asked if they had any objections to working for a fast-food chain that actively contributes to anti-LGBTQ causes. When several employees spoke up, they were later reprimanded and the firm took on the restaurant chain anyway. A diversity and inclusion assessment at IDEO, heralded by the design industry for its genius, found that "men and White employees are most likely to feel that they belong, that they are involved in decision making, and that their voices are heard. Men and White employees are also significantly overrepresented in positions of leadership."

132 *According to Jayshree Seth*: "The STEM Struggle," interview by Mark Reggers, 3M Science of Safety, November 12, 2018, https:/3mscienceofsafety.libsyn.com/episode-18-the-stem-struggle.

132 *3M has been so effective*: Among its data-informed programs, 3M has Inclusion Champions and Inclusion Teams who work closely with the company's Employee Resource Networks to ensure a sort of DEI quality control so that, across geographic and workplace cultures, employees and leaders engage in inclusive behavior and celebrate diversity throughout the business. This includes regular meetings between the Inclusion Champions, Employee Resource Network leaders, and C-level executives. Like SAP, the company has made major financial commitments to support STEM education in a variety of settings, including funding dedicated to creating more educational opportunities for communities of color. 3M's Equity & Community organization is tasked with a variety of functions, including working across the business to ensure equity and inclusion along with social justice support in areas including product development, policy advocacy,

and supplier diversity. In 2020, 3M created two leadership roles to support DEI initiatives—director of Social Justice Strategy & Initiatives, and the vice president, Equity & Community and chief equity officer. The company closely monitors its diversity data, and as of their 2020 report, 3M achieved nearly 50 percent in diversity combined (including 39.7 percent women, 8.7 percent racial and ethnic diversity, 1.4 percent disability-related diversity, and .5 percent LGBTQ+) among global nonproduction workers and nearly 70 percent diversity (including 34.7 percent women and 24.8 percent racial and ethnic diversity) among vice presidents and above. Additionally, 36.4 percent of the company's board of directors were women. In a company survey, 76 percent of 3M employees said they felt like they belonged and were included at the company. "Global Diversity, Equity & Inclusion Report," 3M, 2020, https://multimedia.3m.com/mws/media/1955238O/3m-global-diversity-equity-and-inclusion-report-2020.pdf.

132 *Part of Seth's role*: "The STEM Struggle," interview by Mark Reggers.

133 *At the start of the chapter*: Emerson and Murphy, "Identity Threat at Work"; Emerson and Murphy, "A Company I Can Trust?"

134 *Judith Michelle Williams*: Madeline Bennett, "Black History Month: SAP's Diversity Chief Busts the Talent Pipeline Myth," *Diginomica*, February 2, 2021, https://diginomica.com/black-history-month-saps-diversity-chief-busts-talent-pipeline-myth; Emily Chang, *Brotopia: Breaking Up the Boys' Club of Silicon Valley* (New York: Portfolio, 2018).

134 *"existing pipeline"*: In the United Kingdom, only 4 percent of tech workers are from Black, Asian, and minority ethnic (BAME) backgrounds combined, yet according to data from Colorintech—a London-based nonprofit working to diversify the tech industry—in the 2013–14 academic year, there were more ethnic minority students studying science, engineering, and technology than White students. Today, these former students would ostensibly be available to work in STEM careers. Dion McKenzie, cofounder of Colorintech, says the problem is not the pipeline. "If I'm helping one of my portfolio companies hire someone, we are seeing that applicants that come from a BAME background are not making it even through the screening stage. You've got to ask yourself, why is that?" Douglas, "Lack of Diversity Increases Risk of Tech Product Failures."

135 *Often, I work with*: "Equity Accelerator," https://accelerateequity.org/.

135 *Going on 40 years old, Greyston*: "Open Hiring at Greyston Bakery," YouTube, July 30, 2020, https://www.youtube.com/watch?v=fiKwkh2teQg; "Homepage," Greyston, accessed May 11, 2023, https://www.greyston.org/.

136 Entrepreneur Karen Gross: Karen Gross, interview by Mary Murphy, July 13, 2021; Karen Gross, "A Case for Getting Proximate," University of St. Thomas, accessed May 11, 2023, https://blogs.stthomas.edu/holloran-center/a-case-for-getting-proximate/.

137 *Josh Clarkson, Josh Beck, and I*: Joshua J. Clarkson, Joshua T. Beck, and Mary C. Murphy, "To Repeat or Diversify? The Impact of Implicit Self-Theories and Preferences Forecasting on Anticipated Consumption Variety," (manuscript under review).

138 *Laura Kray, a leading scholar*: L. J. Kray and M. P. Haselhuhn, "Implicit Negotiation Beliefs and Performance: Experimental and Longitudinal Evidence," *Journal of Personality and Social Psychology* 93, no. 1 (2007): 49–64, https://doi.org/10.1037

/0022-3514.93.1.49. Further, in a real-world extension of this work, they measured MBA students' more chronic mindset beliefs about negotiation and examined how these beliefs influenced students' abilities to navigate a challenging bargaining scenario that often ends in failure. The more a duo endorsed growth mindset beliefs, the more they persevered when their back-and-forth became challenging and were able to develop more integrative solutions.

138 *In fact, our study*: Mary C. Murphy, "Cultures of Genius and Cultures of Growth: Effects on Board Gender Diversity in the Fortune 500," unpublished manuscript.

139 *We've worked with more than 300 STEM*: Boucher et al., "Centering the Student Experience"; "Increasing Equity in College Student Experience: Findings from a National Collaborative. A Report of the Student Experience Project," https://studentexperienceproject.org/wp-content/uploads/Increasing-Equity -in-Student-Experience-Findings-from-a-National-Collaborative.pdf; https://studentexperienceproject.org/.

140 *Sanford "Sandy" Shugart*: Sanford Shugart, interview by Mary Murphy, September 23, 2020.

141 *It was similar to the plan*: Louis Wool, interview by Mary Murphy, September 29, 2020.

141 *With tens of thousands of students*: Sanford Shugart, interview by Mary Murphy, September 23, 2020.

143 *Amy Bosley, formerly Valencia's vice president*: Amy Bosley, interview by Kelly Madrone, October 22, 2020.

143 *One of Valencia's great successes*: Sanford Shugart, interview by Mary Murphy, September 23, 2020.

143 *By contrast, in Cultures of Genius*: Courtney L. McCluney, Kathrina Robotham, Serenity Lee, Richard Smith, and Myles Durkee, "The Costs of Code-Switching," *Harvard Business Review*, November 15, 2019, https://hbr.org/2019/11/the-costs -of-codeswitching.

143 *As my research shows, when we bring*: Emerson and Murphy, "A Company I Can Trust?"; Murphy and Reeves, "Personal and Organizational Mindsets at Work"; Emerson and Murphy, "Identity Threat at Work"; Canning et al., "Professors Who Signal a Fixed Mindset"; LaCosse et al., "The Role of STEM Professors' Mindset Beliefs."

143 *Lanaya Irvin, a lesbian who*: "Lanaya Irvin: Talking About Race at Work," interview by Veronica Dagher, *Secrets of Wealthy Women*, Wall Street Journal podcast, June 10, 2020, https://www.wsj.com/podcasts/secrets-of-wealthy-women/lanaya -irvin-talking-about-race-at-work/918158fb-b9a6-422e-b21d-cd6d4a82ffff.

144 *"Proceed intentionally."*: Ibid.

144 *Irvin says that it's important*: Ibid.

145 *Lanaya Irvin says*: Ibid.

146 *Ellen Pao of Project Include*: Ellen Pao, *Reset: My Fight for Inclusion and Lasting Change* (New York: Random House, 2017).

146 *At Karen Gross's Citizen Discourse*: Karen Gross, interview by Mary Murphy, July 13, 2021; "Compassion Contract," Citizen Discourse, accessed May 11, 2023. To learn more, visit Citizen Discourse's website—www.citizendiscourse.org—and download the Compassion contract: https://citizendiscourse.org/compassion-contract/.

147 *As Sara Marcus from Greyston:* "Open Hiring at Greyston Bakery," YouTube.

147 *Nearly all of MIT's:* Mara Leighton, "MIT Offers Over 2,000 Free Online Courses—Here Are 13 of the Best Ones," *Business Insider,* February 9, 2021, https://www.businessinsider.com/guides/learning/free-massachusetts-institute -of-technology-online-courses.

CHAPTER 8: MINDSET MICROCULTURES

152 *After reviewing reams of data:* Mary C. Murphy and Stephanie L. Reeves, "Personal and Organizational Mindsets at Work," *Research in Organizational Behavior* 39 (2019), https://doi.org/10.1016/j.riob.2020.100121.

155 *Situational cues tell us:* Mary C. Murphy, Claude M. Steele, and James J. Gross, "Signaling Threat: How Situational Cues Affect Women in Math, Science, and Engineering Settings," *Psychological Science* 18, no. 10 (October 2007): 879–85, https://doi.org/10.1111/j.1467-9280.2007.01995.x; Katherine T. U. Emerson and Mary C. Murphy, "Identity Threat at Work: How Social Identity Threat and Situational Cues Contribute to Racial and Ethnic Disparities in the Workplace," *Cultural Diversity and Ethnic Minority Psychology* 20, no. 4 (October 2014): 508–20, https://doi.org/10.1037/a0035403; G. M. Walton, M. C. Murphy, and A. M. Ryan, "Stereotype Threat in Organizations: Implications for Equity and Performance," *Annual Review of Organizational Psychology and Organizational Behavior* 2 (2015): 523–50, https://doi.org/10.1146/annurev-orgpsych-032414-111322; Murphy and Taylor, "The Role of Situational Cues in Signaling and Maintaining Stereotype Threat;" Murphy and Reeves, "Personal and Organizational Mindsets at Work"; Elizabeth A. Canning, Mary C. Murphy, Katherine T. U. Emerson, Jennifer A. Chatman, Carol S. Dweck, and Laura J. Kray, "Cultures of Genius at Work: Organizational Mindsets Predict Cultural Norms, Trust, and Commitment," *Personality and Social Psychology Bulletin* 46, no. 4 (2020): 626–42; Elizabeth A. Canning, Elise Ozier, Heidi E. Williams, Rashed AlRasheed, and Mary C. Murphy, "Professors Who Signal a Fixed Mindset about Ability Undermine Women's Performance in STEM," *Social Psychological and Personality Science* 13, no. 5 (2022): 927–37, https://doi.org/10.1177/19485506211030398; J. LaCosse, M. C. Murphy, J. A. Garcia, and S. Zirkel, "The Role of STEM Professors' Mindset Beliefs on Students' Anticipated Psychological Experiences and Course Interest," *Journal of Educational Psychology* 113 (2021): 949–71, https://doi.org/10.1037/edu0000620; K. Muenks, E. A. Canning, J. LaCosse, D. J. Green, S. Zirkel, and J. A. Garcia, "Does My Professor Think My Ability Can Change? Students' Perceptions of Their STEM Professors' Mindset Beliefs Predict Their Psychological Vulnerability, Engagement, and Performance in Class," *Journal of Experimental Psychology: General* 149, no. 11 (2020): 2119–44, https://doi.org/10.1037/xge0000763.

155 *My research shows that different people:* Murphy and Reeves, "Personal and Organizational Mindsets at Work"; Canning et al., "Cultures of Genius at Work"; Emerson and Murphy, "Identity Threat at Work"; Katherine T. U. Emerson and Mary C. Murphy, "A Company I Can Trust? Organizational Lay Theories Moderate Stereotype Threat for Women," *Personality and Social Psychology Bulletin* 41,

no. 2 (February 1, 2015): 295–307, https://doi.org/10.1177/01461672145649; Canning et al., "Professors Who Signal a Fixed Mindset"; LaCosse et al., "The Role of STEM Professors' Mindset Beliefs."

156 *For that, let's look at Daniel "Rudy" Ruettiger*: Dan Scofield, "Daniel 'Rudy' Ruettiger, Notre Dame's Famous Walk-On: The True Story," *Bleacher Report*, January 18, 2010, https://bleacherreport.com/articles/328263-the-true-story-of-notre-dames-famous-walk-on-daniel-rudy-reutigger.

158 *In fact, brain studies reveal*: "How to Change Your Brain with Dr. Andrew Huberman, Episode 533," interview by Rich Roll, *Rich Roll Podcast*, July 20, 2020, https://www.richroll.com/podcast/andrew-huberman-533/.

159 *Also, being familiar with*: Mary C. Murphy and Carol S. Dweck, "A Culture of Genius: How an Organization's Lay Theory Shapes People's Cognition, Affect, and Behavior," *Personality and Social Psychology Bulletin* 36, no. 3 (October 2009): 283–96, https://doi.org/10.1177/0146167209347380; Emerson and Murphy, "A Company I Can Trust?"

159 *However, even here*: Candace Duncan, interview by Kelly Madrone, December 2, 2020.

159 *or with Shell's safety-focused*: Jorrit van der Togt, interview by Mary Murphy, July 8, 2021.

CHAPTER 9: EVALUATIVE SITUATIONS

163 *From our fixed mindset*: L. S. Blackwell, K. H. Trzesniewski, and C. S. Dweck, "Implicit Theories of Intelligence Predict Achievement Across an Adolescent Transition: A Longitudinal Study and an Intervention," *Child Development* 78, no. 1 (2007): 246–63, http://dx.doi.org/10.1111/j.1467-8624.2007.00995.x; Y. Hong, C. Chiu, C. S. Dweck, D. M.-S. Lin, and W. Wan, "Implicit Theories, Attributions, and Coping: A Meaning System Approach," *Journal of Personality and Social Psychology* 77 (1999): 588–99, https://doi.org/10.1037/0022-3514.77.3.588; A. David Nussbaum and Carol S. Dweck, "Defensiveness Versus Remediation: Self-Theories and Modes of Self-Esteem Maintenance," *Personality and Social Psychology Bulletin* 34, no. 5 (March 5, 2008): 599–612, https://doi.org/10.1177/0146167207312960.

165 *As the* Wall Street Journal's: John Carreyrou, *Bad Blood: Secrets and Lies in a Silicon Valley Startup* (New York: Knopf, 2018).

165 *"I kept saying to her"*: The Inventor: Out for Blood in Silicon Valley, directed by Alex Gibney, HBO Documentary Films/Jigsaw Productions, 2019.

165 *Holmes lied to investors*: Avery Hartmans, Sarah Jackson, and Azmi Haroun, "The Rise and Fall of Elizabeth Holmes, the Former Theranos CEO Found Guilty of Wire Fraud and Conspiracy—Who Just Managed to Delay Her Prison Reporting Date," *Business Insider*, April 26, 2023, https://www.businessinsider.com/theranos-founder-ceo-elizabeth-holmes-life-story-bio-2018-4.

165 *Workers falsified test results*: Carreyrou, *Bad Blood*.

166 *Instead, in 2018 the company*: The Inventor, directed by Alex Gibney; Hartmans, Jackson, and Haroun, "The Rise and Fall of Elizabeth Holmes."

166 *Like Holmes, Lake attended Stanford*: "Style Startup to IPO with Katrina Lake at the Commonwealth Club," interview by Lauren Schiller, *Inflection Point*, YouTube, June 20, 2018, https://www.youtube.com/watch?v=69MiU-4v3NU; Jessica

Pressler, "How Stitch Fix CEO Katrina Lake Built a $2 Billion Company," *Elle*, February 28, 2018, https://www.elle.com/fashion/a15895336/katrina-lake-stitch-fix-ceo-interview/.

167 *Two days before the IPO*: "Katrina Lake," interview by Carly Zakin and Danielle Weisberg, *Skimm'd from the Couch*, July 25, 2018, https://www.theskimm.com/money/sftc-katrina-lake.

167 *among Silicon Valley's most successful founders/CEOs*: In the post-pandemic economy, many tech-based companies' valuations suffered, including Stitch Fix. The fact remains that Katrina Lake's growth-minded approach to the evaluative situation of taking her company public made Stitch Fix highly successful for many years. Lake stepped down as CEO in 2021, then returned in 2023. Adriana Lee, "Stitch Fix Plans to Return Focus to What Built the Business," Yahoo!Money, March 8, 2023, https://money.yahoo.com/stitch-fix-plans-return-focus-222156568.html.

168 *Sinek described a meeting*: "These Are Not Uncertain Times: Ways to Pivot, Lead, and Thrive—Simon Sinek with Dave Asprey, #740," *Human Upgrade*, May 21, 2020, https://daveasprey.com/simon-sinek-740/.

169 *As culture writer Anne Helen Petersen*: Anne Helen Petersen, *Can't Even: How Millennials Became the Burnout Generation* (New York: Houghton Mifflin Harcourt, 2020).

170 *In 2020, I engaged in a brief project*: Catherine Poirier, Carina Cheng, Ellora Sarkar, Henry Silva, and Tom Kudrle, "The Culture of Data Leaders," Keystone, February 2, 2021, https://www.keystone.ai/news-publications/whitepaper-the-culture-of-data-leaders/.

170 *This next insight comes from*: Mary Murphy, Stephanie Fryberg, Laura Brady, Elizabeth Canning, and Cameron Hecht, "Global Mindset Initiative Paper 1: Growth Mindset Cultures and Teacher Practices," *Growth Mindset Cultures and Practices* (August 27, 2021), http://dx.doi.org/10.2139/ssrn.3911594; K. Morman, L. Brady, C. Wang, M. C. Murphy, M. Bang, and S. Fryberg, "Creating Identity Safe Classrooms: A Cultural Educational Psychology Approach to Teacher Interventions." Paper presented at the American Educational Research Association Annual Meeting, Chicago, IL, April 2023.

172 *John Mackey, cofounder and former CEO*: John Mackey, Steve McIntosh, and Carter Phipps, *Conscious Leadership: Elevating Humanity Through Business* (New York: Portfolio, 2020).

173 *Or take a tip from Bozoma Saint John*: "Badass Bozoma Saint John," interview by Charli Penn and Cori Murray, *Yes, Girl!*, October 26, 2020, https://www.essence.com/lifestyle/career-advice-uber-cbo-bozoma-saint-john/.

174 *This strategy mirrors something Mark Zuckerberg*: Kurt Wagner, "Mark Zuckerberg Shares Facebook's Secrets with All His Employees, and Almost None of It Leaks," *Vox*, January 5, 2017, https://www.vox.com/2017/1/5/13987714/mark-zuckerberg-facebook-qa-weekly.

CHAPTER 10: HIGH-EFFORT SITUATIONS

176 *A high-effort situation is one*: Mary C. Murphy and Stephanie L. Reeves, "Personal and Organizational Mindsets at Work," *Research in Organizational Behavior* 39 (2019), https://doi.org/10.1016/j.riob.2020.100121.

176 *Hood is the president and CEO*: "Ramona Hood," interview by Carly Zakin and Danielle Weisberg, *Skimm'd from the Couch*, November 11, 2020, https://www.theskimm.com/money/skimmd-from-the-couch-ramona-hood.

178 *Stephen King had been writing*: Stephen King, *On Writing: A Memoir of the Craft* (New York: Scribner, 2000).

178 *King has written*: "Stephen King Books in Order: Complete Series List," *Candid Cover*, May 3, 2023, https://candidcover.net/stephen-king-books-in-order-list/.

178 *writing his 2,000 words per day*: King, *On Writing*.

179 *Hoping to answer this question*: Jason R. Tregellas, Deana B. Davalos, and Donald C. Rojas, "Effect of Task Difficulty on the Functional Anatomy of Temporal Processing," *Neuroimage* 32, no. 1 (April 19, 2006): 307–15, https://doi.org/10.1016/j.neuroimage.2006.02.036.

180 *Research also shows that it's not just*: National Research Council, *How People Learn: Brain, Mind, Experience, and School: Expanded Edition* (Washington, DC: National Academies Press, 2020).

181 *Spending an afternoon*: Cathy O'Neil, "Weapons of Math Destruction," *Discover*, August 31, 2016, https://www.discovermagazine.com/the-sciences/weapons-of-math-destruction.

181 *Neuroscientist David Eagleman*: "The Inside Story of the Ever-Changing Brain," interview by Brené Brown, *Unlocking Us*, December 2, 2020, https://brenebrown.com/podcast/brene-with-david-eagleman-on-the-inside-story-of-the-ever-changing-brain/.

181 *As of 2023, more than 31 million people*: David Curry, "Fitbit Revenue and Usage Statistics (2023)," *Business of Apps*, January 9, 2023, https://www.businessofapps.com/data/fitbit-statistics/.

181 *Yet while wearable tech*: "Fitbit: James Park," interview by Guy Raz, *How I Built This*, April 27, 2020, https://www.npr.org/2020/04/22/841267648/fitbit-james-park.

182 *"Immigrants … we get the job done"*: Lin-Manuel Miranda, Keinan Warsame, Claudia Feliciano, Rizwan Ahmed, René Pérez Joglar, and Jeffrey Penalva, "Immigrants (We Get the Job Done)," *The Hamilton Mixtape*, Atlantic Records, December 2, 2016.

183 *Researcher Julia Leonard*: Julia A. Leonard, Dominique N. Martinez, Samantha C. Dashineau, Anne T. Park, and Allyson P. Mackey, "Children Persist Less When Adults Take Over," *Child Development* 92, no. 4 (July/August 2021): 1325–36, https://doi.org/10.1111/cdev.13492.

183 *You might be familiar with*: "Don't Be a Duck! How to Resist the Stanford Duck Syndrome," Stanford University, accessed May 11, 2023, https://studentaffairs.stanford.edu/focus-dont-be-duck-how-resist-stanford-duck-syndrome.

184 *Cornell has been dubbed*: Jennifer Epstein, "A 'Suicide School'?" *Inside Higher Ed*, March 15, 2010, https://www.insidehighered.com/news/2010/03/16/suicide-school; Trip Gabriel, "After 3 Suspected Suicides, Cornell Reaches Out," *New York Times*, March 16, 2010, https://www.nytimes.com/2010/03/17/education/17cornell.html; Tovia Smith, "Deaths Revive Cornell's Reputation as 'Suicide School,'" NPR, March 18, 2010, https://www.npr.org/templates/story/story.php?storyId=124807724.

184 *During the 2016–17 school year*: Nancy Doolittle, "Cornell Reviews Its Mental

Health Approach, Looks Ahead," *Cornell Chronicle*, January 18, 2018, https://news.cornell.edu/stories/2018/01/cornell-reviews-its-mental-health-approach-looks-ahead.

185 *As researchers Elizabeth and Robert Bjork*: Elizabeth Bjork and Robert A. Bjork, "Making Things Hard on Yourself, but in a Good Way: Creating Desirable Difficulties to Enhance Learning," in *Psychology and the Real World*, ed. Morton Ann Gernsbacher, Richard W. Pew, Leaetta M. Hough, and James R. Pomerantz (New York: Worth, 2009), 56–64.

185 *As cognitive psychologist Nate Kornell*: David Epstein, *Range: Why Generalists Triumph in a Specialized World* (New York: Macmillan, 2019).

185 *Conversely, in China and Japan*: Epstein, *Range*; Harold W. Stevenson and James W. Stigler, *The Learning Gap: Why Our Schools Are Failing and What We Can Learn from Japanese and Chinese Education* (New York: Touchstone, 1992).

185 *Researchers Harold Stevenson and James Stigler*: Stevenson and Stigler, *The Learning Gap*.

185 *As Kornell and his colleagues*: Nate Kornell, Matthew Jensen Hays, and Robert A. Bjork, "Unsuccessful Retrieval Attempts Enhance Subsequent Learning," *Journal of Experimental Psychology* 35, no. 4 (2009): 989–98, https://doi.org/10.1037/a0015729.

186 *Research further clarifies*: Shui-Fong Lam, Pui-shan Lim, and Yee-lam Ng, "Is Effort Praise Motivational? The Role of Beliefs in the Effort–Ability Relationship," *Contemporary Educational Psychology* 33, no. 4 (October 2008): 694–710, https://doi.org/10.1016/j.cedpsych.2008.01.005.

186 *As we've seen, beliefs about*: Lam, Lim, and Ng, "Is Effort Praise Motivational?"; Michael Chapman and Ellen A. Skinner, "Children's Agency Beliefs, Cognitive Performance, and Conceptions of Effort and Ability: Individual and Developmental Differences," *Child Development*, 60, no. 5 (1989): 1229–38, https://doi.org/10.2307/1130796; John G. Nicholls, "The Development of the Concepts of Effort and Ability, Perception of Academic Attainment, and the Understanding that Difficult Tasks Require More Ability," *Child Development* 49, no. 3 (1978): 800–14, https://doi.org/10.2307/1128250.

186 *A young man enrolled*: @sarahelizalewis, "Martin Luther King Jr received two Cs in public speaking. Actually went from a C+ to a C the next term. Here's the transcript. Live your dream." January 11, 2020, 5:09pm, https://twitter.com/sarahelizalewis/status/1216150254120247297?lang=en.

189 *In a series of five studies*: Paul A. O'Keefe, Carol S. Dweck, Gregory M. Walton, "Implicit Theories of Interest: Finding Your Passion or Developing It?" *Psychological Science*, 29, no. 10 (September 6, 2018): 1653–64, https://doi.org/10.1177/0956797618780643.

189 *Sapna Cheryan, a professor*: "Meet the Speakers: Dr. Sapna Cheryan," interview by Andrew Watson, *Learning & the Brain*, October 15, 2017, https://www.learningandthebrain.com/blog/meet-the-speakers-dr-sapna-cheryan/.

190 *gender gap in computer science*: Emily Chang, *Brotopia: Breaking Up the Boys' Club of Silicon Valley* (New York: Portfolio, 2018).

190 *Steve Jobs*: Walter Isaacson, *Steve Jobs* (New York: Simon & Schuster, 2011).

190 *Emma McIlroy*: "The Wildfang Way: Emma McIlroy," interview by Jonathan

Fields, *The Good Life Podcast*, August 7, 2019, https://www.goodlifeproject.com/podcast/emma-mcilroy-wildfang/.

191 *Another barrier to women*: Katherine T. U. Emerson and Mary C. Murphy, "Identity Threat at Work: How Social Identity Threat and Situational Cues Contribute to Racial and Ethnic Disparities in the Workplace," *Cultural Diversity and Ethnic Minority Psychology* 20, no. 4 (October 2014): 508–20, https://doi.org/10.1037/a0035403; Ashley Bittner and Brigette Lau, "Women-Led Startups Received Just 2.3% of VC Funding in 2020," *Harvard Business Review*, February 25, 2021, https://hbr.org/2021/02/women-led-startups-received-just-2-3-of-vc-funding-in-2020; Gabrielle Fonrouge, "Venture Capital for Black Entrepreneurs Plummeted 45% in 2022, Data Shows," CNBC, February 2, 2023, https://www.cnbc.com/2023/02/02/venture-capital-black-founders-plummeted.html; Dana Kanze, Mark A. Conley, Tyler G. Okimoto, Damon J. Phillips, and Jennifer Merluzzi, "Evidence that Investors Penalize Female Founders for Lack of Industry Fit," *Science Advances* 6, no. 48 (2020), https://doi.org/10.1126/sciadv.abd7664; Elsa T. Chan, Pok Man Tang, and Shuhui Chen, "The Psychology of Women in Entrepreneurship: An International Perspective," in *The Cambridge Handbook of the International Psychology of Women*, ed. Fanny M. Cheung and Diane F. Halpern (Cambridge: Cambridge University Press, 2020), https://www.cambridge.org/core/books/abs/cambridge-handbook-of-the-international-psychology-of-women/psychology-of-women-in-entrepreneurship/029B74F2B34330350BF6C72FADC8363D; L. Bigelow, L. Lundmark, J. McLean Parks, and R. Wuebker, "Skirting the Issues: Experimental Evidence of Gender Bias in IPO Prospectus Evaluations," *Journal of Management* 40, no. 6 (2012): 1732–59, https://doi.org/10.1177/0149206312441624; E. H. Buttner and B. Rosen, "Bank Loan Officers' Perceptions of the Characteristics of Men, Women, and Successful Entrepreneurs," *Journal of Business Venturing* 3, no. 3 (1988): 249–58, https://doi.org/10.1016/0883-9026(88)90018-3; Mark Geiger, "A Meta-Analysis of the Gender Gap(s) in Venture Funding: Funder- and Entrepreneur-Driven Perspectives," *Journal of Business Venturing Insights* 13 (2020), https://doi.org/10.1016/j.jbvi.2020.e00167; Candida Brush, Patricia Greene, Lakshmi Balachandra, and Amy Davis, "The Gender Gap in Venture Capital: Progress, Problems, and Perspectives," *Venture Capital* 20, no. 2 (2018): 115–36, https://doi.org/10.1080/13691066.2017.1349266; Michael S. Barr, "Minority and Women Entrepreneurs: Building Capital, Networks, and Skills," Hamilton Project, discussion paper 2015-03 (March 2015), https://www.brookings.edu/wp-content/uploads/2016/07/minority_women_entrepreneurs_building_skills_barr.pdf; Rosanna Garcia and Daniel W. Baack, "The Invisible Racialized Minority Entrepreneur: Using White Solipsism to Explain the White Space," *Journal of Business Ethics* (2022), https://doi.org/10.1007/s10551-022-05308-6.

192 *As* TechCrunch *reports*: Dominic-Madori Davis, "Women-Founded Startups Raised 1.9% of All VC Funds in 2022, a Drop from 2021," *TechCrunch*, January 18, 2023, https://techcrunch.com/2023/01/18/women-founded-startups-raised-1-9-of-all-vc-funds-in-2022-a-drop-from-2021/.

192 *as* PitchBook *states*: Silvia Mah, "Why Female Founders Still Aren't Getting the Big Number Investments—And Why They Should," *Forbes*, November 30, 2022, https://www.forbes.com/sites/forbesbusinesscouncil/2022/11/30/why-female

-founders-still-arent-getting-the-big-number-investments-and-why-they-should /?sh=58c769902761.

192 *In the same year, Black founders*: Dominic-Madori Davis, "Black Founders Still Raised Just 1% of All VC Funds in 2022," *TechCrunch*, January 6, 2023, https:// techcrunch.com/2023/01/06/black-founders-still-raised-just-1-of-all-vc-funds-in -2022/. CNBC offers that, "While investing in diverse teams can often be seen as a moral imperative and something that's done because it's the right thing to do, studies have shown it can lead to higher returns for investors, said John Roussel, the executive director of Colorwave." Fonrouge, "Venture Capital for Black Entre- preneurs Plummeted 45% in 2022, Data Shows."

192 *My own research shows*: Mary C. Murphy, "Mindsets in Entrepreneurship: Mea- surement and Validation Results," report to the G2 Advisory Group and the Kauffman Foundation (April 2020); M. C. Murphy, B. Tauber, C. Samsa, and C. S. Dweck, "Founders' Mindsets Predict Company Culture and Organizational Suc- cess in Early Stage Startups" (working paper).

192 *Katrina Lake*: "Style Startup to IPO with Katrina Lake at the Commonwealth Club," interview by Lauren Schiller, *Inflection Point*, YouTube, June 20, 2018, https://www.youtube.com/watch?v=69MiU-4v3NU.

192 *Calendly founder Tope Awotona*: "Calendly: Tope Awotona," interview by Guy Raz, *How I Built This*, September 14, 2020, https://www.npr.org/2020/09/11/911960189 /calendly-tope-awotona.

192 *The McBride sisters started*: "McBride Sisters Wine (Part 1 of 2): Robin McBride and Andréa McBride John," interview by Guy Raz, *How I Built This*, October 19, 2020, https://www.npr.org/2020/10/15/924227706/mcbride-sisters-wine-part-1-of-2 -robin-mcbride-and-andr-a-mcbride-john; "McBride Sisters Wine (Part 2 of 2): Robin McBride and Andréa McBride John," interview by Guy Raz, *How I Built This*, October 26, 2020, https://www.npr.org/2020/10/23/927158151/mcbride-sist ers-wine-part-2-of-2-robin-mcbride-and-andr-a-mcbride-john.

193 *It's also made the McBride Sisters*: "Our Story," McBride Sisters Wine Company, accessed May 11, 2023, https://www.mcbridesisters.com/Sisters-Story.

193 *But let's hit rewind for a moment*: "McBride Sisters Wine (Part 1 of 2): Robin Mc- Bride and Andréa McBride John," interview by Guy Raz; "McBride Sisters Wine (Part 2 of 2): Robin McBride and Andréa McBride John," interview by Guy Raz.

193 *As Robin pointed out to Guy Raz*: "McBride Sisters Wine (Part 2 of 2): Robin Mc- Bride and Andréa McBride John," interview by Guy Raz.

193 *Superstar climber Alex Megos*: "Rotpunkt: Alex Megos Climbs His Hardest Proj- ect Yet," *Patagonia*, YouTube, accessed May 11, 2023, https://www.youtube.com /watch?v=COuxNFuAS1Q; Michael Levy, "Interview: Alex Megos on 'Bibli- ographie,' (5.15d)," *Rock & Ice*, August 11, 2020, https://www.rockandice.com /climbing-news/inteview-alex-megos-on-bibliographie-5-15d/.

196 *In her bestselling book* Bird by Bird: Anne Lamott, *Bird by Bird: Some Instructions on Writing and Life* (New York: Pantheon, 1994).

196 *To countless others, the prospect*: "McBride Sisters Wine (Part 2 of 2): Robin Mc- Bride and Andréa McBride John," interview by Guy Raz.

197 *Another tactic we can deploy*: Claude M. Steele, "The Psychology of Self- Affirmation: Sustaining the Integrity of the Self," *Advances in Experimental So-*

cial Psychology 21 (1988): 261–2, https://doi.org/10.1016/S0065-2601(08)60229
-4; David K. Sherman and Geoffrey L. Cohen, "The Psychology of Self-Defense:
Self-Affirmation Theory," *Advances in Experimental Social Psychology* 38 (2006):
183–242, https://doi.org/10.1016/S0065-2601(06)38004-5.

197   *according to Gallup, 55 percent of Americans*: Rebecca Riffkin, "In U.S., 55% of
Workers Get Sense of Identity from Their Job," Gallup, August 22, 2014, https://
news.gallup.com/poll/175400/workers-sense-identity-job.aspx.

197   *The process of self-affirmation*: Steele, "The Psychology of Self-Affirmation"; Sherman and Cohen, "The Psychology of Self-Defense."

198   *Again, storytelling is one*: "Jay-Z: The Hip-Hop Billionaire Who Couldn't Even Get
a Record Deal," Black BOSS Channel, YouTube, accessed May 11, 2023, https://
www.youtube.com/watch?v=aVP4NjvuB50.

200   *As I mentioned earlier*: Charles Duhigg, "What Google Learned from Its Quest to
Build the Perfect Team," *New York Times Magazine*, February 15, 2016, https://
www.nytimes.com/2016/02/28/magazine/what-google-learned-from-its-quest-to
-build-the-perfect-team.html.

200   *According to 2022 data from Gallup*: "State of the Global Workplace: 2022 Report,"
Gallup, accessed May 11, 2023, https://www.gallup.com/workplace/349484/state
-of-the-global-workplace-2022-report.aspx#ite-393245.

200   *As any HR exec will tell you*: "The Impact of Employee Engagement on Retention,"
Oak Engagement, April 20, 2023, https://www.oak.com/blog/impact-of-employee
-engagement-on-retention/.

CHAPTER 11: CRITICAL FEEDBACK

202   *As a quote commonly attributed to Aristotle*: According to Wikiquote, the original
quote is actually as follows: "If you would escape moral and physical assassination,
do nothing, say nothing, be nothing—court obscurity, for only in oblivion does
safety lie," from Elbert Hubbard, *Little Journeys to the Homes of American States-
man* (1898), https://en.wikiquote.org/wiki/Aristotle#Misattributed.

202   *When viewed through the lens of our fixed mindset*: Mary C. Murphy and Stephanie L. Reeves, "Personal and Organizational Mindsets at Work," *Research in
Organizational Behavior* 39 (2019), https://doi.org/10.1016/j.riob.2020.100121; J. N.
Belding, K. Z. Naufel, and K. Fujita, "Using High-Level Construal and Perceptions
of Changeability to Promote Self-Change Over Self-Protection Motives in Re-
sponse to Negative Feedback," *Personality and Social Psychology Bulletin*, 41 no. 6
(2015): 822–38, https://doi.org/10.1177/0146167215580776; David Nussbaum and
Carol S. Dweck, "Defensiveness Versus Remediation: Self-Theories and Modes of
Self-Esteem Maintenance," *Personality and Social Psychology Bulletin* 34, no. 5
(March 5, 2008): 599–612, https://doi.org/10.1177/0146167207312960; Y. Trope
and E. Neter, "Reconciling Competing Motives in Self-Evaluation: The Role of
Self-Control in Feedback Seeking," *Journal of Personality and Social Psychology*
66, no. 4 (1994): 646–57, https://doi.org/10.1037/0022-3514.66.4.646.

203   *When we first encounter critical feedback:* "Sadie Lincoln Is Rewriting the Fitness
Story—Thoughts on Movement, Community, Risk & Vulnerability, Episode 501,"
interview by Rich Roll; "How I Built Resilience: Live with Sadie Lincoln," inter-

view by Guy Raz, *How I Built This*, June 20, 2020, https://www.npr.org/2020/06/18/880460529/how-i-built-resilience-live-with-sadie-lincoln.

204 *Neuroscientist Lisa Feldman Barrett*: Lisa Feldman Barrett, "The Theory of Constructed Emotion: An Active Inference Account of Interoception and Categorization," *Social Cognitive and Affective Neuroscience* 12, no. 1 (January 2017): 1–23, https://doi.org/10.1093/scan/nsw154; Lisa Feldman Barrett, *How Emotions Are Made: The Secret Life of the Brain* (New York: Mariner Books, 2017).

204 *Something else that aided Lincoln's shift*: "Sadie Lincoln Is Rewriting the Fitness Story," interview by Rich Roll.

204 *As research shows, our brains*: "All About Amygdala Hijack," PsychCentral, accessed May 11, 2023, https://psychcentral.com/health/amygdala-hijack.

205 *"She helped me process it from a data perspective"*: "Sadie Lincoln Is Rewriting the Fitness Story," interview by Rich Roll.

205 *In response, we become like*: *Seinfeld*, season 9, episode 5, "The Junk Mail," NBC, October 30, 1997.

205 *Jack Nicholson's Colonel Nathan Jessup*: *A Few Good Men*, directed by Rob Reiner, Columbia Pictures/Castle Rock Entertainment/David Brown Productions, 1992.

207 *To answer that question*: Nussbaum and Dweck, "Defensiveness Versus Remediation." Note: Results were similar across two other studies.

208 *However, neuroscience indicates*: Jennifer A. Mangels, Brady Butterfield, Justin Lamb, Catherine Good, and Carol S. Dweck, "Why Do Beliefs about Intelligence Influence Learning Success? A Social Cognitive Neuroscience Model," *Social Cognitive and Affective Neuroscience* 1, no. 2 (September 1, 2006): 75–86, https://doi.org/10.1093/scan/nsl013; Hans S. Schroder, Megan E. Fisher, Yanli Lin, Sharon L. Lo, Judith H. Danovitch, and Jason S. Moser, "Neural Evidence for Enhanced Attention to Mistakes among School-Aged Children with a Growth Mindset," *Developmental Cognitive Neuroscience* 24 (April 2017): 42–50, https://doi.org/10.1016/j.dcn.2017.01.004.

209 *In a 2020 edition*: "The Rise, the Creative Process, and the Difference Between Mastery and Success, with Dr. Sarah Lewis," interview by Brené Brown, *Dare to Lead*, November 30, 2020, https://brenebrown.com/podcast/brene-with-dr-sarah-lewis-on-the-rise-the-creative-process-and-the-difference-between-mastery-and-success/.

209 *When we feel shame*: D. S. Yeager, H. Y. Lee, and J. P. Jamieson, "How to Improve Adolescent Stress Responses: Insights from Integrating Implicit Theories of Personality and Biopsychosocial Models," *Psychological Science* 27 (2016): 1078–91, https://doi.org/10.1177/0956797616649604; D. S. Yeager, K. H. Trzesniewski, K. Tirri, P. Nokelainen, and C. S. Dweck, "Adolescents' Implicit Theories Predict Desire for Vengeance After Peer Conflicts: Correlational and Experimental Evidence," *Developmental Psychology* 47 (2011): 1090–7, https://doi.org/10.1037/a0023769; Weidong Tao, Dongchi Zhao, Huilan Yue, Isabel Horton, Xiuju Tian, Zhen Xu, and Hong-Jin Sun, "The Influence of Growth Mindset on the Mental Health and Life Events of College Students," *Frontiers in Psychology* 13 (2022), https://doi.org/10.3389/fpsyg.2022.821206; L. S. Blackwell, K. H. Trzesniewski, and C. S. Dweck, "Implicit Theories of Intelligence Predict Achievement Across an Adolescent Transition: A Longitudinal Study and an Intervention,"

Child Development 78, no. 1 (2007): 246–63, http://dx.doi.org/10.1111/j.1467
-8624.2007.00995.x; R. W. Robins and J. L. Pals, "Implicit Self-Theories in the Academic Domain: Implications for Goal Orientation, Attributions, Affect, and Self-
Esteem Change," *Self and Identity* 1, no. 4 (2002): 313–36, https://doi.org/10.1080
/15298860290106805; R. B. King, D. M. McInerney, and D. A. Watkins, "How You
Think About Your Intelligence Determines How You Feel in School: The Role of
Theories of Intelligence on Academic Emotions," *Learning and Individual Differences* 22, no. 6 (2002): 814–19, https://doi.org/10.1016/j.lindif.2012.04.005.

210 *Some of the research I've done*: A. Rattan, K. Kroeper, R. Arnett, X. Brown, and
M. C. Murphy, "Not Such a Complainer Anymore: Confrontation that Signals a
Growth Mindset Can Attenuate Backlash," *Journal of Personality and Social Psy-
chology* 124, no. 2 (2003): 344–61, https://doi.org/10.1037/pspi0000399.

210 *If, like Brown, we are triggered*: Betsy Ng, "The Neuroscience of Growth Mindset
and Intrinsic Motivation," *Brain Sciences* 8, no. 2 (2018), https://doi.org/10.3390
/brainsci8020020; Hans S. Schroder, Megan E. Fisher, Yanli Lin, Sharon L. Lo,
Judith H. Danovitch, Jason S. Moser, "Neural Evidence for Enhanced Attention
to Mistakes Among School-Aged Children with a Growth Mindset," *Developmental Cognitive Neuroscience* 24 (April 2017): 42–50, https://doi.org/10.1016
/j.dcn.2017.01.004; J. S. Moser, H. S. Schroder, C. Heeter, T. P. Moran, and Y.-H.
Lee, "Mind Your Errors: Evidence for a Neural Mechanism Linking Growth
Mind-Set to Adaptive Posterror Adjustments," *Psychological Science* 22 (2011):
1484–89, https://doi.org/10.1177/0956797611419520; H. S. Schroder, T. P. Moran,
M. B. Donnellan, and J. S. Moser, "Mindset Induction Effects on Cognitive Control: A Neurobehavioral Investigation," *Biological Psychology* 103 (2014): 27–37,
https://doi.org/10.1016/j.biopsycho.2014.08.004; Mangels et al., "Why Do Beliefs
about Intelligence Influence Learning Success?"

210 *When we're in our growth mindset*: Ibid.

211 *The Dunning-Kruger effect*: Justin Kruger and David Dunning, "Unskilled and
Unaware of It: How Difficulties in Recognizing One's Own Incompetence Lead to
Inflated Self-Assessments," *Journal of Personality and Social Psychology* 77, no. 6
(1999): 1121–34, https://doi.org/10.1037/0022-3514.77.6.1121.

211 *In subsequent work, Joyce Ehrlinger*: Joyce Ehrlinger, Ainsley L. Mitchum, and
Carol S. Dweck, "Understanding Overconfidence: Theories of Intelligence, Pref-
erential Attention, and Distorted Self-Assessment," *Journal of Experimental Psychology* 63 (March 2016): 94–100, https://doi.org/10.1016/j.jesp.2015.11.001.

211 *Some of us are so chronically*: "The Rise, the Creative Process, and the Difference
Between Mastery and Success, with Dr. Sarah Lewis," interview by Brené Brown.

212 *As the first Black ballerina*: "Misty Copeland," interview by Carly Zakin and Danielle Weisberg, 9 to 5ish, Apple Podcasts, https://podcasts.apple.com/us/podca
st/misty-copeland-principal-dancer-american-ballet-theatre/id1345547675?i
=1000493035612.

212 *That it's an acceptable way*: "Misty Copeland on Blackness and Ballet," interview
by Karen Hunter, *Urban View*, SiriusXM, https://www.youtube.com/watch?v=tgn
VHGbnLDQ&t=4s.

212 *As cultural historian and author*: *A Ballerina's Tale*, directed by Nelson George,
Urban Romances/Nice Dissolve/Rumble Audio, 2015.

213 *Copeland says she's learned*: "Misty Copeland," interview by Carly Zakin and Danielle Weisberg.

213 *In one post deriding*: Devon Elizabeth, "Misty Copeland Responds to 'Swan Lake' Performance Criticism," *Teen VOGUE*, March 28, 2018, https://www.teenvogue .com/story/misty-copeland-responds-criticisms-swan-lake-performance.

213 *Recounting the criticism*: "Jessica Hische," interview by Debbie Millman, *Design Matters*, 2020, https://www.designmattersmedia.com/podcast/2020/Jessica -Hische.

214 *When critical feedback shifts*: Blackwell, Trzesniewski, and Dweck, "Implicit Theories of Intelligence Predict Achievement Across an Adolescent Transition"; Carol S. Dweck and Ellen L. Leggett, "A Social-Cognitive Approach to Motivation and Personality," *Psychological Review* 95, no. 2 (1988): 256–73, https://doi.org/10.1037 /0033-295X.95.2.256; Nussbaum and Dweck, "Defensiveness Versus Remediation."

214 *Former Whole Foods Market CEO*: John Mackey, Steve McIntosh, and Carter Phipps, *Conscious Leadership: Elevating Humanity Through Business* (New York: Portfolio, 2020); "Whole Foods CEO John Mackey on Conscious Capitalism, Leadership and Win-Win-Win Thinking," interview by Matt Bodner, *The Science of Success*, September 8, 2020, https://www.successpodcast.com/show-notes/2020 /9/8/b-whole-foods-ceo-john-mackey-on-conscious-capitalism-leadership-and -win-win-win-thinking.

219 *Claude Steele provides*: Claude Steele, interview by Mary Murphy, July 9, 2021; M. C. Murphy, V. J. Taylor, and C. M. Steele, "Stereotype Threat: A Situated Theory of Social Cognition," in *Oxford Handbook of Social Cognition*, ed. K. Hugenberg, K. Johnson, and D. Carlston (New York: Oxford University Press, new edition forthcoming).

220 *I referred earlier to Joyce Ehrlinger's*: Ehrlinger et al., "Understanding Overconfidence."

220 *Steele and his colleagues*: Geoffrey G. Cohen, Claude M. Steele, and Lee Ross, "The Mentor's Dilemma: Providing Critical Feedback Across the Racial Divide," *Personality and Social Psychology Bulletin* 25, no. 10 (October 1999): 1302–18, https:// doi.org/10.1177/0146167299258011.

220 Wise feedback *describes a series*: Cohen et al., "The Mentor's Dilemma"; D. S. Yeager, V. Purdie-Vaughns, J. Garcia, N. Apfel, P. Brzustoski, A. Master, W. T. Hessert, M. E. Williams, and G. L. Cohen, "Breaking the Cycle of Mistrust: Wise Interventions to Provide Critical Feedback Across the Racial Divide," *Journal of Experimental Psychology* 142, no. 2 (2014): 804–24, https://doi.org/10.1037/a0033906; Joel Brockner and David K. Sherman, "Wise Interventions in Organizations," *Research in Organizational Behavior* 39 (2019): 100–25, https://doi.org/10.1016 /j.riob.2020.100125.

222 *Therefore, they don't have to*: Yeager et al., "Breaking the Cycle of Mistrust." In another version of this study, teachers provided an opportunity for students to revise their essays. Of those in the wise criticism group, 71 percent of Black students opted to revise their work (compared to 17 percent of students in the standard feedback group). And not only that, the quality of the revised work was also better. Eighty-eight percent of Black students' scores improved upon revision compared

with only 34 percent of Black students in the standard group. Additionally, the wise intervention was most effective with Black students who were least likely to agree with the statement, "I am treated fairly by teachers and other adults at my school." That is, it was most effective when trust had initially been low. When the teachers clarified why they were giving critical feedback and allayed the concern that students were being treated negatively because of their race, the wise criticism helped Black students feel more trusting, and this trust freed them up to focus on their work, resulting in improved performance.

222 *Journalist Kara Swisher*: "Kara Swisher," interview by Carly Zakin and Danielle Weisberg, 9 to 5ish, Apple Podcasts, https://podcasts.apple.com/us/podcast /kara-swisher-host-pivot-sway-podcasts-co-founder-recode/id1345547675?i =1000503251587.

223 *At Pixar, for example*: Ed Catmull with Amy Wallace, *Creativity, Inc.: Overcoming the Unseen Forces that Stand in the Way of True Inspiration* (New York: Random House, 2014).

224 *For example, when Sadie Lincoln*: "Sadie Lincoln Is Rewriting the Fitness Story," interview by Rich Roll.

224 *When James Park of Fitbit*: "Fitbit: James Park," interview by Guy Raz, *How I Built This*, April 27, 2020, https://www.npr.org/2020/04/22/841267648/fitbit-james -park.

224 *And for her part*: Elizabeth, "Misty Copeland Responds to 'Swan Lake' Performance Criticism."

225 *In research my team undertook in 2020*: K. Muenks, E. A. Canning, J. LaCosse, D. J. Green, S. Zirkel, and J. A. Garcia, "Does My Professor Think My Ability Can Change? Students' Perceptions of Their STEM Professors' Mindset Beliefs Predict Their Psychological Vulnerability, Engagement, and Performance in Class," *Journal of Experimental Psychology: General* 149, no. 11 (2020): 2119–44, https://doi .org/10.1037/xge0000763; K. M. Kroeper, A. Fried, and M. C. Murphy, "Toward Fostering Growth Mindset Classrooms: Identifying Teaching Behaviors that Signal Instructors' Fixed and Growth Mindset Beliefs to Students," *Social Psychology of Education* 25 (2022): 371–98, https://doi.org/10.1007/s11218-022-09689-4; K. M. Kroeper, K. Muenks, E. A. Canning, and M. C. Murphy, "An Exploratory Study of the Behaviors that Communicate Perceived Instructor Mindset Beliefs in College STEM Classrooms," *Teaching and Teacher Education* 114, no. 4 (2022), https://doi.org/10.1016/j.tate.2022.103717.

226 *When I was part of the Faculty Success Program*: "Faculty Success Program: Achieve Academic Success and Better Work–Life Balance," https://www.faculty diversity.org/fsp-bootcamp.

CHAPTER 12: SUCCESS OF OTHERS

229 *When we observe others' achievements*: L. S. Blackwell, K. H. Trzesniewski, and C. S. Dweck, "Implicit Theories of Intelligence Predict Achievement Across an Adolescent Transition: A Longitudinal Study and an Intervention," *Child Development* 78, no. 1 (2007): 246–63, http://dx.doi.org/10.1111/j.1467-8624.2007.00995.x; Carol S. Dweck and Ellen L. Leggett, "A Social-Cognitive Approach to Motiva-

tion and Personality," *Psychological Review* 95, no. 2 (1988): 256–73, https://doi
.org/10.1037/0033-295X.95.2.256; F. Rhodewalt, "Conceptions of Ability, Achievement Goals, and Individual Differences in Self-Handicapping Behavior: On the
Application of Implicit Theories," *Journal of Personality* 62, no. 1 (1994): 67–85,
http://dx.doi.org/10.1111/j.1467-6494.1994.tb00795.x; Carol S. Dweck, "Mindsets
and Human Nature: Promoting Change in the Middle East, the Schoolyard, the
Racial Divide, and Willpower," *American Psychologist* 67, no. 8 (2012): 614–22,
https://doi.org/10.1037/a0029783.

230 *In* Every Other Thursday: Ellen Daniell, *Every Other Thursday: Stories and Strategies from Successful Women Scientists* (New Haven, CT: Yale University Press, 2008).

231 *Yet without a doubt*: 30 for 30, season 1, episode 15, "Unmatched (Evert &
Navratilova)," Disney-ESPN, September 14, 2010, https://www.youtube.com
/watch?v=7eDGNAw97XM&t=62s.

231 *For perspective, Joe Frazier*: Greg Logan, "Muhammad Ali vs. Joe Frazier: A Bru-
tal Trilogy," *Newsday*, June 4, 2016, https://www.newsday.com/sports/boxing
/muhammad-ali-vs-joe-frazier-a-brutal-trilogy-v59775.

231 *while Evert and Navratilova*: 30 for 30, "Unmatched (Evert & Navratilova),"
Disney-ESPN.

232 *Evert was nicknamed*: J. A. Allen, "Queens of the Court: Chris Evert, Never Count
Out the 'Ice Maiden,'" *Sports Then and Now*, December 20, 2009, http://sports
thenandnow.com/2009/12/20/queens-of-the-court-chris-evert-never-count-out
-the-ice-maiden/.

232 *Countering Evert's emotional strength*: 30 for 30, "Unmatched (Evert & Navratilova)," Disney-ESPN.

232 *It's an illustration of something*: Mary C. Murphy and Stephanie L. Reeves, "Personal and Organizational Mindsets at Work," *Research in Organizational Behavior* 39 (2019), https://doi.org/10.1016/j.riob.2020.100121; K. M. Kroeper, A. Fried,
and M. C. Murphy, "Toward Fostering Growth Mindset Classrooms: Identifying
Teaching Behaviors that Signal Instructors' Fixed and Growth Mindset Beliefs
to Students," *Social Psychology of Education* 25 (2022): 371–98, https://doi.org
/10.1007/s11218-022-09689-4; K. M. Kroeper, K. Muenks, E. A. Canning, and
M. C. Murphy, "An Exploratory Study of the Behaviors that Communicate Perceived Instructor Mindset Beliefs in College STEM Classrooms," *Teaching and
Teacher Education* 114, no. 4 (2022), https://doi.org/10.1016/j.tate.2022.103717;
Melissa A. Fuesting, Amanda B. Diekman, Kathryn L. Boucher, Mary C. Murphy, Dana L. Manson, and Brianne L. Safer, "Growing STEM: Perceived Faculty
Mindset as an Indicator of Communal Affordances in STEM," *Journal of Personality and Social Psychology* 117, no. 2 (2019): 260–81, https://doi.org/10.1037
/pspa0000154; K. L. Boucher, M. A. Fuesting, A. Diekman, and M. C. Murphy,
"Can I Work With and Help Others in the Field? How Communal Goals Influence Interest and Participation in STEM Fields," *Frontiers in Psychology* 8 (2017),
https://doi.org/10.3389/fpsyg.2017.00901.

232 *When Des Linden took*: Alisa Chang, "Runner Tells Herself 'Just Show Up for One
More Mile'—and Wins the Boston Marathon," *NPR*, April 17, 2018, https://www
.npr.org/2018/04/17/603189901/runner-tells-herself-just-show-up-for-one-more
-mile-and-wins-the-boston-marathon.

233 *Once she dropped off*: Sarah Lorge Butler and Erin Strout, "Behind the Scenes of Desiree Linden's Incredible Boston Marathon Win," *Runner's World*, May 1, 2018, https://www.runnersworld.com/news/a20087622/behind-the-scenes-of-desiree -lindens-incredible-boston-marathon-win/.

233 *"Just one more mile,"*: Chang, "Runner Tells Herself 'Just Show Up for One More Mile.'"

233 *Linden was not unaware*: Lindsay Crouse, "How the 'Shalane Flanagan Effect' Works," *New York Times*, November 11, 2017, https://www.nytimes.com/2017/11 /11/opinion/sunday/shalane-flanagan-marathon-running.html.

233 *Thomas Edison would likely*: Patrick J. Kiger, "6 Key Inventions by Thomas Edison," *History*, March 6, 2020, https://www.history.com/news/thomas-edison -inventions.

234 *Though Edison was an intellectual giant*: The inventor relied on dozens of so-called muckers—his name for the scores of young, well-educated men who worked 55 hours or more a week receiving sub-par wages to make Edison's ideas a reality. While some described working for Edison as inspiring, he was also known to be critical and domineering. As one mucker described, his boss could "wither one with his biting sarcasm or ridicule one into extinction." Some say that if Edison had a particular gift beyond his very real aptitude for problem solving, it may have been his ability to attract a team of highly engaged employees. Yet Edison seems to have been a darkly charismatic leader and his lab at Menlo Park a Culture of Genius. "The Gifted Men Who Worked for Edison," National Park Service, accessed May 12, 2023, https://www.nps.gov/edis/learn/kidsyouth/the-gifted-men -who-worked-for-edison.htm.

234 *Interestingly, though Edison*: "The Gifted Men Who Worked for Edison," National Park Service.

234 *when it came to identifying the genius*: Tom McNichol, *AC/DC: The Savage Tale of the First Standards War* (New York: Jossey-Bass, 2013).

234 *"Edison's great weakness"*: *American Genius*, season 1, episode 8, "Edison vs Tesla," National Geographic, June 22, 2015.

235 *At one point, Westinghouse*: McNichol, *AC/DC*.

235 *Perhaps no other practice*: Steve Bates, "Forced Ranking," *HR Magazine*, June 1, 2003, https://www.shrm.org/hr-today/news/hr-magazine/pages/0603bates.aspx.

236 *In an article published in 2018, Welch*: Jack Welch, "Rank-and-Yank? That's Not How It's Done," Strayer University, April 12, 2018, https://jackwelch.strayer .edu/winning/rank-yank-differentiation/.

236 *As business journalist Arwa Mahdawi*: Arwa Mahdawi, "30 Under 30-Year Sentences: Why So Many of Forbes' Young Heroes Face Jail," *Guardian*, April 7, 2023, https://www.theguardian.com/business/2023/apr/06/forbes-30-under-30-tech -finance-prison.

236 *Critics of stack ranking*: Jack Welch, "Rank-and-Yank? That's Not How It's Done."

236 *Incidentally, the opposite of schadenfreude*: Juli Fraga, "The Opposite of Schadenfreude Is Freudenfreude. Here's How to Cultivate It," *New York Times*, November 25, 2022, https://www.nytimes.com/2022/11/25/well/mind/schadenfreude -freudenfreude.html.

237 *Competition, itself, may be*: "Fun: What the Hell Is It and Why Do We Need It?,"

interview by Glennon Doyle, *We Can Do Hard Things*, June 1, 2021, https://mo mastery.com/blog/episode-04/.

237 *In a now-famous scandal*: Chris Prentice and Pete Schroeder, "Former Wells Fargo Exec Faces Prison, Will Pay $17 Million Fine Over Fake Accounts Scandal," Reuters, March 15, 2023, https://www.reuters.com/legal/former-wells-fargo -executive-pleads-guilty-obstructing-bank-examination-fined-17-2023-03-15/.

237 *Fierce competition for limited jobs*: Margaret Heffernan, *A Bigger Prize: How We Can Do Better than the Competition* (Philadelphia: PublicAffairs, 2014); Sarah Childress and Gretchen Gavett, "The News Corp. Phone-Hacking Scandal: A Cheat Sheet," *Frontline*, July 24, 2012, https://www.pbs.org/wgbh/frontline/arti cle/the-news-corp-phone-hacking-scandal-a-cheat-sheet/.

237 *And according to former managing director*: Jamie Fiore Higgins, *Bully Market: My Story of Money and Misogyny at Goldman Sachs* (New York: Simon & Schuster, 2022).

237 *A "decade littered with errors"*: Kurt Eichenwald, "Microsoft's Lost Decade," *Vanity Fair*, July 24, 2012, https://www.vanityfair.com/news/business/2012/08/microsoft -lost-mojo-steve-ballmer.

238 *To describe the situation*: Satya Nadella, *Hit Refresh: The Quest to Rediscover Microsoft's Soul and Imagine a Better Future for Everyone* (New York: Harper Business, 2017).

238 *Eichenwald wrote, "Supposing Microsoft"*: Eichenwald, "Microsoft's Lost Decade."

238 *As it happens, one of the*: Peter Cohan, "Why Stacked Ranking Worked Better at GE than Microsoft," *Forbes*, July 13, 2012, https://www.forbes.com/sites/pe tercohan/2012/07/13/why-stack-ranking-worked-better-at-ge-than-microsoft /?sh=62c989d23236.

239 *As Margaret Heffernan emphasizes*: Margaret Heffernan, "Forget the Pecking Order at Work," TEDWomen 2015, May 2015, https://www.ted.com/talks/marga ret_heffernan_forget_the_pecking_order_at_work.

239 *Many years ago, Microsoft's*: "The Moment of Lift with Melinda French Gates," interview by Brené Brown, *Unlocking Us*, January 20, 2021, https://brenebrown .com/podcast/brene-with-david-eagleman-on-the-inside-story-of-the-ever -changing-brain/https://brenebrown.com/podcast/brene-with-melinda-gates-on -the-moment-of-lift/.

239 *In her TED Talk*: Frances Frei, "How to Build (and Rebuild) Trust," TED2018, April 2018, https://www.ted.com/talks/frances_frei_how_to_build_and_rebuild _trust#t-848544.

239 *Before long, the former Microsoft*: "The Moment of Lift with Melinda French Gates," interview by Brené Brown.

240 *In dozens of studies, we find*: Justin M. Berg, Amy Wrzesniewski, Adam M. Grant, Jennifer Kurkoski, and Brian Welle, "Getting Unstuck: The Effects of Growth Mindsets About the Self and Job on Happiness at Work," *Journal of Applied Psychology* 108, no. 1 (January 2023), https://doi.org/10.1037/apl0001021. Mary C. Murphy and Carol S. Dweck, "A Culture of Genius: How an Organization's Lay Theory Shapes People's Cognition, Affect, and Behavior," *Personality and Social Psychology Bulletin* 36, no. 3 (October 2009): 283–96, https://doi.org/10.1177 /0146167209347380; Elizabeth A. Canning, Katherine Muenks, Dorainne J. Green, and Mary C. Murphy, "STEM Faculty Who Believe Ability Is Fixed Have Larger

Racial Achievement Gaps and Inspire Less Student Motivation in Their Classes," *Science Advances* 5, no. 2 (February 15, 2019), https://doi.org/10.1126/sciadv .aau4734; K. Muenks, E. A. Canning, J. LaCosse, D. J. Green, S. Zirkel, and J. A. Garcia, "Does My Professor Think My Ability Can Change? Students' Perceptions of Their STEM Professors' Mindset Beliefs Predict Their Psychological Vulnerability, Engagement, and Performance in Class," *Journal of Experimental Psychology: General* 149, no. 11 (2020): 2119–44, https://doi.org/10.1037/xge0000763; Elizabeth A. Canning, Mary C. Murphy, Katherine T. U. Emerson, Jennifer A. Chatman, Carol S. Dweck, and Laura J. Kray, "Cultures of Genius at Work: Organizational Mindsets Predict Cultural Norms, Trust, and Commitment," *Personality and Social Psychology Bulletin* 46, no. 4 (2020): 626–42; L. Bian, S. Leslie, M. C. Murphy, and A. Cimpian, "Messages about Brilliance Undermine Women's Interest in Educational and Professional Opportunities," *Journal of Experimental Social Psychology* 76 (May 2018): 404–20, https://doi.org/10.1016/j.jesp.2017.11.006; Fuesting et al., "Growing STEM: Perceived Faculty Mindset as an Indicator"; Elizabeth A. Canning, Elise Ozier, Heidi E. Williams, Rashed AlRasheed, and Mary C. Murphy, "Professors Who Signal a Fixed Mindset about Ability Undermine Women's Performance in STEM," *Social Psychological and Personality Science* 13, no. 5 (2022): 927–37, https://doi.org/10.1177/19485506211030398; J. LaCosse, M. C. Murphy, J. A. Garcia, and S. Zirkel, "The Role of STEM Professors' Mindset Beliefs on Students' Anticipated Psychological Experiences and Course Interest," *Journal of Educational Psychology* 113 (2021): 949–71, https://doi.org/10.1037/edu0000620.

240 *A group of researchers from MIT*: Anita Williams Woolley, Christopher F. Chabris, Alex Pentland, Nada Hashmi, and Thomas W. Malone, "Evidence for a Collective Intelligence Factor in the Performance of Human Groups," *Science* 330, no. 6004 (September 30, 2010): 686–88, https://doi.org/10.1126/science.1193147.

241 *At Cultures of Growth such as Pixar*: Catmull with Wallace, *Creativity, Inc.*

241 *As researchers on gender*: Linda L. Carli and Alice H. Eagly, "Gender and Leadership," in *The SAGE Handbook of Leadership*, ed. Alan Bryman, David L. Collinson, Keith Grint, Brad Jackson, and Mary Uhl-Bien (New York: SAGE Publications, 2011), 103–17.

241 *According to behavioral and data scientist*: Paola Cecchi-Dimeglio, "How Gender Bias Corrupts Performance Reviews, and What to Do About It," *Harvard Business Review*, April 12, 2017, https://hbr.org/2017/04/how-gender-bias-corrupts -performance-reviews-and-what-to-do-about-it.

242 *After Uber's culture challenges*: Jeff Miller, "Bozoma Saint John Explains Why She Left Uber," Yahoo! Entertainment, March 13, 2019, https://www.yahoo.com/en tertainment/endeavor-bozoma-saint-john-leaving-210150391.html.

243 *As Carol Dweck and I had shown*: Murphy and Dweck, "A Culture of Genius"; Kroeper et al., "Toward Fostering Growth Mindset Classrooms"; Kroeper et al., "An Exploratory Study of the Behaviors"; Bian et al., "Messages about Brilliance"; Murphy and Reeves, "Personal and Organizational Mindsets at Work."

243 *Subsequently, my team's analysis*: Fuesting et al., "Growing STEM: Perceived Faculty Mindset as an Indicator"; LaCosse et al., "The Role of STEM Professors' Mindset Beliefs"; Muenks et al., "Does My Professor Think My Ability Can Change?"; Bian et al., "Messages about Brilliance."

243 *Cultures of Growth have policies*: Fuesting et al., "Growing STEM: Perceived Faculty Mindset as an Indicator"; Boucher et al., "Can I Work With and Help Others"; Murphy and Reeves, "Personal and Organizational Mindsets at Work."

243 *When Pierre Johnson*: Rochelle Riley, "Trio's Boys-to-Men Journey Leads to Successful Careers as Doctors," *Detroit Free Press*, December 16, 2018, https://www.freep.com/story/news/columnists/rochelle-riley/2018/12/16/riley-doctors-overcome-odds/2324825002/.

243 *According to the Association of American Medical Colleges*: "Diversity in Medicine: Facts and Figures 2019," Association of American Medical Colleges, accessed May 12, 2023, https://www.aamc.org/data-reports/workforce/data/figure-18-percentage-all-active-physicians-race/ethnicity-2018.

244 *As Johnson says*: Riley, "Trio's Boys-to-Men Journey Leads to Successful Careers as Doctors."

244 *Competition undermines psychological safety*: Amy Edmonson, *The Fearless Organization: Creating Psychological Safety in the Workplace for Learning, Innovation, and Growth* (New York: Wiley, 2018).

245 *Pressure to test into gifted and talented*: Heffernan, *A Bigger Prize*.

245 *By that time, social comparison*: Cornell students may also face an additional layer of pressure to prove and perform. Without a doubt, Cornell is a top school, yet in some circles it's thought to fall toward the bottom of the top schools—the least Ivy of the Ivies or even the "Fake Ivy," as some call it. Commonly, people point to a variety of factors to support this claim, from its higher acceptance rate and larger undergraduate enrollment, to its relative youth compared with other Ivy League schools. Additionally, some higher-performing students who applied to Harvard or Yale, for example, applied to Cornell as their fallback, and so while it seems ridiculous to many of us to think of acceptance at Cornell as anything other than a huge accomplishment, some students actually view it as a form of failure.

245 *Cornell launched a massive campaign*: Cornell has one of the best health communication departments in the world, and they engaged the department in an effort to improve campus-wide mental health. In addition to increasing the number of employees of CAPS (the school's psychological and health counseling service) they funneled a further $2.5 million in funding toward the program.

246 *According to data from the National Alliance on Mental Illness*: Nemanja Petkovic, "Top 25 Mental Health Statistics," Health Careers, May 12, 2020, https://healthcareers.co/college-student-mental-health-statistics/.

246 *Additionally, Reuters reports*: Ibid.

246 *More than half of the world's*: "Average Daily Time Spent on Social Media," Broadband Search, accessed May 12, 2023, https://www.broadbandsearch.net/blog/average-daily-time-on-social-media.

246 *As the documentary* The Social Dilemma: *The Social Dilemma*, directed by Jeff Orlowski-Yang, Exposure Labs/Argent Pictures/The Space Program, 2020.

246 *Research shows that while, theoretically*: Judith B. White, Ellen J. Langer, Leeat Yariv, and John C. Welch IV, "Frequent Social Comparisons and Destructive Emotions and Behaviors: The Dark Side of Social Comparison," *Journal of Adult Development* 13, no. 1 (2006): 36–44, https://doi.org/10.1007/s10804-006-9005-0.

A study in the same paper showed that police officers who made frequent social comparisons also displayed more in-group bias and displayed less job satisfaction.

247 *As my team's research on professors' mindsets*: Fuesting et al., "Growing STEM: Perceived Faculty Mindset as an Indicator"; Canning et al., "STEM Faculty Who Believe Ability Is Fixed"; Muenks et al., "Does My Professor Think My Ability Can Change?"; David S. Yeager, Jamie M. Carroll, Jenny Buontempo, Andrei Cimpian, Spencer Woody, Robert Crosnoe, Chandra Muller, Jared Murray, Pratik Mhatre, Nicole Kersting, Christopher Hulleman, Molly Kudym, Mary Murphy, Angela Lee Duckworth, Gregory M. Walton, and Carol S. Dweck, "Teacher Mindsets Help Explain Where a Growth-Mindset Intervention Does and Doesn't Work," *Psychological Science* 33, no. 1 (2022): 18–32, https://doi.org/10.1177/09567976211028984; Canning et al., "Professors Who Signal a Fixed Mindset"; Bian et al., "Messages about Brilliance"; K. Boucher, M. C. Murphy, D. Bartel, J. Smail, C. Logel, and J. Danek, "Centering the Student Experience: What Faculty and Institutions Can Do to Advance Equity," *Change: The Magazine of Higher Learning* 53 (2021): 42–50, https://doi.org/10.1080/00091383.2021.1987804; LaCosse et al., "The Role of STEM Professors' Mindset Beliefs"; Mary Murphy, Stephanie Fryberg, Laura Brady, Elizabeth Canning, and Cameron Hecht, "Global Mindset Initiative Paper 1: Growth Mindset Cultures and Teacher Practices," *Growth Mindset Cultures and Practices* (August 27, 2021), http://dx.doi.org/10.2139/ssrn.3911594.

247 *In the biopic* Itzhak: *Itzhak*, directed by Alison Chernick, American Masters Pictures, 2018.

247 *Toby founded the Perlman Music Program*: "Toby's Dream," Perlman Music Program, accessed May 12, 2023, https://www.perlmanmusicprogram.org/about-pmp.

247 *His parents frequently compared him*: "Itzhak Perlman Teaches Violin," MasterClass, https://www.masterclass.com/classes/itzhak-perlman-teaches-violin.

248 *Social psychophysiologists Jim Blascovich*: Jim Blascovich and Wendy Berry Mendes, "Challenge and Threat Appraisals: The Role of Affective Cues," in *Feeling and Thinking: The Role of Affect in Social Cognition*, ed. Joseph P. Forgas (Cambridge: Cambridge University Press, 1999), 59–81, https://books.google.com/books?hl=en&lr=&id=PSiU9wsJ13QC&oi=fnd&pg=PA59&dq=challenge+and+threat+appraisals&ots=ekJs1IuyUL&sig=RUndkRkiwgeTyewnTWpl1hL7DDI#v=onepage&q=challenge%20and%20threat%20appraisals&f=false. For one of their studies, Blascovich and Mendes cued participants into a challenge or threat state by putting them through a version of the classically stressful situation called the Trier Social Stress Test (TSST). The TSST requires participants to prepare and deliver a speech, and verbally respond to a challenging math problem in the presence of a socially evaluative audience—not my idea of fun! But first, Blascovich and Mendes had participants listen to audiotaped instructions. For the challenge state, the instructions encouraged participants to "try their best and to think of the task as one to be met and overcome." For the threat state, they were told that the task was mandatory and that their performance would be evaluated. Then the researchers administered a series of math tasks and monitored participants' heart rate and blood pressure. While they worked on the math problems,

both groups experienced a similar increase in heart rate. The major difference appeared in the body's mobilization of blood flow. For those in the challenge state, blood mobilized throughout their body in a manner similar to cardiovascular performance during aerobic exercise. The response represented "efficient mobilization of energy for coping" with the stressful situation. But when people had been put in a threat state, the opposite occurred: The body directed blood flow away from the limbs and moved toward the center of the body. They found that our body's physiological response to challenge versus threat is essentially the difference between gearing up for performance or for survival. But the physiological reactions weren't all; challenge and threat actually influenced people's cognitive abilities. When it came to performance, those in the threat group completed fewer problems and, of those they did complete, they got fewer of the problems correct. When it comes to the growth mindset, we recognize the strategies and resources that we have to cope with challenging and stressful situations—and we marshal them to meet the situations' demands. In our fixed mindset, we are much more likely to enter into the threat state—which ultimately undermines our physical well-being and our cognitive performance. One additional item of note is that Blascovich and Mendes say that whether or not we're conscious of the appraisals does not substantially affect the result.

250 *When researcher Ellen Daniell*: Daniell, *Every Other Thursday*.

250 *Daniell didn't magically feel*: Another benefit of the pod as it relates to the success of others is that we can be vulnerable and open up about who we've been measuring ourselves against and how their success is affecting us.

250 *Bozoma Saint John made a splash*: Miller, "Bozoma Saint John Explains Why She Left Uber."

251 *In social psychology, that's an attributional bias*: Kendra Cherry, "Actor–Observer Bias in Social Psychology," *Verywell Mind*, April 1, 2022, https://www.verywell mind.com/what-is-the-actor-observer-bias-2794813.

252 *Atlassian uses corporate storytelling*: Teamistry, Atlassian, accessed May 12, 2023, https://www.atlassian.com/blog/podcast/teamistry/season/season-1.

252 *Itzhak Perlman routinely asks*: "Itzhak Perlman Teaches Violin," MasterClass.

253 *As Simon Sinek defines it*: Simon Sinek, "How Having the Right Kind of Rival Can Help You Thrive in a Changing World," TED, October 15, 2019, https://ideas .ted.com/how-having-the-right-kind-of-rival-can-help-you-thrive-in-a-changing -world/.

254 *Women, in particular, experience*: Daniell, *Every Other Thursday*.

CONCLUSION

257 *In the 1950s*: Humberto R. Maturana and Francisco J. Varela, *The Tree of Knowledge: The Biological Roots of Human Understanding* (Boulder, CO: Shambhala, 1992); S. Hirata, K. Watanabe, and M. Kawai. "'Sweet-Potato Washing' Revisited," in *Primate Origins of Human Behavior*, ed T. Matsuzawa (New York: Springer-Verlag, 2001); Tetsuro Matsuzawa, "Sweet Potato Washing Revisited: 50th Anniversary of the *Primates* Article," *Primates* 56 (2015): 285–87, https://doi.org /10.1007/s10329-015-0492-0.

Index

ability
  addressing, 171
  beliefs about, 171, 181–86
  development of, 12
  effort and, 45–46, 179, 186, 192, 196
  mindset and, 188–89, *188*
Abraaj private equity fund, xviii
academic research, women in, 111
academic sciences, 108–11
accountability, 85, 112, 116–17
accounting, 159
achievement, collective, 243–44
ActOne Group, 129–30
actor-observer asymmetry, 251
actor-observer effect, 251–52, 254
Acumen, 61–63, 69, 119–20
Addison, Joseph, 10
affinity groups, 47, 94, 95
Africa, 60–61
Agarwal, Ankit, 61–62
Ajayi, Luvvie, 173
Ali, Muhammad, 231
Amazon, 98, 238
Amazon Web Services, xv
American Ballet Theatre, 212
Apple, xv, xix, 238
Apple Music, 242
Aristotle, 202
Arnett, Rachel, 210
artificial intelligence, xv
Asprey, Dave, 168
assessments, 5. *See also* evaluative situations
  self-assessment and, 209, 211
  static, 187
Association of American Medical Colleges (AAMC), 243–44
Atlassian, 39–41, 51, 76, 252
auditing, 159
Avis, 65

Awotona, Tope, 192
Aye, George, 132

Backpack Kid (and Adult), 206–7, 225
back-pocket problems, 195, 200
backroom negotiations, 24
Baker, Erica, 131
Ballmer, Steve, 85
Balwani, Ramesh "Sunny," 166
Barre3, 7–8, 203–6
Beck, Josh, 137–38
behavior, learned, 257–58
behavioral norms, 12–13, 20–21, 27–28, 37–38, 58, 71, 76, 112–13
beliefs
  reprogramming core, 198–99
  as self-fulfilling prophecy, 209
Ben & Jerry's, 136
Berrent, Jennifer, 34
Bertozzi, Carolyn, 110
Bezos, Jeff, 98, 238
bias, 244
  feedback and, 212–13, 218–22
  gendered, 218–19
  stack ranking and, 241–42
  translated to products, 131
Bing, xv
Bitcoin, 65
Bjork, Elizabeth, 185–86
Bjork, Robert, 185–86
Black doctors, 243–44
Black Enterprise, 129
Black founders, 192
Black Lives Matter movement, 8
Black men, 243–44
Black people, 125, 243–44. *See also specific groups*
  feedback bias and, 219, 221–22
  identity-based criticism and, 212–13

Black people (*cont.*)
  mistrust of school system, 221
  pipeline myth and, 134–35
Black students, 243–44
  feedback bias and, 219, 221–22
  mistrust of school system, 221
Blackwell, Angela Glover, 78
Black women, 130, 145, 193, 212–13
Blagrove, Courtney, 130
blankness, seizing opportunity of, 209
Blascovich, Jim, 248–49
Bosley, Amy, 143
bottom line, impact of mindset on, 27
"bought" vs. "built" teams, 39–41
B. R., Zan, 130
Braden, Laura, 103–4
brain, growth through challenge, 179–81
brands, organizational mindsets and, 64–67
"brilliant jerks," 101–3, 239
Brown, Brené, 209, 211–12
Brown, Xanni, 210

Calendly, 192
camaraderie, 41
campus-wide campaigns, 245–46, 247
candor, 86
Carli, Linda, 241
Carreyrou, John, 165
Carter, Dean, 49–51, 92–93
Carter, Shawn (Jay-Z), 198
Catmull, Ed, 73
Cecchi-Dimeglio, Paola, 241–42
Center for American Progress, 35
challenge(s), xxi
  growth from, 179–81
  as opportunities, 13
  origin stories and, 251–52
  vs. threat, 248–49
challenge states, 249–50
character, 63
Charpentier, Emmanuelle, 42
chatbots, xv
cheating, 24
Cheryan, Sapna, 189–90
children
  of color, xx
  persistence and, 183
China, 185
Choinard, Yvon, 44–45
Citizen Discourse, 136, 146
clarity pause, 120
Clarkson, Josh, 63–64, 137–38
classical music, 247

classroom agreements, 194
cloud computing, xv
Coca-Cola, 66
code switching, 143–44
cognitive bias, 211
Cohen, Geoff, 197, 220
collaboration, xxi, xxii, 9–10, 12, 23–25,
    27–28, 31–51, 83
  at Atlassian, 76
  vs. competition, 32–33, 36–37, 38, 41–42,
    48, 121
  to cut down on unethical competitive
    behavior, 121
  diversity and, 56
  encouraging, 49, 108–9
  focus on, 33
  innovation and, 54
  measuring, 51
  research and, 110–11
  risk-taking and, 85
collective intelligence, 240–41
collegiality, importance of, 253–54
community, calling on the, 199–200
Compassion Contract, 146
competency, beliefs about, 171
competition, 27, 28, 85, 114–15, 240, 243, 247.
    See also social comparison
  in the classroom, 245–48
  vs. collaboration, 32–33, 36–37, 38, 41–42,
    48, 121
  collaboration to cut down on unethical,
    121
  conflict and, 241
  consequences of, 237–38
  vs. contribution, 168–69
  education and, 245–48
  ethics and, 113–16
  institutionalized, 242
  negative impacts of internal, 41–42
  within organizations, 32–33
  recasting, 48–49
  vs. support, 199
  vs. teamwork, 236, 238
  undermining psychological safety, 244
  unethical behavior and, 113–16
complexity, 11
computer science, gender gap in, 189–90
confirmation bias, 79–80, 241–42
conflict
  competition and, 241
  issues-based, 91
conformity, with organizational mindsets,
    24–25

context, setting the, 168–71
contribution, vs. competition, 168–69
convergent thinking, 59–60
conversations, creating identity-safe
    containers for challenging, 146
Copeland, Misty, 212–13, 224
Coqual, 144
core beliefs, reprogramming, 198–99
Cornell University, 184, 199, 245–46
Cote, David, 238
COVID-19 pandemic, 8, 42–43, 168, 172–73
creativity, 18, 52–80, 85, 170
    how mindset impacts, 58–60
    influence of organizational culture on, 54
Crick, Francis, 42
CRISPR, 42–43, 108
critical thinking, 86
criticism, 203, 213–14. *See also* feedback,
    critical
    actionable, 214–17, *217*
    identity-based, 212–13
    race-based, 212–13
    specific, 214–17, *217*
cues audits, 26–27, 255
    conducting, 47
    fine-tuning, 144–45
cues hypothesis, 123–24
culture creators, 259–60
culture cycle, self-sustaining, 36
Cultures of Genius, xiv, xvii, xviii–xix, 7,
    8–14, 20, 127–28
    adaptive company culture and, 24–25
    artifacts of, 17
    conformity with, 24–25
    data and, 88
    defining, xviii
    DEI and, 125–28
    diversity in, 125–28, 131–37
    employee satisfaction with, 23–24, 35
    employees' trust in and commitment to,
        22–23
    equity in, 125–28, 131–37
    ethnic minorities and, 128
    fear of risk-taking in, 81–82, 83
    focus on performance and outcomes, 116
    genius mythology and, 36
    hiring process at, 134
    inclusion in, 125–28, 131–37
    innovation in, 37
    as leaning organizations, 55
    limited opportunities for development in,
        34–35
    in medical field, 113–14

microcultures of growth within, 173
mission statements and, 17
mistrust of, 126–27, 128, 134
organizational mindsets and, *18*
perfection and, 7, 11
prestige and, 240
racial minorities and, 128
risk-taking in, 37
in science, 110–11
at Shell, 69–71
shifting to Cultures of Growth, 258–60
stakeholder capitalism and, 62
stereotype threat to women and, 127–28
at Theranos, 165–66
from the top, 235–39
unethical behavior and, 100–103, 112
women and, 127–28
Cultures of Growth, xiv, xv, xviii, xix–xx, 7,
    8–14, 16
    adaptive company culture and, 25
    artifacts of, 17
    candor and, 86
    challenge(s) and, 13
    collaboration and, 38, 42–46
    commitment to development in, 40–41
    competition and, 42–46, 114–15
    creating collaborative, 46–51
    creating one's own, 239–40
    critical thinking and, 86
    data and, 87–93
    defining, xv, xvii, xix
    DEI and, 124
    development and, 137
    diversity in, 131–37
    education and, 139–44
    employee satisfaction with, 23–24, 35
    employees' trust in and commitment to,
        22–23
    equitable, 139–44
    equity in, 131–37
    ethical behavior and, 110–12
    factors that influence risk-taking in, 93–95
    focus on collaboration, 33
    focus on progress, 17–18
    fostering, xx–xxi
    HR processes and, 147–48
    inclusion in, 131–37
    innovation and, 258
    language and, 194
    as leaning organizations, 55
    learning and, 116, 120, 124
    as learning organizations, 120
    learning orientation of, 124

Cultures of Growth (*cont.*)
  as listening organizations, 120
  mission statements and, 17
  organizational mindsets and, *18*
  preference for, 240
  psychological safety and, 68–69
  risk-taking in, 82–83
  at Shell, 71–72
  shifting to, 258–60
  STEM classrooms as, 139–40
  striving for growth for everyone, xxii
  sustaining, 259
  teaching, 195
  trustworthiness and, 65
  unethical behavior and, 100–103
customers
  goal-directed vs. task-directed interactions
    with, 106–7
  mindset of, 63–64
cutting corners, 24

Dalen, Kathleen Boyle, 27
Danek, Jennifer, 113–14, 120
Daniell, Ellen, 230, 250
Darwin, Charles, 60
data, 48, 51
  Cultures of Genius and, 88, 170
  Cultures of Growth and, 87–93, 170
  data cultures, 170
  data-driven decision-making, 87–93
  data entry, 159
  de-risking with, 87–93
  engaging people around, 87–93
  examining, 48
  making data your friend, 96–97
  risk-taking and, 87–93
defensiveness, 175, 210
DEI (diversity, equity, inclusion), 12, 28, 91,
    122–48
  DEI-centered policies, 8
  institutionalized scarcity and, 242–43
  mindset culture and, 124, 125–28
  stack ranking and, 242
DeLay, Dorothy, 248
#DeleteUber campaign, 58
de-risking with data, 87–93
development, 12, 137
  commitment to, 37, 40–41
  employees and, 118
  encouraging, 49
  facilitating, 175
  feedback and, 219
  feedback and development goals, 213–14

  growth mindset and, 210
  opportunities for, 34–35
  prioritization of, 187
  of strengths, 201
  willingness to develop oneself, 18
dialogue, 174
differently abled people, 125
Diginomica, 134
DigitalOcean, 49
divergent thinking, 59
diversity, xxi, 8, 12, 28, 91, 111, 122–48, 193.
    See also DEI (diversity, equity, inclusion)
  collaboration and, 56
  in Cultures of Genius, 125–28, 131–37
  in Cultures of Growth, 131–37
  leadership and, 242
  mindset culture and, xx
  organizational mindsets and, 131–44
  scientific insights into, 131–44
  suppression of, 239–44
Dixon, Mark, 214–15
Dixon-Gottschild, Brenda, 212–13
d.light, 62
doctors, 113–14
Dorsey, Jack, 81–82
Doudna, Jennifer, 42–44, 108
dual burden, 211
Duncan, Candace "Candy," 55–56, 57, 159
Dunning, David, 211
Dunning-Kruger effect, 211
Duolingo, 64
Dweck, Carol, xv–xvi, 4, 6–7, 10, 15–16, 63,
    189, 207–9, 211, 243, 245

Eagleman, David, 181
Eagly, Alice, 241
Edison, Thomas, 233–35
Edmondson, Amy, 67–68, 114
education, 139–44, 194–95
  competition and, 245–48
  feedback in, 219–22
  social comparison and, 245–48
  stack ranking and, 245
effective effort, 180, 185, 186, 201, 217
effort
  ability and, 45–46, 179, 186, 192, 196
  dedicated, 11, 12
  effective, 180, 185, 186, 201, 217
  false beliefs about, 181–86
  hiding, 183–85
effort praise, 186
Ehrlinger, Joyce, 211, 220
Eichenwald, Kurt, 237–39

Einstein, Albert, 20
electroencephalographic technology (EEG
    scans), 208–9
Ellison, Larry, 238
Emerson, Katherine, 126–27, 133–34
emotions, theory of constructed, 204
employee performance, measurement of,
    117–18
employees, xvii
    assessments of, 25, 117–18
    biased feedback and, 218–19
    conformity with company culture, 24–25
    critical feedback and, 227
    development and, 118
    in high-effort situations, 197, 200
    institutionalized scarcity and, 242–43
    maintaining growth trajectory of, 200
    receiving feedback, 216–17, 218–19, 224–25
    risk-taking and, 85–87
    stack ranking of, 235–36, 237
    supervisor mindset and, 35–36
    trusting, 174
employee satisfaction, organizational
    mindsets and, 23–24, 35
employee turnover, 27, 35
Enron, 36
entrepreneur, false lore of the, 190–93
entrepreneurship
    barriers to women and minorities in,
        191–92
    fixed mindset beliefs about, 127–28
    fixed vs. growth mindset triggers and,
        190–91
equity, xxi, 8, 12, 28, 91, 112, 122–48. See also
    DEI (diversity, equity, inclusion)
    in academic research, 111
    in Cultures of Genius, 125–28, 131–37
    in Cultures of Growth, 131–37
    organizational mindsets and, 131–44
    scientific insights into, 131–44
Equity Accelerator, xx, 135, 139
Erivo, Cynthia, 173
error correction, 209
errorless learning, 185–86
Esalen Institute, 83–84
ethical behavior, xxi, 12, 25, 28, 99–121
    Cultures of Growth and, 110–12
    how to encourage, 117–22
    management and, 118–19
    organizational mindsets and, 105–12
ethics. See also ethical behavior
    competition and, 113–16
    ethics trainings, 119

integrating everywhere, 119–21
interpersonal competition and, 113–16
through mindset lens, 101–5
ethnic minorities, 128, 134–35. See also
    specific groups
evaluation, xxi. See also assessments; evalu-
    ative situations
evaluation models, 147
evaluative situations, 153, 155, 160, 161–75.
    See also feedback, critical
    anticipatory responses to, 161–63, 171, 175
    on the fixed and growth continuum, 164
    growth mindset and, 168, 172, 174–75
    leaders and, 174–75
    learning from, 175
    mindset triggers and, 171
    modeling a growth mindset in, 174–75
    overdetermination and, 169–70
    questions for reflection, 175–76
    transparency and, 168
Evert, Chris, 231–32, 253
Ewing Marion Kauffman Foundation, 27, 45,
    127–28, 190
experiences, sharing of, 254–55
exploitation, 60
exploration, 60
extraction, focus on, 93

Facebook, 174–75, 218, 238
failures, 98
    embracing, 98
    "fail fast" mantra, 84
    reflecting on, 97
    understanding, 109–10
Fallon, Jimmy, 189
fear
    learning and, 67–68
    of risk-taking, 81–82
FedEx Custom Critical, 176–77
feedback, wise feedback, 220–22, 227
feedback, critical, xxi, 154, 155, 202–28
    ability to change and, 225, 227
    acknowledging, 227
    actionable, 214–17, 217, 225
    bias and, 212–13, 218–22, 224
    corrective, 209
    development and, 219
    emotional responses to, 204–6
    as essential tool for self-awareness, 220
    on fixed and growth continuum, 217
    fixed-minded, 217, 217
    flipping from fixed to growth mindset and,
        212–15, 227–28

feedback, critical (*cont.*)
  fostering a growth mindset in face of, 223
  gender bias and, 218–19
  giving worthwhile, 215–23
  growth-minded, 216–17, *217*
  having a feedback conversation, 224–25
  having multiple avenues for, 223
  how mindset influences the ways we filter, 207–12
  language and, 211–12
  learning and, 219
  mentor's dilemma and, 220
  on mindset continuum, *217*
  modeled by leaders, 224
  negative, 201–2, 208–9
  normalization of as routine, 216–17
  normalizing, 223–24
  ongoing, 216–17
  providing sincere, 224–25
  questions for reflection, 227–28
  racial bias and, 219
  reception of, 204–9, 212–15, 219–22, 226
  relationships and, 222
  routine, 223–24
  salience of, 210
  seeking growth-minded feedback, 225–27, 228
  specific, 214–17, *217, 225*
  stereotypes and, 218–22
  stereotype threat and, 218, 219–22
  storytelling and, 224
  targeted, *225*
  through growth mindset lens, 201–2
  usefulness of, 213–17, *217, 225,* 226
  vulnerability and, 215
  wise feedback, 220–22
feedback bias
  racial minorities and, 219–20
  women and, 218–20
feedback conversation, 219
feedback sandwich, 224
Feldman Barrett, Lisa, 204
file drawer problem, 108
Firestein, Stuart, 109–10
Fitbit, 181–82, 224
fixed-minded organizations. *See also* Cultures of Genius
  mistrust of, 126–27, 128
  prestige and, 65
fixed mindset, 3–6, *4, 14. See also* Cultures of Genius
  confirmation bias and, 79–80
  data cultures and, 170

defensiveness and, 175, 210
evaluative situations and, 163–64, *164*
founders and, 84–85
high-effort situations and, 177–78
how to avoid shifting others toward, 215–23
performance goals and, 64, 163–64
physical tension and, 175
social comparison and, 229–30
success of others and, 254–55
from the top, 235–39
triggers of, 19, 33, 190–91, 201
understanding, 158–60
value of, 159–60
fixed mindset culture. *See* Cultures of Genius
Flanagan, Shalane, 233
flexibility, fostering, 60–63
Flynn, Erin Morrison, 167
formerly incarcerated people, 135–36
fossil fuels, shift away from, 51–52
founders. *See also* entrepreneurs; entrepreneurship
  gender and, 192–93
  growth-minded vs. fixed-minded, 27, 45–46, 84–85
  influence of, 27
  race and, 192–93
Fowler, Susan, 58, 101–2
Frank (company), xviii, 120
Franklin, Rosalind, 42
Frazier, Joe, 231
Frei, Frances, 58, 239
French Gates, Melinda, 239–40
Freud, Sigmund, 207
freudenfreude, 236
Friedman, Eric, 181–82
Friedrich, Bruce, 103, 104
friendships, importance of, 253–54
Fry, Arthur, 76
Fryberg, Stephanie, 170–71

Gadde, Vijaya, 81–82
Gallup, 35, 197, 200
Garber, Marjorie, 10
Gardner, Phyllis, 165
Gates, Bill, 189
Gates, Melinda French, 239–40
GE, 34, 235–36, 238
gender, 125
  barriers to entrepreneurship and, 191–92
  biased feedback and, 218–19
  Cultures of Genius and, 127–28
  feedback bias and, 218–20

fixed mindset culture and, 130
gender gap in STEM fields and, 189–90
institutionalized scarcity and, 242–43
positive assertion and, 241
stack ranking and, 241–42
stereotypes about, 138
stereotype threat and, 126–28, 134, 138, 192
gender bias
feedback and, 218–19
stack ranking and, 241–42
genius
alignment with cultural value of, 184
archetype of, 125, 131, 133–34
idea of, 9–11, 234
stereotypes of, 20
genius mythology, Cultures of Genius and, 36
GitLab, 51
Glassdoor, 23, 35, 41
Goldman Sachs, 102, 237
Good Food Institute (GFI), 103–4
Google, 77, 153–54, 200, 238
GORE-TEX, 77
gratitude, development of, 255
Great Resignation, 35, 93
Greyston, 135–36, 147
Gross, Karen, 136, 146
growth
collective, 243–44
competition and, 33
encouraging, 49
focus on, 172
opportunities for, 34–35
tuning the environment to, 200
growth behaviors, 172
growth mindset, 3–6, 4, 14, 157–58, 201. See also Cultures of Growth
data cultures and, 170
development and, 210
evaluative situations and, 164–65, 164, 172
fostering, 168, 196, 223
fostering in evaluative situations, 168
fostering in high-effort situations, 196
founders and, 84–85
high-effort situations and, 194
learning and, 63–64, 164–65, 210, 211–12
learning goals and, 63–64, 164–65
learning mode and, 211–12
modeling, 174–75
social comparison and, 230
triggered by critical feedback, 210
growth mindset culture. See Cultures of Growth

growth mindset triggers, entrepreneurship and, 190–91
growth potential, 51
guide and release method, 173–74

halo effect, 24
Hamilton, 182
Hardison, Alec, 189
Harnish, Verne, 107–8
Harrison Central School District (HCSD), Westchester County, New York, 88–91, 141
Haselhuhn, Michael, 138
He Jiankui, 108, 110
Heffernan, Margaret, 38, 239
Heinz, 66
help-seeking, 12
heritage brands, 66
Hertz, 65
hierarchy, 10–11, 85
Higgins, Jamie Fiore, 102, 237
high-effort situations, 153–54, 155, 176–201
avoidance of, 176–77
breaking into manageable pieces, 196–97
calling on the community in, 199–200
employees in, 200
fixed mindset and, 177–78
fostering growth mindset in, 196
growth mindset and, 194
leaders in, 200–201
questions for reflection, 201
reflecting on, 201
reprogramming core beliefs in, 198–99
self-affirmation for, 197–98
students and, 193–95
teachers and, 193–95
tuning the environment to growth in, 200
vulnerability and, 177
hiring process, 93–95, 98, 133, 134, 147
hiring criteria, 103–4
hiring models, 147
stereotype threat and, 133–34
Hische, Jessica, 213
Hock, Dee, 75–76
Holmes, Elizabeth, xviii, 84, 165–67
Honest Tea, 79
Honeywell, 238
Hood, Ramona, 176–77, 179, 187
Howroyd, Janice Bryant, 129–30
HR processes. See also specific processes
re-evaluating through growth mindset lens, 147–48

Huddle, Molly, 233
Huffington, Arianna, 101

ideas, surfacing from everywhere, 73–75
identity-based criticism, Black women and, 212–13
IDEO, 132
"I Know!" Kid, 170–71, 175
immigrants, stereotypes of, 182
Imo (monkey), 257–58, 259
incentives, 105
    nonfinancial, 49
inclusion, xxi, 8, 12, 28, 91, 122–48. *See also* DEI (diversity, equity, inclusion)
    in Cultures of Genius, 125–28, 131–37
    in Cultures of Growth, 131–37
    mindset culture and, xx
    organizational mindsets and, 131–44
    scientific insights into, 131–44
inclusivity
    in academic research, 111
    research and, 110–11
India, 61–62
Indigenous people, 125, 170–71
individual mindset continuum, *14*
information
    hoarding, 24, 37, 109, 112
    sharing, 108–9, 112
innovation, xxi, 9, 12, 23–25, 27, 28, 37, 41, 52–80, 159, 170, 257–58
    collaboration and, 54
    competition and, 33
    dedicating time to, 75–77
    encouraging and enabling, 73–80
    fueled or foiled by mindset, 55–69
    influence of organizational culture on, 54
    looking elsewhere and, 78–79
    organizational mindsets and, 66–67
    prioritization of, 187
    risk-taking and, 81–82, 85, 101
    suppression of, 239–44
inspiration, how to encourage, 249–50
integrity, xxi, 12, 23, 24, 28, 99–121
    hiring for, 118–19
    how to encourage, 117–22
    through mindset lens, 101–5
intelligence
    beliefs about, 209
    collective, 240–41
interdependence, 10
intergroup mindsets, 66–67
internal competition, 34–42

interpersonal competition, ethics and, 113–16
investors, 84–85
Irvin, Lanaya, 143–46
Isaac, Mike, 56
Isaacson, Walter, 43
Israel, Paul, 234

James, William, 15
Japan, 115–16, 185
Javice, Charlie, xviii, 120
Jennings, Marianne, 119–20
"Jen-ocides," 34
Jobs, Steve, 189, 190, 238
John, Andréa McBride, 192–93, 196
Johnson, Pierre, 243–44
Johnson & Johnson, 116, 117
JPMorgan Chase, xviii
Juilliard, 248

Kalanick, Travis, 58, 84
Katzman, James, 102
Kauffman Foundation. *See* Ewing Marion Kauffman Foundation
Keystone, 87, 170
Khosrowshahi, Dara, 58
King, Martin Luther, Jr., 186–87
King, Stephen, 178–79
Knowles, Beyoncé, 250–51
Kornell, Nate, 185
KPMG, 55–56, 57, 159
Kray, Laura, 138
Kroeper, Katie, 210
Kroger, 192, 193
Kruger, Justin, 211
Kudrle, Tom, 170

labels, consequences of, 19–20
Lake, Katrina, 166–67, 192
Lamott, Anne, 196
Langer, David, 46
Larson, Sarah, 40–41
Latinas/os, 125
law, 159
leaders, xvii. *See also* managers; teachers
    evaluative situations and, 174–75
    high-effort situations and, 200–201
    modeling feedback, 224
    "recycling," 214–15
    women as, 192, 220
leadership, diversity and, 242
leaning organizations, 55
learned behavior, 257–58

learner mindset, 54, 71–72. *See also* growth
    mindset
"learn fast" mantra, 84–85
learning, 83, 116, 194–95
    anthropology of, 141
    errorless, 185–86
    from evaluative situations, 175
    fear and, 67–68
    feedback and, 175, 219
    goal of, 108
    growth mindset and, 210
    growth through, 107–8
learning behaviors, 172
learning culture, 141
learning goals, 63–65
    feedback and, 213–14
    growth mindset and, 164–65
learning mindset, 94
learning mode, 211–12
learning organizations, 120
learning orientation, 124
learning process
    as rewarding, 157–58
    struggle and, 183–85
Lenox Hill Hospital, 46
Leonard, Julia, 183
Lewis, Sarah, 209
LGBTQ+ community, 125, 145–46, 222
Lincoln, Sadie, 7–8, 203–6, 210, 224
Linden, Des, 232–33, 254
listening organizations, 120
local environment, 155
looking elsewhere, 78–79
Lumosity, 64
lunch-and-learns, 252
Lyft, 57

Mackey, John, 172, 214–15
Mackie, Susan, 106–7, 118, 120
Madhere, Max, 243–44
Magness, Steve, 48
Mahdawi, Arwa, 236
managers
    assessments of employee mindset, 25
    cues from, 26–27
    ethical behavior and, 118–19
    giving feedback, 216–17, 218–19, 224–25
    on growth trajectory, 200
    high-effort assignments from, 197
    institutionalized scarcity and, 243
    mindset beliefs of, 26–27
    normalization of feedback as routine,
        216–17

overdetermination and, 170
    receiving feedback, 227
Marcus, Sara, 136, 147
marketing, to mindset, 63–67
marketplace competition, 32
Maureen (Murphy's sister), 156
McBride, Robin, 192–93, 196
McBride Sisters Collection, 192–93, 196
McDonald's, 67
McIlroy, Emma, 74–75, 96, 116, 190
McKinsey, 129
measurement systems, to identify
        opportunities for development and
        improvement, 117–18
medical schools, 113–14
medicine, field of, 113–14, 159
Medium, 132
Megos, Alex, 193–94, 195, 196
men, 126, 130, 190, 191–92, 239, 241–42
    genius archetype and, 125, 133,
        190–91
    negative assertion and, 241
    White, 129–30
Mendes, Wendy Berry, 248–49
men of color, 132
mental health, 244, 245–46
mentoring, 252, 254–55
mentor's dilemma, 220
messages, paying attention to, 98. *See also*
        cues audits
Meta, 65, 218. *See also* Facebook
microcultures
    prove-and-perform, 168, 169–70, 171
    share-and-support, 168–69
microcultures of growth
    within Cultures of Genius, 173
    peer groups as, 243–44
Microsoft, xiv–xv, xix, 49, 51, 52, 85–87, 95,
        237–40
Millennials, 35, 65
mindset, xv–xvii. *See also* fixed mindset;
        growth mindset; mindset continuum;
        mindset culture
    ability and, 188–89, *188*
    assessments and, 5
    consequences of labeling people by,
        19–20
    core beliefs about, 21
    of customers, 63–64
    Dunning-Kruger effect and, 211
    expressed in mission statements, 23
    false dichotomy view of, 4–6, *4*
    feedback and, 205–10

mindset (*cont.*)
　influence on how we filter feedback, 207–12
　marketing to, 63–67
　personal, 4, *14*
　reception of feedback and, 219–22, 226
　self-assessment and, 209, 211
　as team effort, xxii
　triggers of, xx, xxi
　what mindset feels like, 155–58
mindset beliefs, of managers, 26–27
mindset continuum, 3–14, *6*, *14*, 19, 47, 153, 157–58
　critical feedback on, *217*
　defining, 6–7
　organizational mindsets and, 9
mindset cues, *14*
mindset culture, xvii, 5, 7, *14*
　birth of the concept, 16–17
　as cohesive meaning system, 76
　defining, xix
　DEI and, xx, 124 (*see also* DEI [diversity, equity, inclusion])
　downstream effects of, 27–28
　feedback loop and, 22
　growth and, xx
　how organizations signal, 17–19
　identifying mindset culture cues, 25–27
　shaping of individuals' behavior by, 37–42
　shifting, xxi, 25–26, 69–72, 215–23, 258–60 (*see also* mindset triggers)
mindset culture cycle, 19–27
mindset microcultures, 13, 151–60
　of growth, 173, 243–44
　influence of, 151–52
mindset reset, xxi
　mindset continuum, 3–14
　organizational mindsets, 15–28
mindset set points, 6–7
　evaluating, 19
mindset shifts, xxi, 25–26, 69–72, 215–23. *See also* mindset triggers
mindset triggers, 13–14, 152–58, 169
　critical feedback, 154, 202–28
　evaluative situations, 153, 161–75
　high-effort situations, 153–54, 176–207
　success of others, 154–55, 229–55
　understanding, 158–59
"minoritarian leadership," 78
minorities, 242. *See also* people of color; *specific groups*
　feedback bias and, 219–20
　institutionalized scarcity and, 242–43

pipeline myth and, 134–35
　stereotype threat and, 192
mission statements, 17, 23, 37
mistakes, hiding, 37
MIT, 240–41
Mitchum, Ainsley, 211
motivation, 18, 27–28, 133, 184
　collective, 243–44
Motley Fool, 79
Movement for Open Science, 110–11
Movement for Reproducibility, 110–11
Mudditt, Alison, 109
Murdoch, Rupert, 237
Murray State University, 39
Musk, Elon, 95

Nadella, Satya, xiv–xv, xix, 51, 85–86, 238
Naqvi, Arif, xviii
National Alliance on Mental Health, 246
Navratilova, Martina, 231–32, 253
negative assertion, 241
negotiation ability, 138
Neumann, Adam, 34, 35–36, 84
neural activity, preconscious, 209
neural pathways, 180–81
neurodiverse people, 125
neuroscience, 208–9
News of the World, 237
New York Times, 102
Novogratz, Jacqueline, 60–61, 62, 63, 69, 78, 119–20
Nussbaum, David, 207–9

O'Keefe, Paul, 189, 190
O'Neil, Cathy, 181
Oracle, 238
"organizational introspection," 144–45
Organizational Mindset Culture Cycle, 21–22, *21*
organizational mindsets, xvii, xxi, 8–9, 15–28, *18*
　assessment of, 37–38
　beliefs, 9
　brands and, 64–67
　conformity with, 24–25
　conscious shaping of, xix–xx
　diversity and, 131–44
　employee satisfaction and, 23–24, 35
　equity and, 131–44
　ethical behavior and, 105–12
　inclusion and, 131–44
　innovation and, 66–67
　as meaning-making systems, 13–14

mindset continuum and, 9
perception of, 35–36
power of, 258–59
shaping of behavior norms by, 23–25
signaling of, 17–19
stereotype threat and, 126–27
unethical behavior and, 105–12
organizational transformation, pursuing, 139–44, 161–75
organizations, xvii
commitment and, 23, 38
how organizations signal mindset culture, 17–19
resilience and, 96–98
risks and, 96–98
trust and, 23, 38
vision of, 173–74
organization-wide values, 56–57
origin stories, 251–52
others
elevating, 254–55
identifying, engaging, and learning skills of, 199–200
success of, xxi, 154–55, 229–55
overdetermination, 169–70, 173–74

Page, Larry, 238
Pao, Ellen, 146
parents, "taking-over" behaviors of, 183
Park, James, 181–82, 224
passion(s)
beliefs about, 189
fixed mindset view of, 190
narrative around discovering rather than developing, 190
Patagonia, 44–45, 49–51, 73, 92–93
pecking order, 85, 114
peer groups, as microcultures of growth, 243–44
people of color, 78, 111, 126, 128, 132, 134, 138, 191, 192, 219–20, 226, 239, 242, 243–44. *See also* minorities; *specific groups*
PepsiCo, 49, 242, 250–51
perceptions, impact of mindset on, 27
perfection, 7, 11
performance
evaluation of, 49–51, 248–49 (*see also* evaluative situations)
performance goals, 63–65, 105, 163–64
performance reviews, 49–51
performance targets, 118
pressure and, 41

Perlman, Itzhak, 247–48, 252
Perlman, Toby, 247–48
Perlman Music Program, 247–48
Perrier, 116, 117
persistence, 12, 178–79, 183, 185
personal agency, xvi–xvii
Petersen, Anne Helen, 169
Phillips, Katherine, 128–29
Phool, 61–62
physical tension, fixed mindset and, 175
pipeline myth, 134–35
PitchBook, 192
Pixar, 73–74, 241
"play to your strengths" model, 188–89
PLOS (Public Library of Science), 109–10
PolicyLink, 78
positive assertion, 241
possibility, 11
powerlessness, 217
praise, 213–14
actionable, 214–17, *217*
cues audits of praise practices, 255
specificity of, 214–17, *217*
pressure, performance and, 41
prestige, 65, 240
problem-solving, 18, 196, 240–41
productivity culture, 141
progress, focus on, 17–18
Project Include, 146
promotion models, 147
prove-and-perform microcultures, 168, 169–70, 171
prove-and-perform mindset, 58–59, 163–67
psychological safety, 67–69
growth mindset culture and, 68–69
investing in building, 77–78
teamwork and, 68

quality control, 159
questionable research practices (QRPs), 108–11
Quinn, Kimberly, 79–80

race
feedback bias and, 219–20
fixed mindset culture and, 130
race-based criticism, 212–13
racial bias, 219, 244 (*see also* racism, structural)
racial minorities. *See also specific groups*
barriers to entrepreneurship and, 191–92
Cultures of Genius and, 128
pipeline myth and, 134–35
stereotype threat and, 128, 134

racism, structural, 8
Rae, Issa, 173
rank and yank, 235–39
Rastogi, Karan, 61–62
rating systems, redoing, 49–51
Rattan, Aneeta, 210
Raz, Guy, 8, 181–82, 192–93
recruiting, 98
research
  collaboration and, 110–11
  DEI in, 111
  inclusivity and, 110–11
  questionable research practices (QRPs), 108–11
  replicability and, 108, 110–11
  women in, 111
resilience, xxi, 12, 28, 81–98
Reuters, 246
risks. *See also* risk-taking
  embracing, 91–92, 96–98
  perception of, 83
  re-categorizing, 83–87
  risk aversion, 81–82, 85
  seeking out, 96
  supporting, 98
risk-taking, xxi, 11, 12, 23, 27, 28, 81–98
  collaboration and, 85
  in Cultures of Genius, 37, 81–82, 83
  in Cultures of Growth, 82–83
  data and, 87–93
  employees and, 85–87
  factors that influence, 93–95
  innovation and, 81–82, 85, 101
  as opportunity for learning, 83
rivalries, 231–32, 253, 255
Roc-A-Fella Records, 198
Rockefeller Foundation, 78
Ross, Lee, 220
Rothstein, Jed, 34
Ruettiger, Daniel "Rudy," 156–57

safety, psychological, 67–69
Saint John, Bozoma, 173, 242, 250–51
Salazar, Alberto, 48
Samsa, Christopher, 27
Sandberg, Sheryl, 174–75
SAP, 134
Sarkar, Ellora, 170
Scaling Up, 107–8
scarcity mindset, 229–30, 255
  institutionalized, 242–43
  from the top, 235–44

schedenfreude, 236
Schein, Edgar, 21
Schwab, Katherine, 76–77
science, Cultures of Genius in, 110–11. *See also* academic sciences; STEM culture; *specific fields*
second chances, 136
secrets, keeping, 24
Seiko, 115–16
self-affirmation, 250–51
  activity of, 250–51
  for high-effort situations, 197–98
  to switch from threat state to challenge state, 250
self-assessment, mindset and, 209, 211
self-awareness, 210–11, 220
self-esteem, 205, 207
self-focus, 196, 203, 214, 229, 246
  mental health and, 246
  social comparison and, 228–29
self-perception, accurate, 220
Semien, Joseph, 243–44
Seth, Jayshree, 132, 133
sexual harassment, 58
sexual orientation, 125, 222
Shakespeare, William, 10
Shalane Effect, 233–34, 244, 254
share-and-support microculture, 168–69
Shell, 51–53, 54, 69–72, 95, 159, 252
ShipIt, 76
Shugart, Sanford "Sandy," 140–44
Silicon Valley, 83–85
Sinek, Simon, 168, 253
Singer, David, 88
situational cues, 123–24, 155
skill sharing, grouping for, 252
theSkimm, 177
Slate, 65
social comparison, 58–59, 229–55
  in the classroom, 245–48
  education and, 245–48
  fixed mindset and, 229–30
  growth mindset and, 230
  self-focus and, 228–29
  vs. social connectedness, 246
  social media and, 246–47
  vulnerability and, 231
social connectedness, vs. social comparison, 246
social identity, 155
social media, 246–47
spontaneity, 85

sports. *See also specific athletes*
  growth mindset in, 233
  sports franchises, 39
stack ranking, 34, 36, 49, 235–39, 241, 242,
    245
stakeholder capitalism, 62
Stanford Duck Syndrome, 183–84, 199, 246
Stanford University, 15–16, 51–52, 99–100,
    110, 162, 165–66, 183–84, 189–90, 199
Steele, Claude, 10–11, 123, 197, 198, 219,
    220
STEM classrooms, 139–40
STEM culture, 132–33, 243
STEM faculty, 139–40, 225–26, 230, 243
STEM fields, gender gap in, 189–90
stereotypes. *See also* stereotype threat
  feedback and, 218–20
  of immigrants, 182
  positive, 131
  racial/ethnic minorities and, 128
  women and, 126–27, 138
stereotype threat, 125–26, 192
  feedback and, 218, 219–22
  hiring process and, 133–34
  organizational mindsets and, 126–27
  racial/ethnic minorities and, 128
  women and, 126–27, 138
Stevenson, Harold, 185
Stigler, James, 185
Stitch Fix, 166–67
storytelling, 145–46, 195, 201
  about success of others, 255
  corporate, 252
  feedback and, 224
  to reprogram core beliefs, 198–99
strengths
  assessment of, 187
  development of, 201
  fixed mindset view of, 190
  overfocus on, 186–90
  through growth mindset lens, 201
stress
  evaluation of stressors, 248–49
  learning impaired by, 41
  reframing, 41
structural racism, 8
struggle
  destigmatizing, 171
  learning process and, 183–85
  normalization of, 252
  origin stories and, 251–52
  value of, 183–85, 195
Student Experience Project, 139

students
  critical feedback and, 227
  high-effort situations and, 193–95
  success of others, xxi, 154–55, 229–55
    fixed mindset and, 254–55
    how to react to, 249–50
    inspiring stories of, 255
    recognizing value of, 253–54
    value of, 252, 253–54
    when your success triggers others, 254–55
  supervisors, mindset of, 35–36
  support, 172
    vs. competition, 199
    getting, 172–73
  "surprise journal," 79–80
  surprises, taking note of, 79–80
  sustainable agriculture movement, 49–50
  Swisher, Kara, 222

Taco Bell, 67
talent, 129
  development of, 12
  fixed mindset view of, 190
  genius model and, 133–34
  innate, 215–17, *217*
  overemphasizing, 187
  stereotypes of, 20
  talent assessment programs, 51
  uncovering hidden, 135–36
talent pool, enlarging the, 135–37, 147
task-irrelevant thoughts, 59
Tauber, Ben, 27, 83–84, 85
Tay (chatbot), xv
teachers, 194–95, 206. *See also* STEM faculty
  competition in the classroom and, 245–48
  critical feedback and, 228
  giving feedback, 219–22
  high-effort situations and, 193–95
  impact on students' mindsets and perfor-
    mance, 247
Teamistry, 252
teams, "bought" vs. "built," 39–41
teamwork, 10
  vs. competition, 236, 238
  problem-solving and, 240–41
  psychological safety and, 68
TechCrunch, 192
Tesla, Nikola, 234
Theranos, xviii, 36, 84, 102, 165–66
"thorns and roses" component, 172
threats
  vs. challenge(s), 248–49
  removing, 91

threat states, 249–50
3M, 76–77, 132, 133
time, core beliefs about, 20–21
"time-out cards," 120
Torrance, Wendy, 27
training, 174
transparency, 112, 117, 118, 119–20, 168
trust, 65, 112, 126–27, 128, 133
Twitter, 81–82, 93–95, 98
2008 financial crisis, 102

Uber, 56–58, 84, 101–2, 120, 242
unethical behavior, 24, 27, 37
    competition and, 113–16
    organizational mindsets and, 100–103,
        105–12
    vigilance for and responses to, 116–17
Unilever, 136
University of Cincinnati, 63–64
University of Kansas, 39
U.S. Bureau of Labor Statistics, 134

Valencia College, 140–44
value-implementation gaps, 36
values
    organization-wide, 56–57
    re-creation of, 21–22, 21
Van Beurden, Ben, 52, 70–71
Van der Togt, Jorrit, 51–52, 70, 72, 77
Vanity Fair, 237–38
Vazire, Simine, 108
Vegemite, 67
Velocity Group, 83–84
venture capitalists (VCs), 84–85, 127–28
Virgin, 65–66
Virgin Cola, 66
Virgin Group, 65
Virgin Money, 65
Visa, 75–76
vision, of organizations, 173–74
Volkswagen, 106
vulnerability, social comparison and, 231

Wall Street Journal, 165
Walton, Greg, 189
Wambach, Abby, 237
Watson, James, 42
websites, 9, 37
Welch, Jack, 34, 235–36, 238

Wells Fargo, 36, 237
Westinghouse, George, 234–35
WeWork, 34, 36, 84, 102
Whipped-Urban Dessert Lab, 130
White men, 129–30, 191–92
    genius archetype and, 125, 134
White people, 125, 128–30, 131
Whole Foods, 136, 172, 214–15
Wildfang, 74–75, 96
Williams, Judith Michelle, 134
Williams, Serena, 187
Windows, xv
Winterkorn, Martin, 106
wise criticism. See wise feedback
wise feedback, 220–22, 227
W. L. Gore, 77
women, 125, 126, 129, 190, 242–43
    in academic research, 111
    barriers to entrepreneurship and, 191–92
    biased feedback and, 218–19
    Black, 193
    of color, 126, 145, 193
    Cultures of Genius and, 127–28
    feedback bias and, 218–20
    as founders, 192
    gender gap in STEM fields and, 189–90
    institutionalized scarcity and, 242–43
    as leaders, 192, 220
    pipeline myth and, 134–35
    positive assertion and, 241
    stack ranking and, 241–42
    stereotypes about, 138
    stereotypes and, 126–28, 134, 138, 192
    stereotype threat and, 126–28, 134, 138,
        192
Wool, Louis, 88–91, 95
work ethic, 178–79, 182

Xavier University, 243–44

Yale University, 189
Yeager, David, 221
Yeah, maybe mindset, 74–75, 79
Yerkes-Dodson law, 41

Zalesne, Kinney, 86–87, 104
zero-sum mentality, 58, 229, 233, 235–36,
    245
Zuckerberg, Mark, 174–75, 189, 238

About the Author

Mary C. Murphy is a Class of 1948 Herman B Wells Endowed Professor in the Department of Psychological and Brain Sciences at Indiana University, the founding director of the Summer Institute on Diversity at the Center for Advanced Study in the Behavioral Sciences at Stanford University, and the founder and CEO of the Equity Accelerator, a research and consulting organization that works with schools and companies to create more equitable learning and working environments through social and behavioral science.

Murphy conducts pioneering research on motivation, performance, and intergroup relations focused on how contexts and settings shape our thoughts, feelings, and behavior. She has published more than 100 articles in top academic journals, and her work has been featured in the *New York Times, Forbes, Harvard Business Review, Scientific American*, and *NPR*, among other outlets. The recipient of numerous federal and foundation grants and awards, Murphy received the 2019 Presidential Early Career Award for Scientists and Engineers, the highest award bestowed on early career scholars by the United States government. She has been elected to, and served on, several national and international scientific and policy committees, and she is an elected fellow of the American Association for the Advancement of Science.

Murphy is Latina from San Antonio, Texas. She earned a BA from the University of Texas at Austin and a PhD from Stanford University. She and her partner currently split their time between Bloomington, Indiana, and the San Francisco Bay Area.